THE LETTERS OF
EDGAR ALLAN POE

THE LETTERS OF

Edgar Allan Poe

EDITED BY

JOHN WARD OSTROM

I

WITH NEW FOREWORD
AND SUPPLEMENTARY CHAPTER

NEW YORK

GORDIAN PRESS, INC.

1966

Published by Gordian Press, Inc., by
Arrangement with Harvard University Press
Library of Congress Catalog Card No. 66-20025

Printed in U.S.A. by
E D W A R D S B R O T H E R S , I N C .
Ann Arbor, Michigan

*To AIMÉE who patiently waited the long years
and JODIE who grew up amid facsimiles and
photostats this book is lovingly dedicated*

FOREWORD

I

The present edition of *The Letters of Edgar Allan Poe* reprints the original two-volume edition (1948), page for page, and includes an extensive *Supplement* that brings the work up to date. The *Supplement* not only contains important emendations and additions to the texts and notes as first printed, but also supplies texts and notes for forty-two letters, thirty of which were not in the 1948 edition. It is still true that not all letters written by Poe have come to light, but the number is rapidly decreasing. In the past ten years very few have been listed in the annual records of auction sales, and I am advised that no letters by or to Poe are likely to appear in the 1964–1965 volume of *American Book-Prices Current,* and that no letters by Poe are listed in the sales catalogues covering the period from September, 1965, through May, 1966. Of course, manuscript letters have changed hands privately among individual collectors, but certainly most, if not all, of these have already been printed.

The editorial procedure for letters in the *Supplement* follows that of the original edition (see the *Preface* to Volume I); for the corrections and additions to the original notes, see the headnote to the *Supplement.*

The *Supplement* contains 42 letters: 7 are published for the first time; 23 have been printed in various publications since the 1948 edition; and 12 that were printed in the earlier edition from copies are now reprinted from manuscript. In fact, unless a transcript or copy was the only extant or available source, all letters in the *Supplement* are printed from original manuscripts. Letter 79, for example, is printed from its only extant form, which was released for publication especially for this edition.

The *Supplement* also identifies the present location of manuscripts of letters printed herein and of letters known to have changed hands since 1948. In this connection it is important to note that two very valuable and extensive private collections have been transferred to institutions, one by gift, the other by purchase. Since 1957 the collection of Mr. J. K. Lilly, Jr., of Indianapolis, has been in the Lilly Library, Indiana University. The library of Mr. William H. Koester, of Baltimore, was sold in

1966 and has become associated with the Miriam Lutcher Stark Library, University of Texas. The new locations are cited in the *Supplement* for all manuscript letters in the Lilly collection and for all manuscript letters known to have been acquired by Mr. Koester since 1948; furthermore, all manuscript letters attributed to Mr. Koester in the Notes and Check List of the earlier edition should now be reassigned to the Stark Library.

The Letters of Edgar Allan Poe now includes 369 letters by Poe. The whole Poe correspondence presently numbers 878 items: 837 in *The Letters* of 1948 (this number including the secondary entries in the Check List, such as items 602a and 602b, etc.), 30 new letters by Poe, printed in the *Supplement,* 3 new cited but unlocated letters by Poe, and 8 new cited or implied letters to Poe. About 100 letters known to have been written by Poe still remain unlocated, but most of these must be presumed lost, since they were written in his capacity as editor or as covering letters for his own contributions to various periodicals. Also many letters written to Poe by women of his acquaintance were destroyed after his death, according to his mother-in-law, Mrs. Clemm.

With original Poe letters becoming scarcer each year, the question is often asked, "What is a Poe letter worth?" In many instances, the asked price cannot be taken as the actual selling price, but records of sales through the years give a representative picture. In 1896 one letter brought only $20; in 1929 it sold for $1200. A Poe to Cooke letter sold in 1901 for $210; the same letter in 1929 brought a reported $19,500, a record price for an American literary letter. In 1931 two letters were purchased privately by the same collector for $4400 and $5500 respectively. In the early 1930's two very short letters, significant primarily because they carried Poe's full signature, sold together for about $200. In 1949 a Paris dealer offered them to a private collector for $10,000, which was refused. Eight years later a New York dealer went to Paris, bought them, and subsequently advertised them in the New York *Times* for $5000. They were ultimately sold to the same collector who had turned down the Paris offer. Very recently a Poe to Irving letter brought a reported price of £2000 in England. On the basis of a representative selection of letters sold during the past seventy years at prominent auction galleries (excluding a few single, high-priced items), an average price before 1900 seems to have been about $50; between 1900–1930, about $250; between 1930–1940, about $400; between 1940–1950, about $600; and since 1950, with fewer letters available, nearly $2500.

Other than the famous letters of Poe to Sarah Helen Whitman, purchased with other memorabilia in the early 1930's for $50,000, probably the most important group of letters is composed of Poe's letters to Mrs. Annie L. Richmond. Of the 10 (possibly 11) extant, only 2 (possibly 3) are known to exist in manuscript; the remaining manuscripts are probably lost. Perhaps the most prized item in the whole Poe correspondence would be the manuscript of Poe's letter to his wife Virginia, June 12, 1846. It exists only in printed form. The manuscript has never come to light since Ingram used it (if, indeed, he actually had the original instead of a copy) for his biography of Poe nearly a century ago. In addition to one sentence directed to Virginia before they were married and included in Letter 48 addressed to Mrs. Clemm, Poe is said to have written her many notes, but none are extant either in manuscript or print.

Interesting, too, is the name Poe used in signing his letters. His customary signature is Edgar A. Poe, often with a paraph or flourish. He uses Edgar thirteen times, Edgar Allan Poe eleven, Eddy seven, and Eddie only once. He never signs himself Edgar Poe.

It is often said that one never gets very close to Poe through a reading of his letters. Many of them, to be sure, are quite pedestrian; few are literary gems. But, on the whole, especially to one who sits close to them, they speak of love and hate, hope and despair, frustrations without end, of the joy of friendship and the pain of attack, of an unrelenting nemesis, the desperate need, ever present, of providing for his little family and maintaining a home as a haven to return to. Finally, one grows increasingly aware, explain it as he will, of the *leitmotif* of the letters—the inescapable influence of Virginia Clemm Poe on Edgar Poe's life. We become more knowledgeable about Poe through the biographies and critical works, but, in the final analysis, it is the diapason of the letters that haunts us all.

II

Again, I wish to express grateful help in editing the *Supplement*. Without full cooperation from private collectors, editors, and librarians and staff members this edition could not have been completed. To the following people, therefore, goes my sincere appreciation:

Mr. Charles J. Biddle of Philadelphia, Dr. O. O. Fisher of Detroit,

Col. Richard Gimbel of Yale University, the late Mr. William H. Koester of Baltimore, and Mr. Henry Bradley Martin of New York—all of whom shared with me letters from their private collections.

The editors of the Duke University Press for permission to use material from my two supplements in *American Literature,* XXIV, No. 3, November, 1952, pp. 358–366, and XXIX, No. I, March, 1957, pp. 79–86.

Edward Lazare, editor of *American Book-Prices Current;* Mr. John Alden, Keeper of Rare Books, and Mr. Francis O. Mattson, Assistant in the Department of Rare Books, Boston Public Library; Mrs. Nan Sumner, Assistant to the Curator, Annmary Brown Memorial, Brown University; Mr. Jerome F. Jacob, Head, Language, Literature, and Fine Arts Department, Buffalo and Erie County Public Library, Buffalo; Mr. Lawrence Clark Powell, Director, William Andrews Clark Memorial Library, University of California, Los Angeles; Mr. Kenneth A. Lohf, Assistant Librarian, Butler Library, Columbia University; Mr. Kenneth W. Cameron, Editor, *Emerson Society Quarterly,* Hartford, Connecticut; Mr. Richard Hart, Head, Literature Department, Enoch Pratt Free Library, Baltimore; The Faculty Research Committee, Wittenberg University; Mr. W. H. Bond, Librarian, and Miss Donna Ferguson, Department of Manuscripts, Houghton Library, Harvard University; Mr. David Randall, Librarian, The Lilly Library, Indiana University; Mr. Robert F. Clayton, Librarian, Dawes Memorial Library, Marietta College; Mr. William S. Dix, Librarian, and Mr. Alexander P. Clark, Curator of Manuscripts, Princeton University; Mrs. Clara Sitter, Acting Librarian, Miriam Lutcher Stark Library, University of Texas; Miss Anne Freudenberg, Acting Curator of Manuscripts, and Mr. William G. Ray, Assistant in Manuscripts, University of Virginia Library; Mr. Randolph W. Church, Librarian, Virginia State Library; Mr. Bob Lee Mowery, Librarian, Mrs. Luella Eutsler, Reference Librarian, Miss Ilo Fisher, Chief of Technical Service, and Mrs. Margaret Price, Library Staff, Thomas Library, Wittenberg University.

John Ostrom

Wittenberg University
Springfield, Ohio
May, 1966

PREFACE

This edition of the letters of Edgar Allan Poe supplies the need for an authentic text. Except for photographic reproductions, previous printings of Poe's correspondence have presented, in many instances, inaccurate or incomplete texts, and punctuation that was not Poe's but the editor's.

This collection does not pretend to contain all the letters that Poe wrote, for some are still lost or, if extant, unlocated; but it provides authentic versions of those holographs that were accessible and offers what seem to be the best texts of lost or unavailable originals, accessible now only in printed form or in typescript.

Texts printed herein have been taken from original autograph letters, facsimiles, or photostats; from printed versions in books, magazines, newspapers, and auction catalogues; and from reasonably accurate typescripts. In no instance has a printed or typescript source been used if the original manuscript was extant and available. In those letters printed from holograph, facsimile, or photostat, Poe's original pagination has been preserved, indicated by bracketed figures; also original spelling, punctuation, even manuscript corrections have been followed, except for some idiosyncrasies that defied transference to the printed page. All doubtful readings in photographic reproductions of original letters have been collated with accessible holographs. The paraph or flourish, usually used by Poe under his own signature and under the name of his correspondent, has been omitted; and careted interpolations in the original manuscript have been reduced to their structural position in the sentence. Furthermore, no attempt has been made to indicate the exact spacing of the heading, salutation, or indentions of paragraphs of the original letter.

This edition is a continuation and an expansion of the editor's *A Check List of Letters to and from Poe*, published as No. 4 in the Bibliographical Series sponsored by the Alderman Library of the University of Virginia, 1941. As a result of a complete study of the whole Poe correspondence, the original list has been revised. It now includes all letters known to have been written to or from Poe, arranged chronologically and indexed; citations of letters misdated in various works on Poe, the items being entered chronologically in the list under the date customarily given with a cross-reference to their correct date; the city address, where known, of Poe and his correspondent; the present location of the original letter, if known; an additional printing of the letter, "F" indicating if printed in facsimile; identification of letters for which no original or printed source is known to exist but which are acceptable upon evidence satisfactory to the present editor, these items being explained as "cited" or "implied." Letters that are both entered in the list and printed in this edition are identified by an asterisk next to the date of the item.

The edition proper prints, either in full or in part, 339 letters by Poe. The check list shows that Poe wrote at least 124 others, but of these the editor knows of only a dozen or so that have come down to the present day in manuscript and that are still unlocated. A study of all available sources shows also that at least 373 letters, established by original manuscripts, printed versions, and internal evidence, were written to Poe, exclusive of letters, apparently lost, which were written to him either as editor of a magazine or in connection with his attempt to found the *Penn* or the *Stylus.* A few of these "to the editor" letters appeared, or were referred to, in such periodicals as the *Southern Literary Messenger, Graham's,* and Alexander's *Weekly Messenger,* but they have not been included in the computation. It also follows that Poe wrote letters, now lost, in reply to such correspondents and to subscribers to his proposed magazine, but these, likewise, have been omitted.

Letters in this edition are numbered in sequence. Following the note which appears with the letter is a number in brackets that refers to the chronological position of that letter in the check list. A number of letters which were added to the edition at a late date have been inserted in chronological order with an "a" added to the number; they have been inserted in the same way in the check list.

Notes to the letters conform to the following procedure. With few exceptions each letter has two groups of explanatory comment: first, bibliographical and textual; second, editorial. The bibliographical and textual notes will be found after the text, each group identifiable by the number corresponding to the number given to each letter. The editorial comment accompanies the letter. Both groups of notes should be consulted for a complete understanding of matters pertaining to a specific letter.

In the bibliographical notes appear the source used for printing the letter in the present edition; the number of pages of manuscript, based upon holograph, facsimile, photostat, or notation in an auction catalogue; indication of the first printing of the letter in full or fullest form; comment, if necessary, on a misdated letter, or proposal of a correct or approximate date, if the letter is undated; matters pertaining to an extant envelope or cover, especially if its dating differs from that of the letter, and comment on the addressee, where advisable; irregularities of a known manuscript or of the text used, including any collations made; and, finally, indication of the letter or letters that Poe is answering, with reference to their present accessibility either in manuscript or in printed form.

In the editorial notes accompanying the letter, comment follows, as a rule, the text of the letter. For the first item of an important or extensive series between Poe and a correspondent, the bibliographical note lists the known letters in the correspondence.

A chronology of the main events in Poe's life has been provided for ready reference. Separate lists identifying both general and private collections of Poe letters are given, locations of individual letters being indicated in the bibliographical notes.

Now let me speak *in propria persona*. Not only from a sense of justice, but from a deep appreciation and profound indebtedness, I wish to express my gratitude to Dean James Southall Wilson of the University of Virginia for his Introduction to the present edition and for his valuable guidance during the past seven years in my work of gathering and editing these letters; and to Dr. Thomas Ollive Mabbott of Hunter College for his untiring efforts in compiling data and for generously "lending his mind out" on many of the complexities arising from any study of Poe.

To Dr. Atcheson L. Hench of the University of Virginia, who read the manuscript, I am especially indebted for kindly advice and critical suggestions. I am grateful to Mr. Harry Clemons, Director of the Alderman Library of the University of Virginia, for his whole-hearted coöperation in accumulating material necessary for this edition. I am very much indebted to Mr. John Cook Wyllie, Curator of Rare Books, and to Mr. Francis L. Berkeley, Jr., Curator of Manuscripts, of the Alderman Library, for years of generous coöperation in ways too numerous to mention, as well as to Mr. Jack Dalton, Assistant Librarian, Miss Louise. Savage, Miss Evelyn Dollens, Mr. Harris Williams, and Mr. William Gaines, of the Library staff.

I owe much to Mr. William H. Koester of Baltimore, to Mr. Josiah K.

Lilly, Jr., of Indianapolis, to Mrs. Ralph Catterall and the Trustees of the Valentine Museum of Richmond, to Mr. H. Bradley Martin of New York, and to Mr. Merrill Griswold of Boston, who graciously opened their private collections to me. I am also indebted to Mr. and Mrs. George P. Coleman, Mrs. Sherburne Prescott, Miss Mary Benjamin, Mr. Richard G. Gimble, and Mr. Charles C. Hart for their assistance in making manuscript letters available. I am not unmindful of the assistance given me on many occasions by Dr. Arthur H. Quinn, whose biography of Poe has been referred to frequently; by Dr. David K. Jackson, whose studies of Poe in Richmond were very helpful; by Judge Charles Zimmerman of the Ohio State Supreme Court, Dr. John C. French of Johns Hopkins University, Dr. W. K. Wimsatt of Yale University, Dr. C. William Miller of Temple University, Dr. John G. Varner, of Washington and Lee University, Mr. Edwin B. Hill and Mr. K. L. Daughrity, and Dr. Douglas S. Freeman, former President, and Miss Mary G. Traylor, Secretary until her recent death, of the Poe Foundation in Richmond.

I am indeed grateful to the Syndics of the Harvard University Press, to Mr. Roger L. Scaife, its former Director, and to Mr. Thomas J. Wilson, its present Director, for their interest in this edition, and I am especially indebted to Phoebe deKay Donald, of its editorial staff, for her valuable contributions to the completion of this edition. I want to express my appreciation to the New York Historical Society for making possible my use of the Osgood painting of Poe as a frontispiece.

Though Poe's life was spent almost entirely within two hundred miles of the Atlantic coast, in an area bounded on the north by Boston, on the south by Charleston, the letters of his correspondence have found their way into library crypts as far removed from one another as Boston from San Marino, California, as Charleston from Austin, Texas. Distance, therefore, becomes a veritable wasteland thwarting the progress of the questing knight; and were it not for the generous coöperation of the keepers of original scripts, the armored knight or the editorial squire would be forced to cease his quest, unsuccessful.

It is, therefore, with sincerest appreciation that I here acknowledge — inadequate it must be — the painstaking efforts and hours of research of those who during the past seven years have assisted me: Mr. Clarence S. Brigham, Director of the American Antiquarian Society, for material from the files of the Society; Mr. Zoltán Haraszti, Keeper of Rare Books of the Boston Public Library, and his assistant, Miss Honor McCusker, Curator of English Literature, for hours of labor among the many items of the Griswold Collection; Miss Marie Hamilton Law, Librarian of the Drexel Institute; Mr. William A. Jackson, Librarian of the Houghton Library, Harvard University, and Mr. Herbert C. Schulz, Curator of Manuscripts, Henry E. Huntington Library, both of whom have been at considerable pains to clarify problems arising from textual peculiarities; Mr. St. George L. Sioussat, Chief of the Division of Manuscripts, and Mr. George A. Schwegmann, Jr., Director of the Union Catalogues, Library of Congress; Mr. William D. Hoyt, Jr., Assistant Director of the Maryland Historical Society, for extended investigations among the papers of the Society; Mr. John T. Windle, Head of the Public Service Department, The Newberry Library; Mr. Paul Rice North, Chief of the Reference Department, Mr. Robert W. Hill, Keeper of Manuscripts, and Dr. John D. Gordan, Director of the Berg Collection, New York Public Library, for advice and bibliographical and textual data; Mr. Louis H. Dielman, Librarian Emeritus of the Peabody Institute; Miss Theresa D. Hodges, Librarian of the Petersburg, Virginia, Public Library; Miss Belle da Costa Greene, Librarian of the Pierpont Morgan Library; Mr. Richard H. Hart, Head of the Literature Department of the Enoch Pratt Free Library; Mr. R. W. Church, State Librarian of the Virginia State Library; Lt. Col. W. J. Morton, former Librarian of the United States Military Academy; and Miss Anne S. Pratt, Reference Librarian of the Yale University Library.

I wish to acknowledge the following courtesies for material in print: To D. Appleton-Century Company for permission to reprint material, edited by George E. Woodberry for the *Century Magazine* in 1894 and in 1903; to Thomas Y. Crowell Company, publishers of the Virginia Edition of Poe, edited by James A. Harrison; to J. B. Lippincott Company, publishers of the *Poe Letters Till Now Unpublished*, copyright, 1925, by The Valentine Museum, with commentary by Mary Newton Stanard; to Mrs. Charles D. Woodberry, Boston, for material in George E. Woodberry's *Life of Poe*, 1909; and to Mr. Clarence Gohdes, Editor of *American Literature*, published by the Duke University Press.

Furthermore, I am indebted to librarians and others whose generous assistance has permitted me to reprint in this volume letters in collections under their control: Mr. Harry Clemons of the Alderman Library, University of Virginia, for materials in the Poe and Ingram Collections; Mr. and Mrs. George P. Coleman, for letters now in Colonial Williamsburg Architectural Department; Mr. Milton Edward Lord and Mr. Richard G. Hensley of the Boston Public Library, for correspondence in the Griswold Collection; Mr. Thompson R. Harlow of the Connecticut Historical Society; Mrs. Ethel B. Clark of the Dumbarton Oaks Research Library; Mr. William A. Jackson of the Houghton Library, Harvard University; Miss Anna B. Hewitt of the Haverford College Library, for letters in the Charles Roberts Autograph Collection; Mrs. Sherburne Prescott, whose private collection is in the Hickory Hill Library, Greenwich, Connecticut; Mr. R. N. Williams, II, of the Historical Society of Pennsylvania; Mr. Henry Wadsworth Longfellow Dana, of the Longfellow House, Cambridge, Massachusetts; Mr. Leslie Bliss and Mr. Herbert C. Schulz of the Henry E. Huntington Library; Mr. Emory H. English of the Iowa State Department of History and Archives; Mr. St. George L. Sioussat of the Library of Congress; Miss Viola C. White of the Abernethy Library of American Literature, Middlebury College; Mr. Robert W. Hill, Keeper of Manuscripts, of the New York Public Library — the Poe material of the Manuscript Division having accumulated mainly from the Duyckinck Papers and from gifts by Dr. Thomas Ollive Mabbott, by the late Dr. Alfred W. Anthony, and by others; Dr. John D. Gordan, Director of the Henry W. and Albert A. Berg Collection, of the New York Public Library; Mr. Lloyd A. Brown of the Peabody Institute; Miss Belle da Costa Greene of the Pierpont Morgan Library; Mr. Turner Arrington, President of the Poe Foundation, Richmond; Mr. Emerson Greenaway of the Enoch Pratt Free Library; Miss Fannie Ratchford for material in the Wrenn Library, University of Texas; Mr. R. W. Church and Mr. William J. Van Schreeven of the Virginia State Library; Lt. Col. W. H. Corbett of the United States Military Academy; and Mr. James T. Babb of the Yale University Library.

Wittenberg College
Springfield, Ohio

J. W. O.

CONTENTS

ILLUSTRATIONS

INTRODUCTION

In this new collection of the letters of Edgar Allan Poe, Dr. Ostrom, after years of painstaking labor, has sought to supply an exact and full edition. The task of the editor of such an edition is peculiarly difficult, and perhaps can never result in a definitive work. Poe manuscripts have held an almost unique appeal to wealthy collectors. The prices of Poe letters have advanced to rates prohibitive to most scholars and university libraries. The owner of rare manuscripts often prefers that his possession shall not be publicly known. Sometimes a letter is printed in a newspaper or an auction catalogue and then disappears, occasionally to reappear years later at another auction sale; sometimes no trace of its later ownership can be found.

Time has none the less cleared up many difficulties of publication since 1902, when Professor James A. Harrison of the University of Virginia edited as full an edition of the letters as he could collect and published them in the seventeenth volume of *The Complete Works of Edgar Allan Poe,* known as the "Virginia Poe." That edition, the only inclusive collection hitherto attempted, has until now remained the only available source for most of the correspondence. Dr. Harrison, a scholarly and indefatigable worker, of whom as his former student I speak with deep respect, completed his work under great physical handicaps, especially that of poor eyesight. He had the faults of taste and method common to many nineteenth-century editors. He did not rigidly reproduce the text of the letters, and he omitted or qualified phrases, apparently out of consideration for personalities. Sometimes the omissions had been made in the sources from which he printed; many of the letters had been printed only in part, and he had no access to the originals. Some of the letters had been printed in copyright articles or books, and he did not feel free to reproduce them. In the case of the letters to James Russell Lowell, for example, published by George Edward Woodberry, he gave abstracts of the letters but did not print them in full. Accordingly, the Harrison edition, until now of primary value to students of Poe's life, has long been out of date. Every biographer of Poe has been limited in his judgments by the lack of an adequate and accurate collection of Poe's letters, and every serious student of Poe's life and writings has felt the need of such a collection.

Dr. Ostrom, therefore, has produced a volume of first importance to students of American literature. His editing is painstaking and sympathetic. He has had the generous aid of many people in locating letters or in supplying the text when the location of the letter could not be traced. This edition is, I believe, as complete and as accurate an edition of Poe's letters as can now be made. An occasional uncollected item will, no doubt, from time to time come to light, but it is hardly to be expected that at this late date, practically a hundred years after Poe's death, any large group of his letters remains unknown.

The first important group of Poe's letters consists of those addressed to his foster father, John Allan, which are now in the Valentine Museum at Richmond. They were ably edited by Mrs. Mary Newton Stanard in 1925 under the title *Edgar Allan Poe Letters Till Now Unpublished*. These early letters reveal a highstrung youth who at eighteen considered himself driven from the home of his childhood by the man who had stood in the place of a father. In later years Poe told Mrs. Whitman (as she wrote to the English biographer J. H. Ingram) that Mr. Allan had been as overindulgent at some times as he was severe and withholding at others. Edgar Poe was probably an irritating lad, and in any case he and rough John Allan were bound to grow more and more incompatible. This series of letters runs through Poe's stay at West Point and his earlier hardships in Baltimore, when he worked on the first drafts of his early stories. There is an unexplained hiatus: not a single letter survives for the year 1832, and from December 29, 1831, to November, 1834, there are only two known letters.

The periods in which Poe was actively engaged upon the editing of a magazine are the periods of his most vigorous correspondence. The first of these began in 1835, when after exchanging letters with the proprietor, T. W. White, he became the editor of *The Southern Literary Messenger* in Richmond. From the time he left the *Messenger* in January 1837, to May 1839, when arrangements were discussed with W. E. Burton which led to his editorial connection with *Burton's Gentleman's Magazine*, there are not more than half-a-dozen surviving letters. His correspondence flourished again while he was editor of *Burton's* and later of *Graham's Magazine*. It is probable that the many connections that he formed through his editorship and his efforts to form a subscription list for two dream magazines of his own, the *Penn* and the *Stylus,* were responsible for a large increase in his letter-writing. It is also likely that his celebrity as a figure in the literary world caused a greater proportion of his letters to be preserved.

Among his letters to men, several series are interesting as groups, reflecting, as they do, different phases of the writer. The frankest and most familiar are those to his early friend, F. W. Thomas. With Dr. Snodgrass there is the suggestion of Poe's desire to curry favor and advance his professional interests. In the letters to Lowell, before a personal meeting under unhappy circumstances changed the relations, Poe is revealed as in his earlier, briefer correspondence with P. P. Cooke, as the artist and man of letters addressing himself to a highly idealized fellow poet. Especially remarkable is the series written to George W. Eveleth. The young man was unknown to Poe except as a voluntary correspondent who insisted upon replies. Poe answered his queries almost as he might have done to an intimate friend. He wrote as if he found relief in explaining himself to a sympathetic inquisitor.

The most baffling group among his letters is composed of those written in 1848 and 1849 to Mrs. Sarah Helen Whitman of Providence, Rhode Island, and to Mrs. Charles Richmond ("Annie") of Lowell, Massachusetts. After the death in 1847 of his young wife, Virginia, Edgar Poe seemed to depend upon feminine sympathy for emotional support. It is evident that he attempted to convince himself that a marriage with Mrs. Whitman was desirable, but there can be no doubt that, as far as his unstable emotional condition at this time permitted, he became deeply in love with Mrs. Richmond. The carefully styled letters to Mrs. Whitman are unlike any others that Poe wrote: those to Mrs. Richmond are the passionate outcries of a bewildered man. From the voluminous manuscript collection bought by the University of Virginia from Miss Laura Ingram, the sister of Poe's English biographer, J. H. Ingram, it is apparent that Mrs. Richmond entrusted Ingram with copies of Poe's letters to her, intending that he should read them for his own guidance in the writing of Poe's life, but with no intention that they should be published. One of the few of her copies that Ingram did not destroy, that of the letter dated November 16, 1848, has his note upon it: "This *must* be destroyed. J.H.I." It remains one of the most revealing of all docu-

ments having to do with Poe. If we compare Mrs. Richmond's copy
— here printed by Dr. Ostrom — with the version that Ingram published, and note the changes Ingram made, we are warned that those
letters to Annie that exist only in the form which Ingram printed
may have been equally changed in the editing.

In no other letters is Poe seen so humanly as in those to his mother-
in-law, Mrs. Clemm, from whom he seemed to have no secret reserve.
From the first pathetic pleas not to separate him from Virginia to
almost the last letter he ever wrote, with its despairing cry: "Do not
tell me anything about Annie — I cannot bear to hear it now," he
lays bare to her his tortured soul. The poverty and want he had endured are reflected in the letter of April 7, 1844: "I wish you could
have seen the eggs — and the great dishes of meat." The instability
of his life is shown in his precautions in furnishing Mrs. Clemm with
a fictitious name which she was to use in addressing his letters to
"General Delivery."

Altogether, this correspondence of one of America's first men of
genius suggests the life of a literary hack. His letters, like his personal
life, are subject to the vicissitudes of his fortunes. They give no impression of the continuity of a peaceful and secure personal living,
rather they suggest spasmodic unrest. Many of them are the necessary
drudge-work of a hired pen, and others are written under circumstances painful or humiliating. There are famous names among Poe's
correspondents: William Cullen Bryant, Henry Wadsworth Longfellow, Washington Irving, Charles Dickens, Nathaniel Hawthorne,
James Russell Lowell, and among the magazine celebrities of the
day, N. P. Willis, Sarah J. Hale, R. W. Griswold, and many others.
But it is evident that the relationships represented by these letters are
formal and not intimate. Nowhere in all this collection of the correspondence of a lifetime is there a background of stable, friendly relationship suggesting a circle of real acquaintances who were Poe's intellectual equals. He wrote to John Neal, N. P. Willis, and J. P. Kennedy
as to patrons, and to many of the others as an editor carrying out the
routine of his office.

We do not come very close to Poe through his letters, but we do
come to understand him better. We see more poignantly than in any
story of his life yet written the petty traffic of the literary market,
the uncertainties and the disappointments of his struggle, and the

combination of instability and perseverance within his own person-
ality. The figure that emerges is the same lonely figure of Poe that
has long been known to the imagination of men. It is a humanly
pathetic figure but it is also tragic in the price that the man paid for
his genius.

JAMES SOUTHALL WILSON

University of Virginia

CHRONOLOGY

1809	Jan. 19	Edgar Allan Poe born in Boston.
1811	Dec. 8	Elizabeth Arnold Poe, Edgar's mother, died in Richmond. John and Frances Keeling Allan become Poe's foster-parents.
1815	June–July, 1820	In England with the Allans.
1820	July–Feb. 14, 1826	In Richmond.
1826	Feb. 14–Dec.	At University of Virginia.
1826	Dec.–March 24, 1827	In Richmond. Sailed to Boston, March 24.
1827	May 26	Enlisted in United States Army at Boston. Stationed at Fort Independence, Boston Harbor.
	summer (?)	*Tamerlane and Other Poems* published by Calvin F. S. Thomas in Boston.
	Nov. 8	Poe's battery sailed for Fort Moultrie, Charleston, South Carolina.
1828	Dec. 11	Poe's battery transferred to Fortress Monroe, Virginia.
1829	Feb. 28	Frances Keeling Allan, Poe's foster-mother, died.
	April 15	Discharged from Army. Returned to Richmond.
	May	Left Richmond for Washington and Baltimore, where he may have lived with or near his aunt, Maria Clemm.
	December	*Al Aaraaf, Tamerlane, and Other Poems* published by Hatch and Dunning in Baltimore.
1830	early	Returned to Richmond before May 3.
	May 3–21	Left Richmond en route to West Point as an appointee to the United States Military Academy. Stopped over in Baltimore to visit relatives.
	ca. June 20–Feb. 19, 1831	At West Point until he forced his expulsion. Went to New York.
1831	spring	*Poems* published by Elam Bliss in New York.
	May–July (?), 1835	In Baltimore.
1833	October	Won Baltimore *Saturday Visiter* contest with "A MS. Found in a Bottle."
1834	Mar. 27	John Allan, Poe's foster-father, died.
1835	July–August	Joined *Southern Literary Messenger* in Richmond.
1836	May 16	Poe, aged 27, married his cousin, Virginia Clemm, aged 13.

1837 January	Relinquished editorship of *Southern Literary Messenger,* January 3, but remained in Richmond until at least January 19.
February	In New York.
1838 September	In Philadelphia.
1839 early	*The Conchologist's First Book* published over Poe's name by Haswell, Barrington, and Haswell, in Philadelphia.
June	Became editor of *Burton's Gentleman's Magazine.*
December	*Tales of the Grotesque and Arabesque* published by Carey, Lea, and Carey in Philadelphia.
1840 June	Left editorship of *Burton's* but remained in Philadelphia.
June 13	Prospectus of Poe's projected *Penn Magazine* appeared in the Philadelphia *Saturday Courier.*
1841 February	Became editor of *Graham's Magazine.*
1842 January	Virginia Poe ruptured a blood vessel in her throat, a condition that ultimately led to complications and finally to her death in 1847.
?	Prepared a new publication called *Phantasy Pieces,* which was never published.
April–April, 1844	Gave up editorship of *Graham's* but remained in Philadelphia. Continued his fruitless efforts to establish his own magazine, the title being changed to the *Stylus.*
1843 February 25	Poe's biography, portrait, and announcement that the *Stylus* would be published July 1, 1843, appeared in the Philadelphia *Saturday Museum.*
June	Won the *Dollar Newspaper* prize with "The Gold Bug."
?	*The Prose Romances of Edgar A. Poe* published by William H. Graham in Philadelphia.
1844 April 7	Moved to New York.
1845 Jan. 29	"The Raven" first appeared in the New York *Evening Mirror.*
Feb. 22	Became an editor of the *Broadway Journal.*
ante June 27	*Tales* published by Wiley and Putnam in New York.
July 12	Became sole editor of the *Broadway Journal.*
Oct. 24	Became owner and editor of the *Broadway Journal.*
Nov. 19	*The Raven and Other Poems* published by Wiley and Putnam in New York.

1846	Jan. 3	*The Broadway Journal* expired.
	January–February	*The Raven and Other Poems* . . . *Poe's Tales,* a compound book of Poe's two earlier works, published by Wiley and Putnam in New York.
1847	Jan. 30	Virginia Poe died at Fordham.
	Feb. 17	Won damage suit against the New York *Mirror.*
1848	*ante* Jan. 4	Printed new prospectus of the *Stylus.*
	June	*Eureka* published by George P. Putnam in New York.
	ca. July 17	Went to Richmond to develop interest in the *Stylus.*
	ca. Sept. 5	Returned to New York.
	September	Visited Mrs. S. H. Whitman in Providence, R. I., probably with the thought of offering a proposal of marriage.
	October	In New York.
	ca. Nov. 1–13	In Lowell, Massachusetts, and in Providence.
	Nov. 14–Dec. 19	In New York.
	Dec. 20–23	In Providence for his marriage to Mrs. Whitman. The ceremony never took place.
	Dec. 24	In New York.
1849	May 23–June 1	Visited Mrs. Annie L. Richmond in Lowell, Massachusetts.
	June 29	Left New York for Richmond.
	June 30–July 13	In Philadelphia.
	July 14–Sept. 25	In Richmond. During his stay he made a trip to Norfolk to lecture. Also tried to effect a marriage with his childhood sweetheart, Mrs. Elmira Royster Shelton.
	ca. Sept. 26	Left Richmond for Baltimore by boat.
	Oct. 7	Died in Baltimore.

ABBREVIATIONS

(for fuller information see Bibliography)

[CL]	check list
< >	cancelled matter
[ ]	editorial interpolations
A	Allen, Hervey., *Israfel* (2 vols.).
ABC	*American Book-Prices Current.*
Allen, *Israfel*	Allen, Hervey, *Israfel* (1 vol.).
a.l.s.	autograph letter signed.
Bixby	*Some Edgar Allan Poe Letters in the Collection of W. K. Bixby.*
Cappon	Cappon, Lester J., *Virginia Newspapers: 1821–1935.*
EP and EP (reprint)	Mabbott, Thomas O., "The Letters of George W. Eveleth to Edgar Allan Poe."
Gill	Gill, William F., *The Life of Edgar Allan Poe.*
H	Harrison, James A. *The Complete Works of Edgar Allan Poe.*
Heartman and Canny	Heartman, Charles F., and Canny, James R., *A Bibliography of Edgar Allan Poe.*
Hull	Hull, William D., "A Canon of the Critical Works of Edgar Allan Poe."
Ingram	Ingram, John H., *Edgar Allan Poe.*
LL	Harrison, James A., *Last Letters of Edgar Allan Poe to Sarah Helen Whitman.*
L and L	Harrison, James A., *Life and Letters of Edgar Allan Poe.*
Life	see Ingram
OCL	Ostrom, John W., ed., *Check List of Letters to and from Poe.*
P	Phillips, Mary E., *Edgar Allan Poe, the Man.*
PC	Heartman, Charles F., *A Census of First Editions and Source Materials of Edgar Allan Poe in American Collections.*
PE and PE (reprint)	Wilson, James S., "The Letters of Edgar A. Poe to George W. Eveleth."
Pratt	Quinn, Arthur H., and Hart, Richard H., *Edgar Allan Poe Letters and Documents in the Enoch Pratt Free Library.*
Preface	Griswold, Rufus W., *Works of Edgar Allan Poe,* "Preface" from vol. 1.
Quinn, *Poe*	Quinn, Arthur H., *Edgar Allan Poe.*

Quinn and Hart	see Pratt
SLM	*Southern Literary Messenger.*
SLP	Field, Eugene, *Some Letters of Edgar Allan Poe to E. H. N. Patterson of Oquawka, Illinois.*
Varner	Varner, John G., "Sarah Helen Whitman: Seeress of Providence."
VL	Stanard, Mary Newton., *Edgar Allan Poe Letters Till Now Unpublished.*
Whitty	Whitty, James H., *The Complete Poems of Edgar Allan Poe.*
W	Woodberry, George E., *The Life of Edgar Allan Poe.*
Woodberry (1885)	Woodberry, George E., *Edgar Allan Poe.*
Wyllie, *Poe's Tales*	Wyllie, John C., "A List of the Texts of Poe's Tales."

I

RICHMOND — CHARLOTTESVILLE — BALTIMORE

THE JOHN ALLAN PERIOD

November 1824–April 1833

To his Excellency the Governor & Council of Virg^a

Gentlemen

At the request of the members of the Richmond Junior Volunteers we beg leave to solicit your permission for them to retain the arms which they lately were permitted to draw from the Armory. We are authorized to say that each Individual will not only pledge himself to take proper care of them, but we ourselves will promise to attend strictly to the order in which they are kept by the Company —

We have the honor to be Gentlemen
Your Mo. Obt Serv^{ts}

Richmond 17th Novr 1824   John Lyle   Capt R J V

                                Edgar A. Poe   Lieu^t

> This is Poe's first extant letter (but see Note 3, in which reference is made to a letter to Poe while he and the Allans were in England and to possible notes or letters from Poe, though no MSS. are traceable). Poe was an officer, even at fifteen, of the Junior Morgan Riflemen, a volunteer company of Richmond boys. When General Lafayette visited Richmond in October 1824, the Volunteers served as his bodyguard (see statement of T. H. Ellis, quoted by Quinn, *Poe*, p. 87). [CL 3]

Mr Daniel

Sir

Be so good as to ask the Council for the paper we mentioned to you on Saturday. Our case is this. We had given up our arms to Dr Adams, according to promise when you told us we might keep them until called for by the Executive[.] Immediately upon hearing this we returned and asked Dr Adams for them again. He told us if we brought a communication from the Council stating that we might keep them until called for that he would return them to us without sending them to the Armory otherwise they would immediately be returned to the [*page 2*] the Armory. We applied to you, you said you could not give us such a note, without the consent of the Council —

We beg that you would obtain this for us if possible

And we shall ever remain

Yr. Most Obt. Serv[t]

23rd Nov. 1824

John Lisle   Capt[n] R. J. V.

Edgar A Poe   Lieut.

> It is not known whether the present request was granted. In this connection, see Letter 1. Peter V. Daniel was one of the three members of the Virginia State Council; later he became nationally prominent as an Associate Justice of the Supreme Court. [CL 4]

3 ⊁ TO JOHN ALLAN

University. May [25] 1826

Dear Sir,

I this morning received the clothes you sent me, viz an uniform coat, six yards of striped cloth for pantaloons & four pair of socks — The coat is a beautiful one & fits me exactly — I thought it best not to write 'till I received the clothes — or I should have written before this. You have heard no doubt of the disturbances in College[.] Soon after you left here the Grand Jury met and put the Students in a terrible fright — so much so that the lectures were unattended — and those whose names were upon the Sheriff's list — travelled off into the woods & mountains — taking their beds & provisions along with them — there were about 50 on the list — so you may suppose the College was very well thinned — this was the first day of the fright — the second day, "A proclamation" was issued by the faculty forbidding "any student under pain of a major punishment to leave his dormitory between the hours of 8 & 10 A M — (at which time the Sheriffs would be about) or in any way to resist the lawful authority of the Sheriffs" — This order however was very little attended to — as the fear of the Faculty could not counterbalance that of the Grand Jury — most of the "indicted" ran off a second time into the woods and upon an examination the next morning by the Faculty — Some were reprimanded — some suspended — [*page 2*] and one expelled — James Albert Clarke from Manchester (I went to school with him at Burke's) was suspended for two months, Armstead Carter from this neighbourhood, for the remainder of the session — And Thomas Barclay for ever — There have been several fights since you were here — One between Turner Dixon, and Blow from Norfolk excited more interest than any I have seen — for a common fight is so trifling an occurrence that no notice is taken of it — Blow got much the advantage in the scuffle — but Dixon posted him in very indecent terms — upon which the whole Norfolk party rose in arms — & nothing was talked off for a week, but Dixon's charge, & Blow's explanation — every pillar in the University was white with scratched paper — Dixon made <an> a physical attack upon Arthur Smith one of Blow's Norfolk friends — and a "very fine fellow" — he struck him with a large stone on one side of his head — whereupon Smith drew a pistol (which are all the fashion here) and had it not missed fire would have put an end to the controversy — but so it was — it did miss fire — and the matter has since been more peaceably settled — as the Proctor engaged a Magistrate to bind the whole forces on both sides — over to the peace — Give my love to Ma & Miss Nancy — & all my friends — <&>

I remain
[Your's affecti[onately]

Edgar

Will you be so good as to send me a copy of the Historiae of Tacitus — it is a small volume — also some more soap —

Poe matriculated at the University of Virginia, February 14, 1826, at the start of the second session, and registered in the School of Ancient Languages under Professor George Long and in the School of Modern Languages under Professor George Blaetterman. He gave his home as Richmond and his birth date as January 19, 1809. For an account of the "disturbances" (a result of the Grand Jury's indictment of certain hotel keepers in the spring of 1826), see Quinn, *Poe,* pp. 106–107. Poe had attended William Burke's school in Richmond from April 1, 1823, to (?), according to Quinn, *Poe,* p. 84. "Ma" was Frances Keeling Valentine Allan, Poe's foster-mother; "Miss Nancy" was Anne Moore Valentine, Mrs. Allan's sister (Poe also addressed her as Miss Valentine and Miss V., but never as "Aunt Nancy," as has been stated). There is no evidence that Allan sent the Tacitus or the soap, nor, indeed, that he even answered the letter; the only letters, for which there is any evidence, from Allan to Poe in 1826 are those of *c.* February 24–27 and *c.* December, 1826 (see Letter 28). [CL 7]

University — Septem^r 21^{rst} 1826

Dear Sir,

The whole college has been put in great consternation by the prospect of an examination — There is to be a general one on the first of
December, which will occupy the time of the students till the fifteenth
— the time for breaking up —

It has not yet been determined whether there will be any diplomas,
or doctor's degrees given — but I should hardly think there will be
any such thing, as this is only the second year of the institution & in
other colleges three and four years are required in order to take a
degree — that is, that time is supposed to be necessary — altho they
sometimes confer them before — if the applicants are qualified —

Tho' it will hardly be fair to examine those who have only been
here one session, with those who have been here two — and some of
whom have come from other colleges — still I suppose I shall have to
stand my examination wit[h] the rest —

I have been studying a great deal in order to be prepared, and dare
say I shall come off as well as the rest of them, that is — if I don't get
frightened — Perhaps you will have some business up here about that
time, and then you can judge for yourself —

[*page 2*] They have nearly finished the Rotunda — The pillars of
the Portico are completed and it greatly improves the appearance of
the whole — The books are removed into the library — and we have
a very fine collection[.]

We have had a great many fights up here lately — The faculty
expelled Wickliffe last night for general bad conduct — but more
especially for biting one of the student's arms with whom he was
fighting — I saw the whole affair — it took place before my door —
Wickliffe was much the strongest — but not content with that —
after getting the other completely in his power, he began to bite — I
saw the arm afterwards — and it was really a serious matter — It was
bitten from the shoulder to the elbow — and it is likely that pieces
of flesh as large as my hand will be obliged to be cut out — He is from
Kentucky — the same one that was in suspension when you were up

here some time ago — Give my love to Ma and Miss Nancy — I
remain,

Your's affectionatly

Edgar A Poe

The Faculty Minutes for December 15, 1826, show Poe in the second
group for excellence in Latin and in the first group in French. For a
later letter from Allan, enclosing $100 "towards the close of the ses-
sion," see Letter 28, which implies at least one letter from Poe requesting
funds; both letters are unlocated. [CL 8]

5 ⊁ TO JOHN ALLAN

Richmond   Monday [March 19, 1827]

Sir,

After my treatment on yesterday and what passed between us this
morning, I can hardly think you will be surprised at the contents of
this letter. My determination is at length taken — to leave your house
and indeavor to find some place in this wide world, where I will be
treated — not as *you* have treated me — This is not a hurried determination, but one on which I have long considered — and having so
considered my resolution is unalterable — You may perhaps think that
I have flown off in a passion, & that I am already wishing to return;
But not so — I will give you the reason[s] which have actuated me,
and then judge —
Since I have been able to think on any subject, my thoughts have
aspired, and they have been taught by *you* to aspire, to eminence in
public life — this cannot be attained without a good Education, such
a one I cannot obtain at a Primary school — [*page 2*] A collegiate
Education therefore was what I most ardently desired, and I had been
led to expect that it would at some future time be granted — but in a
moment of caprice — you have blasted my hope <sed> because for-
sooth I disagreed with you in an opinion, which opinion I was forced
to express — Again, I have heard you say (when you little thought
I was listening <) > and therefore must have said it in earnest) that
you had no affection for me —
You have moreover ordered me to quit **your house**, and are con-

tinually upbraiding me with eating the bread of Idleness, when you yourself <m> were the only person to remedy the evil by placing me to some business — You take delight in exposing me before those whom you think likely to advance my interest in this world —

You suffer me to be subjected to the whims & caprice, not only of your white family, but the [*page 3*] complete authority of the blacks — these grievances I could not submit to; and I am gone[.] I request that you will send me my trunk containing my clothes & books — and if you still have the least affection for me, As the last cal[l] I shall make on your bou[nty], To prevent the fulfillment of the Prediction you this morning expressed, send me as much money as will defray <my> the expences of my passage to some of the Northern cit[i]es & then support me for one month, by whic[h] time I [sh]all be enabled to place myself [in] some situation where I may not only o[bt]ain a livelihood, but lay by a sum which one day or another will support me at the University — Send my trunk &c to the Court-house Tavern, send me I entreat you some money immediately — as I am in the greatest necessity — If you fail to comply with my request — I tremble for the consequence

Yours &c

Edgar A Poe

It depends upon yourself if hereafter you see or hear from m[e.]

> For an earlier but less overt estrangement between Poe and John Allan, see Allan's letter to Henry Poe, November 1, 1824 (Quinn, *Poe,* p. 89). There is no evidence that either trunk or money was sent, or that Poe's heroics were more than a youthful threat that ended in his setting sail for Boston — but see the notes to Letter 6, and the comment made by John Allan to his sister in Scotland, March 27, in which he expressed the opinion that Poe had gone to sea, presumably to seek his fortune. See Quinn, *Poe,* p. 116 (also VL, pp. 51–52), from the original letter in the Ellis-Allan Papers, Library of Congress. [CL 12]

6 ⤜ TO JOHN ALLAN

Richmond   Tuesday [March 20, 1827]

Dear Sir,

Be so good as to send me my trunk with my clothes — I wrote to you on yesterday explaining my reasons for leaving — I suppose by my not receiving either my trunk, or an answer to my letter, that you did not receive it — I am in the greatest necessity, not having tasted food since Yesterday morning. I have no where to sleep at night, but roam about the Streets — I am nearly exhausted — I beseech you as you wish not your prediction concerning me to be fulfilled — to send me without delay my trunk containing my clothes, and to lend if you will not give me as much money as will defray the expence of my passage to <bos> Boston (.$12,) and a little to support me there untill I shall be enabled to engage in some business — I sail on Saturday — A letter will be received by me at the Court House Tavern, where be so good as to send my trunk —

Give my love to all at home
I am Your's &c.

Edgar A Poe

I have not one cent in the world to provide any food

> Allan's letter to Poe (March 20, 1827) implies definite refusal of financial aid for the proposed trip to Boston (see VL, pp. 67–68); but Poe's present letter may have evoked the necessary $12, either from Allan or his wife. However, Allan wrote on the verso, after adding an "s" to the signature, "Pretty Letter." If the money was sent, any correspondence concerning it is unknown. The time of Poe's arrival in Boston is uncertain, though a date early in April seems probable. Attempts to name the ship on which he travelled have been inconclusive (see VL, p. 53; Quinn, *Poe*, p. 118; and Mabbott, Introduction to *Tamerlane*, p. xii, and Introduction to *The Raven and Other Poems*, pp. xxvi–xxvii). [CL 13]

7 ➤ TO JOHN ALLAN

Fort Moultrie, Charleston H^r
December 1^{rst} 1828.

Dear Sir,

The letter of Lieut J. Howard left by Mr John, O, Lay for your perusal will explain the cause of my writing from Fort Moultrie. Your note addressed to Mr Lay, & inclosed by him to Lieut: Howard was handed over by the latter to myself. In that note what chiefly gave me concern was hearing of your indisposition — I can readily see & forgive the suggestion which prompted you to write "he had better remain as he is until the termination of his enlistment." It was perhaps under the impression that a *military* life was one after my own heart, and that it might be possible (although contrary to the Regulations of our Army) to obtain a commission for one who had not received his education at West Point, & who, from his age, was excluded that Academy; but I could not help thinking that you beleived me degraded & disgraced, and that any thing were preferable to my returning home & entailing on yourself a portion of my infamy: But, at no period of my life, have I regarded myself with a deeper satisfaction — or did my heart swell with more honourable pride — The time may come (if at all it will come speedily) when much that appears of a doubtful nature will be explained away, and I shall have no hesitation in appearing among my former [*page 2*] connexions — at the present I have no such intention, and nothing, short of your absolute commands, should deter me from my purpose.

I have been in the American army as long as suits my ends or my inclination, and it is now time that I should leave it — To this effect I made known my circumstances to Lieut Howard who promised me my discharge solely upon a re-conciliation with yourself — In vain I told him that your wishes for me (as your letters assured me) were, and had always been those of a father & that you were ready to forgive even the worst offences — He insisted upon my writing you & that if a re-conciliation could be effected he would grant me my wish — This was advised in the goodness of his heart & with a view of serving me in a double sense — He has always been kind to me, and, in many respects, reminds me forcibly of yourself —

The period of an Enlistment is five years — the prime of my life would be wasted — I shall be driven to more decided measures if you refuse to assist me.

You need not fear for my future prosperity — I am altered from what you knew me, & am no longer a boy tossing about on the world without aim or consistency — I feel that within me which will make me fulfil your highest wishes & only beg you to suspend your judgement until you hear *of* me again.

You will perceive that I speak confidently — but when did [*page 3*] ever Ambition exist or Talent prosper without prior conviction of success? I have thrown myself on the world, like the Norman conqueror on the shores of Britain &, by my avowed assurance of victory, have destroyed the fleet which could alone cover my retreat — I must either conquer or die — succeed or be disgraced.

A letter addressed to Lieut: J. Howard assuring him of your re-
conciliation with myself (which you have never yet refused) & desiring my discharge would be all that is necessary — He is already acquainted with you from report & the high character given of you
by Mr Lay.

Write me once more if you do really forgive me [and] let me know
how my Ma preserves her health, and the concerns of the family since
my departure.

Pecuniary assistance I do not desire — unless of your own free &
unbiassed choice — I can struggle with any difficulty. My dearest love
to Ma — it is only when absent that we can tell the value of such a
friend — I hope she will not let my wayward disposition wear away
the love she used to have for me.

Yours respectfully & affectionately

Edgar, A, Poe

P.S. We are now under orders to sail for Old Point Comfort, and will
arrive there before your answer can be received — Your address then
will be to Lieut: J. Howard, Fortress Monroe — the same for myself.

> Poe enlisted in the United States Army at Boston, May 26, 1827, under
> the alias Edgar A. Perry, aged 22, born in Boston, and was assigned to
> Battery H, First Artillery, then stationed at Fort Independence, Boston
> Harbor (see Quinn, *Poe*, p. 119). On November 8, 1827, the battery
> sailed for Fort Moultrie, Charleston Harbor, South Carolina, where it
> arrived on November 18. Poe remained at Fort Moultrie until Decem-
> ber 11, 1828 (see Quinn, *Poe*, p. 129). Mr. Lay's identity, except as
> intermediary, is unknown. John Allan did not reply to Poe's letter.
> Poe's battery reached Fortress Monroe, Virginia, December 15, 1828
> (see Quinn, *Poe*, p. 129). [CL 16]

8 ⊁ TO JOHN ALLAN

Fortress Monroe (Va)

December 22^d 1828 —

Dear Sir;

I wrote you shortly before leaving Fort Moultrie & am much hurt
at receiving no answer. Perhaps my letter has not reached you & under
that supposition I will recapitulate its contents. It was chiefly to
sollicit your interest in freeing me from the Army of the U.S. in

which, (as Mr Lay's letter from Lieut Howard informed you) — I am
at present a soldier. I begged that you would suspend any judgement
you might be inclined to form, upon many untoward circumstances,
until you heard *of* me again — & begged you to give my dearest love
to Ma & solicit her not to let my wayward disposition wear away the
affection she used to have for me. I mentioned that all that was necessary to obtain my discharge from the army was your consent in a
letter to Lieut J. Howard, who has heard of you by report, & the high
character given you by Mr Lay; this being all that I asked at your
hands, I was hurt at your declining to answer my letter. Since arriving
at Fort Moultrie [*page 2*] Lieut Howard has given me an introduction
to Col: James House of the 1^rst Arty to whom I was before personally
known only as a soldier of his regiment. He spoke kindly to me. told
me that he was personally acquainted with my Grandfather Genl Poe,
with yourself & family, & reassured me of my immediate discharge
upon your consent. It must have been a matter of regret to me, that
when those who were strangers took such deep interest in my welfare,
<that> you who called me your son should refuse me even the com-
mon civility of answering a letter. If it is your wish to forget that I
have been your son I am too proud to remind you of it again — I only
beg you to remember that you yourself cherished the cause of my
leaving your family — Ambition. If it has not taken the channel you
wished it, it is not the less certain of its object. Richmond & the
U. States were too narrow a sphere & the world shall be my theatre —

As I observed in the letter which you have not received — (you
would have answered it if you had) you believe me degraded — but
<th> do not believe it — There is that within ny heart which has
no connection with degradation — I can walk among [*page 3*] infec-
tion & be uncontaminated. There never was any period of my life
when my bosom swelled with a deeper satisfaction, of myself & (except in the injury which I may have done to your feelings) — of my
conduct — My father do not throw me aside as *degraded*[.] I will
be an honor to your name.

Give my best love to my Ma & to all friends —

If you determine to abandon me — here take [I my] farewell —
Neglected — I will be doubly [ambi]tious, & the world shall hear of
the son whom you have thought unworthy of your notice. But if you
let the love you bear me, outweigh the offence which I have given —
then write me my father, quickly. My desire is for the present to be

freed from the Army — Since I have been in it my character is one that will bear scrutiny & has merited the esteem of my officers — but I have accomplished my own ends — & I wish to be gone — Write to Lieut Howard — & to Col: House, desiring my discharge — & above all to myself. Lieut Howard's direction is Lieut J. Howard, For⁸⁸ Monroe, Col: House's Col: Jas. House — F⁸⁸ Monroe — my own the same —

[*page 4*] My dearest love to Ma & all my friends

I am   Your affectionate son

Edgar A   Poe

For more on General Poe, see Letter 64, and notes. Poe's promise to become an honor to the Allan name was prompted probably both by ambition and by his having published *Tamerlane*, though anonymously, in Boston, 1827. Apparently Allan did not answer this letter, for the next known communication from him is dated May 18, 1829 (see VL, p. 121). Poe's battery reached Fortress Monroe, Old Point Comfort, Virginia, December 15, 1828 (see the notes to Letter 7). [CL 17]

9 ≻ TO JOHN ALLAN

Fortress Monroe   February 4ᵗʰ 1829,

Dear Sir,

I wrote you some time ago from this place but have as yet received no reply. Since that time I wrote to John Mᶜ Kenzie desiring him to see you personally & desire for me, of you, that you would interest yourself in procuring me a cadets' appointment at the Military Academy.

To this likewise I have received no answer, for which I can in no manner account, as he wrote me before I wrote to him & seemed to take an interest in my welfare.

I made the request to obtain a cadets' appointment partly because I know that — (if <y> my age should prove no obstacle as I have since ascertained it will not) the appointment could easily be obtained either by your personal acquaintance with Mʳ Wirt — or by the recommendation of General Scott, or even of the officers residing at Fortress Monroe & partly because in making the request you would at once see to what direction my "future views & expectations" were inclined.

You can have no idea of the immense [*page 2*] advantages which my present station in the army would give me in the appointment of a cadet — it would be an unprecedented case in the American army, & having already passed thro the practical part even of the higher partion of the Artillery arm, my cadetship would only be considered as a necessary form which I am positive I could run thro' in 6 months.

This is the view of the case which many at this place have taken in regard to myself. If you are willing to assist me it can now be effectually done — if not (as late circumstances have induced me to believe) I must remain contented until chance or other friends shall render me that assistance.

Under the certain expectation of kind news from home I have been led into expences which my present income will not support. I hinted as much in my former letter, and am at present in an uncomfortable situation[.] I have known the time when you would not have suffered me long to remain so.

[*page 3*] Whatever fault you may find with me I have not been ungrateful for past services but you blame me for the part which I have taken without considering the powerful impulses which actuated me — You will remember how much I had to suffer upon my return from the University. I never meant to offer a shadow of excuse for the infamous conduct of myself & others at that place.

It was however at the commencement of that year that I got deeply entangled in difficulty which all my after good conduct in the close of the session (to which all there can testify) could not clear away. I had never been from home before for any length of time. I say again I have no excuse to offer for my [con]duct except the common one of youth & [f***]s — but I repeat that I was unable [if] my life had depended upon it to bear the consequences of that conduct in the taunts & abuse that followed it even from those who had been my warmest friends.

I shall wait with impatience for an [*page 4*] answer to this letter for upon it depend a great many of the circumstances of my future life — the assurance of an honourable & highly successful course in my own country — or the prospect — no *certainty* of an exile forever to another[.]

Give my love to Ma —

I am Yours affectionately

Edgar A Poe

Letters to and from John McKenzie [Mackenzie] of Richmond at this time are otherwise unknown. William Wirt was the author of a biography of Patrick Henry (1817) and had been recently Attorney General of the United States; for Poe's later contact with him, see Wirt to Poe, May 11, 1829 (VL, pp. 131–132) and Letter 11. General Winfield Scott, a friend of the Allans, had known the young Poe in Richmond. Poe's hint for financial assistance appeared in Letter 7. For the reference to the difficulties at the University of Virginia, see Letter 28. Poe's threat of exile to another country does not seem to have been carried out; except for his early visit to England with the Allans, Poe almost certainly never left the United States. [CL 20]

10 ⊁ TO JOHN ALLAN

Fortress Monroe. March 10th 1829.

My dear Pa.

I arrived on the point this morning in good health, and if it were not for late occurrences, should feel much happier than I have for a long time. I have had a fearful warning, & have hardly ever known before what distres[s] was.

The Colonel has left the point this morning [for] Washington to congratulate the President [elect] so I have not yet seen him. He will ret[urn] on Thursday week next[.] In the mean time [I] [a]m employing mys[elf] in preparing for the [tests] [w]hich will engage my [at]tention at W. Point [if I] [s]hould be so fortunate [as] to obtain an appoint[ment.] [I] am anxious to retri[ev]e my good name wi[th my] [frie]nds & especially yo[ur] good opinion. [I] think a letter of reco[mm]endation from Ju[dge Barber,] [Maj]or Gibbon, & Col: P[res]ton forwarded to [Washington] [with] a letter to M^r [Pa]tterson requesting [that if] [nothing] would prev[ent] I may be r[egarded as] [a Bos]tonian.

[*Here probably one line of MS. was burned off.*] [*page 2*] me in the morning of my departure I went to your room to tell you good bye — but, as you were asleep, I would not disturb you.

My respects to M^r & Mrs Galt & Mr Wm Galt[.]

I am, dear Pa,
Your's affectionately

Edgar A. Poe

This letter was very badly burned at both sides, bottom, and center fold; emendations are based on a close study of the letter. This is the first letter to John Allan in which Poe begins, "Dear Pa," or "My dear Pa," as he does in several instances after this date, a fact that shows a new intimacy between Poe and his foster-father (see notes to Letter 3). Poe had just returned from Richmond, where Frances Keeling Allan, his foster-mother, had died on February 28, and had been buried on March 2, 1829; Poe was granted leave, apparently at Mr. Allan's request, but reached Richmond, March 3, "the night after the burial" (see Letter 28). Col. James House, commanding officer of the First Regiment, United States Artillery, Fortress Monroe, had gone to congratulate Andrew Jackson, President-elect. The suggested emendation of the names of Judge John J. Barber and of Col. James P. Preston is based upon John Allan's letter to Poe, May 18, 1829, in which he says: "I was agreeably pleased to hear that the Honourable Jno J Barber [*sic*] did interest himself . . . in your favour" (VL, p. 121), which suggests that Poe had asked that "Ju[dge Barber]" write a letter of recommendation. Furthermore, Allan, in the same letter, says: "Col. Preston wrote a warm letter in your favour to Major Eaton since your departure." This reference, together with Mrs. Stanard's (VL, p. 110) supports the emendation of "Preston." Col. Preston had been a former Governor of Virginia (*ibid.*); and Major Eaton was the Secretary of War (*ibid.*). Allen, *Israfel*, p. 118, identifies Major James Gibbon as a resident of Richmond. James Galt, William Galt, Jr., and John Allan were the chief beneficiaries under the will of William Galt, who died March 26, 1825 (see Allen, *Israfel*, pp. 96, 687–691); Allan was a nephew, James and William, adopted sons. Edgar Poe, son of David and Elizabeth Arnold Poe, was born in Boston, south of the Common and near the Charles river, the exact location of the house being uncertain (see Quinn, *Poe*, p. 31). [CL 21]

11 ⊁ TO JOHN ALLAN

Baltimore. May 20. 1829.

Dear Pa,

I received your letter this morning enclosing a draft for $100 for which liberal allowance you will be sure that I feel grateful. The draft which I drew at Mr Warwick's suggestion will of course be laid aside —

I have succeeded in finding Grandmother & my relations — but the fact of my Grandfather's having been Quater Master Gener[al] of the whole U.S.Army during the Revolutionary war is clearly established — but its being a well known fact at Washington, obviates the necessity of obtaining the certificates you mentioned.

<Not> Presuming upon Mr Wirt's former acquaintance, I intro-

duced myself personally & for a first attempt at self introduction succeeded wonderfully — He treated me with great politeness, and
[*page 2*] invited me to call & see him frequently while I stay in
Baltimore — I have called upon him several times.

I have been introduced to man[y] gentlemen of high standing in
the city. who were formerly acquainted with my grandfather. & have
altogether been treated very handsomely.

Give my best love to Miss Valentine & all at home —

I remain Yours affectionately

Edgar A, Poe

Poe's lost letter apparently spoke of having received a recommendation
to West Point from Judge John J. Barber, and of a successful interview
with the Secretary of War in Washington. Allan, encouraged by the
promise of Poe's appointment to West Point in September, forwarded
$100 in his letter of May 18. Also, his notation on the verso of the
letter printed hereof, "pd his draft," suggests that the order for $50,
which Poe had drawn at Mr. Warwick's "suggestion," was not laid
aside. Corbin Warwick was a relative of John Allan, later serving as an
executor to his will (see Allen, *Israfel*, p. 693). Poe, as Sergeant-Major
Edgar A. Perry, had been discharged from the army, April 15, 1829 (see
Quinn, *Poe*, p. 135). After leaving Fortress Monroe, perhaps directly,
Poe went to Richmond. He seems to have remained at home at least
until May 6, when John Allan gave him a letter of recommendation to
John Eaton, Secretary of War (see VL, pp. 110–111). Following his
"departure" from Richmond (see Allan's letter to Poe, May 18, 1829,
in the VL, p. 121), apparently aided by Allan's advance of $50 (see
Allan's notation on the present letter, above), Poe went to Washington,
then to Baltimore, where he found Mrs. David Poe, widow of General
Poe, Mrs. Maria Clemm, his aunt, and her daughter, Virginia, and his
brother, William Henry. Where they lived is uncertain, for the first
mention of Maria Clemm's residence is found in the Baltimore City
Directory of 1831, the location being Mechanics Row, Wilk Street (now
Eastern Avenue); whether Poe lived with them during the rest of 1829
is also uncertain, but the tone of his letters to Allan implies either that
he did or was in close contact with them, and a document of sale, found
in the Baltimore Court House, shows that he sold a negro slave for
Maria Clemm, December 10, 1829 (see May G. Evans, "Poe in Amity
Street," *Maryland Historical Magazine*, xxxvi (December 1941), 363–
380, especially, pp. 376–377). For William Wirt, see the note to Letter 9. Anne Moore Valentine, sister of Frances Valentine Allan, continued to live at the Allan home after Mrs. Allan's death, February 28,
1829. For more on General David Poe, see the note to Letter 64.
[CL 27]

[Philadelphia, May *ante* 27, 1829]

Dear Sir,

I should have presumed upon the politeness of M^r R- Walsh for a personal introduction to yourself, but was prevented by his leaving town the morning after my arrival — You will be so kind as to consider this as a *literary* introduction until his return from N.Y.

I send you, for your tenderest consideration, a poem —

"Some sins do bear their privilege on earth."

You will oblige me by placing this among the number.

> It was my choice or chance or curse
> To adopt the cause for better or worse
> And with my worldly goods & wit
> And soul & body worship it —

But not to detain you with my nonsense it were as well to speak of "the poem."

Its' title is "Al Aaraaf" — from the Al Aaraaf of the Arabians, a medium between Heaven & Hell where men suffer no punishment, but yet do not attain that tranquil & even happiness which they suppose to be the characteristic of heavenly enjoyment[.]

> Un no rompido
> Un dia puro, allegre, libre
> Quiera —
> Libre de amor, de zelo
> De odio, de esperanza, de re zelo —

[*page 2*] I have placed this "Al Aaraa"f in the celebrated star discovered by Tycho Brache which appeared & dissapeared so suddenly — It is represented as a messenger star of the Deity, &, at the time of its discovery by Tycho, as on an embassy to our world. One of the peculiarities of Al Aaraaf is that, even after death, those who make choice of the star as their residence do not enjoy immortality — but, after a second life of high excitement, sink into forgetfulness. & death — This idea is taken from Job — "I would not live <them>always — let me alone" — I have imagined that some would not be pleased (excuse the bull) with an immortality even of bliss. The poem commences with a sonnet (illegitimate) a la mode de Byron in his prisoner of Chillon. But this is a digression — I have imagined some well known characters of the age of the stars' appearance, as transferred to Al Aaraaf — viz Michael Angelo — and others — of these Michael Angelo as yet, alone appears. I send you parts 1^{rst} 2^d & 3^d. I have reasons for wishing not to publish the 4th at present — for its character depends in a measure upon the success or failure of the others —

As these 3 parts will be insufficient for a [*page 3*] volume, I have wished to publish some minor poems with Al Aaraaf — But as the work would depend for character upon the principal poem it is needless, at present to speak of the rest.

If the poem is published, succeed or not, I am "irrecoverably a poet." But to your opinion I leave it, and as I should be proud of the honor of your press, failing in that I will make no other application.

I should add a circumstance which, tho' no justification of a failure, is yet a boast in success — the poem is by a minor & truly written under extraordinary disadvantages.

> with great respect
> Your ob^t ser^t
>
> Edgar A. Poe

I am staying at Heiskells'. I cannot refrain from adding that M-Wirts' voice is in my favor —

> The year is 1829, for William Wirt's favorable "voice" — a letter of criticism of "Al Aaraaf" — is enclosed in Letter 13. Wirt's autograph MS. in the Boston Public Library is dated May 11, 1829. Thus the Poe to Lea letter can be dated May 11–27, 1829. Quinn, *Poe*, p. 138, identifies R[obert] Walsh as editor of the *American Quarterly Review,* and p. 143, "Heiskell's" as the Indian Queen Hotel, 15 South Fourth Street. The whereabouts of Lea's answer of May 27 is not known. It did not return the poem (see Letter 17). [CL 28]

13 ≻ TO JOHN ALLAN

> Baltimore   May 29th 1829,

Dear Pa,

I am now going to make a request different from any I have ever yet made.

As I wrote you, some time since, I have been several times to visit Mr Wirt, who has treated me with great kindness & attention. I sent him, for his opinion, a day or two ago, *a poem* which I have written since I left home — & in the letter which I now enclose you have his opinion upon its merits — From such a man as Mr Wirt. the flattering character he has given of the work, will surely be to you a recommendation in its favor.

In the conclusion of the letter you will see that he advises me to "get a personal introduction to Mr Walsh" the editor of the American Quaterly Review & get his interest in my favor — that interest, and his highest encomiums on the poem are already obtained — as Editor of the Review he promises to notice it which will assure it, if not of popularity, of success —

Under these circumstances, I have thought [*page 2*] it my duty to write to you on the subject — Believing you to be free from prejudice, I think you will aid me, if you see cause; At my time of life there is much in being *before the eye of the world* — if once noticed I can easily cut out a path to reputation — It can certainly be of no disadvantage as it will not, even for a moment, interfere with other objects which I have in view.

I am aware of the difficulty of getting a poem published in this country — Mr Wirt & Mr Walsh have advised me of that — but the *difficulty* should be no object, with a proper aim in view.

If M^{ssrs} Carey, Lea, & Carey, should decline publishing (as I have no reason to think they will not — they having invariably declined it with all our American poets) that is upon their *own risk* the request I have to make is this — that you will give me a letter to M^{ssrs} Carey, Lea, & Carey saying that if in publishing the poem "Al Aaraaf" [*page 3*] they shall incur any *loss* — you will make it good to them.

The cost of publishing the work, in a style equal to any of our American publications, will at the extent be $100 — This then, of course, must be the limit of any loss supposing not a single copy of the work to be sold — It is more than probable that the work will be profitable & that I may gain instead of lose, even in a pecuniary way —

I would remark, in conclusion that I have long given up *Byron* as a model — for which, I think, I deserve some credit.

If you will help me in this matter I will be always grateful for your kindness.

If you conclude upon giving me a *trial* please enclose me the letter to Messrs Carey, Lea, & Carey — I shall wait anxiously for your answer —

Give my love to Miss Valentine & all

I remain Yours affect^y:

E A. Poe

[*page 4*] Please present my thanks to Col: Preston for his obliging letter.

> John Allan's notation on the right margin of page 4 indicates that the letter of William Wirt was enclosed and that the present letter was answered "8th June 1829"; also Allan wrote just below the last line of the letter, "replied to Monday 8th June 1829/ strongly censuring his conduct — & refusing/ any aid — " Allan's last letter to Poe had been dated May 18, 1829.
>
> For William Wirt, see note to Letter 9. Robert Walsh was editor of the *American Quarterly Review* (March 1827–December 1837), published in Philadelphia (1827–1833) by Carey and Lea (see Mott, *History of American Magazines*, I, 271). Apparently Walsh did not "notice" Poe's poem (see Quinn, *Poe*, p. 144), which was published in Baltimore by Hatch and Dunning, December 1829, as *Al Aaraaf, Tamerlane, and Minor Poems*. For Wirt's letter to Poe, see VL, pp. 131–132, and the note to Letter 12. For Colonel Preston's letter recommending Poe for West Point, see Letter 10, and VL, p. 110. [CL 30]

14 ⊁ TO JOHN ALLAN

Baltimore June 25, 1829.

Dear Pa,

I wrote you on the 10th of June in reply to yours of the 8th in which I urged my reasons in further support of my request to be allowed to publish a poem — & I *did* intend, but forgot to say, in conclusion, that as I had submitted the question of its being expedient to your decision — I should by no means publish it without your approbation — I say this now, because I fear from your silence that I have offended you in pressing my request any farther.

The poem is now in the hands of Carey, Lea & Carey and I am only waiting for your answer to withdraw it or not — It was my wish immediately upon receiving your letter to return home thro' Washington & ascertain the fate of my application — <of> which I am induced to think has succeeded — as there were, I understand several rejected — This I will do immediately upon hearing [*page 2*] from you.

In whatever errors I may have been led into, I would beg you to judge me impartially & to believe that I have acted from the single motive of trying to do something for myself — & with your assistance I trust I may — I have left untried no efforts to enter at W. Point & if I fail I can give you evidence that it is no fault of mine — but I hope to succeed —

I am afraid you will think that I am trying to impose on your good nature & would not except under peculiar circumstances have applied to you for any more money — but it is only a little that I now want.

I will explain the matter clearly — A cousin of my own (Edward Mosher) robbed me at Beltzhoover's Hotel while I was asleep in the same room with him of all the money I had with me (about 46$) [*page 3*] of which I recovered $10 — by searching his pockets the ensuing night, when he acknowledged the theft — I have been endeavouring in vain to obtain the balance from him — he says he has not got it & begs me not to expose him — & for his wife's sake I will not. I have a letter from him referring to the subject, which I will show you on arriving in Richmond.

I have been moderate in my expences & $50 of the money which you sent me I applied in paying a debt contracted at Old Point for my substitute, for [which] I gave my note — the money necessary if Lt Howard had not gone on furlough would have been only 12 $ as a bounty — but when he & Col: House left I had to scuffle for myself — I paid $25 — & gave my note for $50 — in all 75 $.

Since I have been in Baltimore I have learnt something concerning my descent which would have, I am afraid, no very favourable effect if known to the *War* Dep^t: [*page 4*] viz: that I am the grandson of General Benedict Arnold — but this there will be no necessity of telling — [*space reserved for address*]

Give my best love to all my friends — I hope you will give me a favourable answer concerning my poem tho' I will strictly abide by your decision.

I am Yours affect^y

E A. Poe

Poe's letter to Allan, June 10, 1829, is lost, as is Allan's of June 8 (see the note to Letter 13). For the reference to Lea and Carey, see

Letters 12 and 17. According to Wirt's letter to Poe, May 11, 1829 (see VL, p. 131), Poe planned to leave Baltimore for Philadelphia on the day-boat, May 12; thus Poe's letter to Isaac Lea, May *ante* 27, 1829, and the MS. of "Al Aaraaf" were in the hands of the publishers upwards of two weeks, probably, before they acknowledged receipt of the letter or poem; then an interview between Poe and Isaac Lea followed, and hearing nothing more from them Poe wrote Carey, Lea and Carey, July 28, requesting the return of the MS. (It is very possible that John Allan's refusal to give his "approbation" played no small part, especially at this time, in Poe's withdrawing his poem, though the lack of encouragement on the part of the publishers also prompted the step.) The name of Edward Mosher at the end of page 2, above, lacking in both the facsimile and the printing of the letter in the VL, appears in the manuscript letter; Quinn (*Poe*, p. 146) supplies James Mosher Poe, incorrectly. The letter from Edward Mosher, cited by Poe, is lost. John Allan last sent money to Poe on May 18, 1829, to finance in large part Poe's expenses en route to West Point (see the notes to Letter 11). Poe's professed relationship to Benedict Arnold is pure romancing; for Elizabeth Arnold's ancestry, see Quinn, *Poe*, p. 2. Poe's substitute was Samuel Graves (see Quinn, *Poe*, p. 742, and Letter 25). John Allan did not reply to this letter. [CL 34]

15 ➤ TO JOHN ALLAN

Baltimore July 15th 1829

Dear Pa,

I have written you twice lately & have received no answer — I would not trouble you so often with my letters, but I am afraid that being up at the Byrd you might probably not have received them — I am very anxious to return home thro' Washington where I have every hope of being appointed for Sep' & besides by being detained at Baltimore I am incurring unecessary expense as Grandmother is not in a situation to give me any accomodation — I sometimes am afraid that you are angry & perhaps you have reason to be — but if you will but put a little more confidence in me — I will endeavor to deserve it —

[*page 2*] I am sure no one can be more anxious, or would do more towards helping myself than I would — if I had any means of doing it — without your assistance, I have none — I am anxious to abide by your directions, if I knew what they were —

You would relieve me from a great deal of anxiety by writing me

soon — I think I have already had my share of trouble for one so
young —

                                    I am Dear Pa
                                    Yours affectionately

                                        Edgar A. Poe

"Written you twice" refers to the lost letter of June 10, 1829 (see
Letter 14), and the letter of June 25, 1829. For "the Byrd," an estate
of some 6000 acres situated on the James river in Goochland county,
about fifty miles west of Richmond, and willed to John Allan by his
uncle, William Galt, in 1825, see Allen, *Israfel*, p. 687. Poe was unsuccessful in the September appointments to West Point. For "Grandmother," see Letter 11 and note. Allan had not written to Poe since
June 8, that letter being lost (but see Letter 14, and Allan's note on
Poe's letter of May 29, 1829); however, Allan replied to the present
letter, July 19, 1829, but his reply is unlocated. [CL 35]

16 ⇬ TO JOHN ALLAN

                                    Baltimore July 26 — 1829 —

Dear Pa,

I received yours of the 19th on the 22^d ult° & am truly thankful for
the money which you sent me, notwithstanding the taunt with which
it was given "that men of genius ought not to apply to your aid" — It
is too often their necessity to want that little timely assistance which
would prevent such applications —

I did not answer your letter by return of mail on account of my
departure for Washington the next morning — but before I proceed to
tell the event of my application I think it my duty to say something
concerning the accusations & suspicions which are contained in your
letter —

As regards the substitute, the reason why I did not tell you that it
would cost $75 — was that I could not possibly foresee so improbable
an event — The bounty is $12 — & <unless> but for the absence of
Col: House & Lt Howard at the time of my discharge it would have
been all that I should have had to pay — The officer commanding a
company can (if he pleases) enlist the first recruit who offers & muster
him as a substitute for another, of course paying only the bounty of
12 $ but as Lt Howard & Col: House were both absent, this arrange-

ment could not be effected — As I told you it would only cost me $12 I did not wish to make you think me imposing upon you — so upon a substitute, offering for $75 — I gave him $25 & gave him my note of hand for the balance — when you remitted me $100 — thinking I had more than I should want. I thought it my best opportunity of taking up my note — which I did.

[*page 2*] If you will take into consideration the length of time I have been from home, which was occasioned by my not hearing from you (& I was unwilling to leave the city without your answer, expecting it every day) & other expenses, you will find that it has been impossible for me to enter into any extravagancies or improper expense — even supposing I had not lost the $46 — the time which intervened between my letter & your answer in the first instance was 22 days — in the latter one month & 4 days — as I had no reason to suppose you would not reply to my letter as I was unconscious of having offended, it would have been imprudent to leave without your answer — this expense was unavoidable —

As regards the money which was stolen I have sent you the only proof in my possession a letter from Mosher — in which there is an acknowledgement of the theft — I have no other. On receiving your last letter, I went immediately to Washington, on foot, & have returned the same way, having paid away $40 for my bill & being unwilling to spend the balance when I might avoid it, until I could see what prospects were in view — I saw Mr Eaton, he addressed me by name, & in reply to my questions told me — "that of the 47 surplus, on the roll, which I mentioned in my former letters, 19 were rejected [9] dismissed & 8 resigned — consequently there [*page 3*] was yet a surplus of 10 before me on the roll. On asking for my papers of recommendation, which might be of service elsewhere — he told me that in that case my application would be considered as withdrawn, which he strongly advised me not to do — saying that there were still hopes of my obtaining the appointment in Sepr as during the encampment every year there were numerous resignations — if the number exceeded 10 I should be sure of the app^t without farther application in Sepr if not I would at least be among the first on the next roll for the ensuing year — when of course my appointment was certain — when I mentioned that I feared my age would interfere he replied that 21 was the limit — that many entered at that time — & that I might call myself 21 until I was 22 — On leaving the Office he called me back to endorse on my papers the name of my P. Office — I wrote Richmond. He said that I should certainly hear from him & that he regretted my useless trip to Washington — These are his precise words —

Having now explained every circumstance that seemed to require an explanation & shown that I have spared no exertions in the pursuit of my object I write to you for information as to what course I must pursue — I would have returned home immediately but for the words [in] your letter "I am not particularly anxious to see you" — I know not how to interpret them[.]

[*page 4*] I could not help thinking that they amounted to a prohibition to return — if I had any means of support until I could obtain the appointment, I would not trouble you again — I am conscious of having offended you formerly — greatly — but I thought *that had been forgiven.* at least you told me so —

I know that I have done nothing since to deserve your displeasure — [*space reserved for address*]

As regards the poem, I have offended only in asking your approbation — I can publish it upon the terms you mentioned — but will have no more to do with it without your entire approbation — I will wait with great anxiety for your answer[.] You must be aware how important it is that I sho[uld] hear from you soon — as I do not know how to ac[t.]

I am Your's affectionately

Edgar A- [Poe]

John Allan probably sent Poe $50 (see the next to last sentence, page 2). Allan apparently had again criticized Poe's business method in securing Samuel Graves, his army substitute (see Letter 14). In computing the time that intervened between his letter of May 20 and Allan's reply of June 8, 1829, Poe included the day on which he wrote his letter and the day on which he received Allan's; thus he accounted for "22 days"; however, by the same procedure one does not get "one month & 4 days" between Poe's letter of June 10 and Allan's reply of July 19, which seem to be the letters meant. For the letter from Mosher, see the note to Letter 14. In his interview with John Eaton, Secretary of War, Poe was giving his correct age as 21 on January next (January 19, 1809–January, 1830). If correspondence ever existed between Poe and Mr. Eaton, it has been lost. Poe's "offended you formerly" seems to refer to his leaving Richmond in March 1827; and *"that had been forgiven"* undoubtedly alludes to the reconciliation at the time of Mrs. Allan's death. On July 28, 1829, Poe wrote to Carey, Lea and Carey and re-

quested the return of his poem; though the letter of approbation that
Poe requested from Mr. Allan could not have reached Baltimore by that
date, Allan's disapprobation, previously expressed, may have precipitated
the recalling of the manuscript. [CL 37]

17 ➤ TO CAREY, LEA & CAREY

Baltimore   July 28ᵗʰ 1829.

Messrˢ Carey, Lea & Carey

Gentlemen,

Having made a better disposition of my poems than I had any
right to expect, (inducing me to decline publication on my own account) I would thank you to return me the Mss: by <the gentleman
who hands you this> — mail[.]

I should have been proud of having your firm for my publishers &
would have preferred publishing, with your name, even at a disadvantage had my ci[r]cumstances admitted of so doing[.]

Perhaps, at some future day, I may have the honor of your press,
which I most sincerely desire —

Mʳ Lea, during our short interview, at your store, mentioned "the
Atlantic Souvenir" and spoke of my attempting something for that
work[.] I know nothing which could give me greater pleasure than
to see any of my productions in so becoming a dress & in such good
society as "the Souvenir" would ensure them — notwithstanding the
assertions of Mʳ Jⁿᵒ Neal to the contrary, who now & then hitting,
thro' sheer impudence, upon a correct judgement in matters of authorship, is most unenviably ridiculous whenever he touches [*page 2*]
the fine arts —

As I am unacquainted with the method of proceeding in offering
any piece for acceptance (having been sometime absent from this
country) would you, Gentlemen, have the kindness to set me in the
right way—

Nothing could give me greater pleasure than any communication
from Messʳˢ Carey Lea & Carey —

With the greatest respect & best wishes
I am Gentlemen Your most obᵗ servᵗ

Edgar A. Poe

In connection with this letter, see Letter 12. The explanation for Poe's first paragraph may be found in Letter 16, though by inference only, for Allan's letter of July 19, 1829 (location of original unknown) would be essential. No Poe work is known to have appeared in the *Atlantic Souvenir*. Poe's "having been sometime absent from this country" hardly bears up under available evidence; it is belied by the frequency of his known correspondence between December 1, 1828 and July 28, 1829, and though no letters to or from him are known between March 25, 1827, and December 1, 1828, he is known to have been in the army, having enlisted on May 26, 1827. Where he was between March 24, 1827, when he seems to have left Richmond (see Letter 6), and May 26, 1827, is highly conjectural, but the limits of time almost preclude any trip abroad. [CL 38]

18 ➤ TO JOHN ALLAN

Baltimore Aug: 4 — / 29

Dear Sir,

I am unable to account for your not answering — if you are offended with me — I repeat that I have done nothing to deserve your displeasure. If you doubt what I say & think that I have neglected to use any exertions in the procuring my warrant — write yourself to Mr Eaton & he will tell you that more exertions could not have been — the app^t might have been obtained for June if the application had been made 2 months sooner & you will remember that I was under the impression that you were making exertions to obtain the situation for me, while I was at Old Point & so situated as to be unable to use any exertions of my own — On returning home nothing had been done — it is therefore unjust to blame me for a failure, after using every endeavour, when success was impossible rendered so by your own delay —

If you have not forgiven me for my former conduct — that is a different thing — but you told me that you had — I am however aware that I have many enemies at home who fancy it their interest to injure me in your estimation —

[*page 2*] By your last letter I understood that it was not your wish that I should return home — I am anxious to do so — but if you think that I should not — I only wish to know what course I shall pursue —

If you are determined to do nothing more in my behalf — you

will at least do me the common justice to tell me so — I am almost sure of getting the app^t in Sep^r: & certain at any rate of getting it in June. if I could manage until that time I would be no longer a trouble to you —

I think it no more than right that you should answer my letter —

Perhaps the time may come when you will find that I have not deserved ½ the misfortunes which have happened to me & that you suspected me unworthily[.]

I am Yours —

Edgar A. Poe

In connection with this letter see the note to Letter 16. The September quota for West Point did not include Poe. John Allan answered this letter (see Note 19). It should be noted that the salutation of the present letter, for the first time since Poe's visit to Richmond at the time of Mrs. Allan's death, begins "Dear Sir" (see Note 3). [CL 40]

19 ➤ TO JOHN ALLAN

Baltimore August 10th 1829.

Dear Pa,

I received yours this morning which releived me from more trouble than you can well imagine — I was afraid that you were offended & although I knew that I had done nothing to deserve your anger, I was in a most uncomfortable situation — without one cent of money — in a strange place & so quickly engaged in difficulties after the serious misfortunes which I have just escaped — My grandmother is extremely poor & ill (paralytic) [.] My aunt Maria if possible still worse & Henry entirely given up to drink & unable to help himself, much less me —

I am unwilling to appear obstinate as regards the substitute so will say nothing more concerning it — only remarking that they will no longer enlist men for the *residue* of anothers' enlistment as formerly, consequently my substitute was enlisted for 5 years not 3 —

I stated in my last letter (to which I refer you) that Mr Eaton gave me strong hopes for Sepr at any <7> rate that the app^t could be obtained for June next — I can obtain decent board [*page 2*] lodging & washing with other expenses of mending &c for 5 & perhaps even for 4½ $ per week —

If I obtain the app^t by the last of Sepr the am- of expense would
be at most $30 — If I should be unfortunate & not obtain it until
June I will not desire you to allow as much as that per week because
by engaging for a longer period at a cheap boarding house I can do
with much less — say even 10 even 8 $ pr month — any thing with
which you think it possible to exist — I am <not> not <as> so
anxious of obtaining money from your good nature as of preserving
your good will —

I am extremely anxious that you should believe that I have not
attempted to impose upon you — I will in the meantime (if you
wish it) write you often, but pledge myself to apply for no other
assistance than what you shall think proper to allow —

I left behind me in Richmond a small trunk containing books &
some letters — will you forward it on to Baltimore to the care of
H- W. Bool J^r & if you think I may ask so much perhaps you [*page 3*]
will put in it for me some few clothes as I am nearly without —
Give my love to Miss Valentine —

I remain Dear Pa
Yours affectionately

Edgar A. Poe

In reply to Poe's letter of August 4, 1829, Allan apparently sent money;
moreover, Allan's notation on the present letter indicates that he also
sent more funds in his next letter of August 19. It would seem that
Samuel Graves, Poe's substitute, enlisted for "Edgar Perry" at the rate
of $15 a year (see Letters 14 and 16). Though there is no proof, it is
possible that Poe was living with his relatives in Baltimore and that he
sought the weekly allowance both for his benefit and theirs; however,
Allan's contribution of $50, though adequate for six weeks, was quite
insufficient for a period of ten months. This letter and the next four
revert to the familiar salutation. Poe's reference to letters in his trunk
is interesting. Were there any from John Allan, Frances Keeling Allan,
Elmira Royster, or Richmond and University friends? H. W. Bool's
identity is unknown. For Anne Moore Valentine, see Letter 3. [CL 42]

20 ⋗ TO JOHN ALLAN

Balt: Oct: 30. 1829.

Dear Pa —

I received your letter this evening — and am grieved that I can
give you no positive evidence of my industry & zeal as regards the

appᵗ at W. Point: unless you will write to Mʳ Eaton himself who well remembers me & the earnestness of my application.

But you are labouring under a mistake which I beg you to correct by reference to all my former letters — I stated that Mʳ Eaton told me that an appᵗ could be obtained by Sepʳ *provided* there were a sufficient number *rejected* at the June examination & regretted that I had not made an earlier application — that *at all events,* with the strong recommendations I had brought that I should have an appᵗ at the next term which is in June next — So far from having any doubts of my appᵗ at that time, I am as certain of obtaining it as I am of being alive —

If you find this statement to be incorrect then condemn me — otherwise acquit me of any intention to practise upon your good nature — which I now feel myself to be above —

It is my intention upon the receipt of your letter to go again to Washington &, tho' contrary to the usual practice, I will get Mʳ Eaton to give me my letter of appᵗ *now* [*page 2*] — it will consist of an order to repair to W. P. in June for examination &c — & forward it to you that all doubts may be removed — I will tell him why I want it at present & I think he will give it.

I would have sent you the M.S. of ny Poems long ago for your approval, but since I have collected them they have been continually in the hands of some person or another. & I have not had them in my own possession since Carey & Lea took them — I will send them to you at the first opportunity —

I am sorry that your letters to me have still with them a tone of anger as if my former errors were not forgiven — if I knew how to regain your affection God knows I would do any thing I could —

I am Yours affectionately

Edgar A. Poe

John Eaton was Secretary of War. For the letters of recommendation, cited by Poe, see Quinn, *Poe,* pp. 134–137. There is no evidence that Poe made the second trip to Washington to see Eaton. Poe's statement about his poems is hardly correct: Carey, Lea and Carey must have returned the MS. as Poe requested in his letter of July 28, 1829 (Letter 17); Poe's letter, or letters, to John Neal, September–November, 1829, quotes certain passages from his poetry (see Letter 21 and notes); also, Poe apparently sent the poem "Heaven" (later called "Fairyland"), probably with a letter, now lost, to N. P. Willis for inclusion in his new monthly magazine, the *American Monthly* (April 1829–July 1831), published in Boston, for Willis condemned the poem in the issue of November 1829 (see Quinn, *Poe,* p. 156; also Campbell, *Poems of Edgar Allan Poe,* p. 197). However, at the time of the present letter to Allan, Poe's manuscript may have been in the hands of Hatch and Dunning, Baltimore, who published *Al Aaraaf, Tamerlane and Minor Poems* in December 1829; no correspondence between Poe and the publishers is extant. [CL 46]

21 ⤝ TO JOHN NEAL

[Baltimore Oct.–Nov., 1829]

I am young — not yet twenty — *am* a poet — if deep worship of all beauty can make me *one* — and wish to be so in the common meaning of the word. I would give the world to embody one half the ideas afloat in my imagination (By the way, do you remember, or did you ever read the exclamation of Shelley about Shakspeare 'What a number of ideas must have been afloat befor such an author could arise!"). I appeal to you as a man that loves the same beauty which I adore — the beauty of the natural blue sky and the sunshiny earth — there can be no tie more strong than that of brother for brother — it is not so much that they love one another as that they both love the same parent — their affections are always running in the same direction — the same channel and cannot help mingling. I am and have been from my childhood, an idler. It cannot therefore be said that

> 'I left a calling for this idle trade
> 'A duty broke — a father disobeyed —

for I have no father — nor mother.

I am about to publish a volume of "Poems" — the greater part written before I was fifteen. Speaking about 'Heaven', the Editor of the Yankee says, He might write a beautiful, if not a magnificent poem — (the very first words of encouragement I ever remember to have heard). I am very certain that, as yet I have not written *either* — but that I *can,* I will take <my> oath — if they will give me time.

The poems to be published are 'Al Aaraaf' "Tamerlane, one about four, the other about three hundred lines, with smaller pieces. Al Aaraaf has some good poetry and much extravagance which I have not had time to throw away"

Al Aaraaf is a tale of another world — the Star discovered by Tycho Brahe, which appeared and disappeared so suddenly — or rather it is no tale at all. I will insert an extract about the palace of its presiding Deity, in which you will see that I have supposed many of the lost sculptures of our world to have flown (in Spirit) to the star Al Aaraaf — a delicate place more suited to their divinity.

[. . . . .]

[Edgar A. Poe]

Poe's letter is subsequent to Neal's encouraging paragraph in *The Yankee*, III (September 1829), 168 n.s., in which he praised "Heaven" (the earlier title of "Fairyland"). Poe's "Poems" was *Al Aaraaf, Tamerlane, and Minor Poems*, published by Hatch & Dunning, Baltimore, 1829. In the original the ellipsis at the end of the letter was replaced by passages from certain poems, the first and last lines of which were quoted by Neal in a letter to Ingram (see Note 21). [CL 47]

22 ➤ TO JOHN ALLAN

Balt° Nov: 12th 1829

Dear Pa,

I wrote you about a fortnight ago and as I have not heard from you, I was afraid you had forgotten me —

I would not trouble you so often if I was not extremely pinched — I am almost without clothes — and, as I board by the month, the lady with whom I board is anxious for hey money — I have not had any (you know) since the middle of August —

I hope the letter I wrote last was received in which you will see that I have cleared myself from any censure of neglect as regards W. P. —

Hoping that you will not forget to write as soon as you receive this[.]

I am   Dear Pa
Yours affectionately

Edgar A Poe

The "lady" Poe refers to may have been his aunt, Maria Clemm. There is no evidence that John Allan sent either the trunk or clothes requested by Poe in his letter of August 10, 1829, though he did send $50 on August 19. "W. P.," of course, stands for West Point. [CL 48]

23 ≯ TO JOHN ALLAN

Balt° Nov 18ᵗʰ 1829

Dear Pa —

I duly recᵈ your letter enclosing a check for $80, for which I am truly thankful — This will be quite sufficient for all the expenditures you mention but I am afraid if I purchase a piece of linen of which I am much in want I shall have none left for pocket money — & if you could get me a piece or a ½ piece at Mʳ Galts & send it to me by the boat, I could get it made up gratis by my Aunt Maria —

The Poems will be printed by Hatch & Dunning of this city upon terms advantageous to me they printing it & giving me 250 copies of the book: — <they> I will send it on by Mʳ Dunning who is going immediately to Richmond —

I am glad to hear that your trip to the springs was of service in recruiting your health & spirits —

Give my love to Miss V. —

I remain   Dear Pa,
Yours affectionately

Edgar A Poe

Allan's letter, here referred to, is the last known until that of May 21, 1830; and the present letter is Poe's last known letter to Allan until that from West Point, June 28, 1830. Whether Allan sent Poe the linen, or when Poe left Baltimore is unknown; that he did go to Richmond sometime between November 1829, and May 1830, is certain from his next letter to his foster-father, June 28, 1830. Mr. Galt was probably William Galt, Jr., the elder brother of James Galt, who with James and John Allan inherited equal portions of the business left by William Galt, Sr. (see Allen, *Israfel*, p. 689; see also Poe's letter to Allan, October 16, 1831, addressed in care of William Galt). Hatch and Dunning published *Al Aaraaf, Tamerlane, and Other Poems*, December 1829, as an octavo of 72 pages (see Quinn, *Poe*, pp. 156, 164–165). Miss V. was Anne Moore Valentine (see the note to Letter 3). The known Poe–Allan correspondence offers no proof that John Allan helped finance the publication of Poe's poems, but his request to see the manuscript (see Letter 20) indicates an interest newly developed. [CL 50]

24 ➤ TO JOHN NEAL

[Baltimore December 29, 1829]

[. . .] [w]as intended — I mention this merely to assure [y]ou that
the delay was none of mine, as [i]n all matters, however trivial, I
dete[*****]. I now forward them —

I thank you, Sir, for the kind interest you [e]xpress for my worldly
as well as poetical [w]elfare — a sermon of prosing would [h]ave
met with much less attention —

You will see that I have made the alterations you suggest *"ventur'd
out"* in place of *peer-ed* — [w]hich is, at best, inapplicable to a
statue — [a]nd other<s> corrections of the same kind — [there]
[is] much however (in metre) to be corrected — [b]ut I did not
observe it till too late —

I wait anxiously for your notice of [*page 2*]
† the book — I think the best lines for *sound* are these in Al Aaraaf.

> There Nature speaks and even ideal things
> Flap shadowy sounds from visionary wings.

But the best thing (in every other respect) is the small piece headed
"Preface."

I am certain that these lines have never been surpassed.† [1]

> Of late, eternal Condor years
> So shake the very air on high
> With tumult as they thunder by
> I hardly have had time for cares
> Thro' gazing on th' unquiet sky

"It is well to think well of one's self" — so sings somebody —
You will do me justice however —

> I am D Sir,
> Sincerely Yours
>
> Edgar A. Poe

This MS. is a fragment of probably one leaf, the upper portion, not
more than seven or eight lines, having been cut or torn off. A cutting
along the left margin of the MS. has carried away certain initial letters.
The incomplete word (dete[*****]) at the end of the first paragraph
is ink-soaked and illegible, though it may be "determine."

[1] Material between daggers is found in Woodberry (see Note 24).

John Neal's *Yankee and Boston Literary Gazette*, after the issue of
December 1829, was merged with the *New-England Galaxy* (see Mott,
History of American Magazines, I, 355), but that Neal reviewed Poe's
volume (*Al Aaraaf, Tamerlane and Other Poems*) seems evident from
Neilson Poe's letter to his cousin, Josephine Clemm, January 26, 1830,
in which Neilson says Neal has written in a published article that Poe
is a "poet of genius" (see Quinn, *Poe*, p. 165). [CL 53]

25 ➤ TO SERGEANT SAMUEL GRAVES

Richmond May 3ᵈ 1830.

Dear Bully

I have just received your letter which is the first I have ever got
from you — I suppose the reason of my not getting your other was
that you directed to Washington — but I have not been there for
some time — As to what you say about Downey Mʳ A very evidently
misunderstood me, and I wish you to understand that I never sent
any money by Downey whatsoever — Mʳ A is not very often sober —
which accounts for it — I mentioned to him that I had seen Downey
at Balto., as I did, & that I wished to send it on by him, but he did
not intend going to the point.

[*page 2*] I have tried to get the money for you from Mʳ A a
dozen times — but he always shuffles me off — I have been very sorry
that I have never had it in my power as yet to pay either you or
Sᵗ Griffith — but altho' appearances are very much against me, I
think you know me sufficiently well to believe that I have no intention of keeping you out of your money — *the very first opportunity,*
you shall have it (both of you) with interest & my best thanks for
your kindness. — I told Sᵗ Benton why I never had it in ny power —
He will explain it.

[*page 3*] I suppose some of the officers told you that I am a cadet —
If you are, at any time, going to leave the point, write to W. Point
and let me know your station. you need be under no uneasiness about
your money.

Give my respects to the company to Sᵗ Benton & wife & sister in
la[w.]

I remain, Yʳs truly

E A Poe

remember me to Mʳˢ Graves Sᵗ Hooper & Charley — Duke &c

This is the first known letter by Poe since that to John Neal, December 29, 1829, and shows that he had left Baltimore and was in Richmond. Samuel (Bully) Graves became Poe's army substitute on April 17, 1829 (see report of the War Department, in Quinn, *Poe*, pp. 742–743). If Poe paid Graves the $50 balance due him as the substitute (see Letters 14 and 16), then the present letter suggests that Poe was indebted, not only to Sergeant Griffith, but also to Graves, for such "expences" as he mentions to Allan in Letter 9. "Downey" remains unidentified. Poe's unfortunate allusion to Mr. Allan's intemperance had repercussions in Allan's letter to Poe, December 29 (?), 1830, after Graves had written to Allan (see Letter 28). According to Quinn (*Poe*, p. 166), Poe received his appointment to West Point in March 1830; any letter ordering him to report at the Military Academy has disappeared. Those men to whom Poe wished to be remembered were probably members of Poe's former company, Battery H, First U. S. Artillery, stationed at Fortress Monroe. [CL 56]

26 ⊁ TO JOHN ALLAN

West Point June 28th [1830]

Dear Pa,

I take the very first opportunity which I have had since arriving here of acknowledging the receipt of your letter of the 21rst May inclosing a U.S. note for $20[.] I received it 3 days ago — it has been lying some time in the W. P. post office where it was forwarded from Balto by Henry. As to what you say about the books &c I have taken nothing except what I considered my own property.

Upon arriving here I delivered my letters of recommn & was very politely received by Capn Hitchcock & Mr Ross — The examination for admission is just over — a great many cadets of good family &c have been rejected as deficient. Among these was Peyton Giles son of the Governor — James D Brown, son of Jas Brown Jr has also been dismissed for deficiency after staying here 3 years. I find that I will possess many advantages & shall endeavor to improve them. Of 130 Cadets appointed every year only 30 or 35 ever graduate — the rest being dismissed for bad conduct or deficiency the Regulations are rigid in the extreme.

[*page 2*] Please present my respects to Mr and Mrs Jas: Galt, Miss Valentine & Miss Carter.

I remain respectfully & truly Yours

Edgar A Poe —

I will be much pleased if you will answer this letter.

I am in camp at present — my tent mates are Read & Henderson (nephew of Major Eaton) & Stockton of Phil^d

> This is Poe's first known letter to his foster-father since that of November 18, 1829. Poe must have left Richmond between his letter to Samuel Graves, May 3, and Allan's letter of May 21, 1830, stopping over for a visit with his relatives in Baltimore. Entrance examinations for West Point were held during the last week in June (see Quinn, *Poe*, p. 169); thus Poe must have reached the Point during the week of June 20, for by June 28, Monday, the examinations are "just over." The "rejected" students were undoubtedly of Richmond families. For James Galt, see the note to Letter 23; for Anne Moore Valentine, see Letter 3; Miss Carter of a Richmond family, Read, and Stockton escape further identification. Summer encampments were held during July and August (see Quinn, *Poe*, p. 169). No reply by Allan to this letter is known. [CL 58]

27 ⤝ TO JOHN ALLAN

West Point Novr 6th 1830

Dear Sir,

I would have written you long before but did not know where my letters would reach you. I was greatly in hopes you would have come on to W. Point while you were in N. York, and was very much dissapointed when I heard you had gone on home without letting me hear from you. I have a very excellent standing in my class — in the first section in every thing and have great hopes of doing well. I have spent my time very pleasantly hitherto — but the study requisite is incessant, and the discipline exceedingly rigid. I have seen Genl Scott here since I came, and he was very polite and attentive — I am very much pleased with Colonel Thayer, and indeed with every thing at the institution —

If you would be so kind as to send me on a Box of Mathematical Instruments, and a copy of the [*page 2*] Cambridge Mathematics, you would confer a great favor upon me and render my situation much more comfortable, or forward to Col: Thayer the means of obtaining them; for as I have no deposit, my more necessary expenditures have run me into debt.

Please give my respects to M^{rs} A and to Mr and Mrs Jas Galt and Miss V.

Mr Cunningham was also on here some time since, and Mr J. Chevalie and I was indeed very much in hopes that the beauty of the river would have tempted yourself and M^r and Mrs Jas Galt to have paid us a visit.

Yours affectionately

Edgar A Poe

John Allan may have been at "The Byrd," the estate inherited from William Galt, Sr., at the Springs, or in New York. General Winfield Scott was an acquaintance of Mr. Allan; Colonel Sylvanus Thayer was superintendent of the United States Military Academy at West Point. There is no evidence that Allan sent Poe the instruments and books requested. "Mrs A" is the second Mrs. Allan, John Allan having married Miss Louisa Gabriella Patterson, of Elizabeth, New Jersey, October 5, 1830 (see Quinn, *Poe*, pp. 169–170). Mr. Cunningham and Mr. Chevalie were Richmond friends; for the Galts and Miss V[alentine], see the notes to Letters 3 and 23. [CL 59]

28 ➤ TO JOHN ALLAN

West Point Jany 3^d 1830. [1831]

Sir,

I suppose (altho' you desire no further communication with yourself on my part,) that your restriction does not extend to my answering your final letter.

Did I, when an infant, sollicit your charity and protection, or was it of your own free will, that you volunteered your services in my behalf? It is well known to respectable individuals in Baltimore, and elsewhere, that my Grandfather (my natural protector at the time you interposed) was wealthy, and that I was his favorite grandchild — But the promises of adoption, and liberal education which you held forth to him in a letter which is now in possession of my family, induced him to resign all care of me into your hands. Under such circumstances, can it be said that I have no *right* to expect any thing at your hands? You may probably urge that you have given me a liberal education. I will leave the decision of that question to those who know how far liberal educations can be obtained in 8 months at the University of Va. Here you will say that it was my own fault that I did not return — You would not let me return be-

cause bills were presented you for payment which I never wished
nor desired you to pay. Had you let me return, ny reformation had
been sure — as my conduct the last 3 months gave every reason to
believe — and you would never have heard more of my extravagances.
But I am not about to proclaim myself guilty of all that has been
alledged against me, and which I have hitherto endured, simply because I was too proud to reply. I will boldly say that it was wholly
and entirely your own mistaken parsimony that caused all the difficulties in which I was involved while at Charlotte[s]ville. The expences of the institution at the lowest estimate were $350 per annum.
You sent me there with $110. Of this $50 were to be paid immediately for board — $60 for attendance upon 2 professors — and you
even then did not miss the opportunity of abusing me because I did
not attend 3. Then $15 more were to be paid for room-rent — re-
member that all this was to be paid *in advance,* with $110. — $12
more for a bed — and $12 more for room furniture. I had, of course,
the mortification [*page 2*] of running in debt for public property —
against the known rules of the institution, and was immediately regarded in the light of a beggar. You will remember that in a week
after my arrival, I wrote to you for some more money, and for
books — You replied in terms of the utmost abuse — if I had been
the vilest wretch on earth you could not have been more abusive
than you were because I could not contrive to pay $150 with $110.
I had enclosed to you in my letter (according to your express commands) an account of the expences incurred amounting to $149 —
the balance to be paid was $3[9] — You enclosed me $40, leaving
me one dollar in pocket. In a short time afterwards I received a
packet of books consisting of, Gil Blas, and the Cambridge Mathematics in 2 vols: books for which I had no earthly use since I had
no means of attending the mathematical lectures. But books must be
had, If I intended to remain at the institution — and they were
bought accordingly *upon credit.* In this manner debts were accumulated, and money borrowed of Jews in Charlottesville at extravagant interest — for I was obliged to hire a servant, to pay for wood,
for washing, and a thousand other necessaries. It was then that I
became dissolute, for how could it be otherwise? I could associate with
no students, except those who were in a similar situation with myself — alho' from different causes — They from drunkenness, and

extravagance — I, because it was my crime to have no one on Earth who cared for me, or loved me. I call God to witness that I have never loved dissipation — Those who know me know that my pursuits and habits are very far from any thing of the kind. But I was drawn into it by my companions[.] Even their professions of friendship — hollow as they were — were a relief. Towards the close of the session you sent me $100 — but it was too late — to be of any service in extricating me from my difficulties — I kept it for some time — thinking that if I could obtain more I could yet retrieve my character — I applied to James Galt — but he, I believe, from the best of motives refused to lend me any — I then became desperate, and gambled — until I finally i[n]volved myself irretrievably. If I have been to blame in all this — place yourself in my situation, and tell me if you would not have been [*page 3*] equally so. But these circumstances were all unknown to my friends when I returned home — They knew that I had been extravagant — but that was all — I had no hope of returning to Charlottesville, and I waited in vain in expectation that you would, at least, obtain me some employment. I saw no prospect of this — and I could endure it no longer. — Every day threatened with a warrant &c. I left home — and after nearly 2 years conduct with which no fault could be found — in the army, as a common soldier — I *earned*, myself, by the most humiliating privations — a Cadets' warrant which you could have obtained at any time for asking. It was then that I thought I might venture to sollicit your assistance in giving me an outfit — I came home, you will remember, the night after the burial — If she had not have died while I was away there would have been nothing for me to regret — *Your* love I never valued — but she I believed loved me as her own child. You promised me to forgive all — but you soon forgot your promise. You sent me to W. Point l[ike a beggar.] The same difficulties are threateni[n]g me as before at [Charlottesville] — and I must resign.

As to your injunction not to trouble you with farther communication rest assured, Sir, that I will most religiously observe it. When I parted from you — at the steam-boat, I knew that I should nev[er] see you again.

As regards Sergt. Graves — I *did* write him that letter. As to the truth of its contents, I leave it to God, and your own conscience. — The time in which I wrote it was within a half hour after you had embittered every feeling of my heart against you by your abuse of my *family*, and myself, under your own roof — and at a time when you knew that my heart was almost breaking.

I have no more to say — except that my future life (which thank God will not endure long) must be passed in indigence and sickness. I have no energy left, nor health, If it was possible, to put up with the fatigues of this place, and the inconveniences which my absolute want of necessaries subject me to, and [*page 4*] as I mentioned before it is my intention to resign. For this end it will be necessary that you (as my nominal guardian) enclose me your written permission. It will be useless to refuse me this last request — for I can leave the place without any permission — your refusal would only deprive me of the little pay which is now due as mileage. [*space reserved for address*]

From the time of writing this I shall neglect my studies and duties at the institution — if I do not receive your answer in 10 days — I will leave the point without — for otherwise I should subject myself to dismission.

E A Poe

Elizabeth Arnold Poe died December 8, 1811, in Richmond, and within a few days the John Allans took Edgar and the William Mackenzies took Rosalie, Poe's younger sister (see Quinn, *Poe*, p. 45). For the wealth of General David Poe, see Letter 64; see also Eliza Poe to Mrs. Allan, February 8, 1813 (Quinn, *Poe*, pp. 61–62). The letter of John Allan to General Poe is unlocated. Poe attended the University of Virginia for ten months (February 14 to December 15, 1826; see Quinn, *Poe*, pp. 97, 101). For confirmation of Poe's expenses at the University of Virginia, see Quinn, *Poe*, pp. 111–113. Three exchanges of letters (location of originals unknown) are suggested in the present letter: one between Poe and Allan (Poe to Allan, *ca.* February 21, and Allan to Poe, *ca.* February 24, 1826), early in the school year; another between Poe and Allan, late in the University session (Poe to Allan, October–November, and Allan to Poe, *ca.* December 1826); and still another, probably the last of the three, between Poe and James Galt, Galt and Poe. Frances Keeling Allan, Poe's foster-mother, died February 28, 1829, and was buried in Richmond, March 2. Poe's letter to Graves was dated May 3, 1830 (Letter 25). Allan did not write his permission for Poe's resignation from West Point; so Poe left the Academy on February 19, 1831 (see Letter 29), having been ordered dismissed by sentence of Court Martial and the approval of the Secretary of War, to take effect March 6, 1831 (see Quinn, *Poe*, pp. 742–

744). According to the record of Poe's trial, Poe's first neglect of duty was dated January 8 (see Quinn, *ibid.*); moreover he remained at the Point for five weeks longer than he threatened to stay. [CL 61]

29 ⤞ TO JOHN ALLAN

N. York Feb 21, 1831

Dear Sir —

In spite of all my resolution to the contrary I am obliged once more to recur to you for assistance — It will however be the last time that I ever trouble any human being — I feel that I am on sick bed from *which* I never shall get up. I now make an appeal not to your affection because I have lost that but to your sense of justice — I wrote to you for permission to resign — because it was *impossible* that I could [*stay*] — my *ear* has been too shocking for any description — I am wearing away every day — even if my last sickness had not completed it. I wrote to you as I say for permission to resign because without your permission no resignation can be received — My reason for doing so was that I should obtain my mileage amounting to $30,35 — according to the rules of the institution. in my present circumstances a single dollar is of more importance to me than 10,000 are to you and you *deliberately* refused to answer my letter — I, as I told you, neglected my duty when I found it impossible to attend to it, and [*page 2*] the consequences were inevitable — dismissal. I have been dismissed — when a single line from you would have saved it — The whole academy have interested themselves in my behalf because my only crime was being *sick* — but it was of no use — I refer you to Col Thayer to the public records, for my standing and reputation for talent — but it was all in vain if you had granted me permission to resign — all might have been avoided — I have not strength nor energy left to write half what I feel — You one day or other will *felll* how you have treated me. I left [West] Point two days ago and travelling to N. York without a cloak or an[y] other clothing of importance. I have caught a most violen,t cold and am confined to my bed — I have no money — no friends — I have written to my brother — but he cannot help me — I shall never rise from my bed — besides a most violent cold on my lungs my *ear* discharges blood and matter continuall[y] and my headache is

distracting — I hardly know what I am writing — I will [*page 3*]
write no more — Please send me a little money — quickly — and
forget what I said about you —

God bless you

E A Poe

do not say a word to my sister. I shall send to the P.O. every day.

> See Letter 28, which Allan did not answer. The chirography of the
> present letter shows an unsteady hand. Woodberry (I, 77–78) suggests
> that Poe left West Point with only twenty-four cents to his credit, un-
> less he had a portion of the subscription money advanced by the cadets
> for his *Poems* of 1831, published by Elam Bliss in New York. Poe's
> "dismissal" from West Point became effective on March 6, 1831 (see
> the note to Letter 28). Poe's letter to Henry Poe in Baltimore is un-
> located; it is the only letter Poe is known to have written to his brother,
> though Henry wrote to Edgar, October 25, 1824 (see letter of John
> Allan to Henry Poe, November 1, 1824, in Quinn, *Poe*, p. 89); Wil-
> liam Henry Poe was two years Poe's senior and died August 1, 1831
> (see Quinn, *Poe*, p. 16). Apparently, Allan did not reply to the present
> letter. Rosalie Poe, Edgar's sister, lived with the William Mackenzies,
> friends of John Allan, in Richmond. [CL 63]

30 ⊁ TO COLONEL SYLVANUS THAYER

New York March 10th 1831.

Sir,

Having no longer any ties which can bind me to my native country — no prospects — nor any friends — I intend by the first opportunity to proceed to Paris with the view of obtaining, thro' the
interest of the Marquis de La Fayette, an appointment (if possible)
in the Polish Army. In the event of the interference of France in
behalf of Poland this may easily be effected — at all events it will be
my only feasible plan of procedure.

The object of this letter is respectfully to request that you will
give me such assistance as may lie in your power in furtherance of
my views.

A certificate of "standing" in my class is all that I have any right to expect. Any thing farther — a letter to a friend in Paris — or to the Marquis — would be a kindness which I should never forget.

Col: S. Thayer

Sup^t U.S.M.A.

Most respectfully

Yr. Ob^t S^t

Edgar A Poe

In connection with this letter, see the notes to Letters 1 and 28. There is no real evidence to show that Poe ever went to England or the Continent after his return to America with the Allans in 1820. [CL 64]

31 ✈ TO WILLIAM GWYNN

[Baltimore] May 6th 1831.

Mr. W. Gwynn.

Dear Sir,

I am almost ashamed to ask any favour at your hands after my foolish conduct upon a former occasion — but I trust to your good nature.

I am very anxious to remain and settle myself in Balt° as Mr. Allan has married again and I no longer look upon Richmond as my place of residence.

This wish of mine has also met with his approbation.

I write to request your influence in obtaining some situation or employment in this city.

Salary would be a minor consideration, but I do not wish to be idle.

Perhaps (since I understand Neilson has left you) you might be so kind as to employ me in your office in some capacity.

If so I will use every exertion to deserve your confidence.

Very Respectfully

Y^r Ob. S^t

Edgar A. Poe

I would have waited upon you personally but am confined to my room with a severe sprain in my knee.

Gwynn was editor of the *Baltimore Gazette and Daily Advertiser* (W I, p. 55). No letter is extant from Allan to Poe giving "approbation." Neilson, son of Jacob Poe, was Poe's cousin. There is no evidence that Gwynn replied to this letter. [CL 65]

32 ⤻ TO JOHN ALLAN

Baltimore. Octo: 16th 1831.

Dear Sir,

It is a long time since I have written to you unless with an application for money or assistance. I am sorry that it is so seldom that I
hear from you or even *of* you — for all communication seems to be
at an end; and when I think of the long twenty one years that I have
called you father, and you have called me son, I could cry like a
child to think that it should all end in this. You know me too well
to think me interested — if so: why have I rejected your thousand
offers of love and kindness? It is true that when I have been in great
extremity, I have always applied to you — for I had no other friend,
but it is only at such a time as the present when I can write to you
with the consciousness of making no application for assistance, that
I dare to open my heart, or speak one word of old affection. When I
look back upon the past and think of every thing — of how much
you tried to do for me — of your forbearance and your generosity,
in spite of the most flagrant ingratitude on my part, I can not help
thinking <you> myself the greatest fool im [*page 2*] existence, —
I am ready to curse the day when I was born.

But I am fully — truly conscious that all these better feelings have
come too late — I am not the damned villain even to ask you to re-
store me to the twentieth part of those affections which I have so
deservedly lost, and I am resigned to whatever fate is alotted me.

I write merely because I am by myself and have been thinking over
old times, and my only frie[n]ds, until m[y] heart is full — At such
a time the conversation of new acquaintance is like ice, and I prefer
[w]riting to you altho' I know that you care nothing about me, and
perhaps will not even read my letter.

I have nothing more to say — and *this time*, no favour to ask —
Altho I am wretchedly poor, I have managed to get clear of the
difficulty I spoke of in my last, and am *out of debt*, at any rate.

May God bless you —

E A P.

Will you not write one word to me?

This is Poe's first known letter to Allan since February 21, 1831. Poe was undoubtedly living with his aunt, Mrs. Maria Clemm, in Mechanics Row, Wilk Street, Baltimore, at this time; Mrs. Clemm's residence is given in the Baltimore City Directory for 1831, and though there is no proof that Poe lived with her, evidence points to the fact (see May G. Evans, "Poe in Amity Street," *Maryland Historical Magazine*, XXXVI (December 1941), 377). On the basis of Poe's statement in his next letter to Allan, November 18, 1831, namely, "I would rather have done any thing on earth than apply to you again after your late kindness . . ." it would seem that John Allan replied to the present letter, though his letter is unlocated. [CL 66]

33 ⊁ TO JOHN ALLAN

Balt: Novr 18. 1831,

My Dear Pa,

I am in the greatest distress and have no other friend on earth to apply to except yourself if you refuse to help me I know not what I shall do. I was arrested eleven days ago for a debt which I never expected to have to pay, and which was incurred as much on Hy'ˢ account [as] on my own about two years ago.

I would rather have done any thing on earth than apply to you again after your late kindness — but indeed I have no other resource, and I am in bad health, and unable to undergo as much hardships as formerly or I never would have asked you to give me another cent.

If you will only send me this one time $80, by Wednesday next, I will never forget your kindness & generosity. — if you refuse God only knows what I shall do, & all my hopes & prospects are ruined forever —

Yours affectionatel[y]

E A Poe

I have made every exertion but in vain.

This is the first letter from Poe to Allan since June 28, 1830, in which Poe uses the familiar salutation, a fact that not only confirms the "late kindness" of John Allan, but also suggests renewed hope in Poe that relations between them are once again "improved." According to Quinn (*Poe*, p. 190), court evidence of Poe's arrest seems lacking; what obligation he shared with his brother Henry is unknown; moreover, Henry had died August 1, 1831. Poe's next two letters to Allan, and Allan's

notation on the back of the one for December 15, 1831, should be read
in connection with the present letter. It is a coincidence that on November 18, 1829, just two years earlier, Poe wrote to John Allan to
thank him for a check for $80; and though one might seek some con-
nection between the $80 and the two-year period provided by the two
letters, no relation seems to exist on the basis of available evidence.
John Allan did not reply to Poe's letter. [CL 68]

34 ➤ TO JOHN ALLAN

Balt. Dec. 15ᵗʰ, 1831.

Dear Pa,

I am sure you could not refuse to assist me if you were well aware
of the distress I am in. How often have you relieved the distresses
of a perfect stranger in circumstances less urgent than mine. and
yet when I beg and intreat you in the name of God to send me succour
you will still refuse to aid me. I know that I have offended you past
all forgiveness, and I know that I have no longer any hopes of being
again received into your favour, but, for the sake of Christ. do not
let me perish for a sum of money which you would never miss, and
which would relieve me from the greatest earthly misery — especially
as I promise by all that is sacred that I will never under any circumstances apply to you again. Oh! if you knew at this moment how
wretched I am you would never forgive you[r]self for having refused
me. You are enjoying yourself in all the blessings that wealth & happiness can bestow, and I am suffering every extremity of want and
misery without even a chance of escape, or a friend to whom I can
look up to for assistance.

Think for one moment, and if your nature and former heart are
not altogether changed you [*page 2*] will no longer refuse me your
assistance if not for my sake for the sake of humanity.

I know you have never turned a beggar from your door, and I
apply to you in that light, I *beg* you for a little aid, and for the
sake of all that was formerly dear to you I trust that you will
relieve me.

If you wish me to humble myself before you I am humble —
Sickness and misfortune have left me not a shadow of pride,. I own
that I am miserable and unworthy of your notice, but do not leave
me to perish without leaving me still one resource. I feel at the very

bottom of my heart that if you were in my situation and you in mine, how differently I would act.

Yours affect^y

E A P.

In connection with the present letter, see Letter 33, and notes. [CL 69]

35 ⊁ TO JOHN ALLAN

Baltimore Decr 29th 1831

Dear Sir

Nothing but extreme misery and distress would make \<y\> me venture to intrude myself again upon your notice — If you knew how wretched I am I am sure that you would \<ref\> relieve me — No person in the world I am sure, could have undergone more wretchedness than I have done for some time past — and I have indeed no friend to look to but yourself — and no chance of extricating myself without you[r] assistance. I know that I have no claim upon your generosity — and that what little share I had of your affection is long since forfeited, but, for the sake of what once was dear to you, for the sake of the love you bore me when I sat upon your knee and called you father do not forsake me this only time — and god will remember you accordingly —

E A Poe

In connection with this letter, see Letters 33 and 34 and notes. This is Poe's last known letter to Allan, until that of April 12, 1833, which ended their correspondence. [CL 70]

36 ⊁ TO JOHN ALLAN

Baltimore April 12th 1833

It has now been more than two years since you have assisted me, and more than three since you have spoken to me. I feel little hope that you will pay any regard to this letter, but still I cannot refrain from making one more attempt to interest you in my behalf. If you will only consider in what a situation I am placed you will surely pity me — without friends, without any means, consequently of ob-

taining employment, I am perishing — absolutely perishing for want
of aid. And yet I am not idle — nor addicted to any vice — nor have
I committed any offence against society which would render me de-
serving of so hard a fate. For God's sake pity me, and save me from
destruction.

E A Poe

The present letter ends the correspondence between Poe and John Allan,
the known items numbering 42–43 (see Note 3), with one or two
others, supported by internal or external evidence, reasonably certain,
and still others, without any definite support, possible (see the notes to
the individual items in the series). John Allan died March 27, 1834.
Poe's last specific acknowledgment of financial aid from John Allan
occurs in his letter of June 28, 1830; however, Poe's reference to Allan's
"late kindness," in the letter of November 18, 1831, and Allan's note
on the letter of December 15, 1831, contradict the first sentence of
the present letter. Poe last talked with Allan at their parting in Richmond, in May, 1830 (see Letter 28). In connection with the date of
the present letter, it is interesting to read the date and note written by
John Allan at the end of Poe's letter of February 21, 1831. Regarding
Poe's plea of poverty, see the postscript to Letter 37. [CL 71]

II

BALTIMORE — RICHMOND

THE FOLIO CLUB AND SOUTHERN LITERARY MESSENGER

May 1833–January 1837

Baltimore May 4th 1833

Gentlemen,

I send you an original tale in hope of your accepting it for the N. E. Magazine. It is one of a number of similar pieces which I have contemplated publishing under the title of 'Eleven Tales of the Arabesque'. They are supposed to be read at table by the eleven members of a literary club, and are followed by the remarks of the company upon each. These remarks are intended as a burlesque upon criticism. In the whole, originality more than any thing else has been attempted. I have said this much with a view of offering you the entire M.S. If you like the specimen which I have sent I will forward the rest at your suggestion — but if you decide upon publishing all the tales, it would not be proper to print the one I now send until it can be printed in its place with the others. It is however optional with you either to accept them all, or publish 'Epimanes' and reject the rest — if indeed you do not reject them altogether.

Very resp^{ly}
Y^r Ob^t S^t

Messrs Buckingham.   Edgar Allan Poe

Please reply by letter as I have few opportunities of seeing your Magazine.

[Here appears the text of "Epimanes," running to page 4.]

P.S. I am poor.

The *New-England Magazine* was founded by Joseph T. Buckingham and his son, Edwin; its first issue was July 1831; its last, December 1835; it offered $1 a page for contributions (Mott, *History of American Magazines*, I, 599–600). "Epimanes," one of the tales of the Folio Club, was first printed in the SLM, II (March 1836), 235–238 (see Wyllie, *Poe's Tales*, p. 327). If the Messrs. Buckingham replied by letter, in returning the MS., its location is unknown. For supplemental discussions of Poe's tales of the Folio Club, see James Southall Wilson's "The Devil Was in It," *American Mercury*, xxiv (October 1931), 214–220; also Quinn, *Poe*, pp. 745–746. [CL 72]

38 ⇥ TO JOHN P. KENNEDY

Balto: Nov: [*ca.* 19] 1834.

Dᴿ Sir,

I have a favour to beg of you which I thought it better to ask in writing, because, sincerely, I had not courage to ask it in person. I am indeed too well aware that I have no claim whatever to your attention, and that even the manner of my introduction to your notice was, at the best, equivocal.

Since the day you first saw me my situation in life has altered materially. At that time I looked forward to the inheritance of a large fortune, and, in the meantime, was in receipt of an annuity sufficient for my support. This was allowed me by a gentleman of Virginia (Mᴿ Jⁿᵒ Allan) who adopted me at the age of two years, (both my parents being dead) and who, until lately, always treated me with the affection of a father. But a second marriage on his part, and I dare say many follies on my own at length ended in a quarrel between us. He is now dead, and has left me nothing. I am thrown entirely upon my own resources with no profession, and very few friends. Worse than all this, I am at length penniless. Indeed no circumstances less urgent would have induced me to risk your friendship by troubling you with my distresses. But I could not help thinking that if my situation was stated — as you could state it — to Carey & Lea, they might be led to aid me with a small sum in consideration of my M.S. now in their hands. This would relieve my immediate wants, and I could then look forward more confidently to better days. At all events receive assurance of my gratitude for what you have already done.

Most respʸ
Yᴿ Obt Sᵗ

Jno. P. Kennedy Esqᴿ   Edgar Allan Poe

The present letter and that of December 19, 1834, both to Kennedy, are the only known letters by Poe between May 4, 1833, and January 21, 1835, a period in Poe's life about which very little is known. He was probably living at 203 North Amity Street with his aunt Maria Clemm, with whom also lived his grandmother, Mrs. David Poe, and his cousin, Virginia. Mrs. Clemm is first identified as living there in the spring of 1833, by the Baltimore City Directory of that year (there was no Directory for 1832); and according to a notice in the Baltimore *American and Commercial Daily Advertiser,* July 7, 1835, Mrs. David Poe died there (for this information, as well as fuller account, see May G. Evans, "Poe in Amity Street," *Maryland Historical Magazine,* XXXVI (December 1941), 363–380). Poe's first contacts with Kennedy came with his participation in and winning of the Baltimore *Saturday Visiter* contest, announced June 15, and closed October 1, the winners being published October 12, 1833; Kennedy, John H. B. Latrobe, and Dr. James H. Miller were the judges (see Quinn, *Poe,* pp. 201–202). Of course, Poe received no annuity "sufficient for my support" from John Allan. Whether David Poe, Jr., died before or after Poe's "adoption" by John Allan is unknown. The Poe–Allan correspondence hardly supports Poe's statement that Allan "always treated me with the affection of a father"; Allan died March 27, 1834, and left Poe penniless. Concerning Carey and Lea in whose hands were Poe's tales submitted previously for the *Saturday Visiter* prize, see Kennedy to Poe, December 22, 1834 (H, XVII, 3); see also, Kennedy's note, printed with the present letter by H, I, 2 (though the note does not appear on the original MS. letter). [CL 73]

39 ⇥ TO JOHN P. KENNEDY

Balt. Dec. 19 / 34

Dr Sir,

About four weeks ago I sent you a note respecting my Tales of the F. Club, and matters have since occurred to me that make me doubt whether you have recd. it. You would confer upon me the greatest favour by dropping a few words for me in the P.O.

Very resp^y

Jno. P. Kennedy, Esqr.   Edgar Allan Poe

In connection with this letter, see Letter 38. Kennedy's reply is dated December 22, 1834 (see H, XVII, 3). Poe's *Tales of the Folio Club* was submitted in the Baltimore *Saturday Visiter* contest, one tale of which, "The Manuscript Found in a Bottle," won the prize; the series at the time of the contest comprised six tales (see the announcement by the judges, reprinted in Quinn, *Poe,* pp. 202–203). Poe, at Kennedy's suggestion (see H, I, 2, n.; and Kennedy to Poe, H, XVII, 3), submitted the tales to Carey and Lea for publication. Though Carey was willing to publish them, he advised Poe, through Kennedy, first to sell them indi-

vidually to the annuals, and was actually successful in selling one to
Miss Leslie for the *Atlantic Souvenir,* according to Kennedy (but the
Souvenir had merged with the *Token* in 1832 — see Quinn, *Poe,* p. 204,
n.); however neither annual nor Carey and Lea published Poe's work
at this time. The fifteen dollars received by Carey for the tale and forwarded to Kennedy, was undoubtedly called for by Poe (see Kennedy's
December letter, cited above). [CL 74]

40 ✈ TO JOHN P. KENNEDY

[Baltimore]

Sunday — 15ᵗʰ March. [1835]

Dʳ Sir,

In the paper which will be handed you with this note is an advertisement to which I most anxiously solicit your attention. It relates
to the appointment of a teacher in a Public School, and I have marked
it with a cross so that you may readily perceive it. In my present
circumstances such a situation would be most desirable, and if your
interest could obtain it for me I would always remember your kindness with the deepest gratitude.

Have I any hope? Your reply to this would greatly oblige. The
18ᵗʰ is fixed on for the decision of the commissioners, and the advertisement has only this moment caught my eye. This will excuse my
obtruding the matter on your attention to day.

Very respʸ

E A Poe

The present letter undoubtedly led to Kennedy's invitation to Poe to
come to dinner (Kennedy to Poe, Sunday, March 15, 1835, unlocated)
and Poe's subsequent note of Sunday, 15th [March, 1835]. Whether
Kennedy recommended Poe is unknown; a search of the *Baltimore
Patriot* following the close of applications revealed no announcement
of an appointment. [CL 76]

41 ✈ TO JOHN P. KENNEDY

[Baltimore]

Dʳ Sir,

Your kind invitation to dinner to day has wounded me to the
quick. I cannot come — and for reasons of the most humiliating
nature <in> my personal appearance. You may conceive my deep

mortification in making this disclosure to you — but it was necessary. If you will be my friend so far as to loan me $20 I will call on you to morrow — otherwise it will be impossible, and I must submit to my fate.

Sincerely, Yours

J. P. Kennedy Esqʳ   E A Poe

Sunday, 15ᵗʰ [March, 1835]

> For Kennedy's own word about assisting Poe in Baltimore, see Quinn, *Poe*, p. 208; for Poe's statement, see Letter 118. [CL 78]

42 ⤳ TO THOMAS W. WHITE

[Baltimore, April 30, 1835]

[I noticed the allusion in the Doom. The writer seems to compare my swim with that of Lord Byron, whereas there can be no comparison between them. Any swimmer "in the falls" in my days, would have swum the Hellespont, and thought nothing of the matter. I swam from Ludlam's wharf to Warwick, (six miles,) in a hot June sun, against one of the strongest tides ever known in the river. It would have been a feat comparatively easy to swim twenty miles in still water. I would not think much of attempting to swim the British Channel from Dover to Calais . . .] [. . .] to what you said concerning [MS. *torn off*]

A word or two in relation to Berenice. Your opinion of it is very just. The subject is by far too horrible, and I confess that I hesitated in sending it you especially as a specimen of my capabilities. The Tale originated in a bet that I could produce nothing effective on a subject so singular, provided I treated it seriously. But what I wish to say relates to the character of your Magazine more than to any articles I may offer, and I beg you to believe that I have no intention of giving you *advice*, being fully confident that, upon consideration, you will agree with me. The history of all Magazines shows plainly that those which have attained celebrity were indebted for it to articles *similar in nature — to Berenice —* although, I grant you, far superior in style and execution. I say similar in *nature*. You ask me in what does this nature consist? In the ludicrous heightened into the grotesque: the fearful coloured into the horrible: the witty exaggerated into the burlesque: the singular wrought out into the strange and mystical. You may say all this is bad taste. I have my doubts about it. Nobody is more aware than I am that simplicity is the cant of the day — but take my word for it no one cares any thing about simplicity in their hearts. Believe me also, in spite of what people say to the contrary, that there is nothing easier in the world than to be extremely simple. But whether the articles of which I speak are, or are not in bad taste is little to the purpose. To be appreciated you must be *read*, and these things are invariably sought after with avidity. They are, if you will take notice, the articles which find their way into other periodicals, and into the papers, and in this manner, taking hold upon the public mind they augment the reputation of the source where they originated. Such articles are the "M.S. found in a Madhouse" and the "Monos and Daimonos" of the London New Monthly — the "Confessions of an Opium-Eater" and the "Man in the Bell" of Blackwood. The two first were written by no less a man than Bulwer — the *Confessions* [*illegible*] universally attributed to Coleridge — although unjustly. Thus the first men in [England] have not thought writings of this nature unworthy of their talents, and I have go[od] reason to believe that some very high names valued themselves *principally* upon this species of literature. To be sure originality is an essential in these things — great attention must be paid to style, and much labour spent in their composition, or they will degenerate into the tugid or the absurd. If I am not mistaken you will find Mr Kennedy, whose writings you admire, and whose Swallow-Barn is unrivalled for purity of style and thought of my opinion in this matter. It is unnecessary for you to pay much attention to the many who will no doubt favour you with their critiques. In respect to Berenice individually I allow that it approaches the very verge of bad taste — but I will not sin quite so egregiously again. I propose to furnish you every month with a Tale of the nature which I have alluded to. The effect — if any — will be estimated better by the circulation of the Magazine than by any comments upon its contents. This much, however, it is necessary to premise, that no two of these Tales will have the slightest resemblance one to the other either in matter or manner — still however preserving the character which I speak of.

Mrs Butler's book will be out on the 1^{rst}. A life of Cicero is in press by Jn° Stricker of this city — also a life of Franklin by Jared Sparks, Boston. — also Willis' Poems, and a novel by Dr Bird.

Yours sincerely

Edgar A Poe

The bracketed first paragraph has been inserted by the editor from the SLM, 1 (May 1835), 468 (see Note 42). "Mrs. Butler's book" refers to Fanny Kemble Butler's *Journal* (Carey, Lea and Blanchard, 1835), reviewed by Poe in SLM, 1 (May 1835), 524–531. Jared Sparks was professor of history at Harvard; see also Poe's "Autography" in H, xv, 214, and Letter 63. N. P. Willis published *Melanie and Other Poems* in 1835. Dr. Robert M. Bird's *The Infidel* (Carey, Lea and Blanchard, 1835) was reviewed by Poe in SLM, 1 (June 1835), 582–585. [CL 80]

43 ➤ TO THOMAS W. WHITE

Baltimore, May 30, 1835.

Mr T. W. White

Dr Sir,

I duly rec^d, through Mr Kennedy your favour of the 20th enclosing $5: and an order for $4.94. I assure you it was very welcome. Miscarriages of double letters are by no means unfrequent just now, but yours, at least, came safely to hand. Had I reflected a moment I should have acknowledged the rec^t before. I suppose you have heard about Wm Gwynn Jones of this place, late Editor of the Gazette. He was detected in purloining letters from the Office to which the Clerks were in the habit of admitting him familiarly. He acknowledged the theft of more than $2000 in this way at different times. He probably took even more than that, and I am quite sure that on the part of the Clerks themselves advantage was taken of his arrest to embezzle double that sum. I have been a loser myself to a small amount.

I have not seen Mr Kennedy for some days, having been too unwell to go abroad. When I saw him last he assured me his book would reach Rich^d in time for your next number, and under this assurance, I thought it useless to make such extracts from the book as I wished — thinking you could please yourself in this matter. I cannot imagine what delays its publication, for it has been for some time ready for issue. In regard to my critique I seriously feel ashamed of what I have written. I fully intended to have given the work a thorough review, and examine it in detail. Ill health alone prevented me from so doing. At the time I wrote the hasty sketch [*page 2*] I sent you I was so ill as to be hardly able to see the paper on which I wrote, and finished in a state of complete exhaustion. I have therefore, not done any thing like justice to the book, and I am vexed about the matter, for Mʳ K has proved himself a kind friend to me in every respect, and I am sincerely grateful to him for many acts of generosity and attention.

I read the article in the Compiler relating to the "Confessions of a Poet" but there is no necessity of giving it a reply. The book is silly enough of itself, without the aid of any controversy concerning it. In your private ear however I may say a word or two. The writer "I" founds his opinion that I have not read the book simply upon one fact — that I disagree with him concerning it. I have looked over his article two or three times attentively and can see no other reason adduced by him. If this is a good reason. one way it is equally good another — ergo — *He* has not read the book because he disagrees with me — Neither of us having read it then, it is better to say no more about it.

But seriously — I *have* read it from beginning to end and was very much amused at it. My opinion concerning it is pretty much the opinion of the press at large. I have heard no person offer one serious word in its defence.

My notice of your Messenger in the Republican was I am afraid too brief for your views. But I could command no greater space in its editorial columns. I have often wondered at your preferring to insert such notices in the *Republican*. It is a paper by no means in the hands of the first people here. Would not the American suit as well? Its columns are equally at your service. Did you notice the alteration I made in [*page 3*] the name of the authoress of the lines in reply to Mʳ Wilde? They were written by Mʳˢ Dʳ Buckler of this city — not Buckley.

You ask me if I am perfectly satisfied with your course. I reply that I am — entirely. My poor services are not worth what you give me for them.

The high compliment of Judge Tucker is rendered doubly flattering to me by my knowledge of his literary character.

Very sincerely yours

Edgar A Poe

Poe probably received 80 cents per column, and $9.94 was payment in full for contributions to the May SLM (see Hull, p. 21). William Gwynn was the editor of the *Baltimore Gazette and Daily Advertiser* (see Letter 31); William Gwynn Jones was a boy whom the bachelor editor took into his home. "The boy did not appreciate his opportunities and robbed the city post office," according to Florence Belle Ogg, a kinswoman of William Gwynn, in a letter to James Southall Wilson. Kennedy's *Horse-Shoe Robinson* was reviewed by Poe in the SLM, I (May 1835), 522–524, prior to its publication. Poe noticed the April 1835 issue of the SLM in the *Baltimore Republican and Commercial Advertiser*, May 14, 1835 (see David K. Jackson, *Modern Language Notes*, L (1935), 251–256). Eliza Sloan Buckler, wife of Poe's Baltimore physician, published a poem entitled "Answer" in the SLM, I (April 1835), 452, in reply to Richard Henry Wilde's "My Life Is Like the Summer Rose," in the SLM, I (August 1834), 13 (see Jackson, MLN, L (1935), 251). Nathaniel Beverley Tucker was Professor of Law at William and Mary College, Williamsburg, Virginia, and published *George Balcombe* (1836) and *The Partisan Leader* (1836); he was born in 1784 and died in 1851. Poe reviewed Laughton Osborn's *Confessions of a Poet* in the SLM, I (April 1835), 459 (see also Letter 206 and notes). [CL 84]

44 ➤ TO THOMAS W. WHITE

Bal: June 12ᵗʰ 1835.

Mʳ T. W, White.

My Dear Sir.

I take the opportunity of sending this M.S. by private hand. Your letter of June 8ᵗʰ I recᵈ yesterday morning together with the Magazines. In reply to your kind enquiries after my health I am glad to say that I have entirely recovered — although Dʳ Buckler, no longer than 3 weeks ago, assured me that nothing but a sea-voyage would save me. I will do my best to please you in relation to Marshall's Washington if you will send it on. By what time would you wish the M.S. of the Review?

I suppose you have recᵈ Mʳ Calverts' communication. He will prove a valuable correspondent. I will send you on The American & Republican as soon as the *critiques* come out. What I can do farther to aid the circulation of your Magazine I will gladly do — but I must insist on your not sending me any remuneration for services of this nature. They are a pleasure to me & no trouble whatever.

Very sincerely

Edgar A Poe

I congratulate you upon obtaining the services of Mr S. He has a high reputation for talent.

> Poe's Baltimore physician seems to have been Dr. Buckler, whose wife had contributed to the SLM, in April 1835 (see Letter 43). Poe wrote the review of Marshall's *Washington,* but White did not print it (see Letter 46). George H. Calvert, of Baltimore, was author of "German Literature" (SLM, II (May 1836), 373–380) and a scene from *Arnold and Andre* (SLM, I (June 1835), 555–557), to which the above "communication" may have reference. According to David K. Jackson (*Modern Language Notes,* L (1935), 253), Poe's notices of the SLM for May 1835, appeared in the *Baltimore American,* June 15, 1835, and in the *Baltimore Republican,* June 13, 1835 (see also, T. O. Mabbott, *Modern Language Notes,* XXXV (1920), 374). "Mr. S." was Edward V. Sparhawk, announced as editor of the SLM in the May issue (I, 461). [CL 86]

45 ➤ TO THOMAS W. WHITE

Balt: June 22^d 1835

My Dear Sir,

I rec^d your letter of the 18th yesterday, and this morning your re-print of the Messenger No 3. While I entirely agree with you, and with many of your correspondents, in your opinion of this number (it being in fact one of the very best issued) I cannot help entertaining a doubt whether it would be of any advantage to you to have the public attention called to this its second appearance by any detailed notice in the papers. There would be an air of irregularity about it — as the first edition was issued so long ago — which might even have a prejudicial effect. For indeed the veriest trifles — the mere semblance of any thing unusual or outré — will frequently have a pernicious influence in cases similar to this; and you must be aware that of all the delicate things in the world the character of a young Periodical is the most easily injured. Besides it is undeniable that the public will not think of judging you by the appearance, or the merit of your Magazine in November. Its *present* character, whether that be good or bad, is all that will influence them. I would therefore look zealously to the future, letting the past take care of itself. Adopting this view of the case, I thought it best to delay doing any thing until I should hear farther from you — being fully assured that a little reflection will enable you to see the matter in the same light as myself. One important objection to what you proposed is the insuperable dislike entertained by the Daily Editors to notice any but the most recent publications. And although I dare say that I could, if you insist upon it, overcome this aversion in the present case, still it would be trifling to no purpose with your interest in that quarter. If however you disagree with me in these opinions I will undoubtedly (upon hearing from you) do as you desire. Of course the remarks I now make will equally apply to any other of the back numbers.

Many of the Contributors to No 3 are familiarly known to me — most of them I have seen occasionally. Charles B. Shaw the author of the Alleghany Levels is an old acquaintance, and a most estimable and talented man. I cannot say with truth that I had any knowledge of your son. I read the Lines to his memory in No 9 and was much struck with an air of tenderness and unaffected simplicity which pervades them. The verses immediately following, and from the same pen, give evidence of fine poetic feeling in the writer.

I will pay especial attention to what you suggested in relation to the punctuation &c of my future M.S.S.

[*page 2*] You ask me if I would be willing to come on to Richmond if you should have occasion for my services during the coming winter. I reply that nothing would give me greater pleasure. I have been desirous, for some time past, of paying a visit to Richmond, and would be glad of any reasonable excuse for so doing. Indeed I am anxious to settle myself in that city, and if, by any chance, you hear of a situation likely to suit me, I would gladly accept it, were the salary even the merest trifle. I should indeed feel myself greatly indebted to you, if through your means, I could accomplish this object. What you say, in the conclusion of your letter, in relation to the supervision of proof-sheets, gives me reason to hope that possibly you might find something for me to do in your office. If so I should be very glad — for at present a very small portion of my time is employed.

Immediately after putting my last letter to you in the P. O. I called upon M[r] Wood as you desired — but the Magazine was then completed.

Very sincerely yours.

Edgar A Poe

I have heard it suggested that a lighter-faced type in the headings of your various articles would improve the appearance of the Messenger. Do you not think so likewise? Who is the author of the Doom?

> No. 3 of the SLM had been published in November (though delayed), 1834 (see David K. Jackson, *Poe and the Southern Literary Messenger*, p. 30). No. 9 (May 1835) printed Eliza Gookin Thornton's verses in memory of White's son, Thomas H., who had died on October 7, 1832; the verses (SLM, pp. 491–492) were signed "Eliza of Saco, Maine" (see Jackson, *Poe and the Southern Literary Messenger*, p. 18). White's complaint about Poe's careless punctuation probably has reference to a MS. criticism; originals for Poe's SLM criticisms do not seem to exist and collation is therefore impossible. Poe's earliest letters show an erratic punctuation, as do his poems of 1827; but the pointing of the letters improved, especially when he chose to be careful, and in 1845 while preparing the 1829 "Al Aaraaf" for inclusion in *The Raven and Other Poems,* he made only a few changes not involving words (on authority of T. O. Mabbott; see also his edition of "Al Aaraaf" (1933), and the 1845 "Raven" (1942), for the Facsimile Text Society). As time went on, Poe became increasingly careful of his punctuation of his tales, though the pointing often was more rhetorical than logical. Poe joined White in late July or early August 1835 (see the note to Letter 49). Mr. Wood is probably John W. Woods, a Baltimore publisher (see H, IX, 158). "The Doom" appeared in SLM, I (January 1835), 235–240, and was signed "Benedict." White changed his font of type for the issue (Vol. II) of December 1835 (see White to Minor, September 8, 1835 in Jackson, *Poe and the Southern Literary Messenger*, pp. 98–99; see also Jackson, p. 59). [CL 88]

46 ➤ TO THOMAS W. WHITE

Baltimore, July 20. 1835.

My Dear Sir,

I duly rec[d] both your letters (July 14th & 16th) together with the $20. I am indeed grieved to hear that your health has not been improved by your trip — I agree with you in thinking that too close attention to business has been instrumental in causing your sickness.

I saw the Martinsburg Gazette by accident at Mr Kennedy's — but he is now out of town, and will not be back till the fall, and I know not where to procure a copy of the paper. It merely spoke of the Messenger in general terms of commendation. Have you seen the "Young Man's Paper" — and the N. Y. Evening Star?

As might be supposed I am highly gratified with Mr Pleasants' notice and especially with Paulding's. What Mr Pleasants says in relation to the commencement of Hans Phaal is judicious. That part of the Tale is faulty indeed — so much so that I had often thought of remodelling it entirely. I will take care & have the Letter inserted in all the Baltimore papers.

Herewith I send you a Baltimore Visiter of October 12th 1833. It contains a highly complimentary letter from Mr Kennedy, Mr Latrobe, and Dr Miller of Baltimore in relation to myself. The Tales of the Folio Club have only been partially published as yet. *Lionizing* was one of them. If you could in any manner contrive to have this letter copied into any of the Richmond Papers it would greatly advance a particular object which I have in view. If you could find an excuse for printing it in the Messenger it would be still better. You might observe that as many contradictory opinions had been formed in relation to my Tales & especially to Lionizing, you took the liberty of copying the Letter of the Baltimore Committee. One fact I would wish particularly noticed. The Visiter offered two Premiums — one for the best Tale & one for the best Poem — *both* of which were awarded to me. The award was, however, altered and the Premium for Poetry awarded to the second best in consideration of my having obtained the higher Prize. This Mr Kennedy & Mr Latrobe told me themselves. I know you will do me this favour if you can — the manner of doing it I leave altogether to yourself.

[*page 2*] I have taken much pains to procure you the Ink. Only one person in Baltimore had it — and he not for sale. As a great favour I obtained a pound at the price of $1.50. It is mixed with Linseed oil prepared after a particular fashion which renders it expensive. I shall go down to the Steamboat as soon as I finish this letter. and if I get an opportunity of sending it I will do so.

It gives me the greatest pain to hear that my Review will not appear in no 11. I cannot imagine what circumstances y[ou] allude to as preventing you from publishing. The Death of the Chief Justice, so far from rendering the Review useless <wa> is the very thing to attract public notice to the Article. I really wish you would consider this matter more maturely and if *possible* insert it in No 11.

Look over Hans Phaal, and the Literary Notices by me in No 10, and see if you have not miscalculated the sum due me. There are 34 columns in all. Hans Phaal cost me nearly a fortnights hard labour and was written especially for the Messenger. I will not however sin so egregiously again in sending you a long article. I will confine myself to 3 or 4 pages.

Very sincerely yours.

Edgar A. Poe

The *Visiter* cited carried the announcement of a prize of fifty dollars awarded Poe for the "MS. Found in a Bottle," and, in addition, high praises by the judges of its merit; Poe's request that the letter be reprinted was granted by White in SLM, 1 (August 1835), 716. John H. Hewitt, editor of the *Visiter*, won the poetry award with "Song of the Winds" over the pseudonym of Henry Wilton (see Quinn, *Poe*, pp. 202–203). Poe's review of Marshall's *Washington* was not inserted in Number 11. "34 columns in all" was based on "Hans Phaal" (31 columns), a review of *The Infidel* (nearly seven with quoted portions), and possibly other contributions (see Hull, p. 50). Poe's tales of the Folio Club which were published by this date were: "The Assignation," "Berenice," "Bon-Bon," "Duc de L'Omelette," "Lionizing," "Loss of Breath," "MS. Found in a Bottle," "Metzengerstein," and "A Tale of Jerusalem." [CL 91]

47 ➤ TO WILLIAM POE

Richmond Aug: 20, 1835

Dear Sir,

I received your very kind and complimentary letter only a few minutes ago, and hasten to reply.

I have been long aware that a connexion existed between us — without knowing precisely in what manner. Your letter however has satisfied me that we are second cousins. I will briefly relate to you what little I have been able to ascertain, or rather to remember, in relation to our families. That I know but little on this head will not appear so singular to you when I relate the circumstances connected with my own particular history. But to return. My paternal grandfather was Gen: David Poe of Baltimore — originally of Ireland. I know that he had brothers — two I believe. But my knowledge extends only to one, Mr George Poe. My grandfather married, when very young, a Miss Elizabeth Carnes of Lancaster, P^a, by whom he had 5 sons — viz: George (who died while an infant) John, William, David, and Samuel: also two daughters Maria and Eliza. Of the sons none married with the exception of David. He married a Mrs Elizabeth Hopkins, an English lady, by whom he had 3 children, Henry, myself, and Rosalie. Henry died about 4 years ago — Rosalie and myself remain. The daughters of Gen: David Poe, Maria, and Eliza, both married young. Maria married Mr Wm Clemm, a gentleman of high standing and some property in Baltimore. He was a widower with 5 children — and had, after his marriage to Maria Poe 3 others — viz: 2 girls and a boy, of which a girl Virginia, and a boy Henry are still living. Mr Clemm died about 9 years ago without any property whatever, leaving his widow desolate, and unprotected, and little likely to receive protection or assistance from the relatives of her husband — most of whom were opposed to the marriage in the first instances — and whose opposition was no doubt aggravated by the petty quarrels frequently occurring between Maria's children, and M^r C^s children by his former wife. This Maria is the one of whom you speak, and to whom I will allude again presently. Eliza the second daughter of the General, married a Mr Henry Herring of Baltimore, a man of unprincipled character, and by whom she ha[d sever]al children. She is now dead, and Mr Herring, having married ag[ain . . .] communication with the family of his <sisters> wife's sister. M^rs [Eliza Poe] the widow of General D. Poe, and the mother of Maria, died on[ly 6 week]s ago, at the age of 79. She had for the last 8 years of her life been [confine]d entirely to bed — never, i[n] any instance, leaving it during that time. She [h]ad been paralyzed, and suffered from many other complaints — her daughter Maria attending her during her long & tedious illness with a Christian and martyr-like fortitude, and with a constancy of attention, and unremitting affection, which must exalt her character in the eyes of all who know her. Maria is now the only survivor of my grandfather's family.

In relation to my grandfather's brother George I know but little. Jacob Poe of Frederich town, Maryland, is his son — also George Poe of Mobile — and I presume your father Wm Poe. G Jacob Poe has two sons Neilson, and George — also one [*page 2*] daughter Amelia.

My father David died when I was in the second year of my age, and when my sister Rosalie was an infant in arms. Our mother died a few weeks before him. Thus we were left orphans at an age when the hand of a parent is so peculiarly requisite. At this period my grandfather's circumstances were at a low ebb, he from great wealth having been reduced to poverty. It was therefore in his power to do little for us. My brother Henry he took however under his charge, while myself and Rosalie were adopted by gentlemen in Richmond, where we were at the period of our parents' death. I was adopted by Mʳ Jnº Allan of Richmond, Va: and she by Mʳ Wᵐ McKenzie of the same place. Rosalie is still living at Mʳˢ McKˢ still unmarried, and is treated as one of the family, being a favourite with all. I accompanied Mʳ Allan to England in my 7ᵗʰ year, and remained there at school 5 years since which I resided with Mʳ A. until a few years ago. The first Mʳˢ A. having died, and Mʳ A having married again I found my situation not so comfortable as before, and obtained a Cadet's appointment at W. Point. During my stay there Mʳ A died suddenly, and left me — nothing. No will was found among his papers. I have accordingly been thrown entirely upon my own resources. Brought up to no profession, and educated in the expectation of an immense fortune (Mʳ A having been worth $750,000) the blow has been a heavy one, and I had nearly succumbed to its influence, and yielded to despair. But by the exertion of much resolution I am now beginning to look upon the matter in a less serious light, and although struggling still with many embarrassments, am enabled to keep up my spirits. I have lately obtained the Editorship of the Southern Messenger, and may probably yet do well.

Mʳˢ Thompson, your aunt, is still living in Baltimore. George Poe of Baltimore allows her a small income.

In conclusion, I beg leave to assure you that whatever aid you may have it in your power to bestow upon Mʳˢ Clemm will be given to one who well deserves every kindness and attention. Would to God! that I could at this moment aid her. She is now, whi[le] I write, struggling without friends, without money, and without health to support [herself] and 2 children. I sincerely pray God that the words which I am [writing] may be the means of inducing you to unite wit[h] your brothers a[nd . . . fri]ends, and send her that *immediate* relief wh[ich] it is *utterly* out of [my p]ower to give her just now, and which, unless it reach her soon will, [I] am afraid, reach her too late. Entreating your attention to this subject I remain

Yours very truly & affectionately

Edgar A. Poe

It would give me the greatest pleasure to hear from you in reply. To Mr Wm Poe

> In connection with this letter and the family tree, see Mrs. Clemm to William Poe, October 7, 1835, in H, XVII, 379–381 (under the wrong date of 1836: see Quinn, *Poe*, p. 230, n. 16); see also, Quinn, *Poe*, pp. 16–17. The death-date of Edgar's father, David Poe, is unknown (see Quinn, *Poe*, p. 44); his mother died December 8, 1811 (Quinn, *Poe*, p. 45). Edgar went with the Allans to England in June 1815. Poe went to West Point before, not after, John Allan married for the second time; and Mr. Allan died, March 27, 1834 (see the notes to Letter 36), three years after Poe left West Point (see Letter 29). Poe joined the *Southern Literary Messenger* sometime between his letter to White, July 20, and White's letter to Minor, August 18, 1835 (see Jackson, *Poe and the Southern Literary Messenger*, pp. 97–98). William Poe answered Poe's letter, about October 2–4, 1835 (see Mrs. Clemm's letter to William Poe, October 7, 1835, cited above). [CL 93]

---

48 ➤ TO MARIA CLEMM

[Richmond] Aug: 29th [1835]

My dearest Aunty,

I am blinded with tears while writing thi[s] letter — I have no wish to live another hour. Amid sorrow, [MS. *torn*] and the deepest anxiety your letter reached — and you well know how little I am able to bear up under the pressure of grief. My bitterest enemy would pity me could he now read my heart — My last my last my only hold on life is cruelly torn away — I have no desire to live and *will not*. But let my duty be done. I love, *you know* I love Virginia passionately devotedly. I cannot express in words the fervent devotion I feel towards my dear little cousin — my own darling. But what can [I] say; Oh think for me for I am incapable of thinking. Al[l my] thoughts are occupied with the supposition that both you & she will prefer to go with N. Poe; I do sincerely believe that your *comforts* will for the present be secured — I cannot speak as regards your peace — your happiness. You have both tender hearts — and you will always have the reflection that my agony is more than I can bear — that you have driven me to the grave — for love like mine can never be gotten over. It is useless to disguise the truth that when Virginia goes with N. P. that I shall never behold her again — that is absolutely sure. Pity me, my dear Aunty, pity me. I have no one now to fly to — I am among strangers, and my wretchedness is more than I can bear. It is useless to expect advice forom me — what can I say? — Can I, in honour & in truth say — Virginia! do not go! — do not go where you can be comfortable & perhaps happy — and on the other hand can I calmly resign my — life itself. If she had truly loved me would she not have rejected th offer with scorn? Oh God have mercy on me! [*page 2*] If she goes with N. P. what are you to do, my own Aunty,?

I had procured a sweet little house in a retired situation on [ch]urch hill — newly done up and with a large garden and [eve]ry convenience — at only $5 per month. I have been dreaming [MS. *torn*] every day & night since of the rapture I should feel in [havi]ng my only frieids — all I love on Earth with me there, [and] the pride I would take in making you both comfor[table] & in calling her my wife — But the dream is over[.] [Oh G]od have mercy on me. What have I *to live for?* Among strangers with *not one soul to love me.*

The situation has this morning been conferred upon another. Branch T. Saunders. but White has engaged to make my salary $60 a month, and we could live in comparative comfort & happiness — even the $4 a week I am now paying for board would support us all — but I shall have $15 a week. & what need would we have of more? I had thought to send you on a little money every week until you could either hear from Hall or Wᵐ Poe, and then we could get a [little] furniture for a start — for White will not be able [to a]dvance any. After that all would go well — or I would make a desperate exertion & try to borrow enough for that purpose. There is little danger of the house being taken immediately.

I would send you on $5 now — for White paid me the $8 2 days since — but you appear not to have received my last letter and I am afraid to trust it to the mail, as the letters are continually robbed. I have it *for* you & will keep it until I hear from you when I will send it & more if I get an[y] in the meantime. I wrote you that Wᵐ Poe had written to me concerning you & has offered to assist you asking me questions concerning you which I answered. He will beyond doubt aid you shortly & with an effectual aid. Trust in God.

The tone of your letter wounds me to the soul — Oh Aunty, Aunty you loved me once — how can you be so cruel now? You speak of Virginia acquiring accomplishments, and entering into [*page 3*] society — you speak <also of> in so *worldly* a tone. Are you sure she would be more happy. Do you think any one could love her more dearly than I? She will have far — very far better opportunites of entering into society here than with N. P. Every one here receives me with open arms.

Adieu my dear Aunty. I *cannot advise you.* Ask Virginia. Leave it to her. Let me have, under her own hand, a letter, bidding me *good bye* — forever — and I [m]ay die — my heart will break — but I will say no more.

E A P.

Kiss her for me — a million times[.]

For Virginia,
My love, my own sweetest Sissy, my darling little wifey, thi[nk w]ell before you break the heart of your cousin. Eddy.

I open this letter to inclose the 5$ — I have just received another letter from you announcing the rec^t of mine. My heart bleeds for you. Dearest Aunty consider my happiness while you are thinking about your own. I am saving all I can. The only money I have yet spent is 50 cts for washing — I have now 2,25. left. I will shortly send you more, Write immediately. I shall be all anxiety & dread until I hear from you. Try and convince my dear Virg^a how devotedly I love her. I wish you would get me th Republican wh: noticed the Messenger & send it on immediately by mail. God bless & protect you both.

N. Poe and N.P. refer to Neilson Poe, of Baltimore, seven months younger than Poe (see Quinn, *Poe*, p. 725), who had married Josephine Clemm, Virginia's half-sister (see Quinn, *Poe*, p. 219). His daughter, Amelia Poe, in a letter to J. H. Ingram (Ingram collection, University of Virginia), dated March 27, 1912, says that her father would not permit the above letter to be published. William Poe, of Augusta, Georgia, was Mrs. Clemm's first cousin. Poe's letter is carelessly written and shows his extreme agitation. Buried in it is what might be called the only extant letter from him to Virginia, other than Letter 232.
[CL 97]

49 ➤ TO JOHN NEAL

Richmond, Va. Sep. 4. 1835.

My Dear Sir,

Herewith I send a number of the Southern Literary Messenger, a Magazine of which I have lately obtained the Editorship. Do you think you could send me regularly in exchange, The Galaxy or any other paper of wh: you have the control? I should be *extremely* glad to hear from you, altho' I suppose you have almost forgotten our former correspondence. When you reply to this I will write you more fully — for I have much to tell you.

Very truly & respectfully Yours

John Neal.   Edgar A. Poe

Between July 20, 1835, when Poe wrote Thomas W. White from Baltimore, and August 18, when White wrote Lucian Minor, Poe went to Richmond to assist White in editing the *Southern Literary Messenger*. Though Poe in his correspondence speaks of himself as editor of the magazine, White was slow in referring to him in that capacity. In the August 18 letter to Minor he says: "Mr. Poe is here also. — He tarries one month — and will aid me all that lies in his power." (See Jackson, *Poe and the Southern Literary Messenger*, p. 98.) Again to Minor, October 24, 1835, White says: ". . . the paper is now under my own editorial management . . . You may introduce Mr. Poe's name as amongst those engaged to contribute to its columns — taking care not to say as editor" — he had said about the same thing in his letter to Minor, September 8, when he stated that Poe would give him "some assistance . . . in proof-reading" — (see Jackson, *Poe and the Southern Literary Messenger*, pp. 103–104 and 98). However, White wrote to William Scott, proprietor of the New York *Weekly Messenger*, August 25, 1836: "Courtesy to Mr. Poe whom I employ to edit my paper makes it a matter of etiquette with me to submit all articles intended for the *Messenger* to his judgment and I abide by his dicta" (MS. in Middlebury College Library). Furthermore, writing to Tucker, December 27, 1836, White said: "Highly as I really think of Mr. Poe's talents, I shall be forced to give him notice in a week or so at farthest that I can no longer recognize him as editor of my Messenger" (see James Southall Wilson, *Century Magazine*, cvii, 656). "The Galaxy" was the *New England Galaxy* (1817–1837?); Neal claimed editorship of it in 1835 (Mott, *History of American Magazines*, i, 127). There is no evidence that Neal replied to Poe's letter. [CL 98]

50 ➤ TO JOHN P. KENNEDY

Richmond Sep: 11th 1835

Dear Sir,

I received a letter yesterday from Dr Miller in which he tells me you are in town. I hasten, therefore, to write you — and express by letter what I have always found it impossible to express orally — my deep sense of gratitude for your frequent and effectual assistance and kindness. Through your influence Mr White has been induced to employ me in assisting him with the Editorial duties of his Magazine at a salary of $520 per annum. The situation is agreable to me for many reasons — but alas! it appears to me that nothing can now give me pleasure — or the slightest gratification. Excuse me, my dear Sir, if in this letter you find much incoherency. My feelings at this moment are pitiable indeed. I am suffering under a depression of spirits such as I have never felt before. I have struggled in vain against the influence of this melancholy — *You will believe me* when I say that I am still miserable in spite of the great improvement in my circumstances. I say you will believe me, and for this simple reason, that a man who is writing for *effect* does not write *thus*. My heart is open before you — if it be worth reading, read it. I am wretched, and know not why. Console me — for you can. But let it be quickly — or it will be too late. Write me immediately. Convince me that it is worth one's while — that it is at all necessary to live, and you will prove yourself indeed my friend. Persuade me to do what is right. I do not mean this — I do not mean that you should consider what I now write you a jest — oh pity me! for I feel that my words are incoherent — but I will recover myself. You will not fail to see that I am suffering under a depression of spirits which will <not fail to> ruin me should it be long continued. Write me then, and quickly. Urge me to do what is right. Your words will have more weight with me than the words of others — for you were my friend when no one else was. Fail not — as you value your peace of mind hereafter.

E A. Poe.

Mr White desires me to say that if you could send him any contribution for the Messenger it would serve him most effectually. I would consider it a personal favour if you could do so without incommoding yourself. I will write you more fully hereafter.

John P. Kennedy Esqr

(Turn over)

[*page 2*] I see *"the Gift"* is out. They have published the M.S. found in a Bottle (, the prize tale you will remember,) although I not only told Mr Carey myself that it had been published, but wrote him to that effect after my return to Baltimore, and sent him another tale in place of it (Epimanes). I cannot understand why they have published it — or why they have *not* published either "Siope" or "Epimanes."

Mr White is willing to publish my *Tales of the Folio Club* — that is to *print* them. Would you oblige me by ascertaining from Carey & Lea whether they would, in that case, appear nominally as the publishers, the books, when printed, being sent on to them, as in the case of H. S. Robinson.?

Have you seen the "Discoveries in the Moon"? Do you not think it altogether suggested by *Hans Phaal?* It is very singular, — but when I first purposed writing a Tale concerning the Moon, the idea of *Telescopic* discoveries suggested itself to me — but I afterwards abandoned it. I had however spoken of it freely, & from many little incidents & apparently trivial remarks in those *Discoveries* I am convinced that the idea was stolen from myself.

Yours most sincerely

Edgar A. Poe

The letter from Dr. James H. Miller (unlocated), one of the judges in the Baltimore *Saturday Visiter* contest (see Letter 38), suggests an unlocated letter from Poe to Dr. Miller; the letter from Dr. Miller may be dated September 8–9, and Poe's to Dr. Miller, *ante* September 8, 1835. For the date of Poe's joining Thomas W. White and the *Southern Literary Messenger,* see the note to Letter 49; Kennedy had interceded with White to employ Poe in the editing of the magazine (see Quinn, *Poe,* p. 208). Probably within the week following the present letter, White was forced to sever Poe's connection with the *Messenger;* though White, in his letter to Lucian Minor, September 21, 1835 (see Jackson, *Poe and the Southern Literary Messenger,* pp. 99–100), said: "Poe has flew the track already," giving melancholy and drink as the causes; his letter to Poe, September 29 (H, XVII, 20–21), clearly indicates the chief reason for White's action. Moreover, White's letter to Poe indicates a letter from Poe (unlocated), datable about September 15–20, perhaps a few days later, asking reinstatement. Upon receipt of White's letter of September 29, Poe must have gone back to Richmond and the *Messenger*, for by October 8 he was writing to Robert M. Bird, "at the request of" White. Thus the despondency in the first part of the present letter to Kennedy was probably occasioned by the uncertainty of Poe's position on the *Messenger*. Page 2 of the letter, from its more confident tone, seems to have been written a day or two after the first; White may have promised Poe another opportunity to make good. Moreover, the delayed mailing of the letter would tend to account for the elapsed time between the date it was begun and Kennedy's reply, September 19, a reply that Kennedy, under the circumstances, would have been rather quick to send. Nevertheless, Poe was gone from Richmond when Kennedy's letter arrived, and it was forwarded to Baltimore, September 22 (MS. of Kennedy's letter is in the Boston Public Library; it is printed in H, XVII, 19–20). Poe's letter (unlocated) from Baltimore to E. L. Carey, of Carey and Lea, Philadelphia, concerning "MS. Found in a Bottle" (published in *Saturday Visiter*, October 19, 1833; reprinted in the *Gift*, 1836) is authenticated by Carey's letter to Kennedy, May 18, 1835 (see Killis Campbell, "The Kennedy Papers," *Sewanee Review*, XXV (April 1917), 197–198): "Poe has written me to say that the tale selected by Miss Leslie has been printed already . . . I would have written him but that his letter is only now received and I am excessively busy." Thus Poe's letter to Carey may be dated *ante* May 15, 1835. Nothing came of Poe's suggestion about the *Tales of the Folio Club*. Kennedy was the author of *Horse-Shoe Robinson* (1835). Concerning "Hans Phaal" and "Discoveries in the Moon," see Poe's "Literati" article on Richard Adams Locke (H, XV, 126–137). [CL 101]

51 ➤ TO ROBERT M. BIRD

Richmond Oct. 8, 1835

[Dear Sir:]

At the request of Mr. Thomas W. White, Proprietor of the "Southern Literary Messenger," published in this city, I take the liberty of addressing you, and soliciting your aid in the way of occasional or regular contributions to his Magazine. Being well aware that your time is fully occupied, I confess that I have little hope of being able so far to interest you in behalf of a merely Southern Journal as to obtain that assistance which you have refused to your more immediate neighbours. But the value of any contribution you might afford us rendered it incumbent upon me to make the attempt, at all events, in accordance with his desire.

Very respt. Yr. ob. st.

Edgar A. Poe

Only two letters are known from Poe to Bird, and two replies may be assumed: one, October 9 (?) or later, in which a "demi-promise . . . in relation to an article for our Southern Literary Messenger" was made (see Letter 65); two, after June 7 (?), probably a note accompanying his poem "The Pine Wood," contributed to the SLM, II (August 1836), 541. Dr. Bird was primarily a playwright and novelist, Poe having reviewed his *Calavar* in the SLM, I (February 1835), 315, and his *The Infidel*, SLM (June 1835), 582–585. See also Poe's "Autography," SLM, February 1836 (reprinted in H, xv, 156), and his "Chapter on Autography," *Graham's*, November 1841 (reprinted in H, xv, 203–204. [CL 106]

51a ➤ TO LUCIAN MINOR

Richmond, October 31, 1835

[. . . . .]

I will hand your translation to Mr. Poe in the morning, and will attend to your request touching keeping your name secret.

[Thomas W. White]

Lucian Minor (1802–1858) was a lawyer in Louisa County, Virginia. His "Letters from New England" were published in the *Southern Literary Messenger*, owned by Thomas W. White, from November 1834–April 1835, and his "Address of Education" appeared in the SLM in December 1835, while Poe was editor. In 1855 Minor became professor of law at the College of William and Mary (see the *Dictionary of American Biography*, XIII, 27). The present letter is interesting because it shows Poe serving as amanuensis for White (see also the note to Letter 99); however, despite the reference to "Mr. Poe" in the present letter, Poe probably not only wrote the letter but also formulated most of its content, White merely signing it. [CL 107]

52 ➤ TO BEVERLEY TUCKER

Richmond Dec: 1. 35.

Dear Sir,

Mʳ White was so kind as to read me some portions of your letter to himself, dated Nov 29, and I feel impelled, as much by gratitude for

your many friendly expressions of interest in my behalf, as by a
desire to make some little explanations, to answer, personally, the
passages alluded to.

And firstly — in relation to your own verses. That they *are not
poetry* I will not allow, even when judging them by your own rules.
A very cursory perusal enabled me, when I first saw them, to point out
many instances of the ποιησις you mention. Had I the lines before
me now I would particularize them. But is there not a more lofty
species of originality than originality of individual thoughts or individual passages? I doubt very much whether a composition may not
even be full of original things, and still be pure imitation as a whole.
On the other hand I have seen writings, devoid of any new thought,
and frequently destitute of any new expression — writings which I
could not help considering as full of creative power. But I have no
wish to refine, and I dare say you have little desire that I should do so.
What *is*, or *is not*, poetry must not be told in a mere epistle. I sincerely think your lines excellent.

The distinction you make between levity, and wit or humour (that
which produces a smile) I perfectly understand; but that levity is
unbecoming the chair of the critic, must be taken, I think, cum grano
salis. Moreover — are you *sure* Jeffrey was never jocular or frivolous
in his critical opinions? I think I can call to mind some instances of
the purest *grotesque* in his Reviews — downright horse-laughter. Did
you ever see a *critique* in Blackwood's Mag: upon an Epic Poem by a
cockney tailor? Its chief witticisms were aimed not at the poem, but at
the goose, and bandy legs of the author, and the notice ended, after innumerable oddities in — "ha! ha! ha! — he! he! he! — hi! hi! hi! —
ho! ho! ho! — hu! hu! hu"! Yet it was, without exception, the most
annihilating, and altogether the most effective Review I remember to
have read. Of course I do not mean to palliate such indecency. The
reviewer should have been horsewhipped. Still I cannot help thinking
levity *here* was indispensable. Indeed how otherwise the subject could
have been treated I do not perceive. To treat a tailor's Epic seriously,
(and such an Epic too!) would have defeated the ends of the critic, in
weakening his own authority by making himself ridiculous.

Your opinion of 'The MS. found in a Bottle' is just. The Tale was
written some years ago, and was one among the first I ever wrote. I
have met with no one, with the exception of yourself & P. P. Cooke of
Winchester, whose judgment concerning these Tales I place any value

upon. Generally, people praise extravagantly those of which I am ashamed, and pass in silence what I fancy to be praise worthy. The last tale I wrote was Morella and it was my best. When I write again I will write something better than Morella. At present, having no time upon my hands, from my editorial duties, I can write nothing worth reading. What articles I have published *since Morella* were all written some time ago. I mention this to account for the "mere *physique*" of [*page 2*] the horrible which prevails in the "M.S. found in a Bottle". I do not think I would be guilty of a similar absurdity *now*. One or two words more of Egotism.

I do not entirely acquiesce in your strictures on the versification of my Drama. I find that versification is a point on which, very frequently, persons who agree in all important particulars, differ very essentially. I do not remember to have known any two persons agree, thoroughly, about metre. I have been puzzled to assign a reason for this — but can find none more satisfactory than that music is a most indefinite conception. I have made prosody, in all languages which I have studied, a particular subject of inquiry. I have written many verses, and read more than you would be inclined to imagine. In short — I especially pride myself upon the accuracy of my ear — and have established the fact of its accuracy, to my own satisfaction at least, by some odd chromatic experiments. I was therefore astonished to find you objecting to the *melody* of my lines. Had I time just now, and were I not afraid of tiring you, I would like to discuss this point more fully. There is much room for speculation here. Your own verses (I remarked this, upon first reading them, to Mr White) are absolutely faultless, if considered as "pure harmony" — I mean to speak technically — "without the intervention of any dischords". I was formerly accustomed to write thus, and it would be an easy thing to convince you of the accuracy of my ear by writing such at present — but imperceptibly the *love of these dischords* grew upon me as my love of music grew stronger, and I at length came to feel all the melody of Pope's later versification, and that of the present T. Moore. I should like to hear from you on this subject. *The Dream* was admitted solely thro' necessity. I know not the author.

In speaking of my mother you have touched a string to which my heart fully responds. To have known her is to be an object of great interest in my eyes. I myself never knew her — and never knew the affection of a father. Both died (as you may remember) within a few weeks of each other. I have many occasional dealings with Adversity — but the want of parental affection has been the heaviest of my trials.

I would be proud if you would honor me frequently with your criticism. Believe me when I say that *I value it.* I would be gratified, also, if you write me in reply to this letter. It will assure me that you have excused my impertinence in addressing you without a previous acquaintance.

> Very resp^y & sincerely
> Y. ob. S^t
>
> Edgar A Poe

Judge Beverly Tucker.

Nathaniel Beverley Tucker, a native Virginian, was Professor of Law at William and Mary College. He was an early contributor to the *Southern Literary Messenger,* and was the author of *George Balcombe* (1836), reviewed by Poe in the SLM, January 1837 (reprinted in H, IX, 243–265), and of *The Partisan Leader* (1836). Poe's "MS. Found in a Bottle" first appeared in the Baltimore *Saturday Visiter,* October 19, 1833. For Poe's praise of Cooke's critical acumen, see Letter 82. "Morella" first appeared in the SLM, April 1835. Three scenes from Poe's drama *Politian* were published in the SLM, December 1835. To White, Tucker had written, ". . . if I do not mistake his [Poe's] filiation, I remember his beautiful mother when a girl" (see Quinn, *Poe,* p. 235). Mrs. Poe died in Richmond, December 8, 1811; but nothing definite is known concerning the death of David Poe. [CL 110]

53 ➤ TO GEORGE POE

Richmond. Jan: 12, 1836.

Dear Sir

I take the liberty of addressing you in behalf of a mutual relation, Mrs William Clemm, late of Baltimore — and at her earnest solicitation.

You are aware that for many years she has been suffering privations and difficulties of no ordinary kind. I know that you have assisted her at a former period, and she has occasionally received aid from her cousins, William and Robert Poe, of Augusta. What little has been heretofore in my own power I have also done.

Having lately established myself in Richmond, and undertaken the Editorship of the Southern Literary Messenger, and my circumstances having thus become better than formerly, I have ventured to offer my aunt a home. She is now therefore in Richmond, with her daughter Virginia, and is, for the present boarding at the house of a Mrs Yarrington. My salary is only at present, about $800 per ann: and the charge per week for our board, (Mrs Clemm's, her daughter's, and my own,) is $9. I am thus particular in stating my precise situation that you may be the better enabled to judge in regard to the propriety of granting the request which I am now about to make for Mrs Clemm.

It is ascertained that if Mrs C. could obtain the means of opening, herself, a boarding-house in this city, she could support herself and daughter comfortably with something to spare. But a small capital would be necessary for an undertaking of this nature, and many of the widows of our first people are engaged in it, and find it profitable. I am willing to advance, for my own part, $100, and I believe that W^{m} & R. Poe will advance $100. If then you would so far aid her in her design as to loan her, Yourself 100, she will have sufficient to commence with. I will be responsible for the repayment of the sum, in a year from this date, if you can make it convenient to comply with her request.

I beg you, my dear Sir, to take this subject into consideration. I feel deeply for the distresses of Mrs Clemm, and I am sure *you* will feel interested in relieving them.

[signature cut out]

P.S) I am the son of David Poe J^{r}. M^{rs} C^{s} brother

> George Poe was the grandson of John Poe, and the first cousin of William Poe, of Augusta, Georgia, to whom Poe wrote giving family relationships and soliciting aid for Mrs. Clemm, August 20, 1835; thus George Poe was Mrs. Clemm's first cousin, and Edgar's second. He was a banker in Mobile at the time of the present letter and apparently well off (see Quinn, *Poe*, p. 33). Mrs. Clemm and Virginia joined Poe in Richmond, in October 1835. R[obert] Poe was William's brother (see Mrs. Clemm to William Poe, October 7, 1835, printed in H, xvii, 379–381; and see also Letter 97), and lived in Augusta, Georgia. On the verso of the MS. letter, George Poe wrote: "Edgar A. Poe/ 12 Jan. 1836/ rec^{d}/ ans. 12 Feb./ Sent check for/$100"; for William Poe's aid to Mrs. Clemm, see Letter 60. Nothing ever came of the "boarding-house" idea. [CL 112]

54 ✢ TO JOHN P. KENNEDY

Richmond — Jan.ʸ 22. 1836.

Dear Sir,

Although I have never yet acknowledged the receipt of your kind letter of advice some months ago, it was not without great influence upon me. I have, since then, fought the enemy manfully, and am now, in every respect, comfortable and happy. I know you will be *pleased* to hear this. My health is better than for years past, my mind is fully occupied, my pecuniary difficulties have vanished, I have a fair prospect of future success — in a word all is right. I shall never forget to whom all this happiness is in great degree to be attributed. I know that without your timely aid I should have sunk under my trials.

M.ʳ White is very liberal, and besides my salary of 520$ pays me liberally for extra work, so that I receive nearly $800. Next year, that is at the commencement of the second volume, I am to get $1000. Besides this I receive, from publishers, nearly all new publications. My friends in Richmond have received me with open arms, and my reputation is extending — especially in the South. Contrast all this with those circumstances of absolute despair in which you found me, and you will see how great reason I have to be grateful to God — and to yourself.

Some matters in relation to the death of M.ʳˢ Catherine Clemm, who resided at Mount Prospect, four miles from Baltimore, render it necessary for me to apply to an attorney, and I have thought it probable you would be kind enough to advise me.

M.ʳˢ Catherine Clemm was the widow of William Clemm S.ʳ (the owner of Clemm's lot). At his death, one third of Clemm's lot passed to his widow — to be divided at her death among the heirs of M.ʳ C. She is now dead. The heirs are M.ʳ C's surviving children, and the children of his deceased children. He had in all 5 children — William, John, James, Eliza, and Joseph. Of these Eliza and Joseph are living — and inherit each ⅕ of the ⅓. Another ⅕ will be divided among the children of John, another ⅕ among the children of James, and the remaining ⅕ among the children of William. It is in relation to this last ⅕ I desire to call your attention. M.ʳˢ Clemm, the widow of William Clemm J.ʳ is now residing under my protection in Richmond. She has two children who have an interest in this ⅕ — one of them,

Virginia, is living with her here — the other, Henry, is absent (at sea). William Clemm J^r had seven children in all — the ⅕ is to be divided among the seven. 5 of the children are in Baltimore (being M^r C's children by a former wife) the other two Henry & Virginia I have already spoken of. They are the children of M^r C by a second wife & share equally with the rest. Each (Henry & Virginia) then, <ar> is entitled to ⅐ of ⅕ of ⅓ = 1/105 of the whole lot. Mrs Catherine Clemm's ⅓ is to be sold immediately and the money divided as stated. Of this ⅓ Henry and Virginia are entitled (each) to ⅐ of ⅕ = 1/35.

Mr James M. McCulloch, who has an office under Barnums, is the attorney for M^r C's children by his first wife, and what I would wish is that *you* would see justice done to his children by his second.

[*page 2*] I am entirely ignorant of all law matters, and know not what steps should be taken. Mrs Wm Clemm (now living in Richmond) wishes me (if possible) to be appointed the guardian of her 2 children. Henry is seventeen and Virginia 15. Will you be so good as to write me in reply, and give me advice. There is other property of which (I believe) Henry & Virginia are heirs precisely in the same way as of the lot. M^r McCulloch will give every information.

<A> I should be glad to have your opinion in regard to my Editorial course in the Messenger. How do you like my Critical Notices?

I have understood (from the Preface to your 3^d Edition of Horse-Shoe) that you are engaged in another work. If so, can you not send me on a copy in advance of the publication?

Remember me to your family, and believe me with the highest respect and esteem.

Yours very truly

John P Kennedy Esqr   Edgar A- Poe.

For Kennedy's aid to Poe, see the notes to Letter 50. In connection with his income, see Letter 53. According to Quinn (*Poe*, pp. 725–726), William Clemm, Jr., had seven children in all, four by his first wife, Harriet Poe: Georgiana, Harriet, Josephine, and William; and three by his second wife, Maria Poe: Henry, Virginia Maria, and Virginia Eliza (Poe's wife), Virginia Maria having died, aged two. At the time of the present letter, Virginia Eliza was only 14, having been born August 15, 1822. No inheritance came to Maria Clemm's children (see Kennedy to Poe, April 26, 1836; MS. unlocated; but printed in H, XVII, 32–33). Kennedy's new work, to which Poe refers, may have been *Rob of the Bowl* (1838). [CL 114]

55 ⊁ TO LUCIAN MINOR

Richmond February 5. 1836

Dear Sir

At Mr Whites' request I enclose you the sheets of the Messenger. In your article on "The Necessity of Selection in Reading" you will per-ceive that the original heading is abbreviated to "Selection in Reading". This was *necessary* in order to preserve uniformity in the captions throughout — it being impossible to get in what you intended, and what, indeed, would have been most proper, except by making use of smaller type than what is used in the other articles.

Very resp^y and truly yours

Lucian Minor Esqr.   Edgar A Poe

It was thought better upon consideration to omit all passages in "Liberian Literature" at which offence could, by any possibility, be taken. We availed ourselves of your consent to do so.

> "Selection in Reading" (unsigned) was printed in the SLM, II (Feb-ruary 1836), 141; and "Liberian Literature" (unsigned), in the SLM, II (February 1836), 158–159. [CL 117]

56 ⊁ TO STEPHEN G. BULFINCH

Richmond Feb. 9, 1836

[Letter addressed to a Southern author and soliciting] in the name, and for the sake of Southern literature [the interest and contribution of the correspondent].

[Edgar A. Poe]

> Evidence in Letter 69 tends to support the supposition that the cor-respondent in this item is Stephen G. Bulfinch of Augusta, Georgia. [CL 119]

57 ⊁ TO JOHN P. KENNEDY

Dr Sir,

I received your kind letter of the 9th about an hour ago, and went immediately in search of Mr Hubard — but have not been successful in getting the picture. Mr H. does not live in Richmond, but at Gloucester C.H. Va: By the merest accident, however, he was here to-day — having arrived yesterday, and intending to be off tomorrow. Before speaking to him I had ascertained that the picture was not in Richmond. Had it been here I would have obtained it at all hazards. He says that it is on its way to Baltimore — but I do not believe him. He had forgotten the name of the vessel in which he shipped it — thinks it was the Todsbury — and cannot tell who is her captain. It is *possible* that the picture is really on its way to *Norfolk*, where he is bound himself, and where he will exhibit it. But my firm impression is that it is at his house in Gloucester — opposite York. He has evidently no intention to give it up. I know a Mr Colin Clarke who resides in Gloucester — a gentleman of high respectability — and had some idea of writing him, and requesting him to get the picture in your name — but, upon second thoughts, determined to write you first. I will go to any trouble in the world to get it for you — if you will drict me in what manner to proceed.

You are nearly, but not altogether right in relation to the satire of some of my Tales. Most of them were *intended* for half banter, half satire — although I might not have fully acknowledged this to be their aim even to myself. "Lionizing" and "Loss of Breath" were satires properly speaking — at least so meant — the one of the rage for Lions and the facility of becoming one — the other of the extravagancies of Blackwood.

I find no difficulty in keeping pace with the demands of the [*page 2*] Magazine. In the February number, which is now in the binder's hands, are no less than *40 pages* of Editorial — perhaps this is a little *de trop*.

There was *no* November number issued — Mr W. having got so far behind hand in regard to time, as to render it expedient to date the number which *should have been* the November number — December.

I am rejoiced that you will attend to the matters I spoke of in my last.

Mr W. has increased my salary, since I wrote, 104$. for the present year — this is being liberal beyond my expectations. He is exceedingly kind in every respect.

You did not reply to my query touching the "new work." But I do not mean to be inquisitive.

Most sincerely yours

John P Kennedy Esqr   Edgar A Poe

Richmond — Feb: 11. 1836.

In an article called "Autography" in the next Messenger, you will see that I have made a blunder in relation to your *seal*. I could decypher only the concluding portion of the motto on one of your letters — (*le partout*) — and taking the head for a Lion's head, imagined the words to be "il parle partout." Your last letter convinces me of my error. I doubt however if it is a matter of much importance.

> Kennedy's letter, cited in Note 57, should be read in connection with the present one. Kennedy sought possession of a picture of his wife, her sister, and himself, painted by Hubard and valued at $225; Hubard had taken it to Richmond, promising to return it, but, after four years, had failed to keep his word. Concerning Poe's request as to how to proceed, see Kennedy to Poe, April 26, 1836 (H, xvii, 32–33). At the time of the present letter, Poe had published 12 tales, ten of which belonged to the *Tales of the Folio Club*: "Metzengerstein," "The Duc de L'Omelette," "Lionizing," "A Tale of Jerusalem," "Loss of Breath," "Bon-Bon," "MS. Found in a Bottle," "The Visionary," "Morella," "Hans Pfaall," "King Pest," and "Shadow. A Fable" (for dates, see Wyllie, *Poe's Tales*). Concerning the satire or burlesque in Poe's tales, see James Southall Wilson, "The Devil Was in It," *American Mercury*, October 1931. Kennedy's letter of February 9, 1836, promised to see McCulloh about the disposition of the inheritance from the William Clemm, Sr., estate. In the February number of the *Southern Literary Messenger*, Poe began his article on autographs (see H, xv, 139 ff.); he spoke of Kennedy's penmanship as "our *beau ideal*," and of the seal as "nearly square, with a lion's head in full *alto relievo*, surrounded by the motto '*il parle par tout*.'" [CL 120]

58 ⊁ TO JOHN COLLINS MCCABE

[Richmond]

My dear Sir:

A press of other engagements has prevented me, hitherto, from replying to your letter of 24th ult., but I have not the less borne it in mind.

I need not speak to you of the difficulties I have to encounter daily in selecting from the mass of MSS. handed in for the *Messenger*. Personal applications from personal friends of course embarrass me greatly. It is indeed almost impossible to refuse an article offered in this manner without giving mortal offence to the friend who offers it. This offence, however, is most frequently taken by those who have the fewest pretentions of merit. In the present instance I feel perfectly sure that I shall neither wound your feelings nor cause you to think less of me as an acquaintance by returning your poem — which I now enclose.

My reasons for declining it relate as much to yourself, individually, as to the Magazine. I feel exceedingly desirous that you should be even more favorably known to the public than you are at present, and that this object should be accomplished through the medium of the *Messenger*. I have frequently seen pieces from your pen which I would have been happy to insert — one long poem especially, whose title I cannot recall to mind — and some lines lately printed in the Baltimore *Athenaeum* — that great bowl of Editorial skimmed milk and water.

I think you will agree with me that "the Consumptive Girl" is not by any means a fair specimen of your talents. Like all I have seen of your composition, it breathes the true spirit of poetic sentiment and feeling — it has fine and original images — and has the proper material of the Muse, but it is deficient in the outward habiliments. The versification, in especial, is not what you can make it. The lines in most instances are rough, owing to your frequent choice of words abounding in consonants. Thus in the beginning:

"One burning spot blushed on her smooth fair cheek".

In some instances the verses are more seriously defective, and cannot be scanned — or even read. For example:

"To the heart — Hope's death, love's blight, faded joys",

and again:

"Long hair unbound fell o'er her swan like neck, wildly".

I know you will reply, and with some appearance of justice, that much worse verses have appeared in the *Messenger* since my Editorship, and are still appearing; but these are poems which have been long on hand, and to the publication of which Mr. W. had bound himself by promise to their respective authors, before my time. Such difficulties shall not occur again.

Suppose you were to try a series of brief poems — say sonnets — one to appear regularly in each number of the Magazine, embodying multum in parvo, laboured out with scrupulous care in their metre — and signed with your initials. This will not fail, (if done as well as I know you can do them), to gain you a high and permanent position.

Your sincere well wisher,

John C. McCabe, Esq., Richmond.   Edgar A. Poe.

March 3d. 1836.

> John Collins McCabe was a Richmond minister and minor literary figure (see Gordon, *Memories and Memorials of William Gordon McCabe*, I, 22, for the statement that he and Poe were close friends). Mr. W. was, of course, Thomas W. White, owner of the *Southern Literary Messenger*. [CL 125]

59 ⤙ TO LUCIAN MINOR

Richmond, Va. March 10. 1836.

Dʳ Sir,

At Mʳ White's request I reply to yours of the 6ᵗʰ. The Messenger shall be mailed regularly to the Rev. O. A. Stearnes as you desire, and attention shall be paid to the *pencilling*. Your N. E. Letters are forwarded herewith, with the exception of Letter 3 (to be found in No 5 of the Messenger — a number which cannot be procured).

Your Marshall article has been very well received in all directions. Grigesby, of Norfolk, alone spoke ill of it and he speaks ill of every thing[.] His objections were to the passages touching John Randolph and Chapman Johnson. Professor Dew is now here, and thinks the whole article every thing it should be.

Liberian Literature has met a fate very similar. Lauded by all men of sense, it has excited animadversion from the Augusta Chronicle. The scoundrel says it is sheer abolitionism[.]

With high respect,
Yʳ Ob. Sᵗ

Edgar A Poe

Reverend Oliver A. Stearns (1807–1885) was a defender of anti-slavery policies, a prominent New England theologian, and a professor in the Harvard Divinity School (see the *Dictionary of American Biography*, XVII, 546–547). This letter identifies Minor as author of "Letters from New England — No. 3, by a Virginian," in SLM, I (January 1835), 217–220. For the "Marshall article," see SLM, II (February 1836), 181–191, unsigned. Hugh Blair Grigsby (1806–1881) owned and edited the Norfolk *American Beacon*, 1834–1840 (see the *Dictionary of American Biography*, VII, p. 628; also Cappon, p. 134). Thomas R. Dew was president of William and Mary College, 1836–1845. [CL 126]

60 ⊁ TO WILLIAM POE

Richmond, Va.,   April 12, 1836

My dear Sir,

A press of business has hitherto prevented my replying to your kind letter of the 29th March, enclosing $50 to Mrs. Clemm. Your prompt and generous assistance, so frequently manifested, is, I assure you, deeply felt and appreciated by myself as well as by her. I trust that she is now so circumstanced, or that she soon will be so, as to render it unnecessary to tax the kindness of yourself and brothers any further.

On the day before receiving your letter I wrote to Washington Poe, Macon, in reply to a favor of his offering his own assistance. He has become a subscriber to the *Messenger*.

I hope you have received our March number. That for April will follow, I hope, soon.

It is probable that at some future time I may avail myself of your friendly invitation to pay you a visit in Augusta. In the mean time, should business or inclination lead you, or any of our friends, to Virginia, it would afford me the greatest pleasure to show you every attention in my power.

With my best respects to Mrs. Poe and your brother, I remain, dear William,

Yours most sincerely,

Edgar A. Poe.

William's gift probably resulted from a plea by Poe, or possibly Mrs. Clemm, for financial aid; if by Poe, the letter, *ante* March 29, 1836, is unlocated. [CL 132]

61 ≻ TO LYDIA H. SIGOURNEY

Richmond, Vᵃ April 12ᵗʰ 1836.

Mʳˢ L. H. Sigourney,

Madam,

At the request of Mʳ T. W. White, I take the liberty of replying to your letter of the 6ᵗʰ ult.

I am vexed to hear that you have not received the Messenger regularly, and am confident that upon reception of the January number (now again forwarded to your address) you will be fully convinced that your friends, in their zeal for your literary reputation, have misconceived the spirit of the criticism to which you have alluded. To yourself, personally, we commit our review, with a perfect certainty of being understood. That we have evinced any "severity amounting to unkindness" is an accusation of which you will, I sincerely hope, unhesitatingly acquit us. We refer you, especially, to the concluding sentences of the critique.

Mʳ White desires me to express his regret at the mistake in relation to your package of books. He would have placed them immediately in the hands of some bookseller here, but was not sure that your views would be met in so doing. They are now properly disposed of.

You will, I hope, allow us still to send you the [*page 2*] Messenger. We are grieved, and mortified to hear that you cannot again contribute to its pages, but your objection in respect to receiving a copy without equivalent is untenable — any one of your pieces already published in our Journal being more than an equivalent to a subscription *in perpetuo*. This we say as publishers, without any intention to flatter, and having reference merely to the sum usually paid, to writers of far less reputation, for articles immeasurably inferior.

In respect to your question touching the Editor of the Messenger, I have to reply that, for the last six months, the Editorial duties have been undertaken by myself. Of course, therefore, I plead guilty to all the criticisms of the Journal during the period mentioned. In addition to what evidence of misconception on the part of your friends you will assuredly find in the January number, I have now only to say that sincere admiration of the book reviewed was the predominant feeling in my bosom while penning the review.

It would afford me the highest gratification should I find that you acquit me of this "foul charge." I will look with great anxiety for your reply.

> Very resp^ly & truly
> Y^r Ob. S^t
>
> Edgar A. Poe

Mrs. Sigourney's *Zinzendorff, and Other Poems* (1836) was reviewed by Poe in the SLM, January 1836 (reprinted in H, VIII, 122–142). For Poe's joining White and the *Southern Literary Messenger*, see Letter 45 and notes, and the note to Letter 49. [CL 133]

62 ≻ TO BEVERLEY TUCKER

> Richmond May 2. 1836.

Dear Sir,

At Mr White's request I write to apologise for the omission of your verses "To a Coquette" in the present number of the Messenger. Upon making up the *form* containing them it was found impossible to get both the pieces in, and their connection one with the other rendered it desirable not to separate them — they were therefore left for the May number.

I must also myself beg your pardon for making a few immaterial alterations in your article on Slavery, with a view of so condensing it as to get it in the space remaining at the end of the number. One very excellent passage in relation to the experience of a sick bed has been, necessarily, omitted altogether.

It would give me great pleasure to hear your opinion of the *February*, and of the *April* number of the Messenger — I mean of the Editorial articles. It is needless for me to say that I value your good opinion, and wish to profit by your counsel.

Please present my best respects to Professor Dew.

> With the highest esteem
> Y^r Ob. S^t
>
> Edgar A Poe

Will you ask Mr Saunders what has become of the article he promised us?

Tucker's two poems, both entitled "To a Coquette," omitted in the April number of the *Southern Literary Messenger*, appeared in the May issue, though unsigned. Tucker's article on slavery was an unsigned review of J. K. Paulding's *Slavery in the United States*. Both Thomas R. Dew and Robert Saunders were professors at William and Mary College, Williamsburg. [CL 136]

63 ⊱ TO JARED SPARKS

Richmond May 23. 1836.

Dear Sir,

Your letter of the 17ᵗʰ is received, and I reply to it at the request of Mʳ White. Herewith a number of the Messenger is forwarded, containing the Letter of Celia Single.

The M.S.S. from which we publish are not in our immediate possession — but in that of Mʳ Wᵐ Duane Jʳ of Philadelphia. He possesses a M.S. volume containing *many* originals of Franklin. I rather suppose that the articles you allude to (as being suspicious) in Mʳ Duane's edition, are genuine, and are a portion of the collection from which we are now publishing. I mean to say, of course, that this collection is in the hand-writing of Franklin. Mʳ D. transcribes the M.S. for our use.

I would be very glad if you could interest yourself in any manner for the success of our Magazine in Boston.

Very respʸ
Yr Ob. Sᵗ

Jared Sparks Esqr   Edgar A. Poe

Cambridge. Mass.

Jared Sparks was Professor of History at Harvard (see "Autography," in H, xv, 214). "Letter of Celia Single" appeared in SLM, II (April 1836), 296; "MSS. of Benj. Franklin" with a note: "never yet published" appeared in SLM, II (April 1836), 293–295. William J. Duane was Secretary of the Treasury from May to September 1833, under President Jackson, after which he returned to Philadelphia and practically withdrew from public life (see the *Dictionary of American Biography*, v, 469). [CL 137]

64 ⊱ TO JAMES H. CAUSTEN

Richmond, Vᵃ June 3. 1836.

Dʳ Sir,

Understanding that you have been engaged, at different times, in the prosecution of private claims against the Government of the U.S.

I have taken the liberty of addressing you on a subject of this nature.

I believe you were personally acquainted with some branches of my family in Baltimore. I am the son of David Poe J^r of that city. It appears to me (and to some others to whom I have mentioned the subject) that my aunt, Mrs Maria Clemm (who now resides with me in Richmond, I having married her daughter) has a claim against the U.S. to a large amount which might be carried to a successful issue if properly managed. I will state, as briefly as possible, the nature of the claim, of which I pretend to give merely an outline, not vouching for particular dates or amounts.

During the war of the Revolution, M^{rs} C's father, Gen: David Poe, was a quarter-master in what was then called the Maryland line. He, at various times, loaned money to the State of Maryland, and about seventeen years ago died, while engaged in making arrangements for the prosecution of his claim. His widow, Mrs Elizabeth Poe, applied to the State Government, which, finding itself too impoverished to think of paying the whole amount (then nearly $40,000) passed a bill, for the immediate time, granting Mrs Poe an annuity of $240 — thus tacitly acknowledging the validity of the vouchers adduced. Mrs Poe is now dead, and I am inclined to believe, from the successful prosecution of several claims of far less promise, but of a similar nature, that the whole claim might be substantiated before the General Government — which has provided for a liberal interpretation of all vouchers in such cases. Among these vouchers (now in proper form at Annapolis) are, I believe, letters from Washington, La Fayette, & many others speaking in high terms of the services and patriotism of Gen: Poe. I have never seen the bill granting the annuity to Mrs Poe, but it may possibly contain a proviso against any future claim. This however, would be of little moment, if the matter were properly brought before Congress.

My object in addressing you is to inquire if you would be willing to investigate and conduct this claim — leaving the terms for your own consideration. Mrs C. authorizes me to act for her in every respect. I would be glad to hear from you as soon as you can make it convenient.

Very resp^{ly}
Y^r Ob. S^t

James H. Causten Esqr Edgar A. Poe

According to the Anderson Galleries catalogue, cited in Note 64, Causten was associated in Washington with Col. John T. Pickett, who was connected with the French spoliation claims; the letter came up for sale from the Pickett family. The same Catalogue states that Gen. David Poe was appointed Assistant Deputy Quartermaster of the Continental Army in Baltimore, April 8, 1778, and on September 10, 1779, was listed as a Continental agent to purchase for the Army. Though Gen. Poe asked nothing for his services, he asked of the Government $40,000 for actual outlays of money. He received nothing, for letters in his support from Washington, Lafayette, and others, "were not held to be vouchers of technical formalities." Later, however, the State of Maryland granted his widow an annuity. There is no evidence that Poe's letter to Causten had any success. [CL 139]

65 ➤ TO ROBERT M. BIRD

Richmond — V^a June 7th 1836

Dr Sir,

I take the liberty of again addressing you, and of calling your attention to what was not precisely a promise on your part, but a kind of demi-promise made some months ago — in relation to an article for our "Southern Literary Messenger." It would be, indeed, a matter of sincere congratulation with us, if, *by any means* within our power, we could so far interest you in our behalf as to obtain something from the author of "Calavar". We have, just at this moment, a conspiracy on foot, and we would be most happy to engage you in our plans. We wish, if possible, to take the public opinion by storm, in a single number of the Messenger which shall contain a series of articles from all the first pens in the land. Can you not aid us — with a single page if no more? I will trust to the chivalric spirit of him who wrote the "Infidel" for a reply.

With the highest respect
Yr. Ob. S^t

Dr Robert M. Bird   Edgar A Poe

Bird answered Poe's request by sending a poem, "The Pine Wood," published in the SLM, II (August 1836), 541. Poe had reviewed *The Infidel,* commenting on *Calavar,* in the SLM, June 1835 (reprinted in H, VIII, 32–37). [CL 143]

66 ➤ TO JAMES FENIMORE COOPER

Richmond, June 7, 1836

Dr Sir

At the request of Mr. T. W. White, I take the liberty of addressing
you and of soliciting some little contribution to our *Southern Literary
Messenger.* I am aware that you are continually pestered with such
applications, and am ready to believe that I have very little chance of
success in this attempt to engage you in our interest, yet I owe it to
the magazine to make the effort.

One reason will, I think, have its influence with you. Our publication is the first literary attempt of Virginia, and has been for eighteen
months forcing its way, unaided and against a host of difficulties, into
the public attention. We wish, if possible to strike a bold stroke which
may establish us on a surer footing than we now possess, and design to
issue, as soon as possible, a number of the Journal consisting altogether
of articles from distinguished Americans, whose *names* may give
weight and character to this work. To aid us in this attempt would
cost you no effort, as any spare scrap in your port folio would answer
our main purpose and to us your aid would be invaluable.

With highest respect,

Y^r Ob S^t

Edgar A. Poe

Cooper does not seem to have complied with Poe's request. For similar
solicitations, see Letters 65, 67, and 68. [CL 144]

67 ➤ TO FITZ-GREENE HALLECK

Richmond Va. June 7, 1836.

Dear Sir,

At the request of the Proprietor of the "Southern Literary Messenger" I take the liberty of addressing you, and of soliciting some
little contribution to our Journal. It is well known to us that you are
continually pestered with similar applications; we are, therefore, ready
to believe that we have little chance of success in this attempt to
engage you in our interest — yet we owe it to the Magazine to make
the effort.

One consideration, will, we think, have its influence with you. Our
publication is the first successful literary attempt of Virginia, and has

been now, for eighteen months, forcing its way unaided, and against a host of difficulties, into the public view and attention[.]

We wish to issue, if possible, a number of the Messenger consisting altogether of articles from our most distinguished *literati,* and to this end we have received aid from a variety of high sources. To omit your name in the plan we propose would be not only a negative sin on our part — but would be a positive injury to our cause. In this dilemma may we not trust to your good nature for assistance? Send us any little scrap in your port-folio — it will be sure to answer our purpose fully, if it have the name of Halleck affixed[.]

With the highest respect
Yr. Ob. S^t

Edgar A. Poe
Ed. S. L. M.

Fitz-Greene Halleck Esqr

> There is no evidence that Halleck complied with Poe's request. The SLM had been "forcing its way" for more than "eighteen months." White's first number appeared in August 1834, as a bi-weekly periodical "Devoted to Every Department of Literature and the Fine Arts," but it was changed to a monthly with the November issue (see Jackson, *Poe and the Southern Literary Messenger,* pp. 20–21). [CL 146]

68 ➤ TO JOHN P. KENNEDY

Richmond. Va. June 7. 1836.

Dear Sir,

Having got into a little temporary difficulty I venture to ask you, once more, for aid, rather than apply to any of my new friends in Richmond.

Mr White, having purchased a new house, at $10.000, made propositions to my aunt to rent it to her, and to board himself and family with her. This plan was highly advantageous to us, and, having accepted it, all arrangements were made, and I obtained credit for some furniture &c to the amount of $200, above what little money I had. But upon examination of the premises purchased, it appears that the house will barely be large enough for one family, and the scheme is laid aside — leaving me now in debt (, to a small amount,) without the means of discharging it upon which I had depended.

In this dilemma I would be greatly indebted to you for the loan of $100 for 6 months. This will enable me to meet a note for $100 due in 3 months — and allow me 3 months to return your money. I shall have no difficulty in doing this, as, beyond this 100 $, I owe nothing, and I am now receiving 15 $ per week, and am to recieve $20 after November. All Mr White's disposable money has [*page 2*] been required to make his first payment.

Have you heard any thing farther in relation to Mrs Clemm's estate?

Our Messenger is thriving beyond all expectation, and I myself have every prospect of success.

It is our design to issue, as soon as possible, a number of the Magazine consisting entirely of articles from our most distinguished *literati.* To this end we have received, and have been promised, a variety of aid from the highest sources — Mrs Sigourney, Miss Sedgwick, Paulding, Flint, Halleck, Cooper, Judge Hopkinson, Dew, Governor Cass — J. Q. Adams, and many others. Could you not do me so great a favor as to send a scrap, however small[,] from your portfolio? Your name is of the greatest influence in that region where we direct our greatest efforts — in the South. Any little reminiscence, tale, jeu-d'esprit[,] historical anecdote — any thing, in short, *with your name,* will answer all our purposes.

I presume you have heard of my marriage.

With sincere respect and esteem

Yours truly

J. P. Kennedy.   Edgar A Poe

No reply from Kennedy is known. Concerning Mrs. Catherine Clemm's estate, see Letter 54. With one exception, letters from the authors cited in the present letter are unlocated; Mrs. Sigourney's letter to Poe, June 11, 1836 (original in the Boston Public Library), promises a contribution and mentions a letter from Poe, June 4, which is unlocated. Poe and Virginia were married in Richmond, Monday, May 16, 1836 (see Quinn, *Poe,* p. 252). [CL 147]

69 ⇥ TO STEPHEN G. BULFINCH

Richmond June 8, 1836

My dear Sir;

Your kind letter of the 3d ult. is received, and I beg you to accept my thanks for your beautiful translation, and equally beautiful original lines. It would, indeed, be a source of congratulation with me if, by any means within my power I could secure your occasional aid in

the way of contributions. I look, with much interest, for your promised Notice of Mr. Perdicaris' Lectures. You will send it on, I hope,
as soon as possible. The 20 copies shall be attended to. Your verses are
already in the printer's hands, and shall appear, certainly, in the next
number of the Messenger — of which a copy shall be also forwarded
to Mr. Perdicaris.

Do you not think that, through your intercession, Perdicaris himself might be induced to send us something for our Journal. I am well
aware of his abilities, and especially of his critical acquaintance with
the classical Greek. A Romaic song, in the original, by P. with a
translation by yourself, would be an invaluable gem. We would be
glad, indeed, to publish anything either from him or from yourself.

Please give my best respects to my cousins, Robert F. Poe, and
William, and believe me, dear Sir, that I fully reciprocate the many
kind expressions of your letter.

> With the highest respect
> yr. mo. ob. st.
>
> Edgar A. Poe.

The identification of Stephen Greenleaf Bulfinch is based upon investigations by James H. Whitty, who claimed to have seen the letter,
according to information sent to me by David K. Jackson. Stephen
Greenleaf Bulfinch (1809–1870), a native Bostonian, became a Uni-
tarian clergyman in Augusta, Georgia, 1830–1837. He published re-
ligious works and a book of poems. He was the brother of Thomas Bulfinch, author of *The Age of Fable* (see *Appleton's Cyclopedia of
American Biography*, I, 444). The SLM, II (June 1836), 410–411,
carried an article entitled "Perdicaris," consisting of a half column
of biographical information introducing two poems: "From the Romaic
of Christopoulos" (a translation "executed with Mr. Perdicaris's assistance, from Christopoulos"), and "To G. A. Perdicaris" (obviously
written by the author of the introduction, who signs himself at the end
of the second poem: *B*. Robert and William Poe lived in Augusta,
Georgia. [CL 149]

70 ⨾ TO LITTLETON W. TAZEWELL

Richmond. July 16, 1836.

Dʳ Sir,

At the request of Mʳ T. W. White, I take the liberty of soliciting,
for publication in the Messenger, your Reasons for declining to trans-

mit the instructions of the State Legislature to Mess. Tyler & Leigh.

If, as I imagine, these reasons enter into the Constitutional question itself, it would afford us the greatest pleasure to give them publicity, and we should take it as an especial favor if you could let us have them for this purpose.

Very resp^y
Yr ob S^t

Littleton W. Tazewell Esqr   Edgar A. Poe

> Littleton W. Tazewell, of Norfolk, succeeded John Marshall in Congress in 1800, was United States Senator from Virginia in 1824, and was Governor of Virginia, 1834–1836 (see *The South in the Building of the Nation*, XII, 445–446). John Tyler, later President of the United States, and Benjamin W. Leigh were United States Senators from Virginia at the time of the present letter (*ibid.*, pp. 487 and 89–90). Tazewell did not contribute the article to the SLM as Poe requested. [CL 154]

71 ↗ TO MATHEW CAREY

Richmond July 30. 1836

Dr Sir,

Your article on the "study of the learned languages" was duly received, and is already "set up". I am much in hope that it will please the public generally as much as it has done myself. My object in writing you at present is to beg that you will allow us to alter the *heading* which you have affixed to it, from the words "A Looker on in Venice, No 2", to the words *"On the study of the Learned Languages"* or some similar caption. I have many reasons for requesting this favor. First — it would accord with the character of all the other captions made use of in our Magazine — Secondly it would prevent the necessity of making any explanation in regard to the heading of your last article. and explanations are always inconvenient — Thirdly, your article would then stand by itself unconnected with any thing going before, or to come — Fourthly it would prevent our having a series of *continued* articles which you must know by experience are often the cause of some trouble — and Fifthly the *"Looker on in Venice"* is a caption which has been very frequently been made use of before by [*page 2*] Essayists. I submit all, however, to your better judgment, merely saying that Mr White would take it as a personal favor if you would allow us to make the alteration proposed.

I am extremely sorry that the error should have occurred in relation to your *Anthologia* and *The Science of Life*. We did not, however, suppose it necessary to put the Anthologia as a selection — supposing the word *Anthologia* itself sufficiently significant,

> With high respect
> Y^r Ob. S^t
>
> Edgar A Poe

I perceive that your article "National Ingratitude" has attracted great attention, and approbation. The *Charlottesville Jeffersonian* among other papers pays it a merited compliment.

> Carey's article appeared as "The Learned Languages" in SLM, II (August 1836), 557–561. His "last article" refers to "National Ingratitude" in SLM, II (July 1836), 486–488, and not to the very brief "The Science of Life" (*ibid.*, p. 503) or the poem "Anthologia" (*ibid.*). No reply from Carey is known. [CL 156]

72 ⊁ TO HIRAM HAINES

> Richmond — Va. [August 19, 1836]

Dr Sir,

Herewith I send you the August number of the "Messenger" — the best number, by far, yet issued. Can you oblige me so far as to look it over and give your unbiassed opinion of its merits and demerits in the "Constellation"? We need the assistance of *all* our friends and count upon yourself among the foremost.

The contributions have, in most cases, the names of the authors prefixed. All after the word *Editorial* is my own.

If you copy any thing please take my Review of Willis' "Inklings of Adventure" — or some other Review.

> With sincere respect
> Y^r ob. S^t

H. Haines Esqr Edgar A. Poe

> For elaboration of "the best number, by far, yet issued" see Letter 73. "All after the word *Editorial*" includes 2 editorials and 13 reviews. Haines had praised Poe's reviews as early as January 1836, and, subsequently, complimented him upon certain reviews and criticisms and

reprinted portions of Poe's work. (See SLM, II (January 1836), 140; *ibid.* (February 1836), pp. 205–212; *ibid.* (April 1836), p. 347; *ibid.* (July 1836), p. 522. Hiram Haines (1802–1841) was a minor literary figure and publisher of Petersburg, Virginia; he published *Mountain Buds and Blossoms,* a volume of poetry, in 1825; established the democratic tri-weekly *American Constellation* in 1834; edited *Th' Time o' Day,* devoted to news and literature, in 1839; and published the *Virginia Star* (a weekly, then a semi-weekly) from March 4, 1840, until his death, probably in February 1841 (for fuller account, see Ostrom, in *Americana,* XXXVI, No. 1 (January 1942), pp. 67–71). [CL 158]

73 ➤ TO EDITOR OF THE RICHMOND "COURIER AND DAILY COMPILER"

[*ante* September 2, 1836]

To the Editor of the Compiler:
Dear Sir:

In a late paragraph respecting the "Southern Literary Messenger," you did injustice to that Magazine — and perhaps your words, if unanswered, may even do it an injury. As any such wrong is far from your thoughts, you will of course, allow the Editor of the Messenger the privilege of reply. The reputation of a young Journal, occupying a conspicuous post in the eye of the public, should be watched, by those who preside over its interests, with a jealous attention, and those interests defended when necessary and when possible. But it is not often possible. Custom debars a Magazine from answering in its own pages (except in rare cases,) contemporary misrepresentations and attacks. Against these it has seldom, therefore, any means of defence — the best of reasons why it should avail itself of the few which, through courtesy, may fall to its lot. I mean this as an apology for troubling you to-day.

Your notice of the Messenger would generally be regarded as complimentary — especially so to myself. I would, however, prefer justice to a compliment, and the good name of the Magazine to any personal consideration. The concluding sentence of your paragraph runs thus: "The criticisms are pithy, and often highly judicious, but *the editors* must remember that it is almost as injurious to obtain a character for regular cutting and slashing, as for indiscriminate laudation." The italics are my own. I had supposed you aware of the fact that the Messenger has *but one* editor — it is not right that others should be saddled with demerits belonging only to myself. But this is not the

To his Excellency the Governor & Council of Virga

Gentlemen

At the request of the members
of the Richmond Junior Volunteers we beg leave to
solicit your permission for them to retain the arms
which they lately were permitted to draw from
the armory We are authorized to say that each
Individual will not only pledge himself to take
proper care of them, but we ourselves will promise
to attend strictly to the order in which they are
kept by the Company—

We have the honor to be
Gentlemen
Your mo. Obt Servt
John Lyle Capt R J V
Edgar A Poe Lieut

Richmond 17th Novr 1824

POE AND LYLE TO THE GOVERNOR OF VIRGINIA, 17 NOVEMBER 1824
(Letter 1)

JOHN ALLAN

point to which I especially object. You assume that the Messenger has obtained a character for regular "cutting and slashing;" or if you do not mean to assume this, every one will suppose that you do — which, in effect, is the same. Were the assumption just, I would be silent, and set immediately about amending my editorial course. You are not sufficiently decided, I think, in saying that a career of "regular cutting and slashing is *almost* as bad as one of indiscriminate laudation." It is infinitely worse — it is horrible. The laudation may proceed from — philanthropy, if you please; but the "indiscriminate cutting and slashing" only from the vilest passions of our nature. But I wish briefly to examine two points — first, is the charge of indiscriminate "cutting and slashing" just, granting it adduced against the Messenger? — and, second, is such charge adduced at all? Since the commencement of my editorship in December last, 94 books have been reviewed. In 79 of these cases, the commendation has so largely predominated over the few sentences of censure, that every reader would pronounce the notices highly laudatory. In 7 instances, viz: in those of The Hawks of Hawk Hollow, The Old World and the New, Spain Revisited, the Poems of Mrs. Sigourney, of Miss Gould, of Mrs. Ellett, and of Halleck, praise slightly prevails. In 5, viz: in those of Clinton Bradshaw, The Partisan, Elkswatawa, Lafitte, and the Poems of Drake, censure is greatly predominant; while the only reviews decidedly and harshly condemnatory are those of Norman Leslie, Paul Ulric, and the Ups and Downs. — The "Ups and Downs" alone is *unexceptionably* condemned. Of these facts you may satisfy yourself at any moment by reference. In such case the difficulty you will find, in *classing* these notices, as I have here done, according to the predominance of censure or commendation, will afford you sufficient evidence that they cannot justly be called "indiscriminate."

But this charge of indiscriminate "cutting and slashing" has *never been adduced* — except in 4 instances, while the rigid justice and impartiality of our Journal has been lauded even *ad nauseam* in more than four times four hundred. You should not therefore have assumed that the Messenger had obtained a reputation for this "cutting and slashing" — for the asserting a thing to be famous, is a well known method of rendering it so. The 4 instances to which I allude, are the *Newbern Spectator,* to which thing I replied in July — the *Commercial Advertiser* of Colonel Stone, whose Ups and Downs I had occasion (pardon me) to "use *up*" — the *N. Y. Mirror,* whose Editor's Norman

Leslie did not please me — and the *Philadelphia Gazette*, which, being conducted by one of the sub-editors of the Knickerbocker, thinks it its duty to abuse all rival Magazines.

I have only to add that the inaccuracy of your expression in the words — "The August No. of the Southern Literary Messenger has been well received by *most* of the Editorial corps who have noticed it," is of a mischievous tendency in regard to the Messenger. You have seen, I presume, no notices which have not been seen by myself — and you must be aware that there is *not one*, so far, which has not spoken, in the highest terms, of the August number. I cannot, however, bring myself to doubt that your remarks, upon the whole, were meant to do the Messenger a service, and that you regard it with the most friendly feelings in the world.

> Respectfully,
>
> The Editor of the Messenger.

The *Courier* paragraph to which Poe alludes, and which, so far as I know, has not been reprinted, follows: "The August No. of the Southern Literary Messenger has been well received by most of the editorial corps who have noticed it. These commendations may be valued, because they emanate from sources beyond the influence of private friendship; and therefore it is, that suggestions of improvement should be, and we have no doubt will be, duly regarded by the editor and publisher. No periodical in the country has been so successful in obtaining the aid of able and distinguished writers; and the quantity of matter is much greater than need be. We entirely agree with the editor of one of the prints, who thinks a *choice tale* in each number would add to its attraction; as something is due to the tastes of those who have neither time nor relish for the higher grades of literature. Specimens of the writing we refer to, have often been given in the Messenger, but the supply may not be as abundant as needful. The hint, we are sure, is enough to prompt the effort to obtain regular contributions of this sort.

"The criticisms are pithy and often highly judicious, but the editors must remember that it is almost as injurious to obtain a character for regular cutting and slashing as for indiscriminate laudation." The editor's remarks, appended to Poe's letter, protest innocence of any attempt to injure the reputation of the *Messenger;* point out that "editors" was a typographical error and that the paper did not imply that the editor of the *Messenger* was already guilty of cutting and slashing, but merely warned him against such a possibility; and, further, that Poe in his letter chose "to transpose our words, and use the word 'indiscriminate' instead of 'regular,' which makes us say what we did not say."

The editor of the paper cites, "if we remember right," the Baltimore Chronicle as one paper that did not praise unreservedly the August number of the *Messenger*. The *Newbern* [N.C.] *Spectator* article (reprinted in the SLM, II (July 1836), 517) said the SLM was pretentious and that many of its articles were worthy only of an ephemeral sheet, and was answered by Poe, SLM, II, 517–518. Colonel Stone's *Ups and Downs* was severely handled in the SLM, II (June 1836), 455–457. Theodore S. Fay's *Norman Leslie* was reviewed in SLM, II (December 1835), 54–57. For Poe's statement that he is the only editor of the SLM, see the note to Letter 49. [CL 159]

74 ✦ TO HARRISON HALL

Richmond Sep: 2. 1836.

Dr Sir,

Mr White duly received your letter of the 12th August, and I take the liberty of replying for him. The Latin Grammar and Mr Hall's Sketches have come to hand. The latter I have perused, some time ago, with great interest — I have also read the objectionable article in the N. A. Review, and agree with you that some personal pique is at the bottom of it. I cannot republish the reply in the Am. D. Advertiser, but, with your leave, I will make it the basis of another notice for the Sep: Messenger. It is against our rules to republish any thing — otherwise the reply is so good it would save me the trouble of saying more.

Will you now permit me to trouble you with a little business of my own? At different times there has appeared in the Messenger a series of Tales, by myself — in all seventeen. They are of a bizarre and generally whimsical character, and were originally written to illustrate a large work "On the Imaginative Faculties." I have prepared them for republication, in book form, in the [*page 2*] following manner. I imagine a company of 17 persons who call themselves the Folio Club. They meet once a month at the house of one of the members, and, at a late dinner, each member reads aloud a short prose tale of his own composition. The votes are taken in regard to the merits of each tale. The author of the worst tale, for the month, forfeits the dinner & wine at the next meeting. The author of the best, is President at the next meeting. The seventeen tales which appeared in the Mess^r are supposed to be narrated by the seventeen members at one of these monthly meetings. As soon as <one> each tale is read — the other 16 members criticise it in turn — and these criticisms are intended as a burlesque upon criticism generally. The author of the tale adjudged to be the worst demurs from the general judgment, seizes the seventeen M.SS. upon the table, and, rushing from the house, determines to appeal, by printing the whole, from the decision of the Club, to that of the public. The critical remarks, *which have never been published*, will make about ¼ of the whole — the whole will form a volume of about 300 close pages. oct.

I refer you for the reputation of these tales to the covers of the 1ʳˢᵗ & 2ᵈ vols. Lit. Messʳ — A mass of eulogy, in the way of extracts from papers, might be appended if necessary, *such as have never appeared to any volume in the country*. I mention this merely as a matter of business.

My object in stating the nature of these tales &c is to ascertain if you, or any bookseller of your acquaintance, would feel willing to undertake [*page 3*] the publication. I make you the first offer. In regard to remuneration, as ¾ of the book will have been published before, I shall expect none beyond a few copies of the work. My interest with the press throughout the U.S. is perhaps as extensive as that of any man in the country, and would aid the sale, no doubt. Please write me, as soon as possible, on this head. I shall be happy to review, fully, any books you may be pleased to forward.

Very resp ʳ,
Yʳ Ob. Sᵗ

Edgar A Poe

Herewith I forward the published Nos of Vol 2 of the Mess.

Poe answered numerous letters for T. W. White during his editorship of the SLM. Harrison Hall was a Philadelphia printer and had published the *Port Folio*, 1816–1827 (see Mott, *History of American Magazines*, I, 223). For Poe's review of the Latin Grammar, published by Hall, see H, IX, 166–167. The "Sketches" may have been those by Basil Hall, reviewed by Poe in the *Messenger*, October 1836 (see H, IX, 170–174). Contrary to Poe's statement, the SLM did republish material; for example, Poe's tales. The chief interest in the present letter lies in Poe's discussion of the Folio Club. Poe's original plan for the Club was to have a membership "limited to eleven" (see H, II, xxxvii); the present letter shows its expansion to seventeen. By the date of the present letter, Poe had printed in the SLM a total of 14 tales: of these, Quinn (*Poe*, pp. 745–746) accepts all, with the possible exception of "Hans Phaall," as tales of the Club; James Southall Wilson accepts only 12, excepting "Hans Phaall" and "Morella." To make up the total of 17, Quinn adds to the above 14 the following, published later: "Mystification," "Siope," and "A Descent into the Maelström"; Wilson excludes "A Descent into the Maelström," accepts "Mystification," and "Siope" and adds "Never Bet the Devil Your Head" and "Why the Little Frenchman Wears His Hand in a Sling," making a total of 16. (In this connection, see James Southall Wilson, "The Devil Was In It," *American Mercury*, XXIV (October 1931), 214–220.) The "critical remarks," mentioned by Poe, are lost. The 14 SLM tales found republication in the *Tales* of 1840. No reply from Harrison Hall is known. [CL 160]

75 ➤ TO SARAH J. HALE

Richmond Oct: 20. 1837. [1836]

Dear Madam,

I was somewhat astonished to day at receiving a letter addressed to "W. G. Simms Esqr, Editor of the S. L. Messenger", and hesitated about my right to open it, until I reflected that, in forwarding it to Mʳ S., I should place him in a similar dilemma. I therefore broke the seal — but the address, even within, was "W. G. Simms." I could arrive, therefore, at no other conclusion than that, by some missapprehension, you have imagined Mʳ S. to be actually Editor of the Messenger, altho' I wrote you, but lately, in that capacity myself.

Of course, under the circumstances, it is difficult to reply to one portion of your letter — that touching the prose article desired. If however, it was your wish that *I* should furnish it, I am grieved to say that it will be impossible for me to make a definite promise just now, as I am unfortunately overwhelmed with business, having been sadly thrown back by late illness. I regret this the more sincerely as I would be proud to find my name in any publication you edit, and as you have been so kind as to aid the Messenger so effectually in a similar manner yourself. To send you a crude or hastily written article would be injurious to me, and an insult to yourself — and I fear that I could, at present, do little more.

As Editor of the Messenger I can however say that it will afford me sincere pleasure to do you any service in my power. I shall look anxiously for the "Ladies' Wreath."

I am surprised and grieved to learn that your son (with whom I had a slight acquaintance at W. Point) should have been vexed about the autographs. So mere nonsense it was hardly worth while to find fault with. Most assuredly as regards yourself, Madam, I had no intention of giving offence — in respect to the "Mirror" I am somewhat less scrupulous.

                                        With the highest regard
                                        I am Yr Ob S[t]

M[rs] Sarah J. Hale   Edgar A Poe

> Mrs. Hale contributed "A Profession for Ladies" to the SLM, II (August 1836), 571–572. Mrs. Hale, then editor of the *Ladies' Magazine*, Boston, became an editor of Godey's *Lady's Book* when her magazine was merged with his in 1837 (Quinn, *Poe*, p. 269). Though the above letter is the first extant one between Poe and Mrs. Hale, there may have been at least two earlier ones: (1) a note to her as editor of the *Ladies' Magazine*, similar to that sent to Neal, accompanying "Heaven" (see Note 21), and to Willis, who reviewed "Heaven" in the *American Monthly Magazine*, I (November 1829), 587 (see Quinn, *Poe*, pp. 155–156); (2) an unpublished scratch note (original in the Merrill Griswold collection, Boston), which contains, besides other items, almost a copy of Mrs. Hale's review of "Al Aaraaf" in the *Ladies' Magazine*, III (January 1830), 47 (see Quinn, *Poe*, p. 165), but also has at the head of the scratch notes "D[r] Madam." Existence of the full letter, if written, is unknown. Mrs. Hale's son, David E. Hale, had known Poe at West Point, to whom, on one occasion, he had conveyed some message from his mother (see letter of David Hale to Mrs. Hale, February 10, 1831, in Quinn, *Poe*, p. 171). David Hale's concern about the autograph was due to Poe's use of Mrs. Hale's in the "Chapter on Autography" in the SLM, II (February and August 1836). [CL 164]

76 ⊁ TO ALLAN B. MAGRUDER

                                        Richmond, January 9, 1837.

My dear Sir,

Your kind letter of Christmas eve was duly received — with the Essay.

I have read it with great pleasure and, I confess, some degree of surprise — Never having suspected you of any literary designs. It shall certainly appear, entire, in the February number of the "Messenger." Any supervision on my part, I perceive, would be altogether superfluous.

I must apologize for not having made you a reply before. Ill health and a weight of various and harassing business will prove, I trust, a sufficient excuse.

With sincere friendship and esteem,

I am yours, &c.,

Allan B. Magruder, Esq.   Edgar A. Poe

Allan B. Magruder became a lawyer and writer, and lived for some time in Charlottesville, Virginia. His daughter Julia became a writer of some prominence. (Woodberry, I, 70, seems to have confused General John B. Magruder with the present correspondent.) T. W. White, publisher of the SLM, refused to print the essay, though Poe seems to have had it set in type (see White to Poe, January 17, 1837, in H, XVII, 41–42). According to White in a letter to William Scott, January 23, 1837, "Mr. Poe retired from the editorship of my work on the 3d inst. I am once more at the head of affairs" (MS. in Middlebury College Library); but Poe seems to have been in Richmond as late as January 19 (see White to Beverley Tucker, of that date, in Jackson, *Poe and the Southern Literary Messenger,* pp. 111–112), perhaps later. [CL 168]

III

PHILADELPHIA

FROM WEISSNICHTWO TO BURTON'S GENTLEMAN'S MAGAZINE

February 1837–June 1840

New York, Feb. 28, 1837.

To W. H. Carpenter[,] J. S. Norris[,] James Brown

It would give me the greatest pleasure to aid you in your design of a "Baltimore Book" and I would be quite willing to forward an article by the 1st April if so late a period would answer. I am afraid my other engagements would not admit of my sending anything at an earlier date.

I would like to be informed (by return of mail, if possible) what number of pages will be open for me — also what will be the form, etc., of the book, and should like some hint of the nature of the article or articles desired, with any other particulars. In the meantime, I will prepare something in case the theme should be left to my own choice.

Very resp'ly, gentlemen,
Yr. ob. st.

Edgar A. Poe.

W. H. Carpenter and T. S. Arthur edited *The Baltimore Book* of 1838, in which appeared Poe's "Siope — A Fable." It seems reasonable to suppose that Carpenter answered the present letter, though the reply must be lost. [CL 173]

Philadelphia, September 4, 1838.

My Dear Sir:

I duly received your favor with the $10. Touching the review, I am forced to decline it just now. I should be most unwilling not to execute such a task well, and this I would not do at so short notice, at least now. I have two other engagements which it would be ruinous to defer. Besides this, I am just leaving Arch street for a small house, and, of course, somewhat in confusion.

My main reason, however, for declining is what I first alleged, viz.: I could not do the review well at short notice. The truth is, I can hardly say that I am conversant with Irving's writings, having read nothing of his since I was a boy, save his "Granada." It would be necessary to give his entire works a reperusal. You see, therefore, the difficulty at once. It is a theme upon which I would like very much to write, for there is a vast deal to be said upon it. Irving is much over-rated, and a nice distinction might be drawn between his just and his surreptitious and adventitious reputation — between what is due to the pioneer solely, and what to the writer.

The merit, too, of his tame propriety and faultlessness of style should be candidly weighed. He should be compared with Addison, something being hinted about imitation, and Sir Roger de Coverly should be brought up in judgment. A bold and *a priori* investigation of Irving's claims would strike home, take my word for it. The American literary world never saw anything of the kind yet. Seeing, therefore, the opportunity of making a fine hit, I am unwilling to hazard your fame by a failure, and a failure would assuredly be the event were I to undertake the task at present.

The difficulty with you is nothing — for I fancy you are conversant with Irving's works, old and new, and would not have to read for the task. Had you spoken decidedly when I first saw you, I would have adventured. If you can delay the "Review" until the second number I would be most happy to do my best. But this, I presume, is impossible.

I have gotten nearly out of my late embarrassments. Neilson would not aid me, being much pushed himself. He would, no doubt, have aided me, if possible. Present my respects if you see him.

Very truly yours,

Edgar A. Poe.

Suppose you send me proofs of my articles; it might be as well — that is, if you have time. I look anxiously for the first number, from which I date the dawn of a fine literary day in Baltimore.

After the 15th I shall be more at leisure and will be happy to do you any literary service in my power. You have but to hint.

E.A.P.

Brooks started the *American Museum of Literature and the Arts* in Baltimore in September 1838 (see Mott, *History of American Magazines*, I, 345). Poe contributed "Ligeia" to the first number; "The

Psyche Zenobia" and "The Scythe of Time" to the November number;
"Literary Small Talk" to the January and February 1839 numbers;
and "The Haunted Palace" to the April 1839, number. The magazine died with the June issue, 1839 (see the note to Letter 81). The
$10 was undoubtedly payment for "Ligeia," at about eighty cents a
page. Despite Poe's statement about not having read Irving, he had
reviewed *Astoria* (SLM, January 1837) and before that *The Crayon
Miscellany* (SLM, December 1835). Brooks wrote the review of Irving's
works for the first number of the *Museum*. [CL 178]

79 ≻ TO GEORGE POE

[Philadelphia] July 14, 1839

[. . . . .]

There can be no doubt, I think, that our family is originally German, as the name indicates it; it is frequently met with in German
works on Natural History, and a Mr. Poe is now living in Vienna,
who has much reputation as a naturalist. The name there is spelled
with an accent, thus, Poé, and is pronounced in two syllables, 'Po-a.'
As far back, however, as we can trace, our immediate progenitors are
Irish. . . .

John Poe about a century ago was a name of much note in the
financial history of Ireland; he was of ancient and noble family, and
married the sister of the British Admiral McBride, himself of illustrious
descent. . . .

[*Signature missing*]

Poe's German ancestry is uncertain; but John Poe was his great-grand-
father, and he was the son of a tenant-farmer in Dring, Ireland (see
Quinn, *Poe*, p. 13). John Poe came to America about 1750, and settled
first in Lancaster County, Pennsylvania, and later in Baltimore, where
he died in 1756 (*ibid.*, p. 14). [CL 192]

80 ≻ TO J. BEAUCHAMP JONES

Philadelphia August 8th 1839

My Dear Sir,

I have just received your favor of the 6th, and thank you sincerely
for the friendly interest you manifest in my behalf. At some future
time I hope to have the pleasure of making your acquaintance.

In the Sun of the 6th I saw the paragraph to which you allude —
the other attacks have not met my notice. I would be much obliged
to you if you could make it convenient to procure me the paper or
papers, and forward them to me by mail — or, if this cannot be done,
would it be too much to ask you to transcribe the passages referred
to, and send them in a letter?

I presume it is the "Athenaeum" which has honoured me with its
ill-nature. I notice nothing in the Republican, Chronicle, American,
or Patriot.

It is always desirable to know *who are* our enemies, and what are
the nature of their attacks.

I intend to put up with nothing that I can *put down* (excuse the
pun) and I am not aware that there is any one in Baltimore whom I
have particular reason to fear in a regular set-to.

I would take it as a great favor if you would let me know who
edits the "Sun" — also who are the editors of the other papers at-
tacking me — and should be thankful for any other similar information.

You speak of "enemies" — could you give me their names? All
the literary people in Baltimore, as far as I know them, have at least
*profes*sed a friendship.

Very truly Y^r Ob. S^t

E A Poe   (over

[*page 2*]

[I presume the "Sun" has expressed the opinion that the August No:
of the Mag: is not well edited, because it has been more than usually
praised in this respect. No number ever issued from this office has
recd. ¼ of the approbation which this has elicited. We are run
down with puffs especially from the North. . . . Here lies the true
secret of the spleen of the little fish.]

> J. Beauchamp Jones, born in 1810, was a Baltimore journalist. During
> the Civil War he was a government employee in Richmond, and in
> 1866 published his experiences: *A Rebel War Clerk's Diary of the
> Confederate States Capital* (see *The Collector*, cited in Note 80).
> Apparently Poe and Jones never met. In June Poe had become asso-
> ciated with *Burton's Gentleman's Magazine,* and the August number
> contained a number of Poe's writings. [CL 195]

81 ≻ TO JOSEPH EVANS SNODGRASS

Philadel: Sep. 11, [1839]

My Dear Sir,

I have to thank you for your friendly attention in forwarding the St Louis "Bulletin". I was the more gratified, as the reception of the paper convinced me that *you*, of whom I have long thought highly, had no share in the feelings of ill will towards me, which are somewhat prevalent (God only knows why) in Balt:

I should be very much pleased if you would write, and let me know the Balt. news — especially about yourself and Mr Brooks, and the fate of the "Museum".

I have now a great favor to ask — and [th]ink that I may depend upon you[r] friendship. It is to write a [not]ice (such as you think rigidly jus[t] — no more) of the Sep: no of the [Gen]t's Mag: embodying in your art[icl]e the passage concerning myse[lf], from the St Louis Bulletin — in an[y] manner which your good tas[te] may suggest. The critique when written might be handed to Neilson Poe. If you ask him to insert it editorially, it is possible he may do it — but, in fact, I have no great faith in him. If he refuses — then upon your stating the fact to Mr Harker of the "Republican" — you will secure its insertion there. If you will do me this great favor, depend upon any similar good office from me, *"upon demand"*.

I am about to publish my tales collectively — [an]d shall be happy to send you an early [copy. I append the extract from] the Bulletin.

"The general tone [& character of this work (The S. L. Messenger)] impart lustre to our perio[dical literature; and we really congratulate] its publisher upon the so[und and steadfast popularity which it] has acquired. Let it [never be forgotten, however, that the first] impetus to the favor [of *literary men* which it received was] [*page 2*] given by the glowing pen of Edgar A Poe now assistant editor of Burton's Gentleman's Magazine; and, although, since he has left it, has well maintained its claims to respectability, yet there are few writers in this country — take Neal, Irving, & Willis away and we would say *none* — who can compete successfully, in many respects, with Poe. With an acuteness of observation, a vigorous and effective style, and an independence that defies control, he unites a [fervid] fancy and a most beautiful enthusiasm. His is a high destiny."

Will you be kind enough to drop me a line in reply [?]

Yours sincerely

J. E. Snodgrass, Esqʳ   Edgar A Poe.

Did you see the "Weekly Mess[en]ger" (Alexander's) or Noah's Evening Star? They spoke highl[y] of my tale — "The House of Usher". — as also the Pennsylvanian & The U.S. Gazette of this city.

P.S. I have made a profitable engagement with Blackwoods' Mag: and my forthcoming Tales are promised a very commendatory Review in that journal from the pen of Prof. Wilson. Keep this a secret, if you please, for the present.

[Can you not send us some]thing for the Gents' Mag? [Do you know anything of the Pittsbur]g Literary Examiner? [I wrote for it a review of Tortesa in its] 3ᵈ no — but have [not yet recd. No 4.]

[All the criticisms in the Mag: are mine] *with the exception of the 3 first.*

The MS. of this letter is much damaged; all restorations have been made from a collation with William Hand Browne's original transcript made for Ingram. Joseph Evans Snodgrass, a Baltimore physician and minor literary figure, had known Poe probably since Poe's association with the "City of Monuments," 1831–1835. With Nathan C. Brooks, he edited the *American Museum of Science, Literature and the Arts* in 1839, and became proprietor of the *Saturday Visiter* about 1842, probably after being associated with it editorially from late in 1839, and contributed essays and poems to *Burton's, Graham's, Godey's,* and the SLM. He attended Poe during his last illness in Baltimore and was present at his burial. Eighteen years later he wrote "The Facts of Poe's Death and Burial" for Beadle's *Monthly.* The *Museum* died in May 1839. Brooks's editorial farewell, dated May 16, 1839, and printed at the end of the last issue, announced the passing of the editorship to Snodgrass, but Snodgrass printed just below Brooks's announcement that financial inducements more interesting called him elsewhere. L. A. Wilmer, in *Our Press Gang,* pp. 22–29, says that Snodgrass succeeded T. S. Arthur as publisher of the Baltimore *Saturday Visiter,* but allowed it to die soon after, that is, late in 1839 or early 1840; however, Snodgrass was proprietor of the *Visiter* at the time of Poe's letter to him, June 4, 1842 (Letter 137). Snodgrass wrote the "puff" for Poe (see Letter 84). Samuel Harker was editor of the *Baltimore Republican* (see D. K. Jackson, "Four Poe Critiques," *Modern Language Notes,* L,

Richmond - Va
June 7th 1836

Dr Sir.

I take the liberty of again addressing you, and
of calling your attention to what was not precisely a promise
on your part, but a kind of demi-promise made some
months ago — in relation to an article for our "Southern
Literary Messenger". It would be, indeed, a matter of sincere
congratulation with us; if, by any means within our power,
we could so far interest you in our behalf as to obtain
something from the author of "Calavar". We have, just at this
moment, a conspiracy on foot; and we would be most happy
to engage you in our plans. We wish, if possible, to take the
public opinion by storm, in a single number of the Messenger
which shall contain a series of articles from all the first pens
in the land. Can you not aid us — with a single page if no more?
I will trust to the chivalric spirit of him who wrote the "Infidel"
for a reply.

With the highest respect
N. 06. Se
Edgar A Poe

Dr Robert M. Bird.

POE TO R. M. BIRD, 7 JUNE 1836
(Letter 65)

MARIA CLEMM, IN 1849

252). In his letter to F. W. Thomas, November 23, 1840, Poe says that the St. Louis *Bulletin* "has always been very kind to me, and I am at a loss to know who edits it"; but in "Autography" in *Graham's*, December 1841 (see H, xv, 237), Poe identifies G. G. Foster as the editor. Charles Alexander's *Weekly Messenger* (January 1836?–1848; see Mott, *History of American Magazines*, I, 803) was published in Philadelphia, and to its December 18, 1839, number Poe contributed "Enigmatical and Conundrum-ical" that included his offer to solve cryptograms submitted by the readers (see Quinn, *Poe*, p. 326). For Poe's "profitable engagement with Blackwoods' Mag:" see Letter 95. The Pittsburgh *Literary Examiner*, edited by E. Burke Fisher and W. H. Burleigh, was first issued in May 1839; it seems not to have died with the July issue, but later became the *Examiner and Hesperian*, though this lasted only until February 1840 (see Mott, *History of American Magazines*, I, 390). Poe wrote two articles for the *Examiner*: the review of *Tortesa*, I (July 1839), 209–213; and an article on American novel writing, I (August 1839), 316–320 — both were unsigned. Dr. Thomas O. Mabbott first identified Poe's authorship of the second contribution, the material of which was extensively reused in Poe's review of "The Quacks of Helicon," in *Graham's*, August 1841 (reprinted in H, x, 182–195). Poe's discussion of the novel was to serve as an introduction to a series of papers; the first was to have been on Charles Brockden Brown. The first volume of the *Examiner* is in the New York Historical Society, and includes the numbers May–December 1839. In connection with request for puffs to be inserted in the Baltimore papers, see Letter 80. [CL 198]

82 ❯ TO PHILIP P. COOKE

Philadelphia, September 21, 1839.

My Dear Sir:

I received your letter this morning — and read it with more pleasure than I can well express. You wrong me, indeed, in supposing that I meant one word of mere flattery in what I said. I have an inveterate habit of speaking the truth — and had I not valued your opinion more highly than that of any man in America I should not have written you as I did.

I say that I read your letter with delight. In fact I am aware of no delight greater than that of feeling one's self appreciated (in such wild matters as "Ligeia") by those in whose judgment one has faith. You read my inmost spirit "like a book," and with the single exception of D'Israeli, I have had communication with no other person who does. Willis had a glimpse of it — Judge Tucker saw about one half way through — but your ideas are the very echo of my own. I am very far from meaning to flatter — I am flattered and honored. Beside me is now lying a letter from Washington Irving in which he speaks with enthusiasm of a late tale of mine, "The Fall of the House of Usher," — and in which he promises to make his opinion public, upon the first opportunity, — but from the bottom of my heart I assure you, I regard his best word as but dust in the balance when weighed with those discriminating opinions of your own, which teach me that you feel and perceive.

Touching "Ligeia" you are right — all right — throughout. The *gradual* perception of the fact that Ligeia lives again in the person of Rowena is a far loftier and more thrilling idea than the one I have embodied. It offers in my opinion, the widest possible scope to the imagination — it might be rendered even sublime. And this idea was mine — had I never written before I should have adopted it — but then there is "Morella." Do you remember there the *gradual* conviction on the part of the parent that the spirit of the first Morella tenants the person of the second? It was necessary, since "Morella" was written, to modify "Ligeia." I was forced to be content with a sudden half-consciousness, on the part of the narrator, that Ligeia stood before him. One point I have not fully carried out — I should have intimated that the *will* did not perfect its intention — there should have been a relapse — a final one — and Ligeia (who had only succeeded in so much as to convey an idea of the truth to the narrator) should be at length entombed as Rowena — the bodily alterations having gradually faded away.

But since "Morella" is upon record I will suffer "Ligeia" to remain as it is. Your word that it is "intelligible" suffices — and your commentary sustains your word. As for the mob — let them talk on. I should be grieved if I thought they comprehended me here. The "saith Verulam" shall be put right — your "impertinence" is quite pertinent.

I send the "Gentleman's Magazine" (July, August, September). Do not think of subscribing. The criticisms are not worth your notice. Of course I pay no attention to them — for there are two of us. It is not pleasant to be taxed with the twaddle of other people, or to let other people be taxed with ours. Therefore for the present I remain upon my oars — merely penning an occasional paragraph, without care. The critiques, such as they are, are all mine in the July number and all mine in the August and September with the exception of the three first in each — which are by Burton. As soon as Fate allows I will have a Magazine of my own — and will endeavor to kick up a dust. Do you ever see the "Pittsburg Examiner" (a New Monthly)? I wrote a Review of "Tortesa," at some length in the July number. In the October number of the "Gentleman's Magazine," I will have "William Wilson" from "The Gift" for 1840. This tale I think you will like — it is perhaps the best, although not the last, I have done. During the autumn I will publish all in two volumes — and now I have done with my egoism.

It makes me laugh to hear you speaking about "romantic young persons" as of a race with whom, for the future, you have nothing to do. You need not attempt to shake off or to banter off Romance. It is an evil you will never get rid of to the end of your days. It is a part of yourself — a portion of your soul. Age will only mellow it a little, and give it a holier tone. I will give your contributions a hearty welcome, and the choicest position in the magazine.

Sincerely yours,

Edgar A. Poe.

No correspondence between Isaac D'Israeli and Poe is extant, though the above reference implies at least one letter. No correspondence between Willis and Poe at this time is extant. For the reference to Beverley Tucker, see Tucker to T. W. White, November 29, 1835 (James Southall Wilson, "Unpublished Letters of Edgar Allan Poe," *Century Magazine*, cvii (March 1924), 652–653); see also Letter 52, in which Poe implies having received a letter (?) (unlocated) from Cooke giving an intelligent criticism and appreciation of certain tales published by Poe in the SLM. For the reference to Irving, see the note to Letter 113. Poe's "To Ianthe in Heaven" appeared in the July number of *Burton's Gentleman's Magazine*; his "The Man That Was Used Up," in August; his "The Fall of the House of Usher," in September; and his "Morella," in November, reprinted from the SLM, April 1835. "The Pittsburg Examiner" was E. Burke Fisher's *Literary Examiner and Monthly Review* (see Letter 81 and notes); Poe also reviewed Willis's *Tortesa* in *Burton's*, August 1839. The 1840 *Gift* had been copyrighted May 1839. For Poe's *Tales of the Grotesque and Arabesque* (December 1839), see the note to Letter 87. Cooke's answer of December 19, 1839 (MS. in the Boston Public Library; unprinted in full) implies a follow-up letter (unlocated) to Poe's present one. [CL 203]

83 ⊁ TO JOSEPH EVANS SNODGRASS

Phil: Oct: 7, 39

My dear Sir

I recᵈ your kind letter and now write a few hasty words in reply, merely to thank you for your exertions in my behalf, and to say that I send today, the Octo. No. 2. We have been delayed with it, for various reasons.

I *felt* that N. Poe, would not insert the article editorially. In your private ear, I believe him to be the bitterest enemy I have in the world. He is the more despicable in this, since he makes loud professions of friendship. Was it "relationship &c." which prevented him saying *any thing at all* of the 2 or 3 last Nos. of the Gents' Mag? I cannot account for his hostility except in being vain enough to imagine him jealous of the little literary reputation I have, of late years, obtained. But enough of the little dog.

I sincerely thank you for the interest you have taken in my well-doing. The friendship of a man of talent, who is at the same time a man of honorable feeling, is especially valuable in these days of double dealing. I hope I shall always deserve your good opinion.

In the Octo. no: all the criticisms are mine — also the gymnastic article.

My book will be out in the begᵍ of No.ʳ

In haste, yours most truly

Dr. J. E. Snodgrass.   Edgar A Poe

Have you any of the Nos: of the S.Lit. Mess.ʳ from No 7, vol 1 — to No 6. vol 2? both inclusive. Or do you know anyone who has them?

> Poe's strong charge against Neilson Poe here is a more outspoken attack than that in Letter 81; it was prompted, perhaps, by Neilson's objections, on certain grounds, to Edgar's marriage to Virginia Clemm, and by Poe's feeling that Neilson, as editor of a Baltimore daily (H, xvii, 70), could assist in building up Poe's reputation but would not. The "gymnastic article" was entitled "A Chapter on Field Sports and Manly Pastimes," and was the fourth number in a series that began in the July issue and ended in the December number; it was anonymous. Poe's "book," *Tales of the Grotesque and Arabesque*, was published in December 1839 (see Letter 87 and notes). The issues of the SLM requested

by Poe included those from March 1835 (vol. I, no. 7) through May 1836 (vol. II, no. 6), and contained, besides other contributions, thirteen of his tales: "Berenice," "Morella," "Lionizing," "Hans Phaal," "Bon-Bon," "Loss of Breath," "King Pest the First," "Shadow. A Fable," "MS. Found in a Bottle," "Metzengerstein," "Duc de L'Omelette," "Epimanes," and "A Tale of Jerusalem." [CL 209]

84 ➤ TO JOSEPH EVANS SNODGRASS

Nov: 11ᵗʰ Phil. [1839]

My Dear Sir,

I was much pleased this morning by the reception of *two* letters from you — one of which, I presume, has been lying *perdu* in the P. Office for some 10 days — but the Post did not come to hand at all, or, possibly, may have been mislaid among our daily cargo of mail-papers. I have, however, just succeeded in seeing your critique on file in a friend's office — and have to thank you very sincerely for your kindness. The only fault I find is that you say altogether *too much* in my favor. You have overwhelmed me with praise — much of which I truly feel is undeserved. I regret too that you did not preserve the proper order of your initials — I should have been proud of the authority of *your name.*

I am sure you will be pleased to hear that Washington Irving has addressed me 2 letters, abounding in high passages of compliment in regard to my Tales — passages which he desires me to make public — if I think benefit may be derived. It is needless to say that I shall do so — it is a duty I owe myself — and which it would be wilful folly to neglect, through a false sense of modesty. L & Blanchard also urge the publication upon me — so the passages referred to, with others of a similar nature from Paulding, Anthon, &c will be printed in an Appendix of Advertisement to the book — such as publishers are in the habit of appending. Irving's name will afford me a complete triumph over those little critics who would endeavor to put me down by raising the hue & cry of *exaggeration* in style, of *Germanism* & such twaddle. You know Irving heads the school of the *quietists.* I tell you these things in [*page 2*] all confidence, & because I think you will be pleased to hear of my well-doing — not, I assure you, in any spirit of vain-glory — a feeling which I am above.

It grieves me much that I can say not a word touching compensation for articles in Maga. The intense pressure has obliged Mr B.

with nearly every, if not with every, publisher in the country, to discontinue paying for contributions. Mr B. pays for nothing — and we are forced to *fill up* as we can. You know that I appreciate your talents and did we pay *at all* your writings would command in my judgment the highest price. Could we get them, for a while, gratis, how gladly would I use them! — but this is requesting too much.

I have never received the nos of the Museum since the one containing my "Small Talk" — if you have the remaining nos to spare, I would be glad to make my set complete.

I regret that you have not received the Gents' Mag: with regularity — but the fault is my own — as I neglected to have your name put upon the free list; an oversight which I hasten to remedy:

> With high respect & sincere esteem
> Your friend.
>
> Edgar A Poe

Regarding Irving's two letters, see Letter 113, and notes; Poe is overemphasizing Irving's praise of "The Fall of the House of Usher" and "William Wilson," and the passage of compliment, which Poe says Irving wants him to publish, is not to be found in the November 6 letter (cited in Note 84), though it may have been in the earlier, location of which is unknown. Known correspondence of this period does not confirm Poe's implication that James K. Paulding and Charles Anthon wrote Poe in praise of his tales, but Poe may be alluding to Paulding's letter of March 17, 1836 (see H, xvii, 31–32). "Small Talk" appeared in the January and February 1839 issues of the *American Museum*, edited by Nathan C. Brooks and Joseph E. Snodgrass (see title page, volume two) and published in Baltimore (also see Letter 90 and notes). To the *American Museum*, Poe also contributed: "Ligeia" (September), "The Psyche Zenobia" with the pendant "The Scythe of Time" (November), and "The Haunted Palace" (April); the magazine ran only from September 1838, to June 1839, a total of ten issues (Mott, *History of American Magazines*, I, 345). [CL 216]

85 ➤ TO JOHN C. COX

Philadelphia, Dec: 6. 1839

Mr Jno. C. Cox
My Dear Sir,

I am really afraid you will think me the most ungrateful person in the world; as I have not only failed to return you the money so kindly lent nearly a year ago but have never even seen you since, to apologise for my failure. Still, in the face of all appearances, you would be wrong in supposing that I am not deeply sensible of your kindness, and that I do not always bear it in mind. The simple truth is, that the mortification I feel in not being able to repay you, has been the reason of my not calling upon you. From week to week, and from day to day, I have been living in the hope of getting the means of payment, and of calling upon you with the $50 and the apology at once — but my greatest exertions have been in vain; and it was only with the most painful sacrifices that I managed to pay Mrs Jones — which I did about last Christmas. I trust, however, that this state of things cannot last long, and that I shall now soon have it in my power to discharge the claim.

It would give me the most sincere pleasure if you could make it convenient to come & see us. We are still where we were. I could then speak to you more fully, and convince you that the embarrasments under which I have labored are not exaggerated.

Mess. Lea & Blanchard have just issued two vols of Tales, by myself; and may I beg of you to accept a copy with my kindest regards? It would give me great pleasure to hear from you.

Yours most truly,

Edgar A Poe

The identity of Cox is unknown. Mrs. Jones may have been the landlady from whom Poe, Virginia, and Mrs. Clemm rented rooms at 127 Arch Street (see Quinn, *Poe*, p. 273, for the number of the street). Apparently Poe was living in a small house on Sixteenth Street, to which he went from the Arch Street quarters late in 1838 (see Quinn, *Poe*, p. 273). *Tales of the Grotesque and Arabesque* (2 vols.) were published by Lea and Blanchard in Philadelphia, December 1839, as evidenced by this letter, but with an 1840 dating. No reply by Cox is known. [CL 221]

86 ➤ TO E. L. CAREY OR JOHN HART

[Philadelphia]

Dr Sir,

Mr Burton mentioned to me, before going to Charleston, that you were good enough to promise him a Chapter from Marryatt's forthcoming work, for the Jan: No. of our Mag: The Chapter was, I believe, one on "Migration & Emigration". Will you please let me have it, if convenient, by the bearer?

Resp^ly

Mr Carey or Mr Hart.   E A. Poe

Dec 9. [1839]

> No such chapter by Captain Marryat appeared in *Burton's* for January, February, or March 1840; there is, however, a review of his *Diary in America, First and Second Parts* (Philadelphia: Carey and Hart, and T. K. and G. P. Collins) in *Burton's,* VI (February 1840), 103–105, but apparently not written by Poe. Captain Frederick Marryat's novel *Joseph Rushbrook* was reviewed by Poe in *Graham's,* September 1841 (reprinted in H, X, 197–202). [CL 222]

87 ⇸ TO JOSEPH EVANS SNODGRASS

My dear Sir,

I have the pleasure of sending you, through Mess. Lea & Blanchard, a copy of my tales. Not knowing what better plan to pursue, I have addressed the package to you "at the office of the Baltimore American." Will you get it? In the same package is a copy for Mr Carey of the American, which I must beg you to deliver to him with my respects. I have not the pleasure of knowing him personally — but entertain a high opinion of his talents. Please write his full name in his copy — "with the author's respects" — as I forget his *praenomen.*

I do not believe that Lea & B. have sent any of the books to Baltimore as yet — will you be kind enough to forward me any Bal. papers which may contain notices.

Very truly your friend

Dr. J. Evans Snodgrass   Edgar A Poe
Phil: 12 [December] 1839

> *Tales of the Grotesque and Arabesque,* 2 vols. (Philadelphia: Lea and Blanchard, 1840) carried an 1840 dating, but were out by December 6, 1839 (see Letter 85). Lea and Blanchard wrote Poe (September 28, 1839, MS. in the Boston Public Library) that 750 copies were to be printed. Woodberry (II, 376) read the figure correctly. Quinn,

Poe, p. 287, prints 1750. Figures quoted by Charvat in *Publishers'*
Weekly for November 23, 1946, p. 2958, show conclusively that the
correct reading is 750. John L. Carey of the Baltimore *American* was
the author of *Domestic Slavery* (see Letter 90, and note). [CL 223]

88 ⊁ TO JOSEPH EVANS SNODGRASS

Philadelphia. Dec: 19. 1839

My dear Snodgrass,

I presume that upon the 16th (the date of postmark of your last
letter) you received my own dated 2 days before, in which I mentioned having forwarded 2 copies of the "Grotesque & Arab:" one
for yourself & one for Mr. Carey. You will therefore, ere this, have
acquitted me of forgetfulness or neglect.

Touching the Premiums. The Advertisement respecting them was
written by Mr. Burton, and is not, I think as explicit as might [be.]
I can give you no information about their desig[nation furth]er than
is shown in the advertisement itself. The tru[th is,] I object, in toto,
to the whole scheme. — but merely follow[ed in] Mr. B's wake upon
such matters of *business*.

Either of your projected Essays would be, (as you could do it) a
good thing — either that upon American Literature, or upon the
Hints of Science as connected with every-day life. The latter would,
of course, be entirely re-modelled, so as to look *new*.

I am sorry to say that I have been unable to get the "Scenes of
Childhood", in the January number, which is now ready — but it
shall appear in our next. If you look over our columns you will see
that we only put in poetry in the odds and ends of our pages — that
is, to fill out a vacancy left at the foot of a prose article — so that
the length of a poem often determines its insertion. Yours could not
be brôt *to fit* in and was obliged to be left out.

If you see any of the Bal. papers notice my Tales, will you try and
forward them, especially the weeklies which I never see.

The Philadelphians have given me the *very highest possible* praise —
I cd desire nothing further. Have you seen the U.S. Gazette, the Pennsylvanian, or Alexander's Messenger. In the last is a notice by Professor Frost, which I forward you, today, with this. The books have
just reached New York. The Star and the Evening Post have both
capital notices. There is also a promise of one in the New-World —

Benjamin's paper — which I am anxious to see — for, praise or blame,
I have a high op[inion of] that man's ability.

Do not forget to forward [me] the notices — if any appear.

Believe me I am truly yours

Edgar A Poe.

Write soon.

P.S. None of my books have been sent to Richmond as yet — for I
am happy to say that the edition is already very nearly exhausted.

> Regarding Burton's offer of premiums for contributions to the *Gentle-*
> *man's,* see Letter 95. For "Scenes of Childhood," see Letter 90. John
> Frost, a professor of *belles-lettres* in the high school in Philadelphia, is
> included in Poe's "Autography," *Graham's,* December 1841 (reprinted
> in H, xv, 242–243). The *New World,* a monster folio fiction weekly,
> edited by Park Benjamin and Rufus W. Griswold, did not appear until
> June 6, 1840 (Mott, *History of American Magazines,* I, 359–360).
> Poe's postscript was based upon a misapprehension, for on August 16,
> 1841, Lea and Blanchard, his publishers, wrote him that the 1840
> edition of the *Tales* had neither "been got through," nor returned the
> expense of publication (original MS. in Boston Public library). [CL
> 225]

89 ⋗ TO JOSEPH B. BOYD

Philadelphia, Dec 25th 1839.

Dr Sir,

I have only to urge a world of pressing engagements as an excuse
for not sooner attending to your very flattering request of November
the fifteenth. It will now give me great pleasure to copy, as you desire, one of my own poems — selecting a Sonnet for brevity's sake.

Silence — A Sonnet.

There are some qualities — some incorporate things —
    That have a double life — life aptly made
The type of that twin entity which springs
    From matter and light — evinced in solid and shade.

There is a two-fold *Silence* — sea and shore —
    Body and soul. One dwells in desert places
    Newly with grass oergrown. Some solemn graces,
Some human memories (a tearful lore)
Render him terrorless — his name's "No More".

He is the corporate Silence — dread him not.
　No power hath he of evil in himself.
But should some urgent fate (untimely lot!)
　Bring thee to meet *his shadow* — (nameless elf,
Who haunteth the dim regions where hath trod
No foot of man) — commend thyself to God!

With every sentiment of respect,
I am Y^r Ob^t S^t

To Joseph B. Boyd, Esquire,　　　　　Edgar A Poe.
Cincinnati, Ohio.

> Concerning Joseph B. Boyd, see Letter 100 and note. A comparison
> of the present version of the poem with that printed in Campbell,
> *Poems*, pp. 104–105, will show variations in a few words and in punc-
> tuation. The poem was first published in the Philadelphia *Saturday
> Courier*, January 4, 1840. [CL 227]

90 ➤ TO JOSEPH EVANS SNODGRASS

Philadelphia Jan: 20. 1840

My dear Sir

I seize the opportunity afforded me by a temporary lull in a storm
of business, to write you a few hurried words. Your last letter is not
before me — but I refer to it in memory. I received the poem through
Godey, and retain it as you desire. The "Friends of Childhood ["]
is in type for the Feb. no: Mr. Carey's book has not yet reached me.
My own was forwarded by L & Blanchard to Joseph Robinson's —
so they assure me. I presume you have it before this.

I am obliged to decline saying anything of the "Museum" in the
Gent's Mag: however much I feel anxious to oblige yourself, and to
express my own views. You will understand me when I say that I
have no proprietary interest in the Mag: and that Mr Burton is a
warm friend of Brooks — verb. sap. sat.

I have heard, indirectly, that an attempt is to be made by Some
one of capital in Baltimore, to get up a Magazine. Have you heard
anything of it? If you have, will you be kind enough to let me know
all about it *by return of mail* — if you can spare the time to oblige

me — I am particularly desirous of understanding how the matter stands — who are the parties, &c.

Excuse the abruptness of this letter, &

believe me very truly yours,

Edgar A Poe

Though Snodgrass' name does not appear in the letter, his poem "Childhood Scenes" in *Burton's Gentleman's Magazine,* February 1840, identifies Poe's correspondent; Poe had called the poem "Scenes of Childhood" in his letter of December 19, 1839. John L. Carey (not Henry C. Carey, as Woodberry identified him) wrote *Domestic Slavery;* it was published anonymously in Baltimore, 1838, but carried his name as author in the second edition, 1839. (Henry Carey's *The Slave Trade* was not published until 1853.) Concerning Poe's receipt of the book and his unpublished review of it, see Letter 95. Joseph Robinson was probably a book dealer in Baltimore. Poe's reference to the *American Museum of Science, Literature and the Arts* here is curious, for that magazine died in May, 1839, with the June number (see notes to Letter 81); he undoubtedly has reference to the Baltimore *Saturday Visiter.* Perhaps the demise of the *Museum* was attended by a misunderstanding between Snodgrass and Brooks, and Snodgrass' bid for Poe's editorial assistance in revitalizing the *Visiter* was frustrated by Burton's friendship for Brooks. Poe's abbreviation for *verbum sat sapienti (est)* means "A word to the wise (is) sufficient." [CL 229]

---

91 ⊁ TO JOHN KEARSLEY MITCHELL

[Philadelphia, February 29, 1840]

Dr Sir,

It will give me great pleasure to accept your invitation for Feb: 29th — this evening.

Dr J. K. Mitchell   Edgar A Poe

John Kearsley Mitchell, father of S. Weir Mitchell, was a prominent physician and lecturer at various Philadelphia medical institutes. He was also Poe's physician. [CL 231]

---

92 ⊁ TO HIRAM HAINES

Philadelphia April 24. 1840.

My Dear Sir,

Having been absent from the city for a fortnight I have only just received your kind letter of March 24th and hasten to thank you for the "Star", as well as for your offer of the fawn for Mr⁸ P. She desires me to thank you with all her heart — but, unhappily, I cannot point out a mode of conveyance. What can be done? Perhaps some opportunity may offer itself hereafter — some friend from Petersburg may be about to pay us a visit. In the meantime accept our best acknowledgments, precisely as if the little fellow were already nibbling the grass before our windows in Philadelphia.

I will immediately attend to what you say respecting exchanges. The "Star" has my very best wishes, and if you really intend to push it with energy, there cannot be a doubt of its full success. If you can mention anything in the world that I can do here to promote its interests and your own, it will give me a true pleasure.

It is not impossible that I may pay you a visit in Petersburg, a month or two hence.

Till then, believe me,
most sincerely Your friend

H. Haines Esqr   Edgar A Poe

Office Gentleman's Magazine

> This letter is the last known to have been written by Poe to Haines. Haines's letter of March 24, 1840, probably thanked Poe, also, for the "puff" of the *Virginia Star* which he wrote for Alexander's *Weekly Messenger* (Philadelphia), March 18, 1840, p. 2, col. 4 (see Clarence S. Brigham, *Proceedings of the American Antiquarian Society,* LII, pt. 1 (April 1942), pp. 100–101). Dr. T. O. Mabbott informs me that Poe was "contributing to the [*Weekly*] *Messenger* regularly at this time." There is no evidence that the fawn reached Philadelphia. Poe's proposed visit to Petersburg undoubtedly concerned the establishment of the *Penn Magazine*. [CL 233]

93 ➤ TO WILLIAM E. BURTON

[Philadelphia, June 1, 1840]

Sir:

I find myself at leisure this Monday morning, June 1, to notice your very singular letter of Saturday. <I sent George home yesterday without a reply to your letter for I felt somewhat too angry to make one. I have followed the example of Victorine and slept upon the matter>. & you shall now hear what I have to say. In the first place — your attempts to bully me excite in my mind <nothing> scarcely any other sentiment than mirth. When you address me again preserve if you can, the dignity of a gentleman. If by accident you have taken it into your head <by any sad accident> that I am to be insulted with impunity I can only assume that you are an ass. This one point being distinctly understood <we shall be the better able to enter into some arrangement and in regard to myself individually> I shall feel myself more at liberty to be explicit. As for the rest, you do me gross injustice; and you know it. As usual you have wrought yourself into a passion with me on account of some imaginary wrong; for no real injury, or attempt at injury, have you ever received at my hands. As I live, I am utterly unable to say why you are angry, or what true grounds of complaint you have against me. You are a man of <high passions> impulses; have made yourself, in consequence, some enemies; have been in many respects ill treated by those whom you had looked upon as friends — and these things have rendered you suspicious. You once wrote in your magazine [a sharp critique] upon a book of mine — a [very silly book — Pym. Had I written a simi]lar critici[sm] upon a book of yours, you feel that you would [have been] my enemy for life, and you therefore ima[gine in my] bosom a latent hostility towards yourself. This has been a mainspring in your whole conduct towards me since our first acquaintance. It has acted to prevent all cordiality. In a general view of human nature your idea is just — but you will find yourself puzzled in judging me by ordinary motives. Your criticism was essentially correct and therefore, although severe, it did not occasion in me one solitary emotion either of anger or dislike. But even while I write these words, I am sure you will not believe them. Did I not still think you, in spite of the exceeding littleness of some of your hurried actions, a man of many honorable impulses, I should not now take the trouble to send you this letter. I cannot permit myself to suppose that you would say to me in cool blood what you said in your letter of yesterday. You are, of course, only mistaken, in asserting that I owe you a hundred dollars, and you will rectify the mistake at once when you come to look at your accounts. Soon after I joined you, you made me an offer of money, and I accepted $20. Upon another occasion, at my request, you sent me enclosed in a letter $30. Of this 30, I repaid 20 within the next fortnight (drawing no salary for that period.) I was thus still in your debt $30, when not long ago I again asked a loan of $30, which you promptly handed to me at your own house. Within the last 3 weeks, 3$ each week have been retained from my salary, an indignity which I have felt deeply but did not resent. You state the sum retained as $8, but this I believe is through a mistake of Mr Morrell. My postage bill at a guess, might be 9 or 10 $ — and I therefore am indebted to you, upon the whole, in the amount of about $60. More than this sum I shall not pay. You state that you can no longer afford to pay $50 per month for 2 or 3 pp. of M.S. Your error here can be shown by reference to the [Magaz]ine. During my year with you I have writ[ten —]

[in] July —	5 pp		
August	9		
Sept	16		
Octo.	4		
Nov.	5		
Dec.	12		
Jan	9		
Feb	12		
Mar	11		
April	17 +		
May	14 + 5	copied — Miss McMichael, M.S.
June	9 + 3	" Chandlers.
	132		

Dividing this sum by 12 we have an average of 11 pp per month — not 2 or 3. And this estimate leaves out of question everything in the way of extract or compilation. Nothing is counted but bonâ fiede composition. 11 pp. at $3 per p. would be $33, at the usual Magazine prices. Deduct this from $50, my monthly salary, and we have left 17$ per month, or $4 25/100 per week, for the services of proofreading; general superintendence at the printing-office; reading, alteration, & preparation of M.S.S., with compilation of various articles, such as Plate articles, Field Sports &c. Neither has anything been said of my name upon your title page, a small item you will say — but still something as you know. Snowden pays his editresses $2 per week each for their names solely. Upon the whole I am not willing to admit that you have greatly overpaid me. That I did not do 4 times as much as I did for the Magazine, was your own fault. At first I wrote long articles which you deemed inadmissable, & never did I suggest any

to <you> which you had not some immediate and decided objection.
Of course I grew discouraged & could feel no interest in the Journal.
I am at a loss to know why you call me selfish. If you mean that I
borrowed money of you — you know that you offered it — <If>
and you know that I am poor. In what instance has anyone ever
found me selfish? Was there selfishness in the affront I offered Benjamin (whom I respect, and who spoke well of me) because I deemed
it a duty not to receive from any one commendation at your expense?
I had no hesitation in making him my enemy (which he now must
be) through a sense of my obligations as your coadjutor. <No man
can call me selfish & not he> I have said that I could not tell why
you were angry. Place yourself in my situation & see whether you
would not have acted as I have done. You first "enforced", as you say,
a deduction of salary: giving me to understand thereby that you
thought of parting company — You next spoke disrespectfully of me
behind my back — this as an habitual thing — to those whom you
supposed your friends, and who punctually retailed me, as a matter
of course, every ill-natured word which you uttered. Lastly you advertised your magazine for sale without saying a word to me about it.
I felt no anger at what you did — none in the world. Had I not
firmly believed it your design to give up your Journal, with a view of
attending to the Theatre, I should <never> have dreamed of attempting one of my own. The opportunity of doing something for
myself seemed a good one — (I was about to be thrown out of business) — and I embraced it. Now I ask you as a man of honor and
as a man of sense — what is there wrong in all this? What have I
done at which you have any right to take offense? I can give you no
definitive answer (respecting the continuation Rodman's Journal,)
until I hear from you again. The charge of 100 $ I shall not admit for
an instant. If you persist in it our intercourse is at an end, and <I
shall refer you to an attorney, But I cannot bring myself to believe
that you will.> We can each adopt our own measures

In the meantime, I am
Y^r Obt St.

Wm E. Burton Esqr.   Edgar A Poe

"George" perhaps refers to Burton's clerk, Morrell (see Letter 109).
Burton's, III (September 1838), 210-211, reviewed *Pym* (published
by Harper & Brothers, July 1838, according to Quinn, *Poe*, p. 263);

the criticism was derogatory and said, in part, "We regret to find Mr. Poe's name in connexion with such a mass of ignorance and effrontery." Poe's listing of duties is supported by an unpublished letter from Burton to Poe, July 4, 1839 (original in the Boston Public Library), in which Burton, absent in New York, gives Poe orders concerning the August number and exhorts him to see that Morrell and the others get the issue out on time. Park Benjamin's paper, the *New World*, mentioned by Poe on December 19, 1839 (see Letter 88), as if soon to be published, actually appeared in June 1840 (Mott, *History of American Magazines*, I, 359). "Rodman's Journal" ran in *Burton's*, vol. VI (January–June). Poe's arithmetical error in compilation of work done for Burton may have been corrected in the letter actually sent; also Poe apparently counted as full pages those not quite full (see Hull, pp. 151–187). The content of Poe's letter implies that Burton's "letter of Saturday," after making certain accusations against Poe, fired him, but asked about his continuing the "Journal of Julius Rodman" (see ". . . you can no longer afford to pay $50 per month . . ." and "I can give you no definitive answer [respecting . . . Rodman's Journal] until I hear from you again."); or the letter implies some new arrangement whereby Poe will not remain as a full salaried editor; in any event, Poe probably had not resigned when he received Burton's letter. Burton probably answered Poe's letter, and Poe then actually wrote his resignation (see Letter 95), or left *Burton's* and let Snodgrass believe the resignation had been voluntary. Burton's exclusion of reviews (cited in the letter to Snodgrass) may have been due, not to Poe's resignation, but to matters set forth in Burton's "Saturday letter." [CL 235]

IV

PHILADELPHIA

THE PENN AND GRAHAM'S MAGAZINE

June 1840–March 1842

Philadelphia. June 4. [1840]

My Dear Sir

As you gave me the first jog in my literary career, you are in a measure bound to protect me & keep me rolling. I therefore now ask you to aid me with your influence, in whatever manner your experience shall suggest.

It strikes me that I never write you except to ask a favor, but my friend Thomas will assure you that I bear you always in mind — holding you in the highest respect and esteem.

Most truly yours

John Neal Esqʳ   Edgar A Poe

> The "first jog" refers to Neal's notices of Poe's poems in *The Yankee*, September and December 1829. "Thomas" probably refers to Poe's new friend Frederick W. Thomas, who might have known Neal in Baltimore (see the notes to Letter 104). [CL 237]

95 ⇥ TO JOSEPH EVANS SNODGRASS

Philadelphia June 17 [1840]

My dear Snodgrass,

Yours of the 12ᵗʰ was duly received but I have found it impossible to answer it before, owing to an unusual press of business which has positively not left me a moment to myself. Touching your Essay. Burton not only *lies*, but deliberately and wilfully lies; for the last time but one that I saw him I called his attention to the M.S. which was then at the top of a pile of other M.S.S. sent for premiums, in a drawer of the office desk. The last day I was in the office I saw the Essay in the same position, and I am perfectly sure it is there still. You know it is a peculiar looking M.S. and I could not mistake it. In saying it was not in his possession his sole design was to vex you, and through you myself. Were I in your place I would take some summary method of dealing with the scoundrel, whose infamous line of conduct in regard to this whole premium scheme merits, and shall receive exposure. I am firmly convinced that it was never his intention to pay one dollar of the money offered; and indeed his plain intimations to that effect, made to me personally and directly, were the immediate reasons of my cutting the connexion as abruptly as I did. If you could, in any way, spare the time to come on to Philadelphia, I think I could put you in the way of detecting this villain in his rascality. I would go down with you to the office, open the drawer in his presence, and take the M S. from beneath his very nose. I think this would be a good deed done, and would act as a caution to such literary swindlers in future. What think you of this plan? Will you come on? Write immediately in reply.

Mr. Carey's book on slavery was received by me not very long ago, and in last month's number I wrote, at some length, a criticism upon it, in which I endeavored to do justice to the author, whose talents I highly admire. But this critique, as well as some six or seven others, were refused admittance into the Magazine by Mr. Burton, upon his receiving my letter of resignation. [I] allude to the number for June — the one last issued. I fancy, moreover, that he has some private pique against Mr. Carey (as he has against every honest man) for not long ago he refused admission to a poetical address of his which I was anxious to publish.

Herewith you have my Prospectus. You will see that I have given myself sufficient time for preparation. I have every hope of success. As yet I have done nothing more than send a few Prospectuses to the Philadelphia editors, and it is rather early to strike — six months in anticipation. My object, at present, is merely to call attention to the contemplated design. In the meantime be assured that I am not idle — and that if there is any impossibility about the matter, it is the impossibility of *not* succeeding. The world is fond of novelty, and in being absolutely *honest,* I shall be utterly novel.

If you would show the Prospectus to Mr. Carey, or any other editorial friend, when you have done with it, I would be obliged to you.

Touching my Tales, you will scarcely believe me when I tell you that I am ignorant of their fate, and have never spoken to the publishers concerning them since the day of their issue. I have cause to think, however, that the edition was exhausted almost immediately. It was only six weeks since that I had the opportunity I wished of sending a copy to Professor Wilson, so as to be sure of its reaching him directly.

Of course I must wait some time yet for a notice, — if any there is
to be.

Yours most truly

E A Poe

P.S. If you would enclose me Burton's letter to yourself, I will take
it as an especial favor.

> Burton's "lie" was given apparently in a letter to Snodgrass, cited in
> Poe's postscript. Concerning the premiums, see also Letter 88. There
> is no evidence that Snodgrass either went to Philadelphia or answered
> "immediately," as Poe requested. For John L. Carey's *Domestic Slavery*
> (2d. edition, 1839), see the note with Letter 90. Poe's "unusual press
> of business" was in connection with his attempt to establish his *Penn
> Magazine*. Its publication was announced in the Philadelphia *Saturday
> Courier*, June 13, 1840, to appear on January 1, 1841 (see reprint of
> prospectus in Quinn, *Poe*, pp. 306–308). Since Poe's letter to Thomson,
> June 28, 1840, was written on the second leaf of the June 1840, pros-
> pectus (see other letters of this period for similar use of the prospectus),
> the present letter to Snodgrass was undoubtedly written on one of the
> blank pages of the advertisement; thus this evidence refutes Wood-
> berry's statement that the prospectus was sent to press in August (see
> W, I, 260), unless he referred to the revision of the June prospectus
> without recognizing the existence of the earlier one (see Quinn, *Poe*,
> p. 308). No correspondence is known between Lea and Blanchard's
> letter of November 20, 1839 (see W, I, 225) and Poe's, dated August 13,
> 1841, so that Poe may have had no knowledge concerning the sale of
> his *Tales*. Upon their publication, an edition of 750 copies, Poe was to
> keep the copyright (see MS. letter of Lea and Blanchard to Poe, Sep-
> tember 28, 1839, in the Boston Public library) and receive about twenty
> copies for "private distribution" (see their letter to Poe, October 30,
> 1839, in W, II, 376); thus upon receipt of the complimentary copies,
> Poe had no need of further dealing with his publishers until August 15,
> 1841, when he suggested that they publish for him a new collection.
> A search of *Blackwood's Magazine*, subsequent to the date of the present
> letter, failed to reveal any review of Poe's *Tales* by John Wilson ("Chris-
> topher North"), editor of the English magazine, despite the postscript
> in Letter 81. [CL 240]

96 ➤ TO CHARLES W. THOMSON

[Philadelphia] June 28 [1840]

Dr Sir,

On Saturday evening I called twice to see you in relation to your
note of the 26th, but had not the pleasure of finding you at home.

You may have heard that I have declined a farther connexion with the Gentleman's Magazine, and propose to establish one of my own. By the Prospectus you will see that the first number will not be issued until the first of January; th[is] delay being rendered necessary by my want of capital. It is, therefore, at present, altogether out of my power to suggest any employment of the nature you designate.

Desperate as my chances of success may appear, where so many have failed with every advantage of money, and monied interest — still I feel a perfect certainty of accomplishing the task I have deliberately undertaken. I am proposing to myself, however, to form a connexion, as soon as possible, with some gentleman of literary attainments, who could at the same time advance as much ready money as will be requisite for the first steps of the undertaking — to defray, for instance, the expences of visiting the chief northern cities, of printing and distributing circulars, of advertising &c &c — items which, altogether, would demand scarcely $500. Upon receipt of your note the idea suggested itself that you might feel willing to join me in the enterprise, and, if so, there is nothing would give me greater pleasure. Will you let me hear from you upon this topic — if possible this afternoon?

                                        Very Resp^y
                                        Yr Ob S^t
C. W. Thompson Esqr Edgar A Poe

Charles West Thomson (Poe spelled it Thompson) contributed poems to the *Southern Literary Messenger*, the *American Museum, Burton's, Graham's,* and to annuals like the *Atlantic Souvenir*, the *Token*, and the *Gift*. With Burton he issued the *Literary Souvenir* for 1838 and 1839. He became an Episcopal minister in York, Pennsylvania. At the time of Poe's letter he was a clerk in the Bank of the United States in Philadelphia (see Heartman and Canny, p. 39). Poe's "Autography" for December 1841, included Thomson (see H, xv, 226). Concerning Poe's leaving *Burton's,* see Letter 93 and notes. [CL 242]

97 ✶ TO WILLIAM POE

                              Philadelphia, Aug. 15 [14] — 40.

Dear William,

Owing to a temporary absence from town I did not receive your welcome letter of the 28th July until this morning. [I n]ow hasten

to reply; and in the first place let me assur[e y]ou that, if I have
not lately written, it is rather because I have been overwhelmed by
worldly cares, which left me scarce a moment for thought, than that
I do not feel for you the kindest affection, as well as deep gratitude
for the services yourself and brothers have so often rendered me.

Herewith I send you a Prospectus of my contemplated Magazine.
I believe you know that my connexion with the Southern Messenger
was merely that of editor. I had no proprietary interest in it, and
my movements were therefore much impeded[.] The situation was
disagree[a]ble to me in every respect. The drudgery was excessive;
the salary was contemptible. In fact I soon found that whatever
reputation I might personally gain, this reputation would be all.
I stood no chance of bettering my pecuniary condition, while my
best energies were wasted in the service of an illiterate and vulgar,
although well-meaning man, who had neither the capacity to appreciate my labors, nor the will to reward them. For these reasons I
left him, and entered, first, into an engagement with The New-York
Review, and afterwards with The Gentleman's Mag[a]zine, writing
occasionally for [other] journals; my object be[in]g merely to keep
my head a[bove] water, as regards money, until a good opportunity
sh[owed itself] of establishing a Magazine of my own, in which I
sho[uld be] able to carry out my plans to full completion, and
d[uring this] time have the satisfaction of feeling that my exertions
w[ould be] to my own advantage.

I believe that the plans I here speak of, and some of [them you]
will find detailed in the Prospectus, are well devised [. . . sug]gested,
and will meet with the hearty support of the m[ore desi]rable and intelligent portion of the community. Should [I be] able to bring them
fairly be[f]ore the public I feel assured [that my] fortune is made.
The ambition which actuates me [is] now to be no ordinary nor unworthy sentiment, and, knowing this, I take pride in earnestly soliciting your support, and that of your brothers and friends. If I fully
succeed in my purposes I will not fail to produce some lasting effect
upon the growing literature of the country, while I establish for myself individually a name which that country "will not willingly let
die."

It is upon the South that I chiefly rely for aid in the undertaking,
and I have every hope that it will not fail me [*page 2*] in my need.
Yet the difficulties which I have to overcome are great, and I acknowl-

edge to you that my prospects depend very much upon getting together a subscription list previously to the 1ʳˢᵗ of December. If, by
this day, I can obtain 500 names, the w[or]k cannot fail to proceed,
and I have no fear for the [resu]lt.

The friendship you have always evinced, the near relationship
which exists between us, and the kind offer in your last letter, all
warrant me in hoping that you will exert your whole influence for
me in Augusta. Will you oblige me by acting as my agent for the
Penn Magazine in your city, this letter being your authority? If I
am not mistaken you already act in that capacity for the Messenger.

I will write a few lines also by this mail to your brother Robert,
with a Prospectus as you suggest — and also to Washington at Macon.

Mrs Clemm, my aunt, is still living with me, but for the last six
weeks has been on a visit to a friend in the State of N. Jersey. She is
quite well, having entirely recovered her health. Respecting the letter
from Mr Bayard I am quite at a loss to understand it. It is, however,
possible that the letter was written by Mr B. at a period when we
were all in much difficulty in New-York & that Mrs C. concealed the
circumstance from me through delicacy.

Yours truly

E A P.

For White's incapacity to appreciate Poe's labors, see White to Tucker,
April 26, 1837, in Jackson, *Poe and the Southern Literary Messenger*,
pp. 114–115: "If he [Paulding] would have been proud of praise from
Poe, it would have been because he really admired the fellow's talents. —
Like myself he was completely gulled." Caleb S. Henry, editor of the
New York Review from March 1837 (the year it was founded), to
some time in 1838, wrote to the Reverend J. H. Hopkins, who sent the
letter to J. H. Ingram: "Poe was never engaged as a writer on the
New York Review. He contributed of his own accord . . . a review
of Stephen's Incidents of Travel in Egypt, etc . . . in the 2ᵈ number . . . Oct. 1837" (this letter is now in the Ingram collection,
University of Virginia, under the date of March 13, 1875). Poe's letter
to Robert Poe was probably written, though its location is not known.
The identity of Mr. Bayard and the significance of the reference to him
are unknown. William Poe's letter of June 15, 1843, is the only other
item in this correspondence known to be extant; it indicates, however,
that Poe wrote to William, *ante* May 15 ? 1843, that William answered
it on May 15 and again on June 15 (see H, XVII, 145–146, the original

being in the Boston Public Library). There is sometimes cited a letter
from William, dated December 15, 1843; but as the script of the June
15 letter could be read "Decem," the letters are probably the same.
[CL 245]

98 ➤ TO WASHINGTON POE

Philadelphia August 15th [1840]

My Dear Sir,

On the other leaf of this sheet you will find the Prospectus of a
Magazine which I am about attempting to establish, and of which the
first number will be issued on the first of January next[.] When I
was editor of the Southern Messenger you were so kind as to use your
influence in behalf of that Journal, although I had myself no proprietary right in it and derived only a collateral benefit from your
exertions. May I ask you to assist me in the present instance? Your
brothers in Augusta have kindly offered me every aid in their power,
and I have reason to hope that you will also feel inclined to do so
for the sake of the relationship which exists between us, and for the
honor of our family name. Upon looking over my Prospectus I trust
you will find my purposes, as expressed in it, of a character worthy
your support. I am actuated by an ambition which I believe to be an
honourable one — the ambition of serving the great cause of truth,
while endeavouring to forward the literature of the country. You are
aware that hitherto my circumstances, as regards pecuniary matters,
have been bad. In fact, my path in life has been beset with difficulties
from which I hope to emerge by this effort. So far, my exertions have
served only to enhance my literary reputation in some degree and to
benefit *others* so far as money was concerned. If I succeed in the present attempt, however, fortune & fame must go hand in hand — and
for these reasons I now most earnestly solicit your support. My chances
of establishing the Magazine depend upon my getting a certain number of subscribers previously to the first of December. This is rendered
necessary by my having no other capital to begin with than whatever
reputation I may have acquired as a literary man. Had I money, I
might issue the first numbers without this list; but as it is, at least 500
names will be required to enable me to commence. I have no doubt in
the world that this number can be obtained among those friends who
aided me in the Messenger; but still it behooves me to use every exer-

tion to ensure success. I think it very probable that your influence in Macon will procure for me several subscribers, and, if so, you will render me a service for which I shall always be grateful. Remember me kindly to your family, and believe me

Yours most truly

Edgar A Poe

No other letters are extant between Poe and Washington Poe, of Macon, Georgia, though Poe wrote William Poe, April 12, 1836 (see Letter 60), that about March 30, 1836, he replied to a letter from Washington, dated probably about March 28–29. [CL 246]

99 ⊁ TO LUCIAN MINOR

Philadelphia, August 18. 1840.

My Dear Sir,

I have the honor of sending you, herewith, a Prospectus of the Penn Magazine. In setting about the difficult and most ungracious task which I have proposed to myself, it is but natural that I should look around me anxiously for friends among the men of integrity and talent — and I now call to mind, with pride, the many instances of good will, towards myself individually, which you evinced while I edited the Southern Messenger.

I believe that the objects set forth in my Prospectus are such as you will approve; I feel that I am actuated by no ordinary nor dishonest ambition; I know that the disadvantages under which I labor are exceedingly great — and for these reasons I have no hesitation in earnestly soliciting your support — even at the risk of being considered importunate.

It is, indeed, in your power to aid me materially, and I have every hope that you will be inclined to do so. The permanent success of the Magazine depends, chiefly, upon the number of subscribers I may obtain before the first of December. If, through any influence you will be kind enough to exert in my behalf, at Charlottesville, or elsewhere, you can procure me even one or two names, you will render me a service of the greatest importance, and one for which I shall be very grateful.

I trust that you will excuse the abruptness of this letter, and attribute it rather to any cause than to a want of courtesy.

With the highest respect.
Yr. Ob. St.

Mr Lucian Minor   Edgar A Poe
(over)

> The present letter is the last of the four known Poe letters to Minor (October 31, 1835, unlocated but advertised for sale in the Merwin-Clayton catalogue, January 18, 1911, as writen by Poe but signed by T. W. White; February 5 and March 10, 1836, being the other three). It is interesting that the second and third letters were written by Poe for White, publisher of the *Southern Literary Messenger,* and the first one probably was too; only the present letter, therefore, was written by Poe in his own interest. [CL 247]

100 ➤ TO JOSEPH B. BOYD

Philadelphia August 20. 1840.

Dear Sir,

On the other leaf of this sheet you will find a Prospectus of the Penn Magazine. In setting about the difficult and most arduous task which I have proposed, it is but natural that I should look with especial anxiety for the support of those whose friendship may do me honor, and whose influence may further the objects I have in view. I believe that the purposes set forth in this Prospectus are such as your candor will approve; I feel that I am actuated by no dishonest, and certainly by no common-place ambition; the disadvantages under which I labor are, in some respects, exceedingly great — and, for these reasons, I have no hesitation in earnestly soliciting your assistance, even at the risk of being considered importunate.

Placed as you are, it is in your power to aid me most essentially, and I have every hope that you will be inclined to do so. My success depends, mainly, upon the number of subscribers I may obtain before the first of December. If, through any influence you will be kind enough to exert in my behalf, you can procure me even one or two names, you will render me a service of vital importance, and one for which I shall be grateful indeed.

I trust you will pardon whatever of abruptness may appear in this letter, and attribute it to any cause rather than to a want of respect.

Yrobst.

Joseph B. Boyd Esqr   Edgar A Poe

> Quinn, *Poe,* p. 308, n. 2, says that the only Joseph B. Boyd of Cincinnati in 1840 ". . . is a watch maker, an unlikely person for Poe to ask for help." Poe's earlier correspondence with Boyd (see Letter 89) seems sufficient evidence for Poe's solicitation of aid in acquiring subscribers to the *Penn* from one who had asked a favor of Poe; as a "watch maker," Boyd might secure the "one or two names" Poe desired. According to Quinn, the letter is written on a revised form of the June prospectus of the *Penn:* page 1 has the prospectus, page 2 is blank, page 3 has the letter, and page 4, the address. There is no known answer to Poe's letter. [CL 248]

101 ⇝ TO JOHN TOMLIN

Philadelphia Sep. 16. 1840.

Dear Sir,

Your kind letter, with the names of nine subscribers to the Penn Magazine, has only this moment reached me, as I have been out of town for the last week. I hope you will think me sincere when I say that I am truly grateful for the interest you have taken in my welfare. A few more such friends as yourself and I shall have no reason to doubt of success.

What you say about "The Devil's Visit to St Dunstan" gives me great pleasure. I was thinking in what manner I should ask of you some such favor as you propose in sending me this "true history["] — but was afraid of making too many demands at once upon your good nature. Your offer, therefore, is most à propos. I shall look anxiously for the tale, and will assuredly be proud to give it a conspicuous place in the opening number of the Magazine.

With high respect, I am,
YrObS^t

Jno Tomlin Esqr Edgar A Poe

> John Tomlin, postmaster of Jackson, Tennessee, was an admirer of Poe. His first known letter is dated October 16, 1839 (original in the Boston Public Library), his last, February 23, 1844 (original in the Boston Public Library). When the *Penn* was postponed, Tomlin wrote

(April 30, 1841) asking Poe if "The Devil's Visit" might be published in *Graham's*. (The extant letters of Tomlin to Poe are in the Boston Public Library.) [CL 253]

102 ➤ TO PLINY EARLE

Philadelphia, October 10th 1840.

Dear Sir,

Your kind letter, dated the 2^d inst, was postmarked the 8th, and I have only this morning received it. I hasten to thank you for the interest you have taken in my contemplated Magazine, and for the beautiful lines "By an Octogenarian". They shall certainly appear in the first number. You must allow me to consider such offerings, however, as any thing but "unsubstantial encouragement." Believe me that good poetry is far rarer, and therefore far more acceptable to the publisher of a journal, than even that rara avis money itself.

Should you be able to aid my cause in Frankford by a good word with your neighbours, I hope that you will be inclined to do so. Much depends upon the list I may have before the first of December. I send you a Prospectus — believing that the objects set forth in it are, upon the whole, such as your candor will approve.

Very truly & respectfully
Yr Ob. St.

Dr Pliny Earle   Edgar A Poe

Pliny Earle, physician and psychiatrist, became superintendent of Friends' Hospital for the Insane, Frankford, Pennsylvania, in 1840. He published, during his lifetime, works on hospitals for the insane and some poetry (*Dictionary of American Biography*, v, 595–596). Poe's *Penn Magazine*, planned for publication in January 1841, never appeared. [CL 256]

103 ➤ TO RICHARD H. STODDARD

[Philadelphia, November 6, 1840]

. . . and now hasten to comply by transcribing a sonnet of my own composition. . . .

[Signature missing]

Though Stoddard in 1884 edited the works of Poe, he did not print the above Poe letter. The "sonnet" was "To Zante." [CL 257]

104 ➤ TO FREDERICK W. THOMAS

Philadelphia, Novem. 23. 1840.

My Dear Thomas,

I only received yours of the 6th about an hour ago, having been out of town for the last ten days. Believe me, I was very glad to hear from you — for in truth I had given you up. I did not get the "Bulletin" you sent, but saw the notice at the Exchange. The "Bulletin" has always been very kind to me, and I am at a loss to know who edits it — will you let me into this secret when you write again? Neither did "Howard Pinkney" come to hand. Upon receipt of your letter, just now, I called at Congress Hall — but no books. Mr Bateman had been there, and gone, forgetting to leave them. I shall get them upon his return. Meantime, and long ago, I have read the novel, with its predecessors. I like H. P. very well — better than E & W. & not nearly so well as C. B. You give yourself up to your own nature (which is a noble one, upon my soul) in Clinton Bradshaw; but in Howard Pinkney you abandon the broad rough road for the dainty by-paths of authorism. In the former you are interested in what you write & write to please, pleasantly; in the latter, having gained a name, you write to maintain it, and [the] effort becomes apparent. This consciousness of reputation leads you so freq[uently] into those literary and other disquisitions about which we quarrelld at Stude-vant's. If you would send the public opinion to the devil, forgetting that a public existed, and writing from the natural promptings of your own spirit you would do wonders. In a word, abandon is want-ing in "Howard Pinkney" — and when I say this you must know that I mean a high compliment — for they to whom this very abandon may be safely suggested are very few indeed, and belong to the loftier class of writers.

I would say more of "Howard Pinkney"; but nothing in the shape of criticism can be well said in petto, and I intend to speak fully of the novel in the first number of the Penn Magazine — which I am happy to say will appear in January. I may just observe now, however, that I pitied you when I saw the blunders, typographical, and Frost-igraphical — although, to do Frost justice, I do not think he looked at the proofs at all.

Thank you a thousand times for your good wishes & kind offers.

I shall wait anxiously for the promised article. I should like to have it, if possible, in the first sheet, which goes to press early in December. But I know that I may depend upon you, and therefore say no more upon this head. For the rest, your own experience and friendship will suggest the modes by which you may serve me in St Louis. Perhaps you may be able to have the accompanying Prospectus (which you will see differs from the first) inserted once or twice in some of the city papers — if you can accomplish this without trouble I shall be greatly obliged to you.

Have you heard that that illustrious graduate of St John's College, Cambridge, (Billy Barlow,) has sold his Magazine to Graham, of the "Casket"?

Mrs Clemm and Virginia unite with me in the kindest remembrances to yourself and sister — with whom your conversation (always turning upon the "one-loved name") has already made us all so well acquainted.

How long will it be before I see you again? Write immediately.

Yours most truly —

E A P

Poe seems to have met Thomas in the summer of 1840, when the latter was attending a Whig convention in Philadelphia; for Thomas' brief autobiographical sketch, see H, XVII, 95–100, where the date of the letter, incorrectly given as August 3, should read September 3, 1841 (see note to Letter 124). Poe's letters to Thomas ring true and reveal a warmth and sincerity often lacking in those to other correspondents; Thomas proved a real friend to Poe. The St. Louis *Bulletin* was edited by a man named Churchill (see Thomas to Poe, December 7, 1840, in H, XVII, 66). Thomas' *Clinton Bradshaw* (1835) was reviewed, not too favorably, by Poe in the SLM, December 1835 (H, VIII, 109–110); *East and West* (1836) and *Howard Pinckney* (1840) are referred to in Poe's "Autography," December 1841 (see H, XV, 209–210). Thomas sent Poe MS.-extracts from his long poem, "The Adventures of a Poet," for use in the *Penn* (see Thomas' autobiography, cited above, and his letter of December 7, 1840, in H, XVII, 65–66), as well as "terms" from an agent in St. Louis, who would handle the *Penn* (*ibid.*). Graham bought *Burton's Gentleman's Magazine* in November 1840, merged it with his *Casket*, and called the combination *Graham's Magazine* (see Mott, *History of American Magazines*, I, 545); he began the year with a total of some 3,500 subscribers from *Burton's* and some 1,500 from the *Casket* (see Quinn, *Poe*, p. 309). [CL 260]

105 ⪢ TO L. J. CIST

Philadelphia, Dec. 30. 1840.

My Dear Sir,

Your letter of the 7th found me labouring under a severe illness, which has confined me to bed for the last month, and from which I am now only slowly recovering.

The worst result of this illness is that I am forced to postpone the issue of the first number of the Mag. until the first of March next, when it will certainly appear, and I trust under the best auspices.

"Bachelor Philosophy", I am sorry to say, cannot appear until the second number, as at the time of its reception, all the poetry for the first number was already in type.

Would you be kind enough to mention the delay in the issue to your friend Mr Boyd, and if possible to procure me the insertion of this announcement in some one of your city papers.

"THE PENN MAGAZINE" Owing to the severe and continued illness of Mr Poe the issue of the first number of this journal is postponed until the first of March next.

I am very truly & respectfully
Yr. ob. St

L. J. Cist Esqr   Edgar A Poe

> Lewis J. Cist and Joseph B. Boyd, both of Cincinnati, were interested in Poe's proposed *Penn Magazine*. Concerning Cist, see Letter 125 and note; concerning Boyd, see Letter 100 and note. The *Penn Magazine* was never published. [CL 263]

106 ⪢ TO JOHN P. KENNEDY

Philadelphia, Dec. 31. 1840

My Dear Sir,

I am about to commence, in this city, a Monthly Magazine somewhat on the plan of the "Southern Messenger", and of which you may have seen a Prospectus in some of the Baltimore papers. The leading feature proposed is that of an absolutely independent criticism. Since you gave me my first start in the literary world, and since indeed I seriously say that without the timely kindness you once evinced towards me, I should not at this moment be among the living — you will not feel surprise that I look anxiously to you for encouragement in this new enterprise — the first of any importance which I have undertaken on my own account. What I most seriously need, in the commencement, is caste for the journal — I need the countenance of those who stand well in the social not less than in the literary world. I know that you have never yet written for Magazines — and this is a main reason for my now begging you to give me something for my own. I care not what the article be, nor of what length — what I wish is the weight of your name. Any unused scrap lying by you will fully answer my purpose.

The Magazine will be issued on the first of March, and, I believe, under the best auspices. May I ask your influence among your personal friends?

I shall look with great anxiety for your reply to this letter. In the meantime believe me, my dear Sir,

Yours ever gratefully & respectfully.

John P. Kennedy Esqr   **Edgar A Poe**

> Through the summer and fall of 1840 Poe had been working to launch his *Penn Magazine*, often writing letters on the printed prospectuses. He wrote Thomas, November 23, 1840, that the first number would be published January 1, 1841; now to Kennedy, he says March 1. It never was issued, though Poe throughout his life never gave up hope of establishing his dream magazine. No answer to this letter, in the form of contribution or letter from Kennedy, is known. [CL 264]

107 ➤ TO JOSEPH EVANS SNODGRASS

Philadelphia. Jan. 17. 1841.

My Dear Sir,

Your letters are always welcome — albeit "few and far between" (what an infamous tautology is that by the bye, for visits that are few *must* be far between) — and your last letter was especially so. I thought you had forgotten me altogether.

You wish to know my prospects with the "Penn". They are *glorious* — notwithstanding the world of difficulties under which I labored and labor. My illness (from which I have now entirely recovered) has been, for various reasons, a benefit to my scheme, rather than a disadvantage; and, upon the whole, if I do not eminently succeed in this enterprize the fault will be altogether mine own. Still, I am using every exertion to ensure success, and, among other maneuvres, I have cut down the bridges behind me. I must now do or die — I mean in a literary sense.

Thank you for your offer of aid. I shall be delighted to receive any *prose* article from your [p]en. As for poetry I am overs[tock]ed with it. I am particu[l]arly anxious for a paper on the International Copy-Right [l]aw, [or] on the subject of the Laws of Libel in regard to Literary Criticism; but I believe these topics are not "in your line". Your friend, David Hoffman Esqr, has been so kind as to promise me his aid; and perhaps he would not be unwilling to send me something on one or the other of the heads in question. *Will you oblige me by speaking to him upon this subject?* Above all things it is necessary that whatever be done "if done, be done quickly"; for I am about to put the first sheet to press immediately; and the others will follow in rapid succession.

In regard to my plans &c the Prospectus will inform you in some measure. I am resolved upon a good outward appearance — clear type, fine paper &c — double columns, I think, & brevier, with the poetry running across the page in a single column. No steel engravings; but now & then a superior wood-cut in illustration of the text. Thick covers. In the literary way, I shall endeavour, gradually, if I cannot effect the purpose at once to give the Magazine (*page 2*] a reputation for the having *no articles but from the best pens* — a somewhat negative merit, you will say. In criticism I will be bold & sternly, absolutely just, with friend & foe. From this purpose nothing shall turn me. I shall aim at *originality* in the body of the work, more than at any other especial quality. I have one or two articles of my own in statu pupillari that would make you stare, at least, on account of the utter oddity of their conception. To carry out the conception is a difficulty which — may be overcome.

I have not seen the January Messenger; — but "Quotidiana" is a very good title "Quodlibetica" is also good; and even more inclusive than the other. I am fond of such articles as these; and in good hands they may be made very interesting.

Burton that illustrious "graduate of St John's College, Cambridge" is going to the devil with the worst grace in the world, but with a velocity truly astounding. The press here, in a body, have given him the cut direct. So be it — suum cuique. We have said q[u]ite enough about this genius.

Mr Graham is a very g[en]tlemanly personage. I will see him tomorrow, and speak to him in regard to your essay: although, to prevent detection, Burton may have destroyed it.

And now, my dear Snodgrass, *will* you do me a favor? I have heard some mention made of a new Magazine to be established in Baltimore by a Virginian & a practical printer. I am *anxious* to know all the de[t]ails of the project. Can you procure & send me (by return of mail) a Prospectus? If you cannot get one, will you write me all about it — the gentleman's name &c &c &c ?

I have underscored the word "anxious" because I really mean what I say, and because, about a fortnight ago, I made to the Hon. N. C. Brooks A. M. a request just such as I now make to yourself. *He did not reply;* and I, expecting of course the treatment which one gentleman naturally expects from another, have been put to the greatest inconvenience by the daily but fruitless expectation.

Very truly & respectfully yours.

Dʳ J. E. Snodgrass.   Edgar A Poe.

The *Penn* did not appear as scheduled (see Letter 108 and note). David Hoffman was a partner in the Baltimore law firm of Hoffman and Dobbins (see P, I, 645), and an author (see H, XVII, 76). "Quotidiana" was an article by Snodgrass in the current SLM. George R. Graham established *Graham's Magazine* by merging his own *Casket* and *Burton's Gentleman's Magazine,* in November 1840 (Quinn, *Poe,* p. 309). Regarding the essay by Snodgrass, see Letter 109 and note. Failure to hear from Nathan C. Brooks may have been due to Poe's rupture with Burton, a friend of the former editor of the Baltimore *American Museum,* or to Brooks's new duties as principal of the Baltimore city schools. Poe had been a contributor to Brooks's *Museum* (see Letter 78; also note to Letter 90). [CL 267]

108 ➤ TO ROBERT T. CONRAD

Philadelphia January 22. 1841.

Dear Sir,

On the other leaf of this sheet you will find a Prospectus of a new monthly journal which I am about to establish in this city, somewhat on the plan of the Richmond "Southern Literary Messenger". In this latter I had no proprietary right; but "The Penn Magazine" will be my own. I have been led to make the attempt of establishing it through an earnest yet natural desire of rendering myself independent — I mean not so much as regards money, as in respect to my literary opinions and conduct. So far I have not only labored solely for the benefit of others (receiving for myself a miserable pittance) but have been forced to model my thoughts at the will of men whose imbecility was evident to all but themselves.

As a man of the world you will at once understand that what I most need for my work in its commencement (since I am comparatively a stranger in Philadelphia) is *caste*. I need the countenance of those who stand well not less in the social than in the literary world. I, certainly, have no claim whatever upon your attention, and have scarcely the honor of your personal acquaintance — but if I could obtain the influence of your name in an article (however brief) for my opening number, I feel that it would assist me beyond measure — and, without knowing definitely why, I have been induced to hope that you would not be altogether unwilling to aid me. I am the more anxious that you would do me this great favor, as there are two subjects which strike me as exceedingly proper for discussion, at this moment, in a magazine such as I propose — two subjects which could scarcely be so well treated by any one as by yourself. I mean the topics of the International Copy-Right Law, and The Laws of Libel in their relation to Literary Criticism. I am rash, however, in making any suggestions; and should be only too much delighted if you could afford me an article upon any question whatever.

The first number will be put to press on the first of February.

Looking anxiously for your reply,

I am, with high respect
Y^r Ob. S^t

Judge R. T. Conrad   Edgar A Poe

During his lifetime, Robert T. Conrad was a prominent Philadelphian and semi-professional man of letters; he wrote plays and contributed to the magazines of the day. Later he became a judge and a mayor of Philadelphia (see Mott, *History of American Magazines*, I, 551). In 1847–1848, he assisted George Graham in editing the *North American* and *Graham's*. Poe included him in his "Autography," *Graham's*, December 1841 (reprinted in H, xv, 232–233). During the second half of 1840, Poe frequently used a blank page of his printed prospectus for correspondence (see Letters 94, 95, 96, 97, 98, 100, 101, and 107). Regarding the articles desired of Conrad, see also Letter 107 in which he suggests that Snodgrass' friend, David Hoffman, of Baltimore, might contribute articles on the same topics. The *Penn* did not appear (see F. W. Thomas' letter to Poe, March 7, 1841 in H, XVII, 81: ". . . this past week. Dow . . . told me you had given up the idea of the Penn and was engaged with Graham"; see also the note to Letter 109). No reply from Conrad is known. [CL 268]

109 ➤ TO JOSEPH EVANS SNODGRASS

Philadelphia, April 1, 1841.

My Dear Snodgrass —

I fear you have been thinking it was not my design to answer your kind letter at all. It is now April Fool's Day, and yours is dated March 8th; but believe me, although, for good reason, I may occasionally postpone my reply to your favors, I am never in danger of forgetting them.

I am much obliged to you for permitting me to hand over your essay to Mr. Graham. It will appear in the June number. In order to understand this apparent delay, you must be informed that we go to press at a singularly early period. The *May* number is now within two days of being ready for delivery to the mails. I should be pleased to receive a brief notice of Soran's poems for the June number — if you think this will not be too late.

In regard to Burton. I feel indebted to you for the kind interest you express; but scarcely know how to reply. My situation is embarrassing. It is impossible, as you say, to notice a buffoon and a felon, as one gentleman would notice another. The law, then, is my only resource. Now, if the truth of a scandal could be admitted in justification — I mean of what the law terms a *scandal* — I would have matters all my own way. I would institute a suit, forthwith, for his personal defamation of myself. He would be unable to prove the truth of his allegations. I could prove their falsity and their malicious intent by witnesses who, seeing me at all hours of every day, would have the best right to speak — I mean Burton's own clerk, Morrell, and the compositors of the printing office. In fact, I could prove the scandal almost by acclamation. I should obtain damages. But, on the other hand, I have never been scrupulous in regard to what I have said of him. I have always told *him* to his face, and everybody else, that I looked upon him as a blackguard and a villain. This is notorious. He would meet me with a cross action. The truth of the allegation — which I could easily prove as he would find it difficult to prove the truth of his own respecting me — would not avail me. The law will not admit, as justification of my calling Billy Burton a scoundrel, that Billy Burton is really such. What then can I do? If I sue, he sues; you see how it is.

At the same time — as I may, after further reflection, be induced to sue, I would take it as an act of kindness — not to say *justice* — on your part, if you would see the gentleman of whom you spoke, and ascertain with accuracy all that may legally avail me; that is to say, what and when were the words used, and whether your friend would be willing for your sake, for my sake, and for the sake of truth, to give evidence if called upon. Will you do this for me?

So far for the matter inasmuch as it concerns Burton. I have now to thank you for your defence of myself, as stated. You are a physician, and I presume no physician can have difficulty in detecting the *drunkard* at a glance. You are, moreover, a literary man, well read in morals. You will never be brought to believe that I could write what I daily write, *as* I write it, were I as this villain would induce those who know me not, to believe. In fine, I pledge you, before God, the solemn word of a gentleman, that I am temperate even to rigor. From the hour in which I first saw this basest of calumniators to the hour in which I retired from his office in uncontrollable disgust at his chicanery, arrogance, ignorance and brutality, *nothing stronger than water ever passed my lips.*

It is, however, due to candor that I inform you upon what foundation he has erected his slanders. At no period of my life was I ever what men call intemperate. I never was in the *habit* of intoxication. I never drunk drams, &c. But, for a brief period, while I resided in Richmond, and edited the *Messenger*, I certainly did give way, at long intervals, to the temptation held out on all sides by the spirit of Southern conviviality. My sensitive temperament could not stand an excitement which was an everyday matter to my companions. In short, it sometimes happened that I was completely intoxicated. For some days after each excess I was invariably confined to bed. But it is now quite four years since I have abandoned every kind of alcoholic drink — four years, with the exception of a single deviation, which occurred shortly *after* my leaving Burton, and when I was induced to resort to the occasional use of *cider*, with the hope of relieving a nervous attack.

You will thus see, frankly stated, the whole amount of my sin. You will also see the blackness of that heart which could *revive* a slander of this nature. Neither can you fail to perceive how desperate the malignity of the slanderer must be — how resolute he must be to slander, and how slight the grounds upon which he would build up a defamation — since he can find nothing better with which to charge me than an accusation which can be disproved by each and every man with whom I am in the habit of daily intercourse.

I have now only to repeat to you, in general, my solemn assurance that my habits are as far removed from intemperance as the day from the night. My sole drink is water.

Will you do me the kindness to repeat this assurance to such of your friends as happen to speak of me in your hearing?

I feel that nothing more is requisite, and you will agree with me upon reflection.

Hoping soon to hear from you, I am,

Yours most cordially,

Dr. J. E. Snodgrass.   Edgar A. Poe.

P.S. — You will receive the magazine, as a matter of course. I had supposed that you were already on our free list.

P.P.S. — The *Penn*, I hope, is only "scotched, not killed." It would have appeared under glorious auspices, and with capital at command, in March, as advertised, but for the unexpected bank suspensions. In the meantime, Mr. Graham has made me a liberal offer, which I had great pleasure in accepting. The *Penn* project will unquestionably be resumed hereafter.

> Though the *Baltimore American* is the only known source for this letter, all subsequent printings have varied in some degree, either in changes in pointing or in omissions of text. Several papers, including the *New York World* and the *New York Herald*, copied the letter on the same day under a Baltimore release. According to editorial comment in the *American*, the italics are Poe's own. "Poetry: the uncertainty of its appreciation," by Snodgrass, previously submitted to *Burton's* for a premium, was printed in *Graham's*, XVIII (June 1841), 288–289. Unlike *Burton's*, *Graham's* appeared almost a month in advance of date. Within the limits given, Poe's defense of himself against accusations of drunkenness is probably based on truth. When the *Penn* was postponed, Poe joined *Graham's*. George Rex Graham bought Atkinson's

Casket in May, 1839, and merged it with Burton's *Gentleman's* in December 1840, at which time he was also part owner of the *Saturday Evening Post*. After contributing "The Man of the Crowd" to the December number of *Graham's*, Poe joined the editorial staff in February in time for the April issue (see Mott, *History of American Magazines*, I, 544–546). An editorial in the *Saturday Evening Post*, February 20, 1841, speaks of Poe's becoming one of the editors of *Graham's*, and in the April issue of the magazine the proprietor himself speaks of having made certain arrangements with Poe, "commencing with the present number" (see Quinn, *Poe*, p. 310). According to Mott (*History of American Magazines*, p. 549), Poe's salary was $800, which did not include payments made for contributions, such as tales, to "the literary contents." Mott also points out (p. 512) that Graham paid R. W. Griswold $1000 as editor in 1842, and he offered Bayard Taylor the editorship in 1848 at the same salary. "The *Penn* project" was resumed in the early summer of 1841, Poe believing Graham would finance its publication (see Poe's letters to Kennedy, Irving, Halleck, and others, in June). [CL 275]

110 ➤ TO HENRY WADSWORTH LONGFELLOW

Dear Sir,

Mʳ Geo: R. Graham, proprietor of "Graham's Magazine", a monthly journal published in this city, and edited by myself, desires me to beg of you the honor of your contribution to its pages. Upon the principle that we seldom obtain what we *very* anxiously covet, I confess that I have but little hope of inducing you to write for us; — and, to say truth, I fear that Mʳ Graham would have opened the negotiation much better in his own person — for I have no reason to think myself favorably known to you — but the attempt was to be made, and I make it.

I should be overjoyed if we could get from you an article each month — either poetry or prose — length and subject à discretion. In respect to terms we would gladly offer you carte blanche — and the periods of payment should also be made to suit yourself.

Should you be willing to write for the Magazine, it would be an important object with us to have something, as soon as convenient, for the July number, which commences a new volume, and with part of which we are already going to press. With this letter I forward to your address, by mail, the April and May numbers of the journal — that you may form some judgment of the character of the work. It is our design, however, greatly to improve its mechanical appearance;

and, in the new volume, we shall have [*page 2*] an array of contributors not altogether unworthy an association with yourself.

In conclusion — I cannot refrain from availing myself of this, the only opportunity I may ever have, to assure the author of the "Hymn to the Night", of the "Beleaguered City" and of the "Skeleton in Armor", of the fervent admiration with which his genius has inspired me: — and yet I would scarcely hazard a declaration whose import might be so easily misconstrued, and which bears with it, at best, more or less, of niäiserie, were I not convinced that Professor Longfellow, writing and thinking as he does, will be at no loss to feel and to appreciate the honest *sincerity* of what I say.

> With highest respect.
> Y^r Ob. S^t

Prof. H. W. Longfellow   Edgar A. Poe.

Philadelphia,
May 3^d / 41

> This is the first of the two letters Poe wrote to Longfellow, the other being that of June 22, 1841 (see Longfellow to Griswold, September 28, 1850, in H, xvii, 406–407, where Longfellow says, ". . . two letters . . . and these are the only ones I ever received from him"). For Poe's favorable opinion of "Hymn to the Night" and "The Beleaguered City," see his review of *Voices of the Night* in *Burton's*, February 1840 (reprinted in H, x, 71–80). Longfellow's reply to the present letter declined the offer but added that Poe's name was known to him and that he thought highly of Poe's power, especially as a "romance-writer."
> [CL 281]

111 ⊁ TO RUFUS W. GRISWOLD

> [Philadelphia]
> [*ante* May 8, Spring, 1841]

Dr Griswold,

Will you be kind enough to lend me the No. of the Family Magazine of which we spoke — if you have received it?

I w^d be much obliged, also, if you c^d let me take a peep at Stephens' "Yucatan", if you have it, or, if not, at any new book of interest.

> Truly yours
> Poe

Rufus Wilmot Griswold (1815–1857), a native of Vermont, was a licensed Baptist clergyman and had done editorial work in New England and in New York before coming to Philadelphia where in the spring of 1841 he and Poe became acquainted. He became well known as an editor of anthologies, his *Poets and Poetry of America, Prose Writers of America,* and *Female Poets of America* going into numerous editions. Upon Poe's resignation from *Graham's* in April 1842, Griswold succeeded to the editorship. Following Poe's death in Baltimore, October 7, 1849, Griswold wrote for the October 9 issue of the *New York Tribune* his famous "Ludwig" article that did so much to damage Poe's reputation. Then, in 1850, he edited the *Works of the Late Edgar Allan Poe.* Volume 1 included a notice "To the Reader," authorized by Maria Clemm (see Griswold's power of attorney from Mrs. Clemm, Quinn, *Poe,* p. 754), but certainly worded by Griswold: "The late Edgar Allan Poe wrote (just before he left his home in Fordham, for the last time, on the 29th of June, 1849) requests that the Rev. Rufus W. Griswold should act as his literary Executor, and superintend the publication of his works . . ." (see the notes to Letter 321). The *Family Magazine,* a weekly founded in New York by Origen Bacheler in 1833, became a monthly in June 1834, and remained so until suspended in May 1841, serving its readers with "useful and entertaining knowledge" (Mott, *History of American Magazines,* I, 363–364). John L. Stephens wrote several books beginning with the title "Incidents of Travel . . ."; Poe reviewed his *Incidents of Travel in Egypt, Arabia, and the Holy Land* (1837) in the New York *Review,* October 1837, and his *Incidents of Travel in Central America, Chiapas, and Yucatan* (1841) in *Graham's,* August 1841; though Stephens also published *Incidents of Travel in Yucatan* (see *Dictionary of American Biography,* XIX, 579–580), in 1843, the evidence so far adduced points to the 1841 title, Poe merely clipping it in his note to Griswold. [CL 282]

112 ⊁ TO RUFUS W. GRISWOLD

[Philadelphia, May 29, 1841]

R. W. Griswold Esqr,

My Dear Sir,

On the other leaf I send such poems as I think my best, from which you can select any which please your fancy. I should be proud to see one or two of them in your book. The one called "Haunted Palace" is that of which I spoke in reference to Prof. Longfellow's plagiarism. I first published the H. P. in Brooks' "Museum", a monthly journal of Baltimore, now dead. Afterwards, I embodied it in a tale called "The House of Usher" in Burton's Magazine. Here it was, I suppose, that Prof. Longfellow saw it; for, about 6 weeks afterwards, there appeared in the South. Lit. Mess: a poem by him called "The Beleaguered City", which may now be found in his volume. The identity in title is striking; for by the Haunted Palace I mean to imply a mind haunted by phantoms — a disordered brain — and by the Beleaguered City Prof. L. means just the same. But the whole tournure of the poem is based upon mine, as you will see at once. Its allegorical conduct, the style of its versification & expression — all are mine.

As I understood you to say that you meant to preface each set of poems by some biographical notice, I have ventured to send you the above memo — the particulars of which (in a case where an author is so little known as myself) might not be easily obtained elsewhere.

"The Coliseum" was the prize poem alluded to above.

> With high respect and esteem,
> I am yr ob. s^t
>
> Edgar A Poe

The extra "leaf" containing Poe's poems is lost. "The Haunted Palace" was first published in Nathan C. Brooks' *American Museum of Science, Literature and the Arts*, April 1839, and later embodied in "The Fall of the House of Usher" in *Burton's*, vol. v (September 1839). Longfellow's "Beleaguered City" appeared in the SLM, v (November 1839). Regarding the plagiarism charged by Poe but really unfounded, see Longfellow's letter to Griswold, September 28, 1850 (H, XVII, 406–407). The "memo," which is full of inaccuracies, is reprinted in H, I, 344–346. Griswold's *Poets and Poetry of America* (April 18, 1842) printed only three of Poe's poems: "The Haunted Palace," "The Coliseum," and "The Sleeper," all published earlier. "The Coliseum" had been submitted by Poe for the prize offered by the Baltimore *Saturday Visiter* in 1833 at the same time he entered his *Tales of the Folio Club*. His tale, "MS. Found in a Bottle," won the first prize for prose, and apparently the poem would have won first prize in its class except that the judges decided not to award both prizes to the same contestant (see Campbell, *Poems*, pp. 218–219). The "above" refers of course to the "memo," not to the present letter. [CL 289]

113 ⇥ TO WASHINGTON IRVING

> Philadelphia — June 21. 1841.

Dear Sir,

Mr George R. Graham of this city, and myself, design to establish a Monthly Magazine, upon certain conditions, one of which is the procuring your assistance in the enterprise. Will you pardon me for saying a few words upon the subject?

I need not call you attention to the signs of the times in respect to Magazine literature. You will admit the tendency of the age in this direction. The brief, the terse, the condensed, and the easily circulated will take place of the diffuse, the ponderous, and the inaccessible. Even our Reviews are found too massive for the taste of the day — I do not mean for the taste of the merely uneducated, but also for that of the few. In the meantime the finest minds of Europe are beginning to lend their spirit to Magazines. In this country, unhappily, we have not any journal of the class, which either can afford to offer pecuniary inducement to the highest talent, or which would be, in all respects, a fitting vehicle for its thoughts. In the supply of this deficiency there would be a point gained; and the project of which I speak has originated in the hope of supplying it.

Mr Graham is a lawyer, but for some years past has been occupied in publishing. His experience of the business of a periodical is great. He is a gentleman of high social standing, and possessed of ample pecuniary means. You will perhaps remember myself as the original editor of the South: Lit. Messenger, of Richmond, Vᵃ, and I have otherwise had much to do with the editorial conduct of Magazines. Together, we would enter the field with a full understanding of the difficulties to be encountered, and, we hope, with full ability to meet them.

The work will be an octavo of 96 pages. The paper will be of excellent quality — very far superior to that of the N. A. Review. The type will be new (always new) clear and bold, with distinct face. The matter will be disposed in a single column. The printing will be done upon a hand press, in the best manner. There will be a broad margin. We shall have no engravings, except occasional wood-cuts (by Adams) when demanded in obvious illustration of the text; and, when so required, they will be worked in with the type — not upon separate pages, as in "Arcturus." The stitching will be done in the French style, permitting the book to be fully open. Upon the cover, and throughout, the endeavour will be to preserve the greatest [*page 2*] purity of taste, consistent with decision and force. The price will be $5.

The chief feature in the literary department will be that of contributions from the most distinguished pens (of America) *exclu-*

sively; or, if this plan cannot be wholly carried out, we propose, at least, to procure the aid of some five or six of the most distinguished, and to admit *few* articles from other sources — none which are not of a very high order of merit. We shall endeavour to engage the permanent services of yourself, Mr Cooper, Mr Paulding, Mr Kennedy, Mr Longfellow, Mr Bryant, Mr Halleck, Mr Willis, and, perhaps, one or two others. In fact, as before said, our ability to make these arrangements is a condition without which the Magazine will not go into operation; and my immediate object in addressing you now, is to ascertain how far we may look to yourself for aid.

It would be desirable that you agree to furnish one paper each month — either absolute or serial — and of such length as you might deem proper. We leave terms entirely to your own decision. The sums specified would be paid as you might suggest. It would be necessary that an agreement should be made for one year, during which period you should be pledged not to write for any other American Magazine. The journal will be commenced on the first of January 1842, and (should we be so fortunate as to obtain your consent to our proposal) it would be best that we should have in hand, by the first of December 1841, at least two of the papers intended for publication, from each contributor.

With this letter I despatch one of similar tenor to each of the gentlemen above named. If you cannot consent to an unconditional reply, will you be kind enough to say whether you will write for us upon condition that we succeed in our engagements with the others — specifying what others?

> With high respect
> Yr ob S^t

Washington Irving Esqr   Edgar A Poe

This letter should be compared to Letters 113, 115, and 116. [CL 293]

114 ➤ TO JOHN P. KENNEDY

Philadelphia — June [21] 1841

My Dear Sir,

Mr George R. Graham, of this city, and myself, design to establish a Monthly Magazine upon certain conditions — one of which is the procuring your assistance in the enterprise. Will you permit me to say a few words on the subject?

I need not call your attention to the signs of the times in respect to Magazine literature. You will admit the tendency of the age in this direction. The brief, the terse, and the readily-circulated *will* take place of the diffuse, the ponderous, and the inaccessible. Even our Reviews (lucus a non lucendo) are found too massive for the taste of the day — I do not mean merely for the taste of the tasteless, the uneducated, but for that also, of the few. The finest minds of Europe are beginning to deal with Magazines. In this country, unhappily, we have no journal of the class, which can either afford to compensate the highest talent, or which is, in all respects, a fitting vehicle for its thoughts. In the supply of this deficiency there would be a point gained, and the project of which I speak has originated in the hope of supplying it.

Mr Graham is a lawyer, but, for some years past, has been occupied in publishing. His experience of the periodical business is extensive. He is a gentleman of high social standing, and possessed of ample pecuniary means. Together, we would enter the field with a full knowledge of the difficulties to be encountered, and with perfect assurance of being able to overcome them.

The work will be an octavo of 96 pages. The paper will be excellent — far superior to that of the N. A. Review. The type will be new (always new) clear and bold, with distinct face. The matter will be disposed in single column. The printing will be done upon a hand-press, in the best manner. There will be a broad margin. We shall have no engravings except occasional wood-cuts (by Adams) when demanded in obvious illustration of the text; and, when so required, [*page 2*] they will be worked in with the type. The stitching will be done in the French style, permitting the book to lie fully open. Upon the cover, and throughout, the endeavour will be to preserve the greatest purity of taste, consistent with force and decision. The price will be $5.

I believe I sent you, some time ago, a Prospectus of the "Penn Magazine", the scheme of which was broken up by the breaking up of the banks. The name will be preserved — and the general intentions, of that journal. A rigorous independence shall be my watchword still — *truth*, not so much for truth's sake, as for the sake of the novelty of the thing. But the chief feature will be that of contributions from the most distinguished pens (of America) *exclusively;* or if this plan cannot be wholly carried out, we propose at least to procure the aid of some five or six of the most distinguished — admitting few articles from other sources — none which are not of a high order of merit. We shall endeavour to engage the permanent services of yourself, Mr Irving, Mr Cooper, Mr Paulding, Mr Longfellow, Mr Bryant, Mr Halleck, Mr Willis, and, perhaps, one or two more. In fact, as before said; our success in making these engagements, is a condition, without which the Magazine will not go into operation; and my immediate object in addressing you now, is to ascertain how far we may look to yourself for aid.

It would be desirable that you agree to furnish one paper each month — either absolute or serial — of such length as you might think proper. The terms are left entirely to your own decision. Whatever sum you may specify will be paid as you suggest. An agreement should be made for one year, during which period you should be pledged not to write for any other (American) Magazine. The journal will be commenced on the first of January 1842, and (should [*page 3*] we be so fortunate as to obtain your consent to our proposal) it would be necessary that we should have in hand, by the first of December next, at least two articles from each contributor.

I look most anxiously for your answer; for it is of vital importance to me, personally. This you will see at once. Mr Graham is to furnish all supplies, and will give me, merely for editorial service, and my list of subscribers to the old "Penn", a half interest in the proposed Magazine — but he will only engage in the enterprize on the conditions before stated — on condition that I can obtain as contributors the gentlemen above named — or at least the most of them — giving them carte blanche as to terms. Your name will enable me, I know, to get several of the others. You will not fail me at this crisis! If I get this Magazine fairly afloat, with the money to back me as now, I will have every thing my own way.

With this letter I despatch one of similar tenor to each of the gentlemen named. If you cannot reply unconditionally — will you be so kind as to say whether you will write for us if we succeed with others — specifying what others?

Most truly Yours,

John P. Kennedy, Esqr   Edgar A Poe.

N.B. If you have a novel on the tapis, you could not dispose of it in any way so advantageously as by selling it to us. You would get more for it than L & B. would give. It would be printed in finer style than they could afford to print it — and it would have a far wider circulation in our Magazine than in book form. We will *commence* with an edition of 3000.

> In his letter to Cooke, September 21, 1839, Poe said, "As soon as Fate allows I will have a Magazine of my own"; but his dream of the ideal journal was never fulfilled, though on at least three occasions he seemed to be in sight of his goal (see the present letter; Letter 153 and note; and Letter 211 and note. One should also recall his prospectus of the *Penn*, printed in the Philadelphia *Saturday Courier*, June 13, 1840, reprinted in Quinn, *Poe*, pp. 306–308). With the present letter, compare Poe's hopes and plans for the *Stylus*, as the *Penn* came to be called, in Letter 185 and Letter 186. Whatever promises Graham may have made, he never actively participated with Poe in the establishment of a magazine. [CL 294]

115 ➤ TO HENRY WADSWORTH LONGFELLOW

Philadelphia — June 22 1841.

Dear Sir,

Your letter of the 19th May was received. I regret to find my anticipations confirmed, and that you cannot make it convenient to accept M[r] Graham's proposition. Will you now pardon me for making another?

I need not call your attention to the signs of the times in respect to Magazine literature. You will admit that the tendency of the age lies in this way — so far at least as regards the lighter letters. The brief, the terse, the condensed, and the easily circulated will take place of the diffuse, the ponderous, and the inaccessible. Even our Reviews (lucus a non lucendo) are found too massive for the taste of the day: — I do not mean for the taste of the tasteless, but for that of the few. In the meantime the finest minds of Europe are beginning to lend their spirit to Magazines. In this country, unhappily, we have not any journal of the class, which either can afford to offer pecuniary inducement to the highest talent, or which would be, in all respects, a fitting vehicle for its thoughts. In the supply of this deficiency there would be a point gained; and in the hope of at least partially supplying it, Mr Graham and myself propose to establish a Monthly Magazine.

The amplest funds will be embarked in the undertaking. The work will be an octavo of 96 pages. The paper will be of excellent quality — possibly finer than that upon which your "Hyperion" was printed. The type will be new (always new) clear and bold, with distinct face. The matter will be disposed in a single column. The printing will be done upon a hand-press in the best manner. There will be a broad margin. There will be no engravings, except occasional wood-cuts (by Adams) when demanded in obvious illustration of the text; and, when so required, they will be worked in with the type — not upon separate pages as in "Arcturus." The stitching will be done in the French style, permitting the book to lie fully open. Upon the cover, and throughout, the endeavour will be to preserve the greatest purity of taste consistent with decision and force. The price will be $5.

The chief feature in the literary department will be that of contributions from the most distinguished pens (of America) exclusively; or, if this plan cannot be wholly carried out, we [*page 2*] propose, at least, to make arrangements (if possible) with yourself, Mr Irving, Mr Cooper, Mr Paulding, Mr Bryant, Mr Halleck, Mr Paulding, Mr Willis, and one or two others. In fact, our ability to make these arrangements is a condition, without which the Magazine will not go into operation; and my object in writing you this letter is to ascertain how far I may look to yourself for aid.

In your former note you spoke of present engagements. The proposed journal will not be commenced until the 1st January 1842.

It would be desirable that you should agree to furnish one paper each month — prose or poetry — absolute or serial — and of such length as you might deem proper. Should illustrations be desired by you, these will be engraved at our expense, from designs at your own, superintended by yourself. We leave the matter of terms, as before, to your own decision. The sums agreed upon would be paid as you might suggest. It would be necessary that an agreement should be made for one year — during which period you should be pledged not to write for any other (American) Magazine.

With this letter I despatch one of the same tenor to each of the gentlemen before-named. If you cannot consent to an unconditional reply, will you be kind enough to say whether you will write for us

upon condition that we succeed in our engagements with the others —
specifying what others.

With high respect.
Y^r Ob S^t

Prof. H. W. Longfellow.   Edgar A Poe.

> Compare this letter with Letters 113 and 114, and see the notes to these
> letters. In Poe's list of those with whom arrangements were planned
> (see page 2), Kennedy's name probably should have replaced the repe-
> tition of Paulding's. [CL 295]

116 ➤ TO FITZ-GREENE HALLECK

Philadelphia — June 24 — 1841.

Dear Sir,

Mr George R. Graham, of this City, and myself, design to establish
a Monthly Magazine, upon certain conditions — one of which is the
procuring your assistance in the enterprise. Will you pardon me for
saying a few words upon the subject?

I need not call your attention to the signs of the times in respect to
Magazine literature. You will admit the tendency of the age in this
direction. The brief, the terse, and the easily circulated will take place
of the diffuse, the ponderous, and the inaccessible. Even our Reviews
are found too massive for the taste of the day — I do not mean for the
taste of the merely uneducated, but also for that of the few. In the
meantime the finest minds of Europe are beginning to lend their spirit
to Magazines. In this country, unhappily, we have no journal of the
class, which can either afford to compensate the highest talent, or
which is, in all respects, a fitting vehicle for its thoughts. In the supply
of this deficiency there would be a point gained; and the project of
which I speak has originated in the hope of supplying it.

Mr Graham is a lawyer, but for some time past, has been occupied in
publishing. His experience of the periodical business is great. He is a
gentleman of high social standing, and possessed of ample pecuniary
means. Together, we would enter the field with a full understanding
of the difficulties to be encountered, and, I trust, with ability to
meet them.

The work will be an octavo of 96 pages. The paper will be excellent — superior to that of the N. A. Review. The type will be new (always new) clear and bold, with distinct face. The matter will be disposed in single column. The printing will be done upon a hand-press in the best manner. There will be a broad margin. We shall have no engravings, except occasional wood-cuts (by the best artists) when demanded in obvious illustration of the text; and, when so required, they will be worked in with the type — not upon separate pages as in "Arcturus." The stitching will be done in the French style, permitting the book to be fully open. Upon the cover, and throughout, the endeavour will be to preserve [*page 2*] the greatest purity of taste, consistent with decision and force. The price will be 5$.

The chief feature of the literary department will be that of contributions from the most distinguished pens (of America) *exclusively*. Or, if this plan cannot be wholly carried out, we propose, at least, to procure the constant aid of some five or six of the most distinguished, and to admit few articles from other sources — none which are not of a high order of excellence. We shall endeavour to procure the services of yourself, Mr Bryant, Mr Longfellow, Mr Irving, Mr Cooper, Mr Paulding, Mr Kennedy, Mr Willis, and perhaps one or two others. In fact, as before said, our success in making these engagements is a condition, without which the Magazine will not go into operation; and my immediate object in addressing you now is to ascertain how far I may depend upon yourself for assistance.

It would be desirable that you agree to furnish one paper each month — either a complete poem, or a portion of one — and of such length as you deem proper. The terms will be left entirely to your own decision. The sums specified will be paid as you may suggest — in advance if necessary. It would be advisable that an agreement be made for one year, during which you should be pledged to write for no other (American) Magazine. The journal will be commenced on the first of January 1842, and (should we be so fortunate as to obtain your consent to our proposal) it would be proper that we should have in hand by the first of December next, at least two papers from each contributor.

With this letter I despatch one of similar tenor to each of the gentlemen above named. If you cannot make it convenient to give an unconditional reply, will you be kind enough to say whether you

will write for us upon condition that we are able to engage others —
specifying *what* others?

With high respect — yr ob. st.

Fitz-Greene Halleck Esqr   Edgar A Poe

> Compare this letter with Letters 113 and 114, and see the notes to these
> letters. [CL 296]

117 ❯ TO FREDERICK W. THOMAS

My Dear Thomas,

With this I mail you the July No: of the Mag: If you can get us
a notice in the Intelligencer, as you said, I will take it as a particular
favor — but if it is inconvenient, do not put yourself to any trouble
about it.

I have just heard through Graham, who obtained his information
from Ingraham, that you have stepped into an office at Washington —
salary $1000. From the bottom of my heart I wish you joy. You can
now lucubrate more at your ease & will infallibly do something worthy
yourself.

For my own part, notwithstanding Graham's unceasing civility, and
real kindness, I feel more & more disgusted with my situation. Would
to God, I could do as you have done. Do you seriously think that an
application on my part to Tyler would have a good result? My claims,
to be sure, are few. I am a Virginian — at least I call myself one, for
I have resided all my life, until within the last few years, in Richmond.
My political principles have always been as nearly as may be, with the
existing administration, and I battled with right good will for Harrison, when opportunity offered. With Mr Tyler I have some slight
personal acquaintance — although this is a matter which he has possibly forgotten. For the rest, I am a literary man — and I see a disposition in government to cherish letters. Have I any chance? I would
be greatly indebted to you if you [*page 2*] reply to this as soon as you
can, and tell me if it would, in your opinion, be worth my while to
make an effort — and if so — put me upon the right track. This
could not be better done than by detailing to me your own mode of
proceeding.

It appears that Ingraham is in high dudgeon with me because I spoke ill of his "Quadroone." I am really sorry to hear it — but it is a matter that cannot be helped. As a man I like him much, and wherever I could do so, without dishonor to my own sense of truth, I have praised his writings. His "South-West," for example, I lauded highly. His "Quadroone" is, in my honest opinion, trash. If I must call it a good book to preserve the friendship of Prof. Ingraham — Prof. Ingraham may go to the devil.

I am *really* serious about the office. If you can aid me in any way, I am sure you will. Remember me kindly to Dow & believe me

Yours most truly,

F. W. Thomas.   Edgar A Poe

Phil: June 26. 41

It is not impossible that you could effect my object by merely showing this letter yourself personally to the President and speaking of me as the original editor of the Messenger[.]

> The July number of *Graham's* (XIX, 38) carried Thomas' poem, "The Meeting of the Lovers." Poe treated Joseph H. Ingraham in "Autography," *Graham's*, November 1841 (reprinted in H, XV, 188). Strictly speaking, Poe's residence in Richmond may be said to have ended in March 1827, though he may have considered himself a resident until John Allan's death in March 1834. Thomas' letter to Poe, July 1 (MS. in the Boston Public Library), advised Poe to get in touch with J. P. Kennedy, who might aid him in getting a government clerkship. Poe reviewed Ingraham's *Southwest* in the SLM, II (January 1836), 122–123. For Jesse E. Dow, who at one time edited the *Index* (Alexandria, Virginia) and the *Daily Madisonian* (Washington), see Poe's "Autography," *Graham's*, December 1841 (reprinted in H, XV, 228; see also, Note 197 for Thomas' remarks on Poe's letter). In *Graham's* for June 1841 (XVIII, 296), is an unsigned review of *The Quadroone*, obviously by Poe. [CL 298]

118 ⤴ TO FREDERICK W. THOMAS

Phil. July 4 — 41

My Dear Thomas,

I rec^d yours of the 1^rst this morning, and have again to thank you for the interest you take in my welfare. I wish to God I could visit

Washington — but the old story, you know — I have no money —
not even enough to take me there, saying nothing of getting back. It
is a hard thing to be poor — but as I am kept so by an honest motive
I dare not complain.

Your suggestion about Mr Kennedy is well-timed; and here, Thomas
you can do me a true service. Call upon Kennedy — you know him,
I believe — if not, introduce yourself — he is a perfect gentleman and
will give you cordial welcome. Speak to him of my wishes, and urge
him to see the Secretary of War in my behalf — or one of the other
Secretaries — or President Tyler. I mention in particular the Secretary of War, because I have been to W. Point, and this may stand me
in some stead. I would be glad to get almost any appointment — even
a $500 one — so that I have something independent of letters for a
subsistence. To coin one's brain into silver, at the nod of a master, is
to my thinking, the hardest task in the world. Mr Kennedy has been
at all times a true friend to me — he was the first true friend I ever
had — I am indebted to him *for life itself.* He will be willing to help
me now — but *needs urging,* for he is always head and ears in business. Thomas, may I depend upon you? By the way, I wrote to Mr K.
about ten days ago on the subject of a Magazine — a project of mine
in conjunction with Graham — and have not yet heard from him.
Ten to one I misdirected the letter, or sent it to Baltimore — for I am
very thoughtless about such matters.

So you will set me down "a magician" if I decipher your friend's
cryptograph. No sooner suggested than done. Tell him to read this —

"In one of those peripatetic circumrotations I obviated a rustic
whom we subjected to catachetical interrogation respecting the char-
acteristics of the edifice to which he was approximate. With a volu-
bility uncongealed by the frigorific powers of villatin bashfulness he
ejaculated [*page 2*] a voluminous replication from the universal tenor
of whose contents I deduct the subsequent amalgamation of hetero-
geneous facts without dubiety" — &c &c.

The key-phrase is — "But find out this and I give it up". Besides
using this, however, he has interspersed his cypher with such abbre-
viations as £ for *in,* Δ for *of,* ·) for *an,* (for *by,* 9 for *tion,* 7 for *on,*
‡ for *as,* [for *it,* 4 for *to,* 6 for *or,*] for *if,* σ for *he,* † for *is,* $ for *at*
&c &c. This, you will admit, is altogether beyond the limits of my
challenge which extended only to cyphers *such as that of Berryer.*
You will also admit that phrases constructed for purposes of decep-

tion (as your friend's) are *infinitely* more difficult of perusal than a cipher intended for actual conveyance of one's natural ideas. The truth is, that Dr Fraley's cryptograph is inadmissible as such, because it cannot be readily deciphered by the person to whom it is addressed, and who possesses the key. In proof of this, I will publish it in the Mag: with a reward to any one who shall read it *with the key,* and I am pretty sure that no one will be found to do it.

I have not meddled with the first cryptograph — for I thought the D^rs scepticism would be sufficiently set at rest by my solution of the longer one — and to say truth I am exceedingly busy just now. Let him insist however, and read is the word. Nothing intelligible can be written which, with time, I cannot decipher. No more difficult cypher *can* be constructed than the one he has sent. It embodies all the *essentials* of abstruseness. & is very clever.

As I mean to publish it this month, will you be kind enough to get from his own hand an acknowledgment of my solution, adding your own acknowledgment, in such form that I may append both to the cipher by way of note. I wish to do this because I am seriously accused of humbug in this matter — a thing I despise. People *will not* believe I really decipher the puzzles. Write by return of mail.

Yours truly.

E A Poe

[*page 3*] State that I deciphered it by return of mail — as I do.

Thomas' letter of July 1 suggested that Poe enlist the aid of J. P. Kennedy in getting a government clerkship. For Kennedy's friendship, see Letter 50. Poe wrote Kennedy June 21, 1841, and addressed it to Baltimore, where it was readdressed to Washington. Poe published Thomas' letter of July 6 and Frailey's acknowledgment of Poe's solution, the cipher, and a challenge to any reader to solve it, the reward being a year's subscription to *Graham's* and the *Saturday Evening Post,* in *Graham's,* XIX (August 1841), 96 (reprinted in H, XIV, 133–137). In *Graham's,* October 1841, Poe printed the solution of the cipher, after saying that it had "not yet been read by any of our innumerable readers."

Poe's career as a solver of cryptograms began with his issuance of a challenge to all readers, in the December 18, 1839, number of *Alexander's Weekly Messenger,* a Philadelphia newspaper. He said, in part, ". . . we pledge ourselves to read it [a cipher] forthwith — however unusual or arbitrary may be the characters employed." Between December 18, 1839, and May 6, 1840, thirty-six ciphers were announced as received, most of which he solved (for a full discussion, see Clarence S. Brigham, "Edgar Allan Poe's Contributions to Alexander's Weekly Messenger," in *Proceedings of the American Antiquarian Society*, vol. 52, pt. 1 (April, 1942), pp. 45–125, and especially a letter from W. K. Wimsatt quoted in the article, pp. 48–50). Poe continued his articles and challenges on secret writing in *Graham's*, July, August, October, and December 1841 (reprinted in H, XIV, 114–149). The subject is also treated in about a score of the letters in the Poe correspondence. [CL 304]

119 ⇥ TO WILLIAM LANDOR

Philad., July 7. 41.

My Dear Sir,

I duly received both your notes, and, daily, since the reception of the first, have been intending to reply. The cause of my not having done so is my failure to obtain certain definite information from the printer to whom I had allusion, and who still keeps me in momentary expectation of an answer. I merely write these few words now, lest you should think my silence proceeds from discourtesy — than which nothing can be farther from my thoughts. At the first opportunity you shall hear from me in full.

With high respect.
Y^r Ob. S^t

Wm Landor Esqr Edgar A Poe

P.S. You have seen, I believe, the July no: of Mag. Among the critical notices is one on Bolingbroke, the only notice not written by myself. There are passages in that critique which I am sure are *stolen*, although I cannot put my hand upon the original. Your acquaintance with Bolingbroke's commentators is more extensive than my own. Can you aid me in tracing the theft? I am anxious to do so. Has not Bulwer written something like it?

Landor wrote "Sweepings from a Drawer" in *Burton's*, v (November 1839), 236; later he wrote a biography of N. P. Willis (see Letter 173; see also the note by T. O. Mabbott in J. E. Spannuth's *Doings of Gotham*, p. 71, and Poe's reference in Letter 6, *ibid.*). Poe here identifies the notices in *Graham's*, vol. XIX (July 1841). No other letters between Poe and Landor are known. [CL 308]

Philadelphia July 12. 1841.

My Dear Snodgrass,

I have this moment received yours of the 10th, and am really glad
to find that you have not quite given me up. A letter from you now
is a novelty indeed.

The "Reproof of a Bird" shall appear in the September number.
The last sheet of the August no: has already gone to press.

I am innocent of the elision in your quoted lines. Most probably
the syllables were left out by our proof-reader, who looks over the
articles after me, for such things as turned s's & o's, or battered type.
Occasionally he takes strange liberties. In our forthcoming number
he has substituted, (I see), a small for a capital R in Rosinante. Still —
the lines *read* very well as they are, and thus no great harm is done.
Every one is not to know that the last one is a finale to a stanza.

You say some of your monumental writers *"feel small"* — but is
not that, for them, a natural feeling? I never had much opinion of
Arthur. What little merit he has is negative. McJilton I like much
better. He has written one or two *very* good things. As a man, also,
I like him better. Do you know, by the bye, that W. G. Clark re-
proved me in his Gazette, for speaking *too* favorably of McJilton?

I re-enclose the notice of Soran. It was unavoidably crowded from
the July no: and we thought it *out of date,* for the August[.] I have
not read the book — but I would have been willing to take his merits
upon your word.

You flatter me about the Maelström. It was finished in a hurry,
and therefore its conclusion is imperfect. Upon the whole it is neither
so good, nor has it been ½ so popular as "The Murders in the Rue
Morgue". I have a paper in the August no: which will please you.

[*page 2*] Among the Reviews (for August) I have one which will,
at least, surprise you. It is a *long* notice of a satire by a quondam
Baltimorean L. A. Wilmer. You must get this satire & read it — it is
really good — good in the old-fashioned Dryden style. It blazes away,
too, to the right & left — sparing not. I have made it the text from
which to preach a fire-&-fury sermon upon critical independence, and
the general literary humbuggery of the day. I have introduced in this
sermon some portion of a Review formerly written by me for the

"Pittsburg Examiner", a monthly journal which died in the first throes of its existence. It was edited by E. Burke Fisher Esqre — th[a]n whom a greater scamp never walked. He wrote to me offering 4$ per page for criticisms, promising to put them in as contributions — not editorially. The first thing I saw was one of my articles under the editorial head, so altered that I hardly recognized it, and interlarded with all manner of bad English and ridiculous opinions of his own. I believe, however, that the number in which it appeared, being <its> th· last kick of the maga:, was never circulated.

I presume you get our Mag: regularly. It is mailed to your address.

Very cordially your friend,

Edgar A Poe.

Will you do me the favor to call at the Baltimore P.O. and enquire for a letter addressed to John P. Kennedy *at Baltimore*. By some absence of mind I directed it to that city in place of Washington. If still in the P.O. will you forward it to Washington?

"Reproof of a Bird," a poem by Snodgrass, appeared in *Graham's*, September 1841. The "elision" for which Poe apologizes undoubtedly occurred in Snodgrass' article on poetry, in the June issue of *Graham's;* and the reference to "a small for a capital R in Rosinante" has to do with Poe's review of *The Quacks of Helicon*, by L. A. Wilmer, in the August number. T. S. Arthur owned and edited the *Baltimore Monument*, October 1836–October 1839 (Mott, *History of American Magazines*, I, 381), was in Philadelphia by 1841. (*Dictionary of American Biography*), and gained his greatest journalistic fame as editor of *Leslie's* (February 1844–July 1846) and of his own *Arthur's Home Magazine*, from 1853. McJilton, also an editor of the *Monument*, was one of the literary group during Poe's stay in Baltimore; other members included W. H. Carpenter, N. C. Brooks, John Hewitt, and Rufus Dawes. Willis Gaylord Clark edited the Philadelphia *Gazette;* he had just died, and *Graham's* (August 1841) carried a notice of his death. Snodgrass' notice of Soran's poems, requested by Poe in his April 1 letter, came too late, Poe having indicated the June number. "The Murders in the Rue Morgue" had appeared in *Graham's*, for April, and "A Descent into the Maelström," in the May number. The "paper" in the August issue was "The Colloquy of Monos and Una." Poe's review of Wilmer's *The Quacks of Helicon* incorporated portions of his earlier article on American Novel Writing, written for the Pittsburgh *Literary Examiner*, August 1839 number (see the notes to Letter 81). Poe's article on the novel was run editorially by Fisher in the August 1839 issue, which was not the last "kick" of the magazine. Poe's letter to Kennedy (Letter 114) was directed to Baltimore, but had been forwarded to Washington on June 22, according to postmark on the MS. [CL 311]

121 ⊁ TO TIMOTHEUS WHACKEMWELL
   [ADDRESSED TO J. N. MCJILTON]

Philadelphia, August 11./ 41.

Dʳ Sir,

Your letter of yesterday is this moment received. A glance at the cipher which you suppose the more difficult of the two sent, assures me that its translation must run thus —

"This specimen of secret writing is sent you for explanation. If you succeed in divining its meaning, I will believe that you are some kin to Old Nick."

As my solution in this case will fully convince you of my ability to decipher the longer but i[n]f[ini]tely more simple cryptograph, you will perhaps exc[use] me from attempting it — as I am exceedingly occupied with business.

Very truly yours.

Timotheus Whackemwell Esqʳ   Edgar A Poe.

A "Timotheus Whackemwell" of Baltimore sent Poe two ciphers for solution; Poe, believing he had identified "Whackemwell," sent his reply to J. N. McJilton, an acquaintance of Baltimore, under the date of August 11; McJilton, on August 13, wrote disclaiming the identity. McJilton's reply has neither heading nor salutation, and is signed "J. N. M." It reads: "This is certainly intended for some one else. I know nothing of the matter whatever, nor should I be able to tell how the thing happened, but having seen the peice headed secret-writing pubᵈ in Grahams Mag. noticed somewhere I suppose some wag has addressed you anonymously whom you have mistaken for me." In his review of Walsh's translation, *Sketches of Conspicuous Living Characters in France*, in *Graham's* (April 1841, pp. 202–203), Poe had offered to solve any cryptograms submitted; in "A Few Words on Secret Writing," in *Graham's*, XIX (July 1841), 33–38, Poe stated that only "S. D. L." had answered his challenge. In the October number (p. 192), Poe admits McJilton did not write the "Whackemwell" letter; he gives the reading for the cipher, but not the original cipher. [CL 317]

122 ⤳ TO LEA & BLANCHARD

Mess. Lea & Blanchard,

Gentlemen,

I wish to publish a new collection of my prose Tales with some such title as this — "*The Prose Tales of Edgar A. Poe, Including "The Murders in the Rue Morgue", The "Descent into The Maelström", and all his later pieces, with a second edition of the "Tales of the Grotesque and Arabesque"* "

The "later pieces" will be eight in number, making the entire collection thirty-three — which would occupy two *thick* novel volumes.

I am anxious that your firm should continue to be my publishers, and, if you would be willing to bring out the book, I should be glad to accept the terms which you allowed me before — that is — you receive all profits, and allow me twenty copies for distribution to friends.

Will you be kind enough to give me an early reply to this letter, and believe me

Yours very resp^ly

Philadelphia,   Edgar A Poe

Office Graham's Magazine,

August 13./ 41.

> The "later pieces," those published or at least written by the date of the letter, were probably "The Business Man," in *Burton's*, VI (February 1840), 87–89; "The Man of the Crowd," in *Graham's*, VII (December 1840), 267–270; "The Murders in the Rue Morgue," in *Graham's*, XVIII (April 1841), 166–179; "A Descent into the Maelström," *Graham's*, XVIII (May 1841), pp. 235–241; "The Island of the Fay," *Graham's*, XVIII (June 1841), pp. 253–255; "The Colloquy of Monos and Una," *Graham's*, XIX (August 1841), 52–55; "Never Bet the Devil Your Head," *Graham's*, XIX (September 1841), 124–127; "Eleonora," in the *Gift*, 1842, and in the Boston *Notion*, September 4, 1841. Lea and Blanchard had published, in December 1839, Poe's *Tales of the Grotesque and Arabesque* (see letter of Lea and Blanchard to Poe, September 28, 1839, in Quinn, *Poe*, pp. 287–289; but see the note to Letter 87). Lea and Blanchard (August 16) gave Poe an "early reply," declining his suggestion and adding that they had not yet "got through the edition of the other work" (see H, XVII, 101–102). [CL 318]

123 ❯ TO HASTINGS WELD

Philadelphia, August 14, 1841

Hastings Weld, Esqr.,

Dear Sir: —

The proprietor of a weekly paper in this city is about publishing an article (to be written partly by myself) on the subject of American Autography. The design is three-fold: first, to give the Autograph signature — that is, a fac-simile in woodcut — of each of our most distinguished literati; second, to maintain that the character is, to a certain extent, indicated by the chirography; and thirdly, to embody, under each Autograph, some literary gossip about the individual, with a brief critical comment on his writings.

My object in addressing you now is to request that you would favor me with your own Autograph, in a reply to this letter. I would be greatly obliged to you, also, could you make it convenient to give me a brief summary of your literary career.

We are still in want of the Autographs of Sprague, Hoffman, Dawes, Bancroft, Emerson, Whittier, R. A. Locke, and Stephens, the traveller. If among your papers you have the Autographs of either of these gentlemen (the signature will suffice), and will permit me to have an engraving taken from it, I will endeavor to reciprocate the obligation in any manner which you may suggest.

Should you grow weary, at any time, of abusing me in the "Jonathan" for speaking what no man knows to be truth better than yourself, it would give me sincere pleasure to cultivate the friendship of the author of "Corrected Proofs." In the meantime, I am

Very respy. Yours,

Edgar A. Poe.

The Reverend Horatio Hastings Weld was a minor New York literary figure. Besides having written *Corrected Proofs,* a volume of verse and sketches in the Willis manner, and being a regular contributor of serials to the "mammoth" publications like *Brother Jonathan,* he was editor, at the time of the present letter, of the *Dollar Magazine,* a monthly edition containing the same type of material as that in the *Jonathan* and published by the same people (see Mott, *History of American Magazines,* I, 359–360). Poe included Weld in "Autography," *Graham's,*

December 1841 (reprinted in H, xv, 229). The article also included autographs of Sprague, Hoffman, Dawes, Emerson, Whittier, and Locke; but whether Weld provided the signatures is unknown. [CL 320]

124 ⊁ TO FREDERICK W. THOMAS

Philadelphia — Sep. 1. — 41.

My Dear Thomas,

Griswold left a note for me at the office, the other day, requesting me to furnish him with some memoranda of your life; and it will, of course, give me great pleasure to do so; but, upon sitting down to the task, I find that neither myself, nor Mrˢ Clemm, upon whom I mainly depend for information, can give all the necessary points with sufficient precision for G's purpose. Just send me a line, therefore, answering the following queries, and I will put your responses into shape. Most of the points we know, but not with full certainty.

What is your father's Christian name? Had your parents more children than yourself, Lewis, Frances, Susan, Martha, Isabella & Jackson? — if so, what were their names? When & where were you born? With whom did you study law? What was (exactly) the cause of your lameness? How did you first become known to the literary world? Who were your most intimate associates in Baltimore? When did you remove to Cincinnati? With what papers have you been occasionally connected — if with any? Besides answering these queries — give me a list of your writings published & unpublished — and some memoranda respecting your late lectures at Washington. Reply as soon as possible, as the volume is in press.

I understand that Dow has a paper in Alexandria — how does he get on with it?

I am still jogging on in the same old way, and will probably remain with Graham, even if I start the "Penn" in January. Our success (Graham's I mean) is astonishing — we shall print 20,000 copies shortly. When he bought Burton out, the joint circulation was only 5000. I have had some excellent offers respecting the "Penn" and it is more than probable that it will go on.

How do you get on yourself? I have been expecting a letter from you.

Yours truly & constantly —

Edgar A Poe.

The Griswold note to Poe is unlocated. Thomas' autobiographical data (printed in H, xvII, 95–100, under the date of August 3, 1841) is certainly to be dated September 3 (MS. in Boston Public Library), for Thomas prefaces the data (preface omitted by Harrison) with: "Yours of yesterday [September 1] came to hand duly — about the time you were writing me, I was writting you [August 30]." For Jesse E. Dow, see the Poe–Thomas correspondence, *passim*. [CL 325]

125 ⇾ TO LEWIS J. CIST

Philadelphia — Sep: 18 — 41.

My Dear Sir,

I have only this moment received your letter of the 30th ult. having been absent from the city for some time. I feel that I have been guilty of a sad neglect in the matter of your poem; but my conscience absolves me of any intentional disrespect or discourtesy. The facts stand thus. Upon abandoning the design of "The Penn Magazine", and joining M[r] Graham in his own, I handed over to M[r] Peterson (the then editor of that journal and who hereafter was to act as my associate; his especial duty being that of revising MSS for press and attending to the general *arrangement* of the *matter*) — I handed over to this gentleman your "Bachelor Philosophy" together with a large bundle of other articles — sent me for "The Penn." — I assumed no *right* of transferring articles in this manner; and my intention was (as soon as I could steal a moment's leisure from the world of business which just at that period overwhelmed me) to communicate by letter with each of my correspondents, requesting *permission* for such transfer. In many cases I *did* write, and succeeded in obtaining the requisite permission. My impression was that I had secured your consent with that of others — your consent, I mean, for publishing the poem in Graham's Magazine. It remained, therefore, with the rest, in M[r] Peterson's hands — but only for the purpose specified. Mr. Peterson, however, (who has a third interest in the "Saturday Evening Post" and superintends the "getting up" of that paper also) has taken the unwarrantable liberty, it seems, of using the poem to suit his own views — leaving out of question my positive understanding and intention on the subject. I seldom look at the paper, except occasionally at a proof of some of my own articles in it, and the publication of your verses did not meet my eye: otherwise I should have written you at once in explanation and apology. You will not be surprised that I failed to *miss* your article in the Magazine, or to make inquiry respecting it — if you comprehend the nature of the *confusion* attendant upon the joint issue of a paper and Magazine — especially when you consider that the disposition of the MSS — the drudgery of the business — does not fall to my share. I merely write the Reviews, with a tale monthly, and read the last proofs. As to the insertion of your poem in the "Saturday Evening Post" with the words — "writ- [*page 2*] ten for The Post" — it is a downright falsehood on the part of Mr P. which nothing can extenuate — a falsehood wilfully perpetrated — of a kind which he is in the *habit* of perpetrating, and which have before involved me most disagreeably. Not long ago wishing to procure a printed copy of a poem of my own called "A Ballad", and originally published in the "S. L. Mess." I handed it to Mr P. for re-publication in the "Post" with the heading *"From the South. L. Messenger"; and you may imagine my chagrin at seeing it appear with the same caption as your "Bachelor Philosophy."

I make no scruple in thus indicating to you *plainly* the origin of the *contre-temps* which has so justly annoyed you. I must absolve myself, at all hazards, from suspicion of *falsehood* — let the charge fall upon whom it may. Of intentional discourtesy you will, of course, acquit me. To the accusation of neglect I plead guilty, offering only in extenuation, the press of business which has lately harassed and confused me.

> With the highest respect
> I am Yr Ob St.

L. J. Cist Esqr Edgar A Poe

Poe briefly treated Lewis J. Cist, of Cincinnati, in his "Autography," in *Graham's*, December 1841 (reprinted in H, xv, 240), where he spoke of Cist more as a writer of poetry than of prose. For Poe's abandoning the *Penn* project and affiliating himself with Graham, see Letter 109, postscript and note. Charles J. Peterson was an editor of *Graham's*. Poe printed his "Ballad" in the SLM, 1 (August 1835), 705–706 (see Campbell, *Poems of Edgar Allan Poe*, p. 301); his "Bridal Ballad," undoubtedly a revision of the earlier "Ballad," appeared in the SLM, January 1837, and in the *Saturday Evening Post*, July 31, 1841 (see Campbell, *Poems*, p. 234). [CL 329]

126 ➤ TO JOSEPH EVANS SNODGRASS

Philadelphia — Sep. 19. 41.

My Dear Snodgrass,

I seize the first moment of leisure to say a few words in reply to yours of Sep. 6.

Touching the "Reproof of a Bird," I hope you will give yourself no uneasiness about it. *We* don't mind the contre-temps; and as for Godey, it serves him right, as you say. The moment I saw the article in The "Lady's Book", I saw at once how it all happened.

You are mistaken about "The Dial". I have no quarrel in the world with that illustrious journal, nor it with me. I am not aware that it ever mentioned my name, or alluded to me either directly or indirectly. My slaps at it were only in "a general way." The tale in question is a mere Extravaganza levelled at no one in particular, but hitting right & left at things in general.

The "Knickerbocker" has been purchased by Otis Broadus [*Broaders* ?] & co of Boston. I believe it is still edited by Clark the brother of W. Gaylord.

Thank you for attending to the Kennedy matter. We have no news here just yet — something may turn up by & bye. It is not impossible that Graham will join me in The "Penn." He has money. By the way, is it impossible to start a first-class Mag: in Baltimore? Is there no publisher or gentleman of moderate capital who would join me in the scheme? — publishing the work in the City of Monuments.

Do write me soon & tell me the news,

Yours most cordially

Edgar A Poe

"A Bird's Reproof," by Snodgrass, appeared in *Godey's*, XXIII (September 1841), 137; and "Reproof of a Bird," also by Snodgrass, appeared in *Graham's*, XIX (September 1841), 103. Though under slightly different titles, the two printings of the poem are essentially the same in text, except that variations occur in wording and punctuation, and there is an extra stanza in the *Graham's* printing. After receiving the MS., Godey probably delayed printing, and Snodgrass then submitted a revision to *Graham's*, both magazines finally printing the poem in the

same month. The *Dial*, a quarterly published between July 1840, and
April 1844, was at this time edited by Margaret Fuller (see Mott,
History of American Magazines, I, 702), against whom Poe later aimed
several sharp criticisms. Poe's "slaps" apparently were contained in his
"Extravaganza," "Never Bet Your Head," in *Graham's*, September
1841, pp. 124–127. Mott (*History of American Magazines*, I, 606)
gives "L. G. Clark (?)" as the publisher of the *Knickerbocker* for
1840–1841; but if Poe is here correct, Mott's question concerning
Clark's publishing of the magazine is answered; the MS. is not clear,
nor are the letters sufficiently distinct, for the correct spelling of the
new publisher; William Hand Browne transcribed "Broadus," but
others have read "Broaders," and Browne's earlier reading would nor-
mally carry weight. W. Gaylord Clark, brother of Lewis, had been
editor of the Philadelphia *Gazette* until his death, June 13, 1841;
Graham's carried a eulogy in its August 1841 issue. Snodgrass may
have been editor of the Baltimore *Saturday Visiter* at this time (see
Letter 90 and note), and Poe may have meant him as the "publisher or
gentleman of moderate capital." [CL 330]

127 ➤ TO FREDERICK W. THOMAS

Philadelphia — Oct. 27 — 41.

My Dear Thomas,

I received your last some days ago, and have delayed answering it,
in hope that I might say your song was out, and that I might give you
my opinion and Virginia's about its merits. As soon as I received the
MS. I took it forthwith to Willig, who promised me that it should
be ready in a week. I called three or four times, and still the answer
was — "in a day or two". Yesterday I called again; when he positively assured me that it would be out on Monday. As soon as it is
done, he will forward some copies (he did not say how many) to
your address at Washington. Virginia is very anxious to see it, as
your " 'Tis said that absence" &c is a great favorite with her.

I have not your last letter at hand, and cannot therefore reply to it
point by point. You said something about Judge Upshur's book —
or rather about "The Partisan Leader"; for he did not write it —
neither Judge Tucker, I think. It seems to me that it was written
by someone in Petersburg — but I am not sure. I am not personally
acquainted with Judge Upshur; but I have a profound respect for his
talents. He is not only the most graceful speaker I ever heard, but

one of the most graceful & luminous writers. His head is a model for statuary — Speaking of heads — my own *has been* examined by several phrenologists — all of whom spoke of me in a species of extravaganza which I should be ashamed to repeat.

In our autograph article for November your name was crowded out on account of the length of the comment upon it. It heads the list in the December no; which is already finished.

Griswold's book will be issued in January.

I am glad to hear of Dows' success. I wonder he never sends me an "Index".

Our Mag: is progressing at the most astounding rate. When Burton was bought out — you know when that was — the joint list of both Mags. was 5000. In January we print 25000. Such a thing was never heard of before. Ah, if we could only get up the "Penn"! I have made a definite engagement with Graham for 1842 — but nothing to interfere with my own scheme, should I be able by any good luck, to go into it. Graham holds out a hope of his joining me in July. Is there no one among your friends at Washington — no one having both brains & funds who would engage in such an enterprise? Perhaps not. I comfort myself, however, with the assurance that the [time] *must* come when I shall have a journal under my own control. Till then — patience.

Do write me soon, and say something of your own hopes and views. What are you about in the scribbling way?

Sincerely your friend

Edgar A. Poe

Have you read Simm's new book?

Judge Nathaniel Beverley Tucker was the author of the *Partisan Leader* (1836), reviewed (unsigned) by Judge Abel Parker Upshur in the SLM, III (January 1837), 73–89, according to B. B. Minor in *Southern Literary Messenger, 1834–1864*, p. 63. Poe's article on Thomas in "Autography," *Graham's*, December 1841, is reprinted in H, xv, 209–210. Poe probably refers to Griswold's *Poets and Poetry of America*, published in April 1842; for it, Poe apparently wrote a sketch of Thomas, but Griswold did not use it (see Letters 124 and 143). William Gilmore Simms was a rather prolific novelist of this period, several times reviewed by Poe. [CL 334]

128 ⊁ TO LYDIA H. SIGOURNEY

Philadelphia. Nov. 10. 1841.

Dear Madam.

Since my connexion, as editor, with "Graham's Magazine", of this city, I have been sadly disappointed to find that you deem us unworthy your correspondence. Month after month elapses, and, although our list numbers "good names," we still miss that of Mrs Sigourney. Is there no mode of tempting you to send us an occasional contribution? Mr Graham desires me to say that he would be *very especially* obliged if you could furnish, "him with a poem, however brief, for the January number. His compensation — for the days of gratuitous contributions are luckily gone by — will be at least as liberal as that of any publisher in America. May I hope to hear from you in reply? Excuse, dear Madam, this villanous steel pen, and believe me with high respect

Y^r Mo ob S^t

Mrs L. H. Sigourney.   Edgar A Poe

> Mrs. Sigourney contributed a poem, "To a Land Bird at Sea," to *Graham's*, xx (January 1842), 9. According to Poe's article, "The Pay for Periodical Writing," in the *Weekly Mirror*, 1 (October 19, 1844), 28, Graham paid prose writers from $2 to $12 a page, and poets from $5 to $50 an "article" (Quinn, *Poe*, p. 341). Prices were probably much less in 1841; for Poe offered Snodgrass "The Mystery of Marie Rogêt," for the Baltimore *Saturday Visiter*, in his letter of June 4, 1842, at $4 a page, "the usual Magazine price." [CL 342]

129 ⊁ TO LYDIA H. SIGOURNEY

Philadelphia Nov. 16. 1842 [1841]

Dear Madam,

I hasten to reply to yours of the 13th, and to thank you for your consent in the matter of contribution to our January number. We are forced to go to press at a very early period — for our edition is, *in reality*, twenty-five thousand — so that it would be desirable we should have your article in hand by the 1^rst December. We shall look for it with much anxiety, as we are using every exertion to prepare a number of more than ordinary attraction. So far, we have been quite successful. We shall have papers from Longfellow, Benjamin, Willis, Fay, Herbert, Mrs Stephens, Mrs Embury, Dr Reynell Coates, and (what will surprise you) from Sergeant Talfourd, author of "Ion" — besides others of nearly equal celebrity.

Is it not possible that we can make an arrangement with yourself for an article *each* month? It would give us the greatest pleasure to do so; and the terms of Mr Graham will be at least *as* liberal as those of any publisher. Shall we hear from you upon this point?

I regret that I am unable to answer your query touching the "Messenger": — nor do I believe it answerable[.] Since my secession, I *think* that Mr White has had no regular editor. He depends pretty much upon chance, [*page 2*] for assistance in the conduct of the Magazine — sometimes procuring aid from Mr James E. Heath, of Richmond — sometimes (but not of late days) from Judge Beverly Tucker, author of "George Balcombe". Mr. Benjamin has occasionally furnished him with editorial or, rather, critical matters, and Mr R. W. Griswold has lately written much for the Magazine.

I am, Dear Madam, With the highest respect,
Y^r Ob. S^t

Mrs L. H. Sigourney   Edgar A Poe

Following Poe's editorship of the *Southern Literary Messenger*, Thomas W. White edited the magazine, very much as Poe says, from February 1837–December 1839 (?); then he was assisted by Matthew F. Maury, January 1840 (?)–September 1842, after which Maury edited it alone until July 1843 (see Mott, *History of American Magazines*, I, 629). Mr. White died in January 1843, and Benjamin B. Minor took over the SLM interests in July 1843. [CL 345]

130 ⤳ TO RICHARD BOLTON

Philadelphia Nov. 18. 41.

Dear Sir,

Yours of the 4th is this moment received; and I hasten to exonerate myself from a very unpleasant suspicion — the suspicion, no doubt long since entertained by yourself, that I wished to deny you the honors of victory — and a participation in its spoils.

A word in explanation will suffice. You must know, then, that our edition is, *in fact*, exceedingly large. We print 25000 copies. Of course much time is required to prepare them. Our last "form" necessarily goes to press a full month in advance of the day of issue. It often happens, moreover, that the last form *in order* is not the last in press. Our *first* form is usually held back until the last moment on account of the "plate article." Upon this hint you will easily see the possibility of your letter not having come to hand in season for acknowledgment in the November number. Otherwise, I should have had high gratification in sharing with you *then,* the reputation of a bottle-conjurer — for thus the matter seems to stand. In our December number, (which has been quite ready for ten days) you will find an unqualified acknowledgment of your claims — without even allusion to the slight discrepancies for which I believe the printer is chargeable. I mean to say that you have (I believe) solved the cypher as printed. *My* solution follows the MS. — both are correct.

Allow me, Dear Sir, now to say that I was never more astonished in my life than at your solution. Will you honestly tell me? — did you not owe it to the accident of the repetition of the word "itagi?" for "those"? This repetition does not appear in the MS. — at least I [*page 2*] am pretty sure that it was interpolated by one of our compositors — a "genius" who takes much interest in these matters — and many unauthorized liberties.

In Dr Frailey's MS. were many errors — the chief of which I corrected for press — but mere blunders do not really much affect the difficulty of cypher solution — as you, no doubt, perceive. I had also to encounter the embarrasment of a miserably cramped & confused penmanship. Here you had the advantage of me — a very important advantage.

Be all this as it may — your solution *astonished* me. You will accuse me of vanity in so saying — but truth is truth. I make no question that it even astonished yourself — and well it might — for from among at least 100,000 readers — a great number of whom, to my certain knowledge busied themselves in the investigation — you and I are the only persons who have succeeded.

It is unnecessary to trouble yourself with the cipher printed in our Dec. number — it is insoluble for the reason that it is merely type in *pi* or something near it. Being absent from the office for a short time, I did not see a proof and the compositors have made a

complete medley. It has not even a remote resemblance to the MS.
I should be delighted to hear from you at all times — Believe me —

Yours very resp^{ly}

R. Bolton Esqr   Edgar A Poe

Edward S. Sears, author of the article in the *Commercial Appeal* (see
Note 130), also prints Bolton's letter of November 4, 1841, and one
dated "June 10," 1842, which should be January 10, 1842 (according
to a letter to me from W. K. Wimsatt, Jr.; see *Publications of the
Modern Language Association,* LVIII (September 1943), 754–779).
In *Graham's,* XIX (December 1841), 308, Poe says that of the 100,000
readers of the magazine, "one and only one" solved Dr. Frailey's cryptograph, which had appeared in the August number. The honor, he says,
belongs to "Mr. Richard Bolton, of Pontotoc, Mississippi," but adds
that the solution arrived too late for inclusion in the November issue.
In Letter 131 Poe discredits Bolton's first solving of the cryptogram by
saying, "He pretends not to have seen my solution — but his own contains internal evidence of the fact." For an analysis of the problem, see
William F. Friedman, "Edgar Allan Poe, Cryptographer," *American
Literature,* VIII (November 1936), 266–280, where he concludes: "I
must declare that Poe had utterly no foundation for his suspicion [stated
to Thomas]. Internal evidence in Bolton's solution . . . serves to indicate conclusively that his work was accomplished without the key.
Nowhere can one find 'three blunders in mine [Poe's] which are copied
in his own . . .' Poe did not . . . deny having received the latter's
solution mailed on September 9 . . . Poe must have received it by
October 9. The key to the cryptogram did *not* appear in the September number . . . but . . . in the October number, which could not
possibly have arrived before September 9" (*ibid.,* p. 276). No other
letter from Poe to Bolton is known. [CL 346]

131 ➤ TO FREDERICK W. THOMAS

Philadelphia, Nov. 26 — 41.

My Dear Thomas,

I am astonished to hear that you have not yet received the music,
as, upon receipt of your last, I procured it of Willig, and put it into
the hands of Burgess, our Magazine agent here, who promised to
<follow> forward it to Taylor the Magazine agent in Washington.
Taylor was to deliver it to you. You had better call upon him. It is
the same man upon whom you had the draft.

You need not put yourself to trouble about Prentice's autograph, as we have now closed that business. I suppose you have not the December number yet — it has been ready for several weeks. The January no: is nearly prepared — we have an autograph article in each. Should Prentice send on his signature, however, I would be glad to get it.

In the Dec. no: you will see a notice to the effect that a Mr Richard Bolton, of Pontotoc Miss.[1], has solved Dr Frailey's cypher. You must put no great faith in this announcement. Mr Bolton sent me a letter dated at a period long after the reception of our Magazines in Pontotoc, and fully a month after the *preparation* of the number containing the answer by myself. He pretends [*page 2*] not to have seen my solution — but his own contains internal evidence of the fact. Three *blunders* in mine are copied in his own, & two or three *corrections* of Dr Frailey's original, by myself, are also faithfully repeated. I had the alternative of denying his claim and thus appearing invidious, or of sharing with him an honor which, in the eyes of the mob at least, is not much above that of a bottle-conjuror: so I chose the last and have put a *finale* to this business.

Touching your study of the French language. You will, I fear, find it difficult — as, (if I rightly understood you,) you have not received what is called a "classical" education. To the Latin & Greek proficient, the study of all additional languages is mere play — but to the non-proficient it is anything else. The best advice I can give you, under the circumstances, is to busy yourself with the theory or grammar of the language as little as possible & to read *side-by-side* translations continually, of which there are many to be found. I mean French books in which the literal English version is annexed page per page. Board, also, at a French boarding-house, and force yourself to speak French — bad or good — whether you [*page 3*] can or whether you *cannot.*

I have *not* heard from Kennedy for a long time, and I think, upon the whole, he has treated me somewhat cavalierly — professing to be *a friend.*

I would give the world to see you once again and have a little chat. Dow you & I — "when shall we three meet again?" Soon, I hope — for I must try & slip over to Washington some of these days.

Do you hear often from your friends at St Louis? When you write, remember me kindly to your sister Frances — if I may take the liberty of requesting to be remembered where, never having been known personally, there can be nothing to remember. We have had "Clinton Bradshaw" here (the confounded "devils" *will* print it Bradshaw*e*) and the "Dedication" has set us all to thinking & talking about the "dedicatee"[.]

God bless you —

Edgar A Poe

For Thomas' song, see Thomas to Poe, September 22, November 6 and 23, 1841 (MSS. in the Boston Public Library; unpublished), and Letter 127. Poe's "Autography" articles in *Graham's* for December 1841, and January 1842, are reprinted in H, xv, 209–261. For the reference to Bolton, see Letter 130 and note. Poe's early training in classical and modern languages (see Quinn, *Poe*, pp. 71, 99–101) may account for the advice given Thomas. Poe had not received a letter from J. P. Kennedy, apparently, since April 26, 1836. For Jesse E. Dow, see the note to Letter 197. *Clinton Bradshaw* (1835) was Thomas' first novel; Poe may have had it in hand either for the preparation of notes on Thomas' biography requested by Griswold (see Letter 124) or, more likely, for the "Autography" article, which included Thomas, in *Graham's*, December 1841 (see H, xv, 209–210). The dedication to the first edition of *Clinton Bradshaw* reads: "To my sister, Frances Ann / My Dear Sister,/ As a slight acknowledgment of your affection, I / inscribe these volumes with your name./ Your affectionate brother,/ The Author./ Philadelphia, Sept. 17, 1835." (This dedication was supplied through the courtesy of Thomas O. Mabbott, from the first edition copy of the novel in the Yale University Library.) [CL 348]

132 ⇥ TO FREDERICK W. THOMAS

Philadelphia Feb. 3, '42.

My dear Friend:

I am sure you will pardon me for my seeming neglect in not replying to your last when you learn what has been the cause of the delay. My dear little wife has been dangerously ill. About a fortnight since, in singing, she ruptured a blood-vessel, and it was only on yesterday that the physicians gave me any hope of her recovery. You might imagine the agony I have suffered, for you know how devotedly I love her. But to-day the prospect brightens, and I trust that this bitter cup of misery will not be my portion. I seize the first moment of hope and relief to reply to your kind words.

You ask me how I come on with Graham? Will you believe it Thomas? On the morning subsequent to the accident I called upon him, and, being entirely out of his debt, asked an advance of two months salary — when he not only flatly but discourteously refused. Now that man *knows* that I have rendered him the most important services; he cannot help knowing it, for the fact is rung in his ears by every second person who visits the office, and the comments made by the press are too obvious to be misunderstood.

The project of the new Magazine still (you may be sure) occupies my thoughts. *If I live,* I will accomplish it, and in triumph. By the way, there is one point upon which I wish to consult you. You are personally acquainted with Robert Tyler, author of "Ahasuerus." In this poem there are many evidences of power, and, what is better, of nobility of thought & feeling. In reading it, an idea struck me — "Might it not," I thought, "be possible that *he* would, or rather might be induced to feel some interest in my contemplated scheme, perhaps even to *take* an interest in something of the kind — an interest either open or secret?" The Magazine might be made to play even an important part in the politics of the day, like Blackwood; and in this view might be worthy his consideration. Could you contrive to suggest the matter to him? Provided I am permitted a proprietary right in the journal, I shall not be very particular about the extent of that right. If, instead of a paltry salary, Graham had given me a tenth of his Magazine, I should feel myself a rich man to-day. When he bought out Burton, the joint circulation was 4,500, and we have printed of the February number last, 40,000. Godey, at the period of the junction, circulated 30,000, and, in spite of the most strenuous efforts, has not been able to prevent his list from *falling*. I am sure that he does not print more than 30,000 to-day. His absolute circulation is about 20,000. Now Godey, in this interval, has surpassed Graham in all the *externals* of a good Magazine. His paper is better, his type far better, and his engravings fully as good; but I fear I am getting sadly egotistical. I would not speak so plainly to any other than yourself. How delighted I would be to grasp you by the hand!

As regards the French — get into a French family by all means — read much, write more, & give grammar to the dogs.

You are quizzing me about the autographs. I was afraid to say more than one half of what I really thought of you, lest it should be attributed to personal friendship. Those articles have had a great run — have done wonders for the Journal — but I fear have also done me, personally, much injury. I was weak enough to permit Graham to modify my opinions (or at least their expression) in many of the notices. In the case of Conrad, for example; he insisted upon *praise* and worried me into speaking well of such ninnies as Holden, Peterson, Spear, &c., &c. I would not have yielded had I thought it made much difference what one said of such puppets as these, but it seems the error has been made to count against my critical impartiality. Know better next time. Let no man accuse me of leniency again.

I do not believe that Ingraham stole "Lafitte."

No, Benjamin does not write the political papers in the "New World," but I cannot say who does. I cannot bring myself to like that man, although I wished to do so, and although he made some advances, of late, which you may have seen. He is too thorough-souled a time-server. I would not say again what I said of him in the "Autography."

Did you read my review of "Barnaby Rudge" in the Feb. No.? You see that I was right throughout in my predictions about the plot. Was it not you who said you believed I would find myself mistaken?

Remember me kindly to Dow. I fear he has given me up; never writes; never sends a paper.

Will you bear in mind what I say about R. Tyler?

God bless you.

F. W. Thomas.   Edgar A. Poe.

Poe still hoped to publish the *Penn Magazine* and was trying to enlist the aid of Robert Tyler, son of the President of the United States and a friend of Thomas. For Robert Tyler's high opinion of Poe as a critic, see Thomas to Poe, February 26, 1842 (MS. in the Boston Public Library; printed under the wrong date of February 6 in both H, xvii, 105–106, and W, i, 318–321). Poe's "Autography" in *Graham's* for December 1841, included articles on Thomas G. Spear, Ezra Holden, Robert T. Conrad, and Charles J. Peterson (see H, xv, 210–211, 212, 232–233, 235). Poe reviewed Joseph H. Ingraham's *Lafitte* in the SLM, August 1836 (reprinted in H, ix, 106–116). Poe included Park Benjamin, editor of the *New World*, in his "Autography," *Graham's*, November 1841 (reprinted in H, xv, 183–184). In a "prospective notice" in the *Saturday Evening Post*, May 1, 1841, Poe anticipated the plot of Dickens's *Barnaby Rudge;* he reviewed the book at length, recalling his earlier analysis, in *Graham's*, February 1842 (reprinted in H, xi, 38–64). [CL 356]

133 ⇥ TO JOHN N. MCJILTON

Philadelphia — March 13, 1842.

My Dear Sir,

I duly received your letter of the 14th ult, accompanying Miss Wetherald's Translation. My silence, for so long an interval, will have assured you that the article is accepted with pleasure. Mr Graham, however, desires me to say that it will be out of his power to pay more than 2$ per printed page for translations. Should these terms meet the views of Miss Wetherald, we should be glad to receive from her, each month, an article similar to the one sent, and not exceeding three or four pages in length.

It will be inconvenient, just now, to furnish French periodicals, as suggested: — but the task of selection may well be left in the hands of Miss Wetherald, of whose abilities as a French translator I am fully satisfied, and of whose taste I am well assured by the character of the paper now furnished. *Similar* pieces would suit my own views better than others "more in the story-telling style of the day."

Why do I not hear from you occasionally as in "the olden time?"

With the Highest Respect,
Y[r]Ob S[t]

Rev. J. N. M[c]Jilton.   Edgar A Poe

"Russian Revenge," translated from the French, by Esther Wetherald appeared in *Graham's*, xx (June 1842), 322–325. For the only other known correspondence between Poe and McJilton, see the note to Letter 121. [CL 361]

V

PHILADELPHIA

THE POST–GRAHAM'S PERIOD

May 1842–March 1844

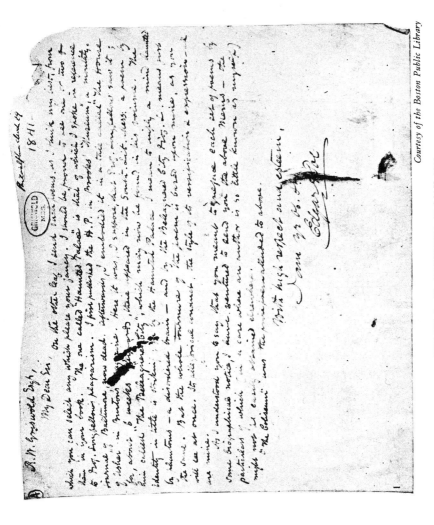

POE TO R. W. GRISWOLD, 29 MAY 1841

(Letter 112)

ELMIRA ROYSTER SHELTON, PROBABLY ABOUT 1845

Philadelphia   May 25.   1842.

My Dear Thomas,

Through an accident I have only just now received yours of the 21ʳˢᵗ. Believe me, I never dreamed of doubting your friendship, or of reproaching you for your silence. I knew you had your reasons for it; and, in this matter, I feel that you have acted for me more judiciously, by far, than I should have done for myself. You have shown yourself, from the first hour of our acquaintance, that rara avis in terris — a *true friend.* Nor am I the man to be unmindful of your kindness.

What you say respecting a situation in the Custom House here, gives me new life. Nothing could more precisely meet my views. Could I obtain such an appointment, I would be enabled thoroughly to carry out all my ambitious projects. It would relieve me of all care as re-gards a mere subsistence, and thus allow me time for thought, which, in fact, is action. I repeat that I would ask for nothing farther or better than a situation such as you mention. If the salary will barely enable me to live I shall be content. Will you say as much for me to Mʳ Tyler, and express to him my sincere gratitude for the interest he takes in my welfare?

The report of my having parted company with Graham, is correct; although, in the forthcoming June number, there is no announcement to that effect; nor had the papers any authority for the statement made. My duties ceased with the May number. I shall continue to contribute occasionally. Griswold succeeds me. My reason for re-signing was dis- [*page 2*] gust with the namby-pamby character of the Magazine — a character which it was impossible to eradicate — I allude to the contemptible pictures, fashion-plates, music and love tales. The salary, moreover, did not pay me for the labor which I was forced to bestow. With Graham who is really a very gentle-manly, although an exceedingly weak man, I had no misunder-standing.

I am rejoiced to say that my dear little wife is much better, and I have strong hope of her ultimate recovery. She desires her kindest regards — as also Mr^s Clemm.

I have moved from the old place — but should you pay an unexpected visit to Philadelphia you will find my address at Graham's. I would give the world to shake you by the hand; and have a thousand things to talk about which would not come within the compass of a letter.

Write immediately upon receipt of this, if possible, and do let me know something of yourself, your own doings and prospects: — see how excellent an example of egotism I set you. Here is a letter nearly every word of which is about myself or my individual affairs.

You saw White — little Tom. I am anxious to know what he said about things in general. He is a *character* if ever one was.

God bless you —

F. W. Thomas.   Edgar A Poe

> Thomas' silence was directly due to his trying to interest Robert Tyler in Poe's welfare. Poe's salary with Graham was $800 a year for his editorial duties; he probably received extra pay for his contributions, varying, according to references in his correspondence, from four to five dollars "a *Graham* page"; Graham was forced to be more liberal with men like Lowell, Longfellow, Cooper, and Willis (see Mott, *History of American Magazines*, I, 506–507). For Poe's change of residence, see Quinn, *Poe*, pp. 273–274. Thomas W. White was the editor and publisher of the *Southern Literary Messenger*. [CL 365]

135 ➤ TO JAMES HERRON

[Philadelphia, early June, 1842.]

[. . .] anticipated my design, and a notice had already been inserted, but only as a *communication* — not editorially.

Believe me that I sincerely rejoice in your good fortune; or rather in the success which you so well earned and deserved; but my means of serving you through the papers have been less than my desire to do so. You have learned, perhaps, that I have retired from "Graham's Magazine". The state of my mind has, in fact, forced me to abandon for the present, all mental exertion. The renewed and hopeless illness of my wife, ill health on my own part, and pecuniary embarrassments, have nearly driven me to distraction. My only hope of relief is the

"Bankrupt Act", of which I shall avail myself as soon as possible. Had I resolved upon this at an earlier day, I might now have been doing well — but the struggle to keep up has, at length, entirely ruined me. I have left myself without even the means of availing myself of the act, [*page* 2] [. . .]

You will be pleased to hear that I have the promise of a situation in our Custom-House. The offer was entirely unexpected & gratuitous. I am to receive the appointment upon removal of several incumbents — the removal to be certainly made in a month. I am indebted to the personal friendship of Robert Tyler. If I *really* receive the appointment all may yet go well. The labors of the office are by no means onerous and I shall have time enough to spare for other pursuits. Please mention nothing of this — for, after all, I may be disappointed.

Mrs Poe is again dangerously ill with hemorrhage from the lungs. It is folly to hope.

With sincere esteem & friendship
Yours

Jas. Herron Esqre   Edgar A Poe

> James Herron, an engineer, invented a trellis railway structure; he described it in a book: *A Practical Description of Herron's Patent Trellis Railway Structure* (Philadelphia: Carey and Hart, 1841), which was reviewed in *Graham's*, October 1841, p. 192. Poe left *Graham's* "with the May number," published about April 15. Poe never received the appointment to an office in the Philadelphia Custom House. Virginia Poe ruptured a blood vessel, while she was singing, about the middle of January 1842, and for some time doctors despaired of her recovery (see Letter 132); Poe is here referring to a recurrence of her illness. [CL 367]

136 ⤷ TO GEORGE ROBERTS

Philadelphia — June 4 1842.

My Dear Sir.

It is just possible that you may have seen a tale of mine entitled "The Murders in the Rue Morgue," and published, originally, in "Graham's Magazine" for April 1841. Its *theme* was the exercise of ingenuity in the detection of a murderer. I have just completed a

similar article, which I shall entitle "The Mystery of Marie Rogêt —
a Sequel to the Murders in the Rue Morgue". The story is based
upon the assassination of Mary Cecilia Rogers, which created so vast
an excitement, some months ago, in New-York. I have, however,
handled my design in a manner altogether *novel* in literature. I have
imagined a series of nearly exact *coincidences* occurring in Paris. A
young grisette, one Marie Rogêt, has been murdered under precisely
similar circumstances with Mary Rogers. Thus, under pretence of
showing how Dupin (the hero of "The Rue Morgue unravelled the
mystery of Marie's assassination, I, in reality, enter into a very long
and rigorous analysis of the New-York tragedy. No point is omitted.
I examine, each by each, the opinions and arguments of the press upon
the subject, and show that this subject has been, hitherto, *unap-
proached*. In fact, I believe not only that I have demonstrated the
fallacy of the general idea — that the girl was the victim of a gang
of ruffians — but have *indicated the assassin* in a manner which
will give renewed impetus to investigation. My main object, nevertheless, as you will readily understand, is an analysis of the true principles which should direct inquiry in similar cases. From the nature
of the subject, I feel convinced that the article will excite attention,
and it has occurred to me that you would be willing to purchase it
for the forthcoming Mammoth Notion. It will make 25 pages of
Graham's Magazine; and, at the usual price, would be worth to me
$100. For reasons, however, which I need not specify, I am de-
sirous [*page 2*] of having this tale printed in Boston, and, if you
like it, I will say $50. Will you please write me upon this point? —
by return of mail, if possible.

Yours very truly,

George Roberts Esqr   Edgar A Poe

Compare this letter with Letter 137, in which the tale is offered for
$40. Also, Poe seems to have written a similar letter (unlocated) to
the editor of the *Southern Literary Messenger* (then edited by T. W.
White and Matthew F. Maury; see *Publications of the Modern Language
Association*, LVI (March 1941), 233, n.). For publication of the new
tale, see the note to Letter 137. Roberts' *Notion* was one of the mam-
moth papers of the day, which included the *Brother Jonathan*, *New-
Yorker*, *New World*, and *Dollar Magazine*, edited by such men as Park
Benjamin, Rufus W. Griswold, Horace Greeley, and L. Fitzgerald
Tasistro. [CL 368]

137 ➤ TO JOSEPH EVANS SNODGRASS

Philadelphia — June 4. 1842.

My Dear Snodgrass,

How does it happen that, in these latter days, I never receive an epistle from yourself? Have I offended you by any of my evil deeds? — if so, how? Time was when you could spare a few minutes occas-<s>ionally for communion with a friend.

I see with pleasure that you have become sole proprietor of the "Visiter"; and this reminds me that I have to thank your partiality for many flattering notices of myself. How is it, nevertheless, that a *Magazine* of the highest class has never yet succeeded in Baltimore? I have often thought, of late, how much better it would have been had you joined me in a Magazine project in the Monumental City, rather than engage with the "Visiter" — a journal which has never yet been able to recover from the *mauvais odeur* imparted to it by Hewitt. Notwithstanding the many failures in Baltimore, I still am firmly convinced that <B> your city is the best adapted for such a Magazine as I propose, of any in the Union. Have you ever thought seriously upon this subject.

I have a proposition to make. You may remember a tale of mine published about a year ago in "Graham" and entitled the "Murders in the Rue Morgue". Its *theme* was the exercise of ingenuity in detecting a murderer. I am just now putting the concluding touch to a similar article, which I shall entitle "The Mystery of Marie Rogêt — a Sequel to 'The Murders in the Rue Morgue'." The story is based upon that of the real murder of Mary Cecilia Rogers, which created so vast an excitement, some months ago, in New-York. I have handled the design in a very singular and [*page 2*] entirely *novel* manner. I imagine a series of nearly exact *coincidences* occurring in Paris. A young grisette, one *Marie Rogêt,* has been murdered under precisely similar circumstances with *Mary Rogers.* Thus under pretence of showing how Dupin (the hero of the Rue Morgue) unravelled the mystery of Marie's assassination, I, in fact, enter into a very rigorous analysis of the *real* tragedy in New-York. *No point* is omitted. I examine <d>, each by each, the opinions and arguments of our press on the subject, and show (I think satisfactorily) that this subject has never yet been *approached.* The press has been entirely on a wrong scent. In fact, I really believe, not only that I have demonstrated the falsity of the idea that the girl was <not> the victim of a gang <as supposed>, but have *indicated the assassin*. My main object, however, as you will readily understand, is the analysis of the *principles of investigation* in cases of like character. Dupin *reasons* the matter throughout.

The article, I feel convinced, will be one of general interest, from the nature of its subject. For reasons which I may mention to you hereafter, I am desirous of publishing it *in Baltimore,* and there would be no channel so proper as the paper under your control. Now the tale is a long one — it would occupy twenty-five pages of Graham's Magazine — and is worth to me a hundred dollars at the usual Magazine price. Of course I could not afford to make you an absolute present of it — but if you are willing to take it, I will say $40. Shall I hear from you on this head — if possible by return of mail?

Have you seen Griswold's Book of Poetry? It is a most outrageous humbug, and I sincerely wish [*page 3*] you would "use it up".

If you have not yet noticed my withdrawal from Graham's Magazine, I would take it as a great favor if you would do so in something like the following terms. Even if you *have* noticed it, this might go in.

We have it from *undoubted authority* that Mr Poe *has* retired from the editorship of "Graham's Magazine", and that his withdrawal took place with the *May* number, notwithstanding the omission of all announcement to this effect in the number for June. We observe that the "Boston Post", in finding just fault with an exceedingly ignorant and flippant review of "Zanoni" which appears in the June number, has spoken of it as from the pen of Mr Poe[.] We will take it upon ourselves to say that M͏ʳ P. neither did write the article, nor could have written any such absurdity. The slightest glance would suffice to convince us of this. Mr P. would never be guilty of the grammatical blunders, to say nothing of the mere twattle, which disgrace the criticism. When did <Mr P.> he ever spell *liaison, liason,* for example, or make use of so absurd a phrase as *"attained to"* in place of attained? We are also fully confident that the criticism in question is not the work of Mr Griswold, who(, whatever may be his abilities as the compiler of a Book of Poetry,) is at all events a decent writer of English. The article appears to be the handiwork of some underling who has become imbued with th[e] fancy of *aping* <some of> Mr Poe's pe-

culiarities of diction. A pretty mess he has made of it! Not to announce Mr P's withdrawal in the [*page 4*] June number, was an act
of the rankest injustice; and as such we denounce it. A man of talent
may occasionally submit to the appropriation of his articles by others
who *insinuate* a claim to the authorship, but it is a far different and
vastly more disagreeable affair <matter> when he finds <th> himself called upon to father the conceit, ignorance and flippant impertinence of an ass.

Put this in editorially, <ny> my dear S., and oblige me eternally.
You will acknowledge that it will be an act of justice. [*space reserved
for mailing address*]

Write immediately and believe me[,]

Your friend.

Edgar A Poe

If you put in th[e] paragraph send me the no: of the Visiter.

Poe's hint that Snodgrass join him in publishing the dream magazine
fell on barren ground. John H. Hewitt had won the poetry prize offered
by the Baltimore *Saturday Visiter*, in 1833, at the same time Poe won
the prose premium; Wilmer, then editor, was subsequently replaced by
Hewitt, who gained the favor of McCloud, the owner (see Wilmer,
Our Press Gang, pp. 22–29). "The Murders in the Rue Morgue" appeared in *Graham's*, April 1841. Poe also offered "The Mystery of Marie
Rogêt" to George Roberts, editor of the Boston *Times and Notion*, in a
letter of the same date (Letter 136); neither editor took the story, and
it was published in Snowden's *Ladies' Companion*, November, December 1842, and February 1843 (Wyllie, *Poe's Tales*, p. 332). On April
18, 1842, Carey and Hart announced the publication of Griswold's
Poets and Poetry of America, and for Poe's attitude toward it, see
the note to Letter 143. Apparently Poe withdrew from *Graham's* during the first part of April, since the magazine appeared in advance of
date. Graham wrote to Griswold, April 20, asking if he intended to
give up all editorial work, and if not to state whether he would consider coming to Philadelphia. On May 3 Graham wrote Griswold, con-
firming his appointment as editor of *Graham's*, at $1000 a year. Gris-
wold must have accepted and gone to Philadelphia within a few days,
for on May 16 Greeley wrote him to return to New York and work
four days for him (see *Passages in the Correspondence of R. W. Griswold*, ed. W. M. Griswold, pp. 106–107). This is the last known letter
in the correspondence between Poe and Snodgrass. [CL 369]

138 ⇥ TO JAMES HERRON

Philadelphia, June 30. 1842.

My Dear Mr Herron.

Upon return from a brief visit to New-York, last night, I found here your kind letter from Washington, enclosing a check for $20, and giving me new life in every way. I am more deeply indebted to you than I can express, and in this I really mean what I say. Without your prompt and unexpected interposition with Mr Tyler, it is by no means improbable that I should have failed in obtaining the appointment which has <now> become so vitally necessary to me; but now I feel assured of success. The $20, also, will enable me to overcome other difficulties — and, I repeat, that I thank you from the bottom of my heart. You have shown yourself a true friend.

My wife's health has slightly improved and my spirits have risen in proportion; but I am still *very* unwell — so much so that I shall be forced to give up and go to bed.

Your own brilliant prospects *must* be realized; for it is not Fate which makes such men as yourself. You make your own Fate. There is such a thing as compelling Fortune, however reluctant or averse. As regards myself — I will probably succeed too. So let us both keep a good heart.

Wishing you the high success which you deserve,

I am your sincere friend,

Jas. Herron Esqre   Edgar A Poe

> In connection with this letter, see Letter 135 and note. The letter just cited and the present one, with the two from Herron, are the only known items in the Poe–Herron correspondence. [CL 376]

139 ⇥ TO DANIEL BRYAN

Philadelphia, July 6. 1842.

My Dear Sir,

Upon my return from a brief visit to New-York, a day or two since, I found your kind and welcome letter of June 27.

What you say in respect to "verses" enclosed to myself has occasioned me some surprise. I have certainly received none. My connexion with "Graham's Magazine" ceased with the May number, which was completed by the 1ʳˢᵗ of April — since which period the editorial conduct of the journal has rested with Mr Griswold. You observe that the poem was sent about three weeks since. Can it be possible that the present editors have thought it proper to open letters addressed to myself, because addressed to myself as "Editor of Graham's Magazine"? I know not how to escape from this conclusion; and now distinctly remember that, although in the habit of receiving many letters daily, before quitting the office, I have not received more than a half dozen during the whole period since elapsed; and none of those received were addressed to me as "Editor of G's Magazine". What to say or do in a case like this I really do not know. I have no quarrel with either Mr Graham or Mr Griswold — although I hold neither in especial respect. I have much aversion to communicate with them in any way, and, perhaps, it would be best that you should address them yourself, demanding the MS.

Many thanks for your kind wishes. I hope the time is not far distant when they may be realized. I am making earnest although *secret* exertions to resume my project of the "Penn Magazine", and have every confidence that I shall succeed in issuing the first number on the first of January. [*page 2*] You may remember that it was my original design to issue it on the first of January 1841. I was induced to abandon the project at that period by the representations of Mr Graham. He said that if I would join him as a salaried editor, giving up, for the time, my own scheme, he himself would unite with me at the expiration of 6 months, or certainly at the end of a year. As Mr G. was a man of capital and I had no money, I thought it most prudent to fall in with his views. The result has proved his want of faith and my own folly. In fact, I was continually laboring against myself. Every exertion made by myself for the benefit of "Graham", by rendering that Mag: a greater source of profit, rendered its owner, at the same time, less willing to keep his word with me. At the time of our bargain (a verbal one) he had 6000 subscribers — when I left him he had more than 40,000. It is no wonder that he has been tempted to leave me in the lurch.

I had nearly 1000 subscribers with which to have started the "Penn", and, with these as a beginning, it would have been my own fault had I failed. There may be still 3 or 4 hundred who will stand by me, of the old list, and, in the interval between this period and the first of January, I will use every endeavor to procure others. You are aware that, in my circumstances, a single name, *in advance,* is worth ten after the issue of the book; for it is upon my list of subscribers that I must depend for the bargain to be made with a partner possessing capital, or with a publisher. If, therefore, you can aid me in Alexandria, with even a single name, I shall feel deeply indebted to your friendship.

I feel that *now* is the time to strike. The delay, after all, will do me no injury. My conduct of "Graham" has rendered me better and (I hope) more favorably known than [*page 3*] before. I am anxious, above all things, to render the journal one in which the *true,* in contradistinction from the merely *factitious,* genius of the country shall be represented. I shall yield nothing to great names — nor to the circumstances of position. I shall make war to the knife against the New-England assumption of "all the decency and all the talent" which has been so disgustingly manifested in the Rev. Rufus W. Griswold's "Poets & Poetry of America". But I am boring you with my egotism.

May I hope to hear from you in reply?

I am with sincere respect & esteem,
Yr Ob^t Ser^t

Danl Bryan Esqre   Edgar A Poe.

P.S. I have not seen the "attack" to which you have [re-]ference. Could it have been in a Philadelphia paper[?]

> Daniel Bryan was postmaster at Alexandria, Virginia (see "Autography" for December 1841, reprinted in H, xv, 218). He wrote at least six letters to Poe (the three in addition to those given in the bibliographical section are: July 11 and 26, and August 4, 1842, original MSS. being in the Boston Public Library; no Bryan to Poe letter has been published). Poe wrote to Bryan on July 6 and apparently again between July 27 and August 3, for Bryan's letter of August 4 speaks of following Poe's suggestion that Bryan get his critique of Griswold's *Poets and Poetry of America* published through the aid of F. W. Thomas or Jesse E. Dow; no known letter by Poe, in MS. or print, gives this information. The whole correspondence, containing at least eight letters, seems to have lasted a little less than three months. Bryan on May 13, 1842, sent a poem, "The Crowning of the May Queen," for *Graham's;* he also spoke of not knowing Edgar Poe personally, but of having known Poe's "lamented Brother." The "verses"

sent to Poe "three weeks since" seem to have been another poem (see reference to Bryan's letter of June 27, above). Though 40,000 was probably high for *Graham's* list, the figure was advertised in the magazine for March 1842 (see Mott, *History of American Magazines*, I, 552). [CL 377]

140 ➤ TO DR. THOMAS H. CHIVERS

Philadelphia, July 6, 1842.

My Dear Sir:

I fear you will have accused me of disrespect in not replying to either of your three last letters; but, if so, you will have wronged me. Among all my correspondents there is *not one* whose good opinion I am more anxious to retain than your own. A world of perplexing business has led me to postpone from day to day a duty which it is always a pleasure to perform.

Your two last letters I have now before me. In the first you spoke of my notice of yourself in the autograph article. The paper had scarcely gone to press before I saw and acknowledged to myself the injustice I had done you — an injustice which it is my full purpose to repair at the first opportunity. What I said of your grammatical errors arose from some imperfect recollections of one or two poems sent to the first volume of the *Southern Literary Messenger*. But in more important respects I now deeply feel that I have wronged you by a hasty opinion. You will not suppose me insincere in saying that I look upon some of your late pieces as the finest I have *ever read*. I allude especially to your poem about Shelley, and the one of which the *refrain* is, "She came from Heaven to tell me she was blest." Upon reading these compositions I felt the necessity of our being friends. Will you accept my proffer of friendship?

Your last favor is dated June 11, and, in writing it, you were doubtless unaware of my having resigned the editorial charge of *Graham's Magazine*. What disposition shall I make of the "Invocation to Spring?" The other pieces are in the hands of my successor, Mr. Griswold.

It is my intention now to resume the project of the *Penn Magazine*. I had made every preparation for the issue of the first number in January, 1841, but relinquished the design at Mr. Graham's representation of joining me in July, provided I would edit his magazine in the meantime. In July he put me off until January, and in January until July again. He now finally declines, and I am resolved to push forward for myself. I believe I have many warm friends, especially in the South and West, and were the journal fairly before the public I have no doubt of ultimate success. Is it possible that you could afford me any aid, in the way of subscribers, among your friends in Middletown?

As I have no money myself, it will be absolutely necessary that I procure a partner who has some pecuniary means. I mention this to you, for it is not impossible that you yourself may have both the will and the ability to join me. The first number will not appear until January, so that I shall have time to look about me.

With sincere respect and esteem, yours,

Edgar A. Poe.

At the time of his correspondence with Poe, Dr. Thomas Holley Chivers lived at Oaky Grove, Georgia, but made frequent visits in the North. Though he graduated in medicine, he professed himself a poet and gained a modicum of distinction; his last volume of verse, *The Lost Pleiad* (1845), was called "monotonous" by the Charleston (South Carolina) *Southern Patriot*, which, in general, damned the book with faint praise (August 7, 1845, p. 2, col. 2). He often charged that Poe borrowed ideas and metrical effects from his poetry. At one time, Chivers encouraged Poe to settle in the South, even to come and live with him in Washington, Georgia, where he went from Oaky Grove. When Poe died, he planned to write a life of his "hero," but the work was never completed (for fuller account of Dr. Chivers, see W, II, 376–390). The Poe–Chivers correspondence numbers at least 36 letters, 10 of which are by Poe; only 8 of Poe's and 11 of Chivers' are extant.

This is the earliest Poe to Chivers letter extant. Chivers' letter of August 27, 1840, says, "I received your letter this evening . . ." This, Poe's first known letter to Chivers, contained a prospectus of the *Penn*, in fact, was probably written on the verso (see other Poe letters in August 1840). Though no definite date for the first letter is possible, it was probably about August 20, the prospectus sent being the revision of the June one. On the envelope of the present letter, addressed to Dr. Thomas Holley Chivers, Middletown, Connecticut, was the following note, according to James Grant Wilson: "The 'grammatical errors' to which Poe alludes here is the want of s in a verse in the poem entitled 'Song to Isa Singing,' as follows: 'The song which none can know,' etc. Song ought to have been written songs, evidently a mistake in copying. The poem was published in the *Broadway Journal*. In the original it's 'Sweet songs.' " Chivers was an early devotee of

Shelley; as Woodberry (II, 381) put it, "Chivers was one of the first of Americans to be 'Shelley-mad.'" Poe left *Graham's* in April 1842. Chivers seems to have got four subscribers among his Middletown friends (see Letter 145). [CL 378]

141 ⊁ TO ELIZABETH R. TUTT

[Philadelphia] July 7, 1842

. . . My dear little wife grew much better from the very first day after taking the Jew's Beer. It seemed to have the most instantaneous and miraculous effect. . . . About ten days ago, however, I was obliged to go on to New York on business . . . she began to fret . . . because she did not hear from me twice a day. . . . What it is to be pestered with a wife! . . . I have resigned the editorship of "Graham's Magazine" . . . .

[No signature]

Mrs. Elizabeth Rebecca Tutt, wife of Andrew Turner Tutt, was Poe's cousin, the former Elizabeth Rebecca Herring, of Baltimore (see Campbell, *Poems*, p. 297). She apparently continued to aid the Poe family until Virginia's death, for a letter from Mrs. Clemm (February, 1847 (?), in the Ingram collection, University of Virginia) thanks "you for your timely aid my dear Mrs. T . . . Eddie has quite set his heart upon the wine going back to you . . . for the sick artist you mentioned." To Virginia, says Mrs. Clemm, "the wine was a great blessing while she needed it . . . We look for you on a train earlier tomorrow . . . Mr. C. [H. D. Chapin (?)] will tell you of our condition, as he is going to call for this note in an hours time." Mrs. Tutt seems to have been living in New York at the time of Mrs. Clemm's letter; but when Poe wrote the above letter, according to the catalogue, she was living in Woodville, Rappahannock County, Virginia. For Poe's visit to New York, see Letter 138. The present letter suggests lost letters from Poe to Virginia Poe. For Virginia's illness, see Letters 132 and 135, and notes. [CL 379]

142 ⊁ TO FREDERICK W. THOMAS

Philadelphia, August 27, '42.

My Dear Thomas,

How happens it that I have received not a line from you for these four months? What in the world is the matter? I write to see if you are still in the land of the living, or have gone your way to the "land o' the leal."

I wrote a few words to you, about two months since, from New York, at the importunate demand of W. Wallace, in which you were requested to use your influence, &c. He overlooked me while I wrote, & therefore I could not speak of private matters. I presume you gave the point as much consideration as it demanded, & no more.

What have you been doing for so long a time? I am anxious to learn how you succeed in Washington. I suppose Congress will have adjourned by the time you get this. Since I heard from you I have had a reiteration of the promise, about the Custom-House appointment, from Rob Tyler. A friend of mine, Mr. Jas. Herron, having heard from me casually, that I had some hope of an appointment, called upon R. T., who assured him that I should *certainly* have it & desired him so to inform me. I have, also, paid my respects to Gen. J. W. Tyson, the leader of the T. party in the city, who seems especially well disposed — but, notwithstanding *all this*, I have my doubts. A few days will end them. If I do not get the office, I am just where I started. Nothing more can be done to secure it than has been already done. Literature is at a sad discount. There is really nothing to be done in this way. Without an international copyright law, American authors may as well cut their throats. A good magazine, of the true stamp, would do wonders in the way of a general revivification of letters, or the law. We must have — both if possible.

What has become of Dow? Do you ever see him?

Write immediately & tell me the Washington news.

My poor little wife still continues ill. I have scarcely a faint hope of her recovery.

Remember us all to your friends & believe me your true friend,

F. W. Thomas, Esq.   Edgar A. Poe.

> William Ross Wallace was a New York poet. For Poe's "casual" remark to Herron, see Letter 135, and for Herron's interview with Robert Tyler, see Letter 138. Jesse E. Dow is frequently mentioned in the Poe–Thomas correspondence. For the beginning of Virginia's illness, in January, see Letter 132. [CL 386]

143 ➤ TO FREDERICK W. THOMAS

Philadelphia, Sep. 12 1842

My Dear Thomas,

I did not receive yours of the 2ᵈ until yesterday — why God only knows, as I either went or sent every-day to the P. Office. Neither have I seen Mr Beard, who, I presume, had some difficulty in finding my residence: since you were here I have moved out in the neighborhood of Fairmount. I have often heard of Beard, from friends who knew him personally, and should have been glad to make his acquaintance.

A thousand sincere thanks for your kind offices in the matter of the appointment. So far, nothing has been done here in the way of *reform*. Thos. S. Smith is to have the Collectorship, but it appears has not yet received his commission — a fact which occasions much surprise among the quid-nuncs.

Should I obtain the office — and of course I can no longer doubt that I shall obtain it — I shall feel that to you alone I am indebted. You have shown yourself a true friend, and I am not likely to forget it, however impotent I may be, now or hereafter, to reciprocate your many kindnesses. I would give the world to clasp you by the hand & assure you, personally, of my gratitude. I hope it will not be long before we meet.

In the event of getting the place, I am undetermined what *literary* course to pursue. Much will depend upon the salary.

Graham has made me a good offer to return. He is not [*page 2*] especially pleased with Griswold — nor is any one else, with the exception of the Rev. gentleman himself, who has gotten himself into quite a hornet's nest, by his "Poets & Poetry". It appears you gave him personal offence by *delay* in replying to his demand for information touching Mr⁵ Welby, I believe, or somebody else. Hence his omission of you in the body of the book; for he had prepared quite a long article from my MS. and had selected several pages for quotation. He is a pretty fellow to set himself up as an *honest* judge, or even as a capable one. — About two months since, we were talking about the book, when I said that I had thought of reviewing it in full for the "Democratic Review", but found my design anticipated by an article from that ass O'Sullivan, and that I knew no other work in which a notice would be readily admissible. Griswold said, in reply — "You need not trouble yourself about the publication of the review, should you decide upon writing it; for I will attend to all that. I will get it in some reputable work, and look to it for the usual pay; in the meantime handing you whatever your charge would be". This, you see, was an ingenious insinuation of a *bribe* to puff his book. I accepted his offer forthwith, wrote the review, handed it to him and received from him the compensation: — he never daring to look over the M.S. in my presence, and taking it for granted that all was right. But that review has not yet appeared, and I am doubtful if it ever will. I wrote it precisely as I would have written under ordinary circumstances; and be sure there was no predominance of praise.

Should I go back to Graham I will endeavor to bring about [*page 3*] some improvements in the general appearance of the Magazine, & above all, to get rid of the quackery which now infects it.

If I do *not* get the app^t I should not be surprised if I joined Foster in the establishment of a Mag: in New-York. He has made me an offer to join him. I suppose you know that he now edits the "Aurora".

Touching your poem. Should you publish it, Boston offers the best facilities — but I feel sure that you will get no publisher to print it, except on your own account. Reason — Copy-Right Laws. However, were I in your place, and could contrive it in *any* way, I would print it at my own expense — of course without reference to emolument, which is not to be hoped. It would make only a small volume, & the cost of publishing it even in such style as Hoffman's last poems, could not be much, absolutely. It should be handsomely printed or not at all.

When is Rob. Tyler to issue his promised poem?

Have you seen how Benjamin & Tasistro have been playing Kilkenny cats with each other? I have always told Graham that Tasistro stole every thing, worth reading, which he offered for sale.

What is it about Ingraham? He has done for himself, in the opinion of all honest men, by his chicaneries.

I am happy to say that Virginia's health has slightly improved. My spirits are proportionately good. Perhaps all will yet go well. Write soon & believe me ever your true friend

Edgar A Poe

For Poe's change of residence, see Quinn, *Poe*, pp. 273–274. Thomas visited Philadelphia and Poe during the week in which the present letter was written (see Thomas' endorsement in Note 143 and Letter 144). Rufus W. Griswold succeeded Poe as an editor of *Graham's*. For the Poe MS., based on Thomas' autobiographical notes, designed for Griswold's use in *Poets and Poetry of America*, see Letter 124 and note. Poe's review of Griswold's second edition of the *Poets and Poetry of America* (1842) was printed in the *Boston Miscellany*, ΙΙ (November 1842), 218–221; on the whole it was a very favorable review, contain-

of its proprietor which hampered & controlled me at all points, I ~~obtained~~ in 15 months. increased the circulation in 15 months to 5.500. subscribers. ~~this number after journal~~ ~~had, when I left it.~~ when I left it. This number was never ~~sur~~exceeded by the journal which rapidly went down & ~~is~~ may now be said to be extinct. Of "Graham's Magazine" you have no doubt heard. It had been in existence under the name of the "Casket" for 8 years, when I became its editor. ~~with a subscription list of about 5000~~ On about 18 months afterward its circulation amounted to no less than 50.000 — astonishing as this may appear. ~~At this period I left it.~~ ~~as~~ It is now 2 years since, and the number of subscribers is now not more than 25.000. — but possibly very much less. In 3 years it will be extinct. The nature of this journal, however, was such, that even its 50. 000 subscribers could not make it a very profitable to its proprietors. Its price was $3 — but not only were its expenses immense owing to the employment of abound ~~that~~ steelplates ~~but recourse was had~~ ~~& other extravagances which tell not at all~~ to innumerable agents who recd it — at a discount of ~~50~~ per cent & whose dishonesty — occasional ~~no less than~~ ~~morning~~ ~~frequent~~ ~~for a 3/6 Maga-~~ great loss. Thus, if 50.000 can be obtained among a class of readers who really read little, why may not 50.000. be procured ~~for a 3/ journal~~ among the true and permanents readers of the land? Astor House ~~found~~

Holding steadily in view my ultimate purpose — to establish a Magazine of my own, or in which at least I might have a proprietary right, — it has been my constant endeavour ~~in the meantime~~ not so much to establish a reputation great in itself as ~~of it~~ one of that particular character which should best further my ~~secret~~ objects, and draw attention to my exertions as Editor of a ~~oo~~ Magazine ~~&~~ I have ~~thus~~ written no books and ~~have been~~ ~~& been~~ so far essentially a Magazinist. — ~~aoe'oe~~ That ~~a o-oe~~ / ~~8~~ That

Courtesy of the Henry E. Huntington Library

POE TO G. ANTHON, ANTE 2 NOVEMBER 1844 (page 5)
(Letter 186)

POE, SELF-PORTRAIT, PROBABLY ABOUT 1845

ing such a passage as: "We know of no one in America who could, or *who would*, have performed the task here undertaken, at once so well in accordance with the judgment of the critical, and so much to the satisfaction of the public . . . We are proud to find [in general] his decisions our own [as to critical estimates]." Still, Poe objected to certain of Griswold's evaluations and omissions (see H, XI, 147–156, for reprint of the article). Griswold, it seems, paid Poe for the review in advance, promised the article to Bradbury and Soden, publishers of the *Miscellany*, then found himself committed to send it on when Poe completed it. (A passage from Griswold's letter to James T. Fields, August 12, 1842, supplied by Thomas O. Mabbott, reads: "I have sent today the article by Poe about my book to Bradbury & Soden for the magazine, with a request that if it be not acceptable they will return it to you. I thought it likely the name of Poe — gratuitously furnished — might be of some consequence, though I care not a fig about the publication of the criticism as the author and myself not being on the best terms, it is not decidedly as favorable as it might have been. Will you see to it though"; original MS. in Harvard College Library.) There is, therefore, a possibility that Poe's adverse comments were "edited" in part. Thus Poe writing a rather fair review accepted Griswold's money but knew that the notice would not please him fully and that the review would probably not find publication. The name of Poe and the gratuitous article may account for the printing, even against Griswold's hope that the review would be suppressed. Poe probably refers to George G. Foster, later editor of *Yankee Doodle* and *John-Donkey*, but nothing came of the offer here alluded to. Thomas' poem was probably *The Beechen Tree*, finally published in the fall of 1844. Park Benjamin, at this time, was an editor of the *New World*, and Count L. Fitzgerald Tasistro, a contributor to periodicals of the day. For other comments on Joseph H. Ingraham, see Letter 117, and "Autography," *Graham's*, November 1841 (reprinted in H, xv, 188). [CL 388]

144 ➤ TO FREDERICK W. THOMAS

Philadelphia, Sep. [21] 1842.

My Dear Thomas,

I am afraid you will think that I keep my promises but indifferently well, since I failed to make my appearance at Congress Hall on Sunday, and I now, therefore, write to apologise. The will to be with you was not wanting — but, upon reaching home on Saturday night, I was taken with a severe chill and fever — the latter keeping me company all next day. I found myself too ill to venture out, but, nevertheless, would have done so had I been able to obtain the consent of all parties. As it was I was quite in a quandary, for we keep no servant and no messenger could be procured in the neighbourhood. I contented myself with the reflection that you would not think it necessary to wait for me very long after 9 o'clock, and that you were not quite as implacable in your resentments as myself. I was much in hope that you would have made your way out in the afternoon. Virginia & Mr⁸ C. were much grieved at not being able to bid you farewell.

I perceive by Du Solle's paper that you saw him. He announced your presence in the city on Sunday, in very handsome terms.

I am about going on a pilgrimage, this morning [*page 2*] to hunt up a copy of "Clinton Bradshaw" & will send it to you as soon as procured.

Excuse the brevity of this letter, for I am still very unwell, & believe me most gratefully & sincerely your friend,

F, W, Thomas. Esqʳ   Edgar A. Poe

> Poe's apology suggests a letter from Thomas announcing his proposed
> visit to Philadelphia and making an appointment with Poe; but the letter
> is unlocated and otherwise unknown. Du Solle's "paper" was the *Spirit
> of the Times. Clinton Bradshaw* (1835) was Thomas' first novel.
> [CL 391]

145 ⤳ TO DR. THOMAS H. CHIVERS

Philadelphia Sep. 27. 1842.

My Dear Sir,

Through some accident, I did not receive your letter of the 15ᵗʰ inst: until this morning, and now hasten to reply.

Allow me, in the first place, to thank you sincerely for your kindness in procuring me the subscribers to the Penn Magazine. The four names sent will aid me most materially in this early stage of the proceedings.

As yet I have taken no overt step in the measure, and have not even printed a Prospectus. As soon as I do this I will send you several. I do not wish to announce my positive resumption of the original scheme until about the middle of October. Before that period I have reason to believe that I shall have received an appointment in the Philadelphia Custom House, which will afford me a good salary and leave the greater portion of my time unemployed. With this appointment to fall back upon, as a certain resource, I shall be enabled to start the Magazine without difficulty, provided I can make an arrangement with either a practical printer possessing a small office, or some one not a printer, with about $1000 at command. (over[ )]

[*page 2*] It would, of course, be better for the permanent influence and success of the journal that I unite myself with a gentleman of education & similarity of thought and feeling. It was this consciousness which induced me to suggest the enterprise to yourself. I know no one with whom I would more readily enter into association than yourself.

I am not aware what are your political views. My own have reference to no one of the present parties; but it has been hinted to me that I will receive the most effectual patronage from Government, for a journal which will admit occasional papers in support of the Administration. For Mr Tyler personally, & as an honest statesman, I have the highest respect. Of the government patronage, upon the condition specified, *I am assured* and this alone will more than sustain the Magazine.

The only real difficulty lies in the beginning — in the pecuniary means for getting out the two (or three) first numbers; after this all is sure, and a great triumph may, and indeed *will* be achieved. If you can command about $1000 and say that you will join me, I will write you fully as respects the details of the plan, or we can have an immediate interview.

It would be proper to start with an edition of 1000 copies. For this number, the monthly expense, including paper (of the finest quality) composition, press-work & stitching will be about 180$. I calculate *all* expenses at about $250 — which is $3000 per annum — a *very* [*page 3*] liberal estimate. 1000 copies at $5 = 5000$ — leaving a nett profit of 2000$, even supposing we have only 1000 subscribers. But I am sure of *beginning* with at least 500, and make no doubt of obtaining 5000 before the expiration of the 2ᵈ year. A Magazine, such as I propose, with 5000 subscribers will produce us each an income of some $10,000; and this you will acknowledge is a game worth playing. At the same time there is no earthly reason why such a Magazine may not, eventually, reach a circulation as great as that of "Graham's" at present — viz 50,000.

I repeat that it would give me the most sincere pleasure if you would make up your mind to join me. I am sure of our community of thought & feeling, and that we would accomplish *much*.

In regard to the poem on Harrison's death, I regret to [say] that nothing can be done with the Philadelphia publishers. The truth is that the higher order of poetry is, and always will be, in this country, unsaleable; but, even were it otherwise, the present state of the Copy-Right Laws will not warrant any publisher, in *purchasing* an American book. The only condition, I am afraid, upon which the poem can be printed, is that you print at your own expense.

I will see Griswold and endeavour to get the smaller poems from him. A precious fellow is he!

Write as soon as you receive this & believe me

Yours most truly

Edgar A Poe

Chivers' autograph notes at the end of the letter show that "the poem on Harrison's death" referred to his "The Mighty Dead"; and regarding the poems held by Griswold, Chivers noted: "Alluding to his not having returned the poem, — although requested so often — which he never did." In Chivers' letter of July 12, 1842 (H, XVII, 115-117), Chivers said he would try to get subscribers to the *Penn*, promised to send on his poem "The Mighty Dead," and asked Poe to hand Graham the "Invocation to Spring," the poem that Griswold failed to return. Poe failed to get the appointment to the Custom House. Though nothing ever came of Poe's suggestion that Chivers join him in publishing a magazine, Chivers wrote Poe, June 15, 1844, that upon coming into his inheritance he would like to become Poe's partner. [CL 394]

146 ➤ TO JOHN TOMLIN[?]

Philadelphia, Oct. 5, 1842.

My Dear Sir, —

I have just received your kind letter of the 21st ult., and hasten to reply.

It *is* my firm determination to commence the "Penn Magazine" on the first of January next. The difficulties which impeded me last year have vanished, and there will be now nothing to prevent success.

I am to receive an office in the Custom House in this city, which will leave me the greater portion of my time unemployed, while, at the same time, it will afford me a good salary. With this to fall back upon as a certain resource until the Magazine is fairly afloat, all must go well. After the elections here (2d Tuesday in this month,) I will issue my new prospectuses and set to work in good earnest. As soon as printed, I will send you some. In the meantime, may I ask you to do what you can for me? Every new name, in the *beginning* of the enterprise, is worth five afterwards. My list of subscribers is getting to be quite respectable, although, as yet, I have positively taken no overt steps to procure names.

It is my firm intention to get up such a journal as *this* country, at least, has never yet seen.

Truly your friend

Edgar A Poe

In connection with this letter, referring to Poe's expectation of the customs house appointment, see Letter 148. [CL 396]

147 ≻ TO JAMES R. LOWELL

Dr Sir,

Learning your design of commencing a Magazine, in Boston, upon the first of January next, I take the liberty of asking whether some arrangement might not be made, by which I should become a regular contributor.

I should be glad to furnish a short article each month — of such character as might be suggested by yourself — and upon such terms as you could afford "in the beginning".

That your success will be marked and permanent I will not doubt. At all events, I most sincerely wish you well; for no man in America has excited in me so much of admiration — and, therefore, none so much of respect and esteem — as the author of "Rosaline".

May I hope to hear from you at your leisure? In the meantime, believe me,

Most Cordially yours

James Russell Lowell Esqre   Edgar Allan Poe

Philadelphia Novem: 16. 1842.

Lowell and Robert Carter were about to publish the *Pioneer*. It was launched with great hopes and commendable standards, but lived for only three numbers, and when it died left Lowell heavily in debt. Poe contributed to each number (see subsequent letters). [CL 398]

Philadelphia Nov. 19.   42

My Dear Friend

Your letter of the 14ᵗʰ gave me new hope — only to be dashed to the ground. On the day of its receipt some of the papers announced four removals and appointments. Among the latter I observed the name — Pogue. Upon inquiry among those behind the curtain, I soon found that no such person as — Pogue has any expectation of an appᵗ and that the name was a misprint or rather a misunderstanding of the reporters, who had heard *my own* name spoken of at the Custom-House. I waited 2 days, without calling on Mʳ Smith, as he had twice told me that "he would send for me, when he wished to swear me in." To-day, however, hearing nothing from him, I called. I asked him if he had no good news for me yet. He replied — "No, I am instructed to make no more removals." At this, being much astonished, I mentioned that I had heard, through a friend, from Mr. Rob. Tyler, that he was requested to appoint me. At these words he said [*page 2*] roughly, — "From *whom* did you say?" I replied from Mʳ Robert Tyler. I wish you could have seen the scoundrel — for scoundrel, my dear Thomas in your private ear, *he is* — "From *Robert* Tyler!" says he — "hem! I have received orders from *President* Tyler to make no more appᵗˢ and shall make none." Immediately afterward, he acknowledged that he *had* made one appᵗ *since* these instructions.

Mr. Smith has excited the thorough disgust of every Tyler man here. He is a Whig of the worst stamp and will appoint none but Whigs if he can possibly avoid it. People here laugh at the idea of his being a Tyler man. He is notoriously not such[.]

As for me, he has trialed me most shamefully. In my case, there was no need of any political shuffling or lying. I proffered my willingness to postpone my claims to those of political claimants, but he told me, upon my first interview after the Election, that if I would call on the fourth day he would swear me in. I called & he was not at home. On the next day I called again & saw him, when he told me that he would send a Messenger for me when ready: — this [*page 3*] without even inquiring my place of residence — showing that he had, from the first, no design of appointing me. Well, I waited nearly a month, when, finding nearly all the appts made, I again called. He did not even ask me to be seated — scarcely spoke — muttered the words "I will *send* for you Mr Poe" — and that was all. My next and last interview was to-day — as I have just described.

The whole *manner* of the man, from the first, convinced me that he would not appoint me if he could help it. Hence the uneasiness I expressed to you when here.

Now, my dear Thomas, this insult is not *to me,* so much as to your friend Mr. Robert Tyler, who was so kind as to promise, and who requested my appointment.

It seems to me that the only way to serve me *now,* is to lay the matter once again before Mr. T. and, if possible through him, to procure a few lines *from the President,* directing Mr. Smith to give me the place. With these credentials he would scarcely again refuse — But I leave all to your better judgment[.]

You can have no idea of the low ruffians and boobies — men, two, without a shadow of political [*page 4*] influence or *caste* — who have received office over my head. If Smith had the feelings of a gentleman, he would have perceived that from the very character of my claim — by which I mean my *want* of claim — he should have made my appt. an early one. It was a gratuitous favor intended me by Mr Rob Tyler — and he (Smith) has done *his* best to deprive this favor of all its grace, by delay[.] I could have forgiven all but the innumerable and altogether *unnecessary* falsehoods with which he insulted my common sense day after day —

I would write more, my dear Thomas, but my heart is too heavy. You have felt the misery of hope deferred & will feel for me.

Believe me ever your true friend

Edgar A Poe

Write soon & if possible relieve my suspense. You cannot imagine the trouble I am in, & have been in for the past 2 months — unable to enter into any literary arrangements — or in fact to do anything — being in hourly expectation of getting the place —

There is no extant proof that Thomas acted in Poe's behalf, upon receipt of this letter, but Thomas' letter of February 1, 1843 (see H, XVII, 128–129) implies that he did. No Thomas letter replying to the present one is known; however, it is very likely that he did write. [CL 399]

149 ⇢ TO JAMES R. LOWELL

[Philadelphia, December 25, 1842]

My Dear Friend

I send you a brief poem for No 2, with my very best wishes.

I duly received yours of the 19ᵗʰ and thank you for reversing the judgment of Mr Tuckerman — the author of the "Spirit of Poesy" — which, by the way, is somewhat of a misnomer — since no spirit appears.

Touching the "Miscellany" — had I known of Mr Tˢ accession, I should not have ventured to send an article. Should he, at any time, accept an effusion of mine, I should ask myself what twattle I had been perpetrating, so flat as to come within the scope of his approbation. He writes, through his publishers, — "if Mr Poe would condescend to furnish more quiet articles he would be a most desirable correspondent." All I have to say is that if Mr T. persists in his *quietude,* he will put a quietus to the Magazine of which Mess. Bradbury & Soden have been so stupid as to give him control.

I am all anxiety to see your first number. In the meantime, believe me

[*Rest of MS. cut off*]

Poe sent "Lenore"; it was printed in the *Pioneer,* February 1843. Henry T. Tuckerman (see "Autography," *Graham's,* December 1841, reprinted in H, xv, 217) succeeded Mrs. Sarah J. Hale as editor of the *Boston Miscellany* with the number for January 1843 (see the last issue for 1842). Lowell's getting "The Tell-Tale Heart" presents a problem. Lowell's letter to Poe, December 17, 1842, says the tale came from Tuckerman and "will appear in my first number." Apparently Poe sent the tale to Bradbury and Soden, publishers of the *Boston Miscellany;* Tuckerman, who assumed the editorship with the January number, refused to print it. Poe's present letter suggests the publishers or Tuckerman wrote to Poe (in an unlocated letter), early in December (the submission of the tale by Poe also suggests a letter to the publishers). The MS. still in the hands of the publishers, Poe probably wrote to them to give it to Lowell (such a letter is also unlocated); or if he wrote to Lowell to get the tale from Bradbury and Soden, the letter is unlocated. Thus the history of the tale, at this time, suggests several lost letters. [CL 407]

150 ⊁ TO JAMES RUSSELL LOWELL

[Philadelphia]

My dear Sir,

If not too late, I would be glad to substitute the lines here given, for what I sent you some days since.

Should the long line "To friends above &c" not come conveniently within the breadth of the page, it may be made to commence farther to the left, so as to correspond with "But waft the angel &c"

Most truly yours,

James Russell Lowell Esqre   Edgar A Poe
Dec 27, 42

> In his letter of December 25 (?), 1842, Poe had sent Lowell "a brief poem ["Lenore"] for No 2" of the *Pioneer*, the February issue; the lines here referred to appear in the fourth stanza of the poem at that time. Lowell printed the poem with short lines, spreading it over two pages (see Quinn, *Poe*, p. 365). [CL 408]

151 ⊁ TO JAMES R. LOWELL

Philadelphia February 4 1843.

My Dear Mr Lowell,

For some weeks I have been daily proposing to write and congratulate you upon the triumphant début of the "Pioneer", but have been prevented by a crowd of more worldly concerns.

Thank you for the compliment in the footnote. Thank you, also, for your attention in forwarding the Magazine.

As far as a $3 Magazine can please me at all, I am delighted with yours. I am especially gratified with what seems to me a certain coincidence of opinion & of taste, between yourself and your humble servant, in the minor arrangements, as well as in the more important details of the journal. For example — the poetry in the same type as the prose — the designs from Flaxman — &c. As regards the contributors our thoughts are one. Do you know that when, some time since, I dreamed of establishing a Magazine of my own, I said

to myself — "If I can but succeed in engaging, as permanent contributors, Mʳ Hawthorne, Mʳ Neal, and two others, with a certain
young poet of Boston, who shall be nameless, I will engage to produce the best journal in Ame- [*page 2*] rica." At the same time,
while I thought and still think highly of Mʳ Bryant, Mʳ Cooper, and
others, I said nothing of *them*.

You have many warm friends in this city — but the reforms you
propose require time in their development, and it may be even a year
before "The Pioneer" will make due impression among the Quakers.
In the meantime, persevere.

I forwarded you, about a fortnight ago I believe, by Harnden's
Express, an article called "Notes upon English Verse". A thought has
struck me, that it may prove too long, or perhaps too dull, for your
Magazine — in either case, use no ceremony, but return it in the same
mode (thro' Harnden) and I will, forthwith, send something in its
place.

I duly received, from Mʳ Graham, $10 on your account, for which
I am obliged. I would prefer, however, that you would remit directly
to myself through the P. Office.

I saw, not long ago, at Graham's, a poem without the author's
name — but which for many reasons I take to be yours — the chief
being that it was *very* beautiful. Its title I forget — but it slightly
veiled a lovely Allegory in which "Religion" was typified, and the
whole painted the voyage of some wanderers & mourners in search of
some far-off isle. Is it yours?

Truly your friend

E A Poe

The *Pioneer*, edited by Lowell and Robert Carter, later an editor of
Appleton's Journal, appeared in January 1843, and received many commendations from the press. The prospectus read in part: "The object
of the Subscribers in establishing the *Pioneer*, is to furnish the intelligent and reflecting portion of the Reading Public with a rational substitute for the enormous quantity of thrice-diluted trash, in the shape
of namby-pamby love tales and sketches, which is monthly poured
out to them by many of our popular magazines . . . Each number will
contain 48 pages, royal octavo, double columns, handsomely printed on
fine paper, and will be illustrated with Engravings of the highest character, both on wood and steel. Terms: Three Dollars a year" (see Mott,
History of American Magazines, I, 735–736). "Notes on English

Verse" (later the "Rationale of Verse") was published in the March issue. Lowell, in his letter of November 19, 1842, had promised Poe $10 at first for each article; thus the ten dollars here referred to was in payment for "The Tell-Tale Heart," printed in the January *Pioneer*. [CL 412]

152 ⊁ TO ROBERT CARTER

[Philadelphia, February 16, 1843]

My Dear Sir,

I send you the above trifle, in hope that I may be in time for your fourth number.

What you tell me about Mr Lowell's health, grieves me most sincerely — but we will hope for the best. Diseases of an opthalmic character, are, by no means, so intractable now, as they were a few years ago. When you write, remember me kindly to him.

When you have leisure, it will give me great pleasure to hear from you at all times. With the warmest wishes for your success, I am, dear Sir,

Yrs truly,

R. Carter Esqr   Edgar A Poe.

This is the first of two known letters from Poe to Carter, who with Lowell edited the *Pioneer's* three numbers, January–March 1843; the fourth number was not issued. However, Carter is known to have written Poe at least three letters: *ante* February 16, 1843 (unlocated), June 19, 1843 (MS. unlocated; printed in H, XVII, 146–148), and September 14–October 18, 1843 (unlocated; but see Letter 164). The version of "Eulalie" accompanying the present letter (see Note 152) antedates by more than two years the first printed form in the *American Whig Review*, July 1845 (see Campbell, *Poems of Edgar Allan Poe*, pp. 114, 259; also Quinn, *Poe*, pp. 381–382). [CL 415]

153 ⊁ TO FREDERICK W. THOMAS

Philadelphia, Feb. 25, 1843.

My Dear Thomas,

Herewith I forward a "Saturday Museum" containing a Biography and caricature, both of myself. I am ugly enough God knows, but not *quite* so bad as that. The biographer is H. W. Hirst, of this city.

I put into his hands your package, as returned, and he has taken the liberty of stating his indebtedness for memoranda to yourself — a slight extension of the truth for which I pray you to excuse him. He is a warm friend of yours by the bye — and a warm friend is a matter of moment at all times <,> but especially in this age of luke-warmness. *I* have also been guilty of an indiscretion in quoting from a private letter of yours to myself — I could not forego the tempta-tion of letting the world know how well you thought of me.

On the outside of the paper you will see a Prospectus of "The Stylus" — my old "Penn" revived & remodelled under better auspices. I am anxious to hear your opinion of it. I have managed, *at last*, to secure, I think, the great object — a partner possessing ample capital, and, at the same time, so little self-esteem, as to allow me entire control of the editorial conduct. He gives me, also, a half inter-est, and is to furnish funds for all the business operations — I agreeing to supply, for the first year, the literary matter. This will puzzle me no little, but I must do my best — write as much as pos-sible myself, under my own name and pseudonyms, and hope for the casual aid of my friends, until the first stage of infancy is surpassed.

The articles of copartnership have been signed & sealed for some weeks, and I should have written you before, informing you of my good luck, but that I was in hope of sending you, at the same time, a specimen-sheet. Some little delay has occurred in getting it out, on account of paper. In the meantime all arrangements are progress-ing with spirit. We *shall* make the most magnificent Magazine as regards externals, ever seen. The finest paper, bold type, in single column, and superb wood-engravings (in the manner of the French illustrated [*page 2*] edition of "Gil Blas" by Gigoux, or "Robinson Crusoe" by Grandville.

There are 3 objects I would give a great deal to accomplish. Of the first I have some hope — but of the 2 last exceedingly little, unless you aid me. In the first place, I wish an article from yourself for my opening number — in the second, one from Mr Rob. Tyler — in the 3^d one from Judge Upshur. If I could get all this, I should be made — but I despair. Judge Upshur wrote some things for "The Messenger" during my editorship, and if I could get him interested in the scheme he *might*, by good management, be induced to give me an article, I care not how brief, or on what subject, *with his name*. It would be worth to me at least $500, and give me *caste* at once. I think him

<both> as a reasoner, as a speaker, and as a writer, absolutely unsurpassed. I have the *very highest* opinion of his abilities. There is no man in America from whom I so strongly covet an article. Is it procurable?

In a few weeks, at farthest, I hope to take you by the hand. In the meantime write & let me know how you come on.

About a week since I enclosed an introductory letter to yourself in one to a friend of mine (Professor Wyatt) now in Washington. I presume you have seen him. He is much of a gentleman & I think you will be pleased with him. Virginia & Mrs Clemm beg to be remembered.

Truly your friend,

F. W. Thomas Esqre   Edgar A Poe

P.S. Smith not rejected yet! — Ah, if I could only get the Inspectorship, or something similar, *now* — how completely it would put me out of all difficulty.

> The *Saturday Museum* of February 25, 1843, carried the biographical sketch of Poe, done by Hirst with the aid of Poe's own notes formerly sent to Thomas but returned. The prospectus of the *Stylus* is reprinted in Quinn, *Poe,* pp. 375–376; the partner was Thomas C. Clarke, and the magazine was to appear July 1, 1843. The articles of partnership were signed January 31, 1843 (see Quinn, *Poe,* p. 369). Judge Abel Parker Upshur wrote several articles for the SLM, but only one, a review of *The Partisan Leader,* January 1837 (III, 73–89), unsigned but identified by B. B. Minor (*Southern Literary Messenger,* p. 63), can be said to have been contributed during Poe's editorship. For Professor Thomas Wyatt, see Letter 249. Concerning Smith, see Letter 148. [CL 418]

153a ≻ TO ROBERT CARTER

Philadelphia
March 7, 1843.

My Dear Sir,

Could you do me a *very* great favor? I am obliged to go on to Washington on Saturday morning — this is Tuesday — and am in sad need of means. I believe there is due me from "The Pioneer" $30, and if you could, by any management, send me the amount so as to

reach me, here, by that period, I would feel myself under deep obligation. If you cannot spare 30$ I would be exceedingly glad of $20.

Your fourth — or rather your third number, has not yet reached
this city — although I see it is out in N. York. I am anxious to
get it.

I sincerely hope that Mr Lowell is recovering. When you write
remember me kindly.

In great haste.
Yours truly

R. Carter Esqre Edgar A Poe

Apparently Carter did not reply to this letter, but Lowell did though
he was unable to send the money due Poe (see Lowell's letter to Poe,
March 24, 1843, in H, xvii, 138–139). In connection with this letter,
see Letter 152 and note. For some reason Poe changed his plans and
arrived in Washington before Saturday (see Letter 154 and note).
[CL 419a]

154 ⇥ TO JOHN KIRK TOWNSEND

Fuller's Hotel [Washington]
Thursday Morning, March 9, '43

Dr. Sir,

I have the honor to inclose two letters and the bearer will deliver
a case containing an air gun. In a day or two I will do myself the
pleasure of calling,

With High Respect yr. ob. s^t

Edgar A. Poe.

Poe's friend, F. W. Thomas, lived at Fuller's Hotel. Sometime, early in
March, Poe went to Washington (see Letter 155 and note). Poe's
friend, Jesse E. Dow, wrote to Thomas C. Clarke, March 12, that Poe
had arrived in Washington "a few days ago"; the text of Dow's letter
seems to indicate that Poe was there before March 9, 1843 (see Quinn,
Poe, p. 378). Thus the date and place of the letter appear genuine.
John Kirk Townsend (1809–1851) was a Philadelphia ornithologist;
he was in Washington from 1842–1845 "engaged in securing and
mounting birds for the National Museum, with its collections housed
in the Patent Office (see the *Dictionary of American Biography*, xviii,
618). In 1839 he had written "Narrative of a Journey across the Rocky

Mountains"; in *Burton's*, January–June 1840, Poe published his "The Journal of Julius Rodman, being an account of the first passage across the Rocky Mountains." If the letter to Townsend is genuine, it may contain a humorous reference to the earlier work. [CL 420]

155 ➤ TO THOMAS C. CLARKE

Washington — March 11. 1843.

My Dear Sir,

I write merely to inform you of my will-doing — for, so far, I have done nothing. My friend Thomas, upon whom I depended, is sick. I suppose he will be well in a few days. In the meantime, I shall have to do the best I can. I have not seen the President yet.

My expenses were more than I thought they would be, although I have economised in every respect, and this *delay* (<Thomas'>) being sick) puts me out sadly. *However* all is going right. I have got the subscriptions of *all* the Departments — President, [*illegible*] &c[.] I believe that I am making a *sensation* which will tend to the benefit of the Magazine.

Day [after] to-morrow I am to lecture.

Rob. Tyler is to give me an article — also Upsher.

Send me $10 by mail, as soon as you get this. I am grieved to ask you <ask you> for money, in this way. — but you will find your account in it — twice over.

Very truely yours

Thos. C. Clarke Esqre   Edgar A Poe.

Poe was in Washington not only to seek a government position, but to solicit subscriptions for the *Stylus*, scheduled to appear in July 1843 (see Letter 157), with Poe as editor and Clarke as co-publisher (see *Saturday Museum*, March 4, 1843, p. 3; reprinted in Quinn, *Poe*, pp. 375–376). On February 8, 1843, F. W. Thomas wrote Poe that illness prevented his presenting Poe to President John Tyler, but sent Poe a letter of introduction to the President's son, Robert, who already knew of Poe through Thomas and through Poe's favorable criticism of a poem he had written (see Thomas to Poe, February 26, 1842, original in Boston Public Library; printed in H, XVII, 105–106, under the wrong date. For the February 8, 1843, letter, *supra*, see Quinn, *Poe*, p. 377, where the date and location — Boston Public Library — only are given). Poe in a letter to F. W. Thomas, February 25, stated he wanted an article from Thomas, from Robert Tyler, and from Judge Abel Parker Upshur (then Secretary of the Navy) for the first issue of the *Stylus*. According to Quinn (*Poe,* p. 378), the lecture was never delivered. [CL 421]

156 ≻ TO FREDERICK W. THOMAS AND JESSE E. DOW

Philadelphia   March 16.   1843.

My Dear Thomas, & Dow

I arrived here, in perfect safety, and *sober,* about half past four last evening — nothing occurring on the road of any consequence. I shaved and breakfasted in Baltimore and lunched on the Susquehannah, and by the time I got to Philᵃ felt quite decent. Mrˢ Clemm was expecting me at the car-office. I went immediately home, took a warm bath & supper & then went to Clarke's. I never saw a man in my life more surprised to see another. He thought by Dow's epistle that I must not only be dead but buried & would as soon have thought of seeing his great-great-great grandmother. He received me, therefore, very cordially & made light of the matter. I told him what had been agreed upon — that I was a little sick & that Dow, knowing I had been, in times passed, given to spreeing upon an extensive scale, had become unduly alarmed &c&c. — that when I found he had written I thought it best to come home. He said my trip had improved me & that he had never *seen me looking so well!!!* — and I don't believe I ever did.

This morning I took medicine, and, as it is a snowy day, will avail myself of the excuse to stay at home — so that by to-morrow I shall be *really* as well as ever.

Virginia's health is about the same — but her distress of mind has been even more than I had anticipated. She desires her *kindest* remembrances to both of you — as also does Mrˢ C.

[*page 2*] Clarke, it appears, wrote to Dow, who must have received the letter this morning. Please re-inclose the letter to me, here — so that I may know how to guide myself. — and, Thomas, do write immediately as proposed. If *possible,* enclose a line from Rob. Tyler — but I fear, under the circumstances, it is not so — I blame no one but myself.

The letter which I looked for & which I wished returned, is not on its way — reason, no money forthcoming — Lowell had not yet sent it — he is ill in N. York of opthalmia. Immediately upon receipt of it, or before, I will forward the money you were both so kind as to lend — which is 8 to Dow — and 3½ to Thomas — What a confounded business I have got myself into, attempting to write a letter to two people at once!

However — this is for Dow. My dear fellow — Thank you a thousand times for your kindness & great forbearance, and don't say a word about the cloak turned inside out, or other peccadilloes of that nature. Also, express to your wife my deep regret for the vexation I must have occasioned her. Send me, also, if you can the letter to Blythe. Call, also, at the barber's shop just above Fuller's and pay for me a levy which I believe I owe. And now God bless you — for a nobler fellow never lived.

And this is for Thomas. My dear friend. Forgive me my petulance & don't believe I think all I said. Believe me I am very grateful to you for your many attentions & forbearances — and the time will never come when I shall forget either them or you. Remember me most kindly to Dʳ Lacey — also to the Don, whose mustachios I *do* admire after all, and who has about the finest figure I ever beheld — also to Dʳ Frailey. Please express my regret to Mr Fuller for making such a fool of <him> myself in his house, and say to him (if you think it necessary) that I should not have got half so drunk on his excellent Port wine but for the rummy [*page 3*] coffee with which I was forced to wash it down. I would be glad, too, if you would take an opportunity of saying to Mr Rob. Tyler that if he *can* look over matters & get me the Inspectorship, I will join the Washingtonians forthwith. I am as serious as a judge — & much so than many. I think it would be a feather in Mr Tyler's cap to save [fr]om the perils of mint julap — & "Port wines" — a young man of whom all the world thinks so well & who thinks so remarkably well of himself.

And now, my dear friends, good bye & believe me

Most Truly Yours.

Mess Dow & Thomas. Edgar A Poe

Upon getting here I found numerous letters of subscribers to my Magazine — for which no canvas has yet been made. This was unexpected & cheering. Did you say Dow that Commodore Elliot had desired me to put down his name? Is it so or did I dream it? At all events, when you see him, present my respects & thanks. Thomas, you will remember that D[r] Lacey wished me to put him down — but I don't know his first name — please let me have it.

At the end of page 3 and across the address on the cover, Thomas wrote a long note (see H, XVII, 137–138), which included: "Poor fellow a place had been promised his friends for him, and in that state of suspense . . . he presented himself in Washington certainly not in a way to advance his interests. I have seen a great deal of Poe, and it was his excessive, and at times marked sensibility which forced him into his 'frolics', rather than any mere marked appetite for drink, but if he took but one glass of week wine or beer or cider the Rubicon of the cup was passed with him, and it almost always ended in excess and sickness. But he fought against the propensity as hard as ever Coleridge fought against it." Thomas added as a last sentence, "And moreover there is a great deal of heartache in the jestings of this letter."

In connection with this letter, see Letter 155 and note; see also Jesse E. Dow to Clarke, March 12, 1843 (Quinn, *Poe*, p. 378). Apparently, Clarke's letter to Dow was not sent to Poe (see Thomas to Poe, March 27, 1843, in H, XVII, 140–141). The expected letter from James R. Lowell was that of March 24, 1843 (see H, XVII, 138–139), in which he explained why he could not send Poe money that was due him from contributions. Thomas lived at Fuller's Hotel in Washington. For Dr. Frailey, see Letter 118 and note. None of the "numerous letters" from prospective subscribers to the *Stylus* is extant. Poe probably reached Washington on or before Wednesday, March 8 (see Letter 154, and Dow's letter to Clarke, cited above). Neither Dow nor Thomas seems to have supplied Poe with the desired information about Commodore Elliot and Dr. Lacey. [CL 424]

157 ➤ TO PETER D. BERNARD

Philadelphia March 24, 1843.

My Dear Sir,

With this letter I mail to your address a number of the "Philadelphia Saturday Museum", containing a Prospectus of "The Stylus", a Magazine which I design to commence on the first of July next, in connexion with M[r] Thomas C. Clarke, of this city.

My object in addressing you is to ascertain if the list of "The South: Lit: Messenger" is to be disposed of, and, if so, upon what terms. We are anxious to purchase the list and unite it with that of "The Stylus," provided a suitable arrangement could be made. I should be happy to hear from you upon the subject.

I hear *of* you occasionally, and most sincerely hope that you are doing well. Mrs Clemm & Virginia desire to be remembered to all our old acquaintances. Believe me,

Yours truly

P. D. Bernard Esqre　　　　　　　　　　Edgar A Poe

> Bernard was Thomas W. White's son-in-law. The prospectus of the *Stylus* appeared in the issue of March 4, 1843, p. 3 (see Quinn, *Poe*, p. 376). White, publisher of the SLM, died January 19, 1843 (see B. B. Minor, *The Southern Literary Messenger*, p. 98; see also the *Dictionary of American Biography*, xx, 120. No reply from Bernard is known. [CL 425]

158 ➤ TO JAMES R. LOWELL

Philadelphia March 27. 43.

My Dear Friend,

I have just received yours of the 24th and am deeply grieved, first that you should have been so unfortunate, and, secondly, that you should have thought it necessary to offer me any apology for your misfortunes. As for the few dollars you owe me — give yourself not one moment's concern about *them*. I am poor, but must be very much poorer, indeed, when I even think of demanding them.

But I sincerely hope all is not as bad as you suppose it, and that, when you come to look about you, you will be able to continue "The Pioneer". Its decease, just now, would be a most severe blow to the good cause — the cause of a Pure Taste. I have looked upon your Magazine, from its outset, as the best in America, and have lost no opportunity of expressing the opinion. Herewith I send a paper, "The Phil: Sat. Museum", in which I have said a few words on the topic.

I am *not* editing this paper, although an announcement was prematurely made to that effect; but have the privilege of inserting what I please editorially. On the first of July next I hope to issue the first number of "The Stylus" a new monthly, with some novel features. I send you, also, a paper containing the Prospectus. In a few weeks I hope to forward you a specimen sheet. I [*page 2*] am anxious to get a poem from yourself for the opening number, but, until you recover your health, I fear that I should be wrong in making the request.

Believe me, my dear friend, that I sympathise with you *truly* in your affliction. When I heard that you had returned to Boston, I hoped you were entirely well, and your letter disappoints and grieves me.

When you find yourself in condition to write, I would be indebted to you if you could put me in the way of procuring a brief article (also for my opening number) from Mr Hawthorne — whom I believe you know personally. Whatever you gave him, we should be happy to give. A part of my design is to illustrate, whatever is fairly susceptible of illustration, with finely executed wood-engravings — after the fashion of Gigoux's "Gil Blas" or "Grandville's Gulliver" — and I wish to get a tale from Mr Hawthorne as early as possible (if I am so fortunate as to get one at all) that I may put the illustration in the hands of the artist.

You will see by the Prospectus that we intend to give a series of portraits of the American literati, with critical sketches. I would be glad if I could so arrange matters as to have you *first* — provided you yourself have no serious objection. Instead of the "full-length portraits" promised in the Prospectus (which will be modified in the specimen-sheet) we shall have medallions, about 3 inches in diameter. Could you put me in possession of any likeness of yourself? — or could you do me the same favor in regard to Mr Hawthorne? — You perceive [*page 3*] I proceed upon the ground that you are intimate with M^r H, and that making these inquiries would not subject you to trouble or inconvenience.

I confess that I am by no means so conversant with your own compositions (especially in prose) as I should be. Could you furnish me with some biographical & critical data, and tell me where or how I could be put in possession of your writings generally? — but I fear I am asking altogether too much.

If the 4th number of "The Pioneer" is printed, I would be obliged if you would send me an early copy through the P.O.

> Please remember me to Mr Carter & believe me
> Most sincerely Your friend,

J. Russell Lowell Esqre Edgar A Poe

Lowell's *Pioneer* ceased with the March issue, owing to its high editorial standards and the rigorous terms of the contract between Lowell and Carter and the publishers, Leland and Whiting (see Mott, *History of American Magazines,* I, 735–736), and to Lowell's ophthalmia. Even if Lowell had paid Poe for "Lenore," in the February number, he still owed $10 for the "Notes on English Verse" (see Letter 163 and note and Letter 164). For Poe's prospectus of the *Stylus,* see Letter 153 and note. For the promise of likenesses of Hawthorne and Lowell, see Lowell to Poe, April 17, 1843 (W, II, 23–24). For the "biographical & critical data" concerning Lowell, see Lowell to Poe, May 8, 1843 (*ibid.,* pp. 25–27). Robert Carter had been co-editor of the *Pioneer.* [CL 427]

159 ⊁ TO WILLIAM MACKENZIE

[Philadelphia, April (?), 1843]

[. . . . .]

I write to get you to do me a gre[at] favor — that is, to ascertain from the heirs, or successors, of Mr White, whether, The subscription list of "The S. L. Messenger" is for sale or not, and, if for sale, upon what terms. A capitalist of this place is anxious to purchase, if possible, and, as I am interested, I will take it as a *very* great favor if you will make the necessary inquiries, and write me *as soon as possible.*

We are all well. Virginia is nearly recovered — indeed I may say quite so — with the exception of a slight cough, which is only noticeable in the morning.

Tell Rose I hope to see her before long, and that I will write her soon. Give my best love to all.

In great hastie
Yours truly

[W]^m Mackenzie Esqre   Edgar A Poe

The upper portion of this MS. is missing (see Note 159). In connection with this letter, see Poe's similar request to Bernard in Letter 157; no reply from either correspondent is known. Thomas W. White died on January 19, 1843, and B. B. Minor bought his interest in the *Southern Literary Messenger,* July 15, 1843 (see Minor, *The Southern Literary Messenger,* pp. 98, 104). The William Mackenzies took the orphan Rosalie Poe at the same time that the Allans took Edgar; whether Poe visited his sister in Richmond, as he here promises, is not known, nor is there any known letter from Poe to Rosalie. [CL 432]

160 ≻ TO LUCY D. HENRY

Philadelphia June 20, 1843.

Dear Madam,

It gives me pleasure to comply with the very flattering request contained in your letter to my sister of March 26ᵗʰ.

With the Highest Respect I am, Madam,
Yr Mo. Ob. Sᵗ

Miss Lucy D. Henry.   Edgar A Poe

> Lucy Dorothea Henry, daughter of Edward Winston Henry, was the granddaughter of Patrick Henry, of Red Mill, Charlotte County, Virginia. As a young girl, while living with her grandfather, she developed an ardent desire to possess the autographs of writers of her time. Why she wrote to Rosalie Poe, and not to Poe directly, is not known. Later she married Octave Laighton, and they went to Quincy, Illinois, where they published a paper. After 1857 they moved to Springdale, near Petersburg, Virginia. Her album, including the letter, was given to the Poe Foundation by her daughter, Fayetta Henry Laighton. [CL 442]

161 ≻ TO JAMES R. LOWELL

Philadelphia June 20, 1843.

My Dear Friend,

I owe you fifty apologies for not having written you before — but sickness and domestic affliction will suffice for all.

I received your poem, which you undervalue, and which I think truly beautiful — as, in fact, I do all you have ever written — but, alas! my Magazine scheme has exploded — or, at least, I have been deprived, through the imbecility, or rather through the idiocy of my partner, of all means of prosecuting it for the present. Under better auspices I may resume it next year.

What am I to do with the poem? I have handed it to Griswold, subject to your disposition.

My address is 234, North Seventh Sᵗ above Spring Garden, West Side. Should you ever pay a visit to Philadelphia, you will remember that there is no one in America whom I would rather hold by the hand than yourself.

With the sincerest friendship
I am yours.

Edgar A Poe

For the troubles referred to in paragraph one, see William Poe to Poe, June 15, 1843, in H, XVII, 145–146. Lowell's poem was sent as Poe had requested in Letter 158, for the first number of the *Stylus*. Poe's "partner" had been Thomas C. Clarke (see Letter 153 and note). Rufus W. Griswold succeeded Poe as an editor of *Graham's*, with the June number, 1842, remaining until October 1843 (see Mott, *History of American Magazines*, I, 544). For more about Poe's North Seventh Street home, see Quinn, *Poe*, pp. 384–386. [CL 443]

162 ⨾ TO JOHN TOMLIN

Phila., August 28, 1843.

My dear Sir,

I have just recᵈ your letter, enclosing one in hieroglyphical writing from Mr. Meek, and hasten to reply, since *you* desire it; although, some months ago, I was obliged to make a vow that I would engage in the solution of no more cryptographs. The reason of my making this vow will be readily understood. Much curiosity was excited throughout the country by my solutions of these cyphers, and a great number of persons felt a desire to test my powers individually — so that I was at one time absolutely overwhelmed; and this placed me in a dilemma; for I had either to devote my whole time to the solutions, or the correspondents would suppose me a mere boaster, incapable of fulfilling my promises. I had no alternative but to solve all; but to each correspondent I made known my intentions to solve no more. You will hardly believe me when I tell you that I have lost, in time, which to me is money, more than a thousand dollars, in solving ciphers, with no other object in view than that just mentioned. A really difficult cipher requires vast labor and the most patient thought in its solution. Mr. Meek's letter is very simple indeed, and merely shows that he misapprehends the whole matter. It runs thus: — [*Here follows the solution*]

This is the whole of Mr. Meek's letter — but he is mistaken in supposing that I "pride myself" upon my solutions of ciphers. I feel little pride about anything.

It is very true, as he says, that cypher writing is "no great difficulty if the signs represent invariably the same letters and are divided into separate words." But the fact is, that most of the criptographs sent to me (Dr. Frailey's for instance) were *not* divided into words, and moreover, the signs *never* represented the same letter twice.

But here is an infallible mode of showing Mr. Meek that he knows nothing about the matter. He says cipher writing "is no great difficulty if the signs represent invariably the same letters and are divided into separate words." This is true; and yet, little as this difficulty is, he cannot surmount it. Send him, as if from yourself, these few words, in which the conditions stated by him are rigidly preserved. I will answer for it, he cannot decipher them for his life. They are taken at random from a well-known work now lying beside me: — [*Here follows Poe's cryptograph*]

And now, my dear friend, have you forgotten that I asked you, some time since, to render me an important favor? You can surely have no scruples in a case of this kind. I have reason to believe that I have been maligned by some envious scoundrel in this city, who has written you a letter respecting myself. I believe I know the villain's name. It is Wilmer. In Philadelphia no one speaks to him. He is avoided by all as a reprobate of the lowest class. Feeling a deep pity for him, I endeavoured to befriend him, and you remember that I rendered myself liable to some censure by writing a review of his filthy pamphlet called the "Quacks of Helicon." He has returned my good offices by slander behind my back. *All* here are anxious to have him convicted — for there is scarcely a gentleman in Phila[a] whom he has not libelled, through the gross malignity of his nature. Now, I ask you, as a friend and as a man of noble feelings, to send me his letter to you. It is your *duty* to do this — and I am sure, upon reflection, you will so regard it.

I await your answer impatiently.

Your friend,

E. A. Poe.

For Tomlin, see the note to Letter 101. Tomlin sent Poe the cipher from Alexander B. Meek of Tuscaloosa, Alabama, with the comment that Poe should "make something out of it," since "many of our learned citizens have endeavored but in vain to solve it." On the envelope of Tomlin's letter are symbols representing, apparently, part or all of those found in the Meek cipher, and beside each is Poe's suggested alphabetical equivalent:

⊓ = p   □ = t   ‡ = h   = e   ⊔ = o   ∨ = f   > = n   + = b
△ = L   ∧ = \<h\>g   < = s   £ = a   § = m   ⁊ = w   ʒ = r   ? = l
ω = u   ·X· = c   ÷ = j   † = d   ·⊢ = y   ! = L   L = v

Poe's solution to Meek's cipher is lost, as is his cipher sent to Meek. Poe's suspicion that Wilmer had written Tomlin was correct, for Tomlin sent Poe the letter on September 10, 1843 (see Tomlin's letter in W, II, 42, and Wilmer's letter to Tomlin, *ibid.*, pp. 42–43). For Poe's review of Lambert A. Wilmer's *The Quacks of Helicon*, see *Graham's Magazine*, August 1841 (reprinted in H, x, 182–195). In connection with the present letter and Poe's skill as a solver of ciphers, see W. K. Wimsatt, Jr., "What Poe Knew about Cryptography," *Publications of the Modern Language Association*, LVIII (September 1943), 754–779. [CL 448]

163 ⊁ TO JAMES R. LOWELL

Philadelphia September 13. 1843.

My Dear Friend,

Since I last wrote you I have suffered much from domestic and pecuniary troubles, and, at one period, had nearly succumbed. I mention this by way of apology to the request I am forced to make — that you would send me, if possible, $10 — which, I believe, is the amount you owe me for contribution. You cannot imagine how sincerely I grieve that any necessity can urge me to ask this of you — but I ask it in the hope that you are now in much better position than myself, and can spare me the sum without inconvenience.

I hope ere long to have the pleasure of conversing with you personally. There is no man living with whom I have so much desire to become acquainted.

Truly your friend,

J. R. Lowell Esqre   Edgar A Poe

C. E. Norton, having placed an asterisk after "contribution," wrote, in the right margin: "To the Pathfinder [*Pioneer*]. The cost of supporting this journal was much greater than the receipts from its publica·· tion, and the balance came out of Lowell's [*continued in the left mar-*

gin, over Poe's writing] pocket. The four [three] numbers left him
heavily in debt [*$1800, according to Mott,* History of American Maga-
zines, I, *738*]. By a letter of Poe's of Oct — [19, 1843] it appears that
the $10 was paid to him. C. E. Norton. *1884."* Poe "last wrote"
June 20, 1843. Poe met Lowell only once, probably in May, 1845
(see W, II, 137). [CL 450]

164 ⋟ TO JAMES R. LOWELL

Philadelphia, Oct. 19. 1843.

My Dear Friend,

I was upon the point of fulfilling a long neglected duty and replying
to Mr Carter's letter, enclosing $5, when I received yours of the 13th,
remitting 5 more. Believe me I am sincerely grateful to you both for
your uniform kindness and consideration.

You say nothing of your health — but Mr C. speaks of its perfect
restoration, and I see, by your very M S., that you are well again, body
& mind. I need not say that I am rejoiced at this — for you must
know and feel that I am. When I thought of the possible loss of your
eye-sight, I grieved as if some dreadful misfortune were about happening to myself.

I shall look with much anxiety for your promised volume. Will it
include your "Year's Life" and other poems already published? I hope
that it may; for these have not yet been fairly placed before the eye
of the world. I am seeking an opportunity to do you justice in a
review, and may find it, in "Graham," when your book appears. No
poet in America has done so much. I have maintained this upon all
occasions. Mr Longfellow has genius, [*page 2*] but by no means equals
you in the true spirit. He is moreover so prone to imitation that I
know not how to understand him at times. I am in doubt whether he
should not be termed an arrant plagiarist. You have read his "Spanish
Student"? I have written quite a long notice of it for Graham's December number. The play is a poor composition, with some fine poetical passages. His "Hymn to the Night", with some strange blemishes,
is glorious. — How much I should like to interchange opinions with
you upon poems and poets in general! I fancy that we should agree,
usually, in results, while differing, frequently, about principles. The
day may come when we can discuss everything at leisure, in person.

You say that your long poem has taught you a useful lesson "that
you are unfit to write narrative — unless in a dramatic form". It is

not you that are unfit for the task — but the task for you — for any poet. Poetry must eschew narrative — except, as you say, dramatically. I mean to say that the *true poetry* — the highest poetry — must eschew it. The Iliad is *not* the highest. The connecting links of a narration — the frequent passages which have to serve the purpose of binding together the parts of the story, are necessarily prose, from their very explanatory nature. To color them — to gloss over their prosaic nature — (for this is the most which can be done) requires great skill. Thus Byron, who was no artist, is always driven, in his narrative, to fragmentary passages, eked out with asterisks. Moore succeeds better than any one. His "Alciphron" is wonderful in the force, grace, and nature of its purely narrative passages: — but pardon me for prosing.

I send you the paper with my life and portrait. The former is true in general — the latter particularly false. [*page 3*] It does not convey the faintest idea of my person. No one of my family recognised it. But this is a point of little importance. You will see, upon the back of the biography, an announcement that I was to assume the editorship of the "Museum". This was unauthorized. I never did edit it. The review of "Graham's Magazine" was written by H. B. Hirst — a young poet of this city.

Who is to write your life for "Graham?" It is a pity that so many of these biographies were entrusted to Mr Griswold. He certainly lacks independence, or judgment, or both.

I have tried in vain to get a copy of your "Years Life" in Philadelphia. If you have one, and could spare it, I would be much obliged.

Do write me again when you have leisure, and believe me,

Your most sincere friend,

J. R. Lowell Esqre   Edgar A Poe

Carter's letter, *ante* October 19, 1843, is unlocated, but like Lowell's enclosed $5 due Poe for his contribution, probably "Notes on English Verse," in the third and last number of the *Pioneer*, March 1843; Poe had requested the payment in his letter to Lowell, September 13. Carter had written Poe on June 19 (see W, II, 28–31), saying that Lowell's "eyes have nearly recovered their usual strength." The letter says nothing of the $5 due Poe, and being written in June before Poe's request for payment, is almost certainly separate from the one alluded to above. Lowell's *Poems* (1844) was reviewed by Poe in *Graham's*, March 1844 (reprinted in H, XI, 243–249). Poe's review of Longfellow's *Spanish*

Student did not appear in *Graham's* (but see Letter 179; Poe's "The American Drama," in the *American Review*, August 1845, reprinted in H, xiii, 33–73; and Poe's replies to "Outis," reprinted in H, xii, 41–106, especially pp. 96–104). Poe's biography and portrait appeared in the Philadelphia *Saturday Museum*, February 25, 1843, and was reprinted March 4. *A Year's Life* (1841) was Lowell's first volume of poetry. [CL 457]

165 ❯ TO JOSEPH H. HEDGES

[Philadelphia] November 16, 1843

[. . . . .]

I presume the request you make, in your note of the 14th, has reference to my grandfather Gen. David Poe, and not to my father David Poe, Jr. I regret to say, however, that, owing to peculiar circumstances, I have in my possession no autograph of either. . . .

[*No signature*]

The identity of Joseph H. Hedges is not known. No other letters are known to have been exchanged between Poe and Hedges. [CL 460]

166 ❯ TO JOEL B. SUTHERLAND

J. B. Sutherland Esqre

My Dear Sir,

Will you permit me to introduce to you my friend Mr Robert Travers, of this city, who will hand you this note? He is an applicant for a post in the Revenue Service. If you could further his views in any regard, I would consider myself as under the *very deepest* personal obligation.

Mr Travers is of the Hughes' family, of Southwark, which has always possessed much political influence. As an experienced seaman, he is, also, well qualified for the appointment he solicits.

Very truly & respectfully Yours,

Philadelphia. Jan: 13. 1844.   Edgar A. Poe

Joel Barlow Sutherland was a Philadelphia lawyer and United States Congressman from Pennsylvania in 1836, having served five terms. As chairman of the committee on commerce he had interested himself in river and harbor development and in the promotion of Philadelphia projects, especially the navy yard and the Delaware breakwater (see the *Dictionary of American Biography*, XVIII, 222–223). Nothing further is known of Robert Travers, nor of Poe's association with him or Mr. Sutherland. [CL 462]

167 ⇂ TO MR. CLARK

[*ante* January 31, 1844

or early 1846]

My Dear Mr Clark

I am exceedingly anxious to try my fortune in Baltimore with a lecture or two, and wish, if possible, to go immediately. I have some little money —

[. . . . .]

Very truly yours

E A Poe.

The identity of Mr. Clark is not known. In connection with the proposed lectures, see Note 167. [CL 463]

168 ⇂ TO ISAAC MUNROE

[Baltimore, January 31, 1844]

My dear Sir,

I have been endeavouring for the last two days to see you and beg of you to do me the kindness to call attention, in the "Patriot" to a lecture on "American Poetry", which I propose to deliver this evening (Wednesday) at the Odd Fellows' Hall in Gay Street. I hope yet to have the honor of seeing you before I leave town.

If not too late, will you say a good word for me in this afternoon's paper.

Most respectfully yours,

Wednesday morning   Edgar A. Poe
Mr. Isaac Munroe.

The *Baltimore Sun* of January 31, 1844, carried the following announcement: "A Lecture on American Poetry by Edgar A. Poe in Odd Fellows Hall, in Gay Street, on this evening 31st, at half-past 7 o'clock" (see

P, I, 850). Elsewhere in the same paper appears: ". . . the lecture by Mr. Poe . . . this evening in the Egyptian Saloon of Odd Fellows' Hall. The name of the lecturer, the subject of the lecture, and the well known adaptation of the talents of the one to the material of the other, form a combination of attractions which will irresistibly result in a crowded audience — and our word for it a delighted one" (excerpt supplied through the courtesy of William D. Hoyt, Jr., Maryland Historical Society, Baltimore). The *Baltimore American* also carried a puff; but no issue of the *Patriot* of that date has been located. [CL 464]

168a ✶ TO JOHN P. KENNEDY

[Baltimore, Feb. 1, 1844]

Thursday Morning, 7 a.m.

Some matters which would not be put off, have taken me to Elkton — so that I shall not have the pleasure of dining with you today, as proposed. Before leaving Baltimore, however, I hope to give you another call.

Most truly yours,

Edgar A. Poe

Poe lectured in Baltimore on Wednesday evening, January 31, 1844 (see Letter 168 and note), and probably had made a visit to his friend Kennedy who invited Poe to dinner before his return to Philadelphia. There is little to clarify the "matters" that took Poe to Elkton, Maryland, unless, perhaps, it had something to do with the lectures he was giving at this time (see Letters 170 and 171). [CL 464a]

169 ✶ TO GEORGE LIPPARD

Philadelphia, Feb. 18, 1844.

My Dear Lippard —

It will give me pleasure to attend to what you suggest. In a day or two you shall hear from me farther.

Touching the "Ladye Annabel," I regret that, until lately, I could find no opportunity of giving it a thorough perusal. The opinion I expressed to you, personally, was based, as I told you, upon a very cursory examination. It has been confirmed, however, by a subsequent reading at leisure. You seem to have been in too desperate a hurry to give due attention to details; and thus your style, although generally nervous, is at times somewhat exuberant — but the work, as a whole, will be admitted, by all but your personal enemies, to be richly inventive and imaginative — indicative of *genius* in its author.

And as for these personal enemies, I cannot see that you need put yourself to any especial trouble about THEM. *Let a fool alone — especially if he be both a scoundrel and a fool — and he will kill himself far sooner than you can kill him by any active exertion. Besides — as to the real philosophy of the thing — you should regard small animosities — the animosities of small men — of the literary animalculae (who have their uses, beyond doubt) — as so many tokens of your ascent — or, rather as so many stepping stones to your ambition. I have never yet been able to make up my mind whether I regard as the higher compliment, the approbation of a man of honor and talent, or the abuse of an ass or a blackguard. Both are excellent in their way — for a man who looks steadily up.*

If my opinion of "The Ladye Annabel" can be of *any* service to you whatever, you have my full permission to publish this letter, or any portion of it you may deem proper.

With respect and friendship,

Yours,

To George Lippard, Esq.   EDGAR A. POE.
Chestnut and Seventh Sts.

George Lippard, of Philadelphia, became very popular as a writer and a lecturer on "legends" of the Revolution, though his literary works were not generally recognized by American critics. He was on the staff of the *Spirit of the Times* from late in 1841 until some time in 1842. In his "Bread Crust Papers" he was responsible for naming Thomas Dunn English, "Thomas Done Brown" and Henry Beck Hirst, "Henry Bread Crust." *Herbert Tracy*, his second novel, began as a serial in the *Saturday Evening Post*, October 22, 1842. "The Ladye Annabel" was contributed in 1843 to *The Citizen Soldier*, a new weekly with which he was associated (see the *Dictionary of American Biography*, XI, 285–286). In printing Poe's letter to him at the end of *Herbert Tracy*, Lippard wrote a brief introduction under the caption, "A Word to the Reader," in which he said that an author's enemies sometimes need a rebuke such as that given "in certain italicized portions of the following letter from the author of 'Tales of the Grotesque and Arabesque' — Edgar A. Poe, Esq., universally confessed one of the most gifted men in the land." [CL 466]

170 ⤅ TO JOHN C. MYERS, SAMUEL WILLIAMS, OR WILLIAM GREAFF, JR.

Philadelphia   March 1.   44.

Gentlemen,

Through some accident which I am at a loss to understand, your letter dated and postmarked Decr 29, has only this moment come to hand; having been lying, ever since, in the Phil^a P. Office. I hope, therefore, you will exonerate me from the charge of discourtesy in not sooner replying to your very flattering request.

I presume that your Lectures are over for the season; but, should this not be the case, it will give me great pleasure to deliver a Discourse before your Society at any period you may appoint; not later than the 9th inst:

With High Respect
Yr Ob S^t

Mess: Jno: C. Myers   Edgar A Poe
  Sam: Williams
  Wm Greaff J^r

In connection with this letter, see Letter 171 and note. [CL 468]

171 ⤅ TO SAMUEL WILLIAMS AND WILLIAM GRAEFF, JR.

Philadelphia March 7, 1844.

Gentlemen:

I have just received your favor of the 5th, and will be pleased to deliver a Lecture on "American Poetry" in Reading, on Tuesday the 12th inst., if convenient. Please reply by return of mail and let me know at what place I shall meet the Committee.

Very Resp^{ly},
Yr. Ob. Svt.,

Mess. Sam. Williams   Edgar A. Poe
  Wm. Graeff Jr.

The lecture was delivered on March 13, 1844; for, according to the *Baltimore Sun*, Thursday, March 21, 1844: "Edgar A. Poe . . . distinguished writer delivered his much extolled lecture, 'Poets and Poetry of America' at Reading, Pa., Wednesday last. He was greeted by a large audience and they testified their appreciation by repeated bursts of applause." — This note was furnished through the courtesy of Thomas O. Mabbott. [CL 471]

172 ⊁ TO CORNELIUS MATHEWS

Philadelphia March 15, 1844.

Dʳ Sir,

I have a letter and small parcel for Mʳ Horne, your friend, and the author of "Orion". Would you be so kind as to furnish me with his address? — and to put me in the best way of forwarding the package securely?

I am reminded that I am your debtor for many little attentions, and embrace this opportunity of tendering you my especial thanks for your able pamphlet on the International Copy-Right Question, and for the admirable Adventures of Puffer Hopkins.

Could I imagine that, at any moment, you regarded a certain impudent and flippant critique as more than a matter to be laughed *at*, I would proffer you an apology on the spot. Since I scribbled the article in question, you yourself have given me fifty good reasons for being ashamed of it.

With the Highest Respect & Esteem
Yr Ob Sᵗ

To Cornelius Mathews Esqʳᵉ   Edgar A Poe

Cornelius Mathews of New York was associated with Evert A. Duyckinck. Poe's apology refers to a review of Mathews' *Wakondah*, in *Graham's* for February 1842 (see Quinn, *Poe*, p. 403). In Letter 259 Poe speaks of Mathews' play *Witchcraft*, and in Letter 304 calls him Margaret Fuller's "protégé." R. H. Horne, a poet of London, England, became a Poe correspondent; the "letter and small parcel" refer to Poe's first letter to Horne, late in March 1844, and the MS. of "The Spectacles," which Horne was to try to place in some English magazine (Poe's letter is not extant, but see Horne's reply, April 16, 1844, original in Boston Public Library); Horne's letter of April 27, not a reply to a Poe letter, but a follow-up of his earlier one, identifies the MS. tale (the original letter is in the Boston Public Library; printed in H, XVII, 167–169). This MS. of "The Spectacles" apparently was not the one from which the tale was printed in the *Dollar Newspaper*, x, no. 2, March 27, 1844 (see also "A List of the Texts of Poe's Tales," ed. by

John Cook Wyllie, pp. 335–336). Instead it was the 38-page MS. of "The Spectacles" sold in 1920 from the library of Buxton Forman, Horne's executor (described in the Anderson Galleries catalogue, No. 1480, March 17, 1920, p. 130). T. O. Mabbott informs me he collated the MS. for verbal variants, and that the MS. "never went through the hands of a printer. The story is unchanged, but the phrases differ [considerably]." Mathews must have replied to Poe's letter (though location of original MS. is unknown), for Poe wrote to Horne within the next week or ten days. [CL 473]

173 ⊁ TO JAMES R. LOWELL

Philadelphia March 30. 1844.

My Dear Friend,

Graham has been speaking to me, lately, about your Biography, and I am anxious to write it at once — always provided you have no objection. Could you forward me the materials within a day or two? I am just now quite disengaged — in fact positively idle.

I presume you have read the Memoir of Willis, in the April No: of G. It is written by a Mr Landor — but I think it full of hyperbole. Willis is *no* genius — a graceful trifler — no more. He wants force & sincerity. He is very frequently far-fetched. In me, at least, he never excites an emotion. Perhaps the best poem he has written, is a little piece called "Unseen Spirits", beginning "The Shadow lay — Along Broadway".

You inquire about my own portrait. It has been done for some time — but is better as an engraving, than as a portrait. It scarcely resembles me at all. When it will appear I cannot say. Conrad & Mrs Stephens will certainly come before me — perhaps Gen: Morris. My Life is not yet written, and I am at a sad loss for a Biographer — for Graham insists upon leaving the matter to myself.

[*page 2*] I sincerely rejoice to hear of the success of your volume. To sell eleven hundred copies of a bound book of American poetry, is to do wonders. I hope every thing from your future endeavours. Have you read "Orion"? Have you seen the article on "American Poetry" in the "London Foreign Quarterly"? It has been denied that Dickens wrote it — but, to me, the article affords so strong internal evidence of his hand that I would as soon think of doubting my existence. He tells much truth — although he evinces much ignorance and more spleen. Among other points he accuses myself of "metrical imitation" of Tennyson, citing, by way of instance, passages from poems which were written & published by me long before Tennyson was heard of: — but I have, at no time, made any poetical pretension. I am greatly indebted for the trouble you have taken about the Lectures, and shall be very glad to avail myself, next season, of any invitation from the "Boston Lyceum." Thank you, also, for the hint about the North A. Review: — I will bear it in mind. I mail you, herewith, a "Dollar Newspaper", containing a somewhat evtravagant tale of my own. I fear it will prove little to your taste.

How dreadful is the present condition of our Literature! To what are things tending? We want two things, certainly: — an International Copy-Right Law, and a well-founded Monthly Journal, of sufficient [*page 3*] ability, circulation, and character, to control and so give tone to, our Letters. It should be, externally, a specimen of high, but not too refined Taste: — I mean, it should be boldly printed, on excellent paper, in single column, and be illustrated, not merely embellished, by spirited wood designs in the style of Grandville. Its chief aims should be Independence, Truth, Originality. It should be a journal of some 120 pp, and furnished at $5. It should have nothing to do with Agents or Agencies. Such a Magazine might be made to exercise a prodigious influence, and would be a source of vast wealth to its proprietors. There *can* be no reason why 100,000 copies might not, in one or two years, be circulated: but the means of bringing it into circulation should be radically different from those usually employed.

Such a journal might, perhaps, be set on foot by a coalition, and, thus set on foot, with proper understanding, would be irresistible. Suppose, for example, that the élite of our men of letters should combine secretly. Many of them control papers &c. Let each subscribe, say $200, for the commencement of the undertaking; furnishing other means, as required from time to time, until the work be established. The articles to be supplied by the members solely, and upon a concerted plan of action. A nominal editor to be elected from among the number. How could such a journal fail? I would like very much to hear your opinion upon this matter. Could not the "ball be set in motion"? If we do *not* defend [*page 4*] ourselves by some such coalition, we shall be devoured, without mercy, by the Godeys, the Snowdens, et id genus omne.

Most truly your friend

Edgar A Poe

William Landor wrote the biographical sketch of Willis (see the note to Letter 119). Poe is referring to Robert T. Conrad, Mrs. Ann S. Stephens, and George P. Morris, minor literary figures of the day (see Poe's "Autography," reprinted in H, xv, 232–233, 246, and 221). Although Poe never wrote Lowell's biography, Lowell wrote Poe's; it was published in *Graham's*, February 1845. For Lowell's *Poems* (1844), see Lowell to Poe, March 6, 1844, and the note to Letter 164. R. H. Horne's *Orion* was reviewed by Poe in Graham's, March 1844 (reprinted in H, xi, 249–275). For more on the "American Poetry" article, see Letter 175. For Poe's lecture before the Boston Lyceum, October 16, 1845, see Letter 185. Lowell's letter of March 6 had suggested that Poe write for the *North American Review* and that Lowell would get him "introduced there." The *Dollar Newspaper* published "The Spectacles," March 27, 1844. Louis A. Godey's *Lady's Book* (Philadelphia) and William W. Snowden's *Ladies' Companion* (New York) were popular magazines of the day; Poe contributed to both. [CL 476]

VI

EARLY STRUGGLES

April 1844–January 1845

New-York, Sunday Morning
April 7. [1844] just after breakfast.

My dear Muddy,

We have just this minute done breakfast, and I now sit down to write you about everything. I can't pay for the letter, because the P.O. won't be open to-day. — In the first place, we arrived safe at Walnut S^t wharf. The driver wanted to make me pay a dollar, but I wouldn't. Then I had to pay a boy a levy to put the trunks in the baggage car. In the meantime I took Sis in the Depôt Hotel. It was only a quarter past 6, and we had to wait till 7. We saw the Ledger & Times — nothing in either — a few words of no account in the Chronicle. — We started in good spirits, but did not get here until nearly 3 o'clock. We went in the cars to Amboy about 40 miles from N. York, and then took the steamboat the rest of the way. — Sissy coughed none at all. When we got to the wharf it was raining hard. I left her on board the boat, after putting the trunks in the Ladies' Cabin, and set off to buy an umbrella and look for a boarding-house. I met a man selling umbrellas and bought [o]ne for <56> 62 cents. Then I went up Greenwich S^t and soon found a boarding-house. It is just before you get to Cedar S^t on the west side going up — the left hand side. It has brown stone steps, with a porch with brown pillars. "Morrison" is the name on the door. I made a bargain in a few minutes and then got a hack and went for Sis. I was not gone more than ½ an hour, and she was quite astonished to see me back so soon. She didn't expect me for an hour. There were 2 other ladies waiting on board — so she was'nt very lonely. — When we got to the house we had to wait about ½ an hour before the room [was ready]. The house is old & looks buggy, b[*excision* t]he landlady is a nice chatty ol[*excision* g]ave us the back room on th[*excision* e] night & day & attendance, f[or 7 $ — the cheapest board I] ever knew, taking into consideration the central situation and the *living*. I wish Kate could see it — she would faint. Last night, for supper, we had the nicest tea you ever drank, strong & hot — wheat bread

& rye bread — cheese — tea-cakes (elegant) [*page 2*] a great dish
(2 dishes) of elegant ham, and 2 of cold veal, piled up like a mountain and large slices — 3 dishes of the cakes, and every thing in the
greatest profusion. No fear of starving here. The landlady seemed
as if she could'nt press us enough, and we were at home directly. Her
husband is living with her — a fat good-natured old soul. There are
8 or 10 boarders — 2 or 3 of them ladies — 2 servants. — For breakfast we had excellent-flavored coffe, hot & strong — not very clear
& no great deal of cream — veal cutlets, elegant ham & eggs & nice
bread and butter. I never sat down to a more plentiful or a nicer
breakfast. I wish you could have seen the eggs — and the great dishes
of meat. I ate the first hearty breakfast I have eaten since I left our
little home. Sis is delighted, and we are both in excellent spirits. She
has coughed hardly any and had no night sweat. She is now busy
mending my pants which I tore against a nail. I went out last night
and bought a skein of silk, a skein of thread, & 2 buttons a pair of
slippers & a tin pan for the stove. The fire kept in all night. — We
have now got 4 $ and a half left. Tomorrow I am going to try
& borrow 3 $ — so that I may have a fortnight to go upon. I feel
in excellent spirits & have'nt drank a drop — so that I hope so[on]
to get out of trouble. The very instant I scrape together enough
money I will send it on. You ca'nt imagine how much we both do
miss you. Sissy had a hearty cry last night, because you and Catterina
weren't here. We are resolved to get 2 rooms the first moment we can.
In the meantime it is impossible we could be more comfortable or
more at home than we are. — It looks as if it was going to clear up
now. — Be sure and go to the P.O. & have my letters forwarded. As
soon as I write Lowell's article, I will send it to you, & get you to get
the money from Graham. Give our best loves to Catter[ina.]

[*three line excision for autograph*]

Be sure & take home the Messenger, [to Hirst]. We hope to send for
you *very* soon.

> Poe's departure from Philadelphia must have been sudden, for in his
> letter to Lowell, March 30, 1844 (the last known letter by Poe prior
> to the one above), he asked that Lowell send "within a day or two" the
> material needed by Poe for a biography. Poe found lodgings at 130
> Greenwich Street (according to Pratt, p. 19; and Quinn, *Poe*, pp. 407–

408). "Sis" was Virginia Clemm Poe. "Kate" was Catterina, the family cat. Apparently Mrs. Clemm did not return to Henry B. Hirst the borrowed volume of the SLM, and the owner, William Duane, later accused Poe of selling it to Leary's Book Store (see W, II, 365–368; and Quinn, *Poe*, pp. 408–410). Mrs. Clemm's having rejoined Poe and Virginia is first mentioned in Poe's letter to F. W. Thomas, September 8, 1844. [CL 477]

175 ⤳ TO JAMES R. LOWELL

New-York, May 28, 44.

My Dear Friend,

I received yours last night — forwarded from Philadelphia to this city, where I intend living for the future: Touching the Biography — I would be very proud, indeed, if you would write it — and did, certainly, say to myself, and I believe to Graham — that such was my wish; but as I fancied the job might be disagreeable, I did not venture to suggest it to yourself. Your offer relieves me from great embarrasment, and I thank you sincerely. You will do me justice; and that I could not expect at all hands.

Herewith, I mail you a Life written some time since by Hirst, from materials furnished principally by Thomas and Mr T. W. White. It is correct, I think, in the main, (barring extravagant eulogy,) and you can select from it whatever you deem right. The limit is 6 pp of Graham — as much less as you please. Besides the Tales enumerated in the foot-note, I have written "The Spectacles"; *"The Oblong Box"*; "A Tale of the Ragged Mountains"; *"The Premature Burial"*; *"The Purloined Letter"*; *"The System of Doctors Tar and Fether"*; "The Black Cat"; "The Elk"; "Diddling Considered as one of the Exact Sciences;" *"Mesmeric Revelation*; "The Gold-Bug;" *"Thou art the Man;* — about 60 altogether, including the "Grotesque & Arabesque.["] Those Italicized are as yet unpublished — in the hands of different editors. Of the "Gold-Bug" (my most successful tale) more than 300,000 copies have been circulated.

There is an article on "American Poetry" in a late number of the London Foreign Quarterly, in [*page 2*] which some allusion is made to me as a poet, and as an imitator of Tennyson. I would like you to say (in my defence) what is the fact; that the passages quoted as imitations were written & published, in Boston, before the issue of even Tennyson's first volume. Dickens (*I know*) wrote the article — I have private personal reasons for knowing this. The portrait prepared, does not in the least resemble me.

I wrote you a long letter from Phil: about 7 weeks since — did you get it? — you make no allusion to it.

In great haste.
Your most sincere friend.

Edgar A Poe

For Poe's arrival in New York, see Letter 174. For "the Biography" see the note to Letter 173; for Poe's "Life" see the note to Letter 164. The tales cited by Poe were published as follows: "The Spectacles," *Dollar Newspaper*, March 27, 1844; "The Oblong Box," *Godey's*, September 1844; "A Tale of the Ragged Mountains," *Godey's*, April 1844; "The Premature Burial," *Dollar Newspaper*, July 31, 1844; "The Purloined Letter," *The Gift*, 1845; "The System of Dr. Tarr and Prof. Fether," *Graham's*, November 1845; "The Black Cat," *United States Saturday Post*, August 19, 1843; "The Elk" ("Morning on the Wissahiccon"), *The Opal*, 1844; "Diddling Considered as One of the Exact Sciences," *Saturday Courier*, October 14, 1843; "Mesmeric Revelation," *Columbian*, August 1844; "The Gold Bug," *Dollar Newspaper*, June 21 and 28, 1843; "Thou Art the Man," *Godey's*, November 1844 (for all references, see Wyllie, *Poe's Tales, passim*). Concerning Poe's total of "about 60" see Letter 186 and note. For the article in the *London Foreign Quarterly*, see Letter 173; this letter is also the one of "about 7 weeks since." [CL 481]

176 ➤ TO SARAH J. HALE

[New York, May 29, 1844]

[. . . . .]

Mr. W. was pleased to express himself in very warm terms of the article, which he considers the best I have written and urged me to offer it to Mr. Riker, for the next Opal; promising to speak to Mr. R. and engage him (if possible) to accept the Tale. . . . I have thought it best to write you this letter, and to ask you if you could accept an article — whether you would wish to see the one in question — or whether you could be so kind as to take it, unseen, upon Mr. Willis's testimony in its favor. It cannot be improper to state that I make the latter request to save time, because I am, as usual, exceedingly in need of a little money. . . .

[*Signature missing*]

Mr. W. is N. P. Willis. The 1845 *Opal: a pure gift for the holy days,* was edited by Sarah J. Hale and published in New York by John C. Riker (copy in the Newberry Library). Occasionally, Poe used *article* and *tale* interchangeably; however, in this letter he may have had a short story in mind, for Mrs. Hale's reply seems to have suggested that Poe submit something more particularly suited to the *Opal* (see Letter 177). The "tale," if tale it was, may have been "The Oblong Box" or "Thou Art the Man" (see the note to Letter 177). [CL 482]

---

177 ➤ TO SARAH J. HALE

New-York. May 31ʳˢᵗ 44.

My Dear Madam,

I hasten to reply to your kind and very satisfactory letter, and to say that, if you will be so good as to keep open for me the ten pages of which you speak, I will forward you, in 2 or 3 days, an article which will about occupy that space, and which I will endeavour to adapt to the character of "The Opal." The price you mention — 50 cts per page — will be amply sufficient; and I am exceedingly anxious to be ranked in your list of contributors.

Should you see Mʳ Godey very soon, will you oblige me by saying that I will write him in a few days, and forward him a package?

With sincere respect.
Yʳ Ob. Sᵗ

Mʳˢ Sarah J. Hale.   Edgar A Poe

Poe's "A Chapter of Suggestions" appeared in the *Opal,* 1845, pp. 164–170. Mrs. Hale was editor of the *Opal* and of *Godey's.* The "package" to Godey probably contained "The Oblong Box" (*Godey's,* XXIX (September 1844), 132–136) and/or "Thou Art the Man" (*ibid.,* November 1844, pp. 219–224). No other letter, which would likely have accompanied the MSS., is known from Poe to either Mrs. Hale or Godey until after 1844. [CL 484]

---

178 ➤ TO ELI BOWEN

[New York, June 4, 1844]

My Dear Mr. Brown:

I would take it as a very great favor if you could mail me an X by return of mail, if possible.

Yours truly,
P.

Eli Bowen and Jacob L. Gossler were the editors and publishers of the Columbia, Pennsylvania, *Spy*. On May 18, 1844, Bowen announced that "Poe . . . will . . . be a regular contributor to the *Spy*." (See Spannuth and Mabbott, *Doings of Gotham*). "Brown" is an error either by Poe or by the newspaper. Whether Bowen sent Poe the ten dollars is unknown. No other correspondence between Poe and Bowen is known, though some must have existed. [CL 487]

179 ⇀ TO JAMES R. LOWELL

New-York, July 2. 44.

My Dear Mʳ Lowell,

I can feel for the "constitutional indolence" of which you complain — for it is one of my own besetting sins. I am excessively slothful, and wonderfully industrious — by fits. There are epochs when any kind of mental exercise is torture, and when nothing yields me pleasure but solitary communion with the "mountains & the woods" — the "altars" of Byron. I have thus rambled and dreamed away whole months, and awake, at last, to a sort of mania for composition. Then I scribble all day, and read all night, so long as the disease endures. This is also the temperament of P. P. Cooke, of Vᵃ the author of "Florence Vane", "Young Rosalie Lee", & some other sweet poems — and I should not be surprised if it were your own. Cooke writes and thinks as you — and I have been told that you resemble him personally.

I am *not* ambitious — unless negatively. I, now and then feel stirred up to excel a fool, merely because I hate to let a fool imagine that he may excel me. Beyond this I feel nothing of ambition. I really perceive that vanity about which most men merely prate — the vanity of the human or temporal life. I live continually in a reverie of the future. I have no faith in human perfectibility. I think that human exertion will have no appreciable effect upon humanity. Man is now only more active — not more happy — nor more wise, than he was 6000 years ago. The result will never vary — and to suppose that it will, is to suppose that the foregone man has [*page 2*] lived in vain — that the foregone time is but the rudiment of the future — that the myriads who have perished have not been upon equal footing with ourselves — nor are we with our posterity. I cannot agree to lose sight of man the individual, in man the mass. — I have no belief in spirituality. I think the word a *mere* word. No one has really a conception of spirit. We cannot imagine what is not. We deceive ourselves by the idea of infinitely rarefied matter. Matter escapes the senses by degrees — a stone — a metal — a liquid — the atmosphere — a gas — the luminiferous ether. Beyond this there are other modifications more rare. But to all we attach the notion of a constitution of particles — atomic composition. For this reason only, we think spirit different; for spirit, we say is unparticled, and *therefore* is not matter. But it is clear that if we proceed sufficiently far in our ideas of rarefaction, we shall arrive at a point where the particles coalesce; for, although the particles be infinite, the infinity of littleness in the spaces between them, is an absurdity. — The unparticled matter, permeating & impelling, all things, is God. Its activity is the thought of God — which creates. Man, and other thinking beings, are individualizations of the unparticled matter. Man exists as a "person", by being clothed with matter (the particled matter) which individualizes him. Thus habited, his life is rudimental. What we call "death" is the painful metamorphosis. The stars are the habitations of rudimental beings. But for the necessity of the rudimental life, there would have been no worlds. At death, the worm is the butterfly — still material, but of a matter unrecognized by our organs — recognized, occasionally, perhaps, by the sleep-waker, directly — without organs — through the mesmeric medium. Thus a sleep-waker may see ghosts. Divested of the rudimental covering, the being inhabits *space* — what we suppose to be the immaterial universe — passing every where, and act- [*page 3*] ing all things, by mere volition — cognizant of all secrets but that of the nature of God's volition — the motion, or activity, of the unparticled matter.

You speak of "an estimate of my life" — and, from what I have already said, you will see that I have none to give. I have been too deeply conscious of the mutability and evanescence of temporal things, to give any continuous effort to anything — to be consistent in anything. My life has been *whim* — impulse — passion — a longing for solitude — a scorn of all things present, in an earnest desire for the future.

I am profoundly excited by music, and by some poems — those of Tennyson especially — whom, with Keats, Shelley, Coleridge (occa-

sionally) and a few others of like thought and expression, I regard as
the *sole* poets. Music is the perfection of the soul, or idea, of Poetry.
The *vagueness* <and> of exultation arous[ed by] a sweet air (which
should be strictly indefinite & never too strongly suggestive) is precisely what we should aim at in poetry. Affectation, within bounds, is
thus no blemish.

I still adhere to Dickens as either author, or dictator, of the review.
My reasons would convince you, could I give them to you — but I
have left myself no space. I had two long interviews with Mʳ D. when
here. Nearly every thing in the critique, I heard from <D> him or
suggested to him, personally. The poem of Emerson I read to him.

I have been so negligent as not to preserve copies of any of my
volumes of poems — nor was either worthy preservation. The best
passages were culled in Hirst's article. I think my best poems, "The
Sleeper", "The Conqueror Worm", "The Haunted Palace", "<A
Paen">" "Lenore", "Dreamland" & "The Coliseum" — but all have
been hurried & unconsidered. My best tales are "Ligeia"; The "Gold-
Bug"; The "Murders in the [*page 4*] Rue Morgue", "The Fall of the
House of Usher", The "Tell-Tale Heart", The "Black Cat", "William
Wilson", & "The Descent into the Maelström." "The Purloined Let-
ter," forthcoming in the "Gift", is, perhaps, the best of my tales of
ratiocination. I have lately written, for Godey, "The Oblong-Box",
and "Thou art the Man" — as yet unpublished. With this, I mail you
"The Gold-Bug", which is the only one of my tales I have on hand.

Graham has had, for 9 months, a review of mine on Longfellow's
"Spanish Student", which I have "used up", and in which I have ex-
posed some of the grossest plagiarisms ever perpetrated. I can't tell
why he does not publish it. — I believe G. intends my Life for the
September number, which will be made up by the 10ᵗʰ August. Your
article shᵈ be on hand as soon as convenient.

Believe me your true friend.

E A Poe.

In connection with Poe's discussion of "spirit" and "matter," especially
for similarity of the phrasing, see "Mesmeric Revelation" (H, v, 241–
254). In his letter, Lowell attributed the review (see Letter 175) to
Dickens' friend, and future biographer, John Forster. "Hirst's article"
refers to the biographical sketch of Poe in the *Saturday Museum*,
February 25, 1843. For the publication of the tales Poe cites "as yet

unpublished," see Letter 175 and note. Concerning Longfellow's *Spanish Student*, see the note to Letter 164. Lowell sent the biography late in September (see Letter 185 and note). [CL 490]

180 ✈ TO DR. THOMAS H. CHIVERS

New-York July 10. 44.

My Dear Friend,

Yours of June 15 was forwarded here to me on the 25th [ul]t. Believe me, I am truly pleased to h[ea]r from you again. The two letters of which you speak were received; but, in the hurry of mere business, I chanced to file them away among a package of letters endorsed "answered," and thus it was that I failed to reply. For many months I have been haunted by the sentiment of some duty unperformed, but was unable to say what it was.

Touching the "Penn Magazine" or rather the "Stylus", (for this is the title I should finally adopt) — I have by no means given up the intention of issuing it; my views respecting it are only confirmed by time, and more intimate acquaintance with our literature, as well as with the business of Magazine publication. I am only "biding my time" — awaiting m[e]ans and opportunity. Should you conclude to join me, we will not fail to make fame and fortune. When you feel ready to attempt the enterpriz[e], you will find me here — at New-York — where I live, [at] present, in strict seclusion, busied with books and [ambiti]ous thoughts, until the hour shall arrive when I may come forth with a [*page 2*] certainty of success. A Magazine like Graham's will never do. We must do something far better — but we will talk of these matters personally. When you come to New-York, put a letter to my address in the P. Office, and we will thus find each other.

I have been lately lecturing on "American Poetry" and have drawn profuse tears from large and intellectual audiences by the recital of your "Heavenly Vision" — which I can never weary of repeating.

You mistake me in supposing I dislike the transcendentalists — it is only the pretenders and sophists among them. My own faith is indeed my own. You will find it, somewhat detailed, in a forthcoming number of the "Columbian Magazine", published here. I have written for it an article headed "Mesmeric Revelation," which see. It may be out in the August or September number.

I disagree with you in what you say of man's advance towards perfection. Man is now only more active, not wiser, nor more happy,
than he was 6000 years ago. To say that we are better than ou[r]
progenitors, is to make the foregone age[s] only the rudiment of the
pre[se]nt & future; whereas each individual man is the rudiment of a
future material (*not* spiritual) being. It were to suppose God unjust
to suppose those who have died before us possessed of less advantage
than ourselves.

[*page 3*] There is no such thing as spirituality. God is material.
All things are material; yet the matter of God has all the qualities
which we attribute to spirit: thus the difference is scarcely more than
of words. There is a matter without particles — of no atomic composition: this is God. It permeates and impels all things, and thus *is* all
things in itself. Its agitation is the thought of God, and creates. Man
and other beings (inhabitants of stars) are portions of this unparticled
matter, individualized by being incorporated in the ordinary or particled matter. Thus they exist rudimentally. Death is the painful
metamorphosis. The worm becomes the butterfly — but the butterfly
is still material — of a matter, however, which cannot be recognized
by our rudimental organs. But for the necessity of the rudimental
life, there would have been no stars — no worlds — nothing which we
term material. These spots are the residences of the rudimental things.
At death, these, taking a n[e]w form, of a n[o]vel matter, pass every
where, and act all things, by mere volition, and are cognizant of all
secrets but *the one* — the nature of the volition of God — of the
agitation of the unparticled matter.

Write upon receipt of this — and *do not* affront me by paying postage or speaking of these trivialities at all. There is nothing which gives
me more sincere pleasure than the receipt of your letters.

Your friend most sincere[l]y.

E A Poe.

As a title for Poe's dream magazine, the old *Penn* gave way to the new
Stylus, as early as January 1843, if not earlier (see Quinn, *Poe*, p. 369).
Chivers' "Heavenly Vision" may have been "To Allegra Florence in
Heaven," a poem on the death of his daughter, written in December
1842 (for newspaper printing, see Miller-Townsend Scrapbook, pp. 58–
59). "Mesmeric Revelation" appeared in the *Columbian*, II (August
1844), 67–70 (see Wyllie, *Poe's Tales*, p. 331). [CL 491]

181 ⇥ TO JAMES R. LOWELL

New-York: August 18. 1844

My Dear Friend,

With this letter I take the liberty to mail you a number of the "Columbian Magazine," in which you will find a paper on "Mesmeric Revelation". In it I have endeavoured to amplify some ideas which I suggested in my last letter.

You will observe many corrections & alterations. In fact the article was wofully misprinted; and my principal object in boring you with it now, is to beg of you the favor to get it copied (with corrections) in the Brother Jonathan — I mean the Boston Notion — or any other paper where you have interest. If you can do this without trouble, I would be very deeply indebted to you. I am living so entirely out of the world, just now, that I can do nothing of the kind myself.

In what are you occupied? — or is it still the far niente? For myself I am very industrious — collecting and arranging materials for a Critical History of Am. Literature. Do you ever see Mr Hawthorne? He is a man of rare genius. A day or two since I met with a sketch by him called "Drowne's Wooden Image" — delicious. The leading idea, however, is suggested [*page 2*] by Michäel Angelo's couplet:

Non ha l'ottimo artista alcun concetto
Chè un marmo solo in se non circunscriva

To be sure Angelo half-stole the thought from Socrates.

How fares it with the Biography? I fear we shall be late.

Most truly your friend.

Edgar A Poe

For publication of "Mesmeric Revelation," see the note to Letter 175. Though Lowell failed to have the tale republished in the Boston *Notion*, it did appear in the *New World*, August 3, and in the Philadelphia *Saturday Museum*, August 31, 1844 (see Wyllie, *Poe's Tales*, p. 331). For Poe's "Critical History" see Letter 240 and note. The quotation from Michaelangelo is, of course, not a couplet, and may be freely translated: "The best artist has no concept which a single marble does not contain within itself." Lowell's biography of Poe was delayed another month (see Lowell to Poe, September 27, 1844, cited in Note 181). [CL 493]

182 ⇥ TO FREDERICK W. THOMAS

New York, September 8, 1844.

My Dear Thomas,

I received yours with sincere pleasure, and nearly as sincere surprise; for while you were wondering that I did not write to *you,* I was making up my mind that you had forgotten *me* altogether.

I have left Philadelphia, and am living, at present, about five miles out of New York. For the last seven or eight months I have been playing hermit in earnest, nor have I seen a living soul out of my family — who are well and desire to be kindly remembered. When I say "well," I only mean (as regards Virginia) as well as usual. Her health remains excessively precarious.

Touching the "Beechen Tree," I remember it well and pleasantly. I have not yet seen a published copy, but will get one forthwith and notice it as it deserves — and it deserves much of high praise — at the very first opportunity I get. At present I am so much out of the world that I may not be able to do anything *immediately.*

Thank God! Richard (whom you know) is himself again. Tell Dow so: but he won't believe it. I am working at a variety of things (all of which you shall behold in the end) — and with an ardor of which I did not believe myself capable.

You said to me hurriedly, when we last met on the wharf in Philadelphia, that you believed Robert Tyler really wished to give me the post in the Custom House. This I also really think; and I am confirmed in the opinion that he could not, at all times, do as he wished in such matters, by seeing —— —— at the head of the "Aurora" — a bullet-headed and malicious villain who has brought more odium upon the Administration than any fellow (of equal littleness) in its ranks, and who has been more indefatigably busy in both open and secret vilification of Robert Tyler than any individual, little or big, in America.

Let me hear from you again very soon, my dear Thomas, and believe me *ever*

Your friend,

Poe.

Thomas' letter of September 2 asks why Poe has not written (probably since March 16, 1843). Poe was living at the home of Patrick Brennan (see the note to Letter 189). For more about *The Beechen Tree,* see Letter 189 and note. In 1844, Thomas Dunn English edited the *Aurora,* and for the same year, he wrote in his autobiography: "I was President of a political club and did a good deal of stumping. I dare say that I was unnecessarily offensive in my remarks at times, and provoked a deal of ill-will" (see the *Dictionary of American Biography,* VI, 166). [CL 496]

183 ➤ TO SAMUEL D. CRAIG

Sir,

Proceed. There are few things which could afford me more pleasure than an opportunity of holding you up to that public admiration which you have so long courted; and this I think I can do to good purpose — with the aid of some of the poor labourers and other warm friends of yours about Yorkville.

The tissue of written lies which you have addressed to myself individually, I deem it as well to retain. It is a specimen of attorney grammar too rich to be lost. As for the letter designed for Mr Willis (who, beyond doubt, (will feel honoured by your correspondence), I take the liberty of re-inclosing it. The fact is, I am neither your footman nor the penny-post.

With all due respect, nevertheless,
I am Y^r Ob, S^t

S.D, Craig Esqr   Edgar A Poe
Quoque. [Quogue]
New-York. Oct, 24, 44,

Samuel D. Craig was a lawyer, who practiced in New York City in 1842 but who lived, not in "Quoque" but in Quogue, on Long Island, according to T. O. Mabbott. Just what the present letter refers to is unknown. Yorkville is the section of New York City around 86th Street and the East River, and in 1844 was probably a small community. [CL 502]

184 ➤ TO WILLIAM DUANE

New-York Octo. 28. 44

My Dear Sir,

Owing to my absence from this city, (where I am now residing), I did not receive your letter of the 15th until this morning.

I regret exceedingly that circumstances should have led you to think me negligent, or uncourteous, in not returning the volume of the "Messenger" — for one or the other (perhaps both) you must long since have considered me. The facts are these: Some eight months ago, I believe, I chanced to mention, in Mr Hirst's hearing, that I wished to look over a particular article in the "Messenger". He immediately volunteered to procure me the desired volume from you. I would much rather have borrowed it personally — but he seemed to make a point of the matter, and I consented. Soon afterwards he handed me the book, which I retained a very short time. It is now certainly more than seven months since I returned it to Mr Hirst, through my mother in law (Mrs Clemm), who informs me that she left it at his office, with one of his brothers. Most probably it was deposited in a book-case, and thus over-looked and forgotten. May I trouble you to send for it?

Very truly Yours,

William Duane Esqr Edgar Allan Poe.

In connection with this letter, see Poe's postscript to Letter 174, and Quinn, *Poe*, pp. 408–410. Unknown to Poe, Mrs. Clemm seems to have sold the volume of the SLM to Leary's bookstore in Philadelphia, instead of returning it to Henry B. Hirst as Poe's postscript requested (for another interpretation, see P, II, 916–919). On the verso of the enclosing cover of the letter Duane wrote: "N.B. The Statement contained in this letter that the/ volume of 'the Southern Literary Messenger' in question was/ returned to Henry B. Hirst Esq. was pronounced by Mr./ Hirst to be 'a damned lie' and subsequent events showed that/ Mr. Hirst was right in denying it — Mr. Poe having sold the/ book — I hope unintentionally — to William A. Leary the book-/ -seller in Second Street./ W.D." (For more on this episode, see Letter 191.) [CL 503]

185 ⇥ TO JAMES R. LOWELL

New-York: Oct. 28. 44.

My Dear Friend,

A host of small troubles growing from the *one* trouble of poverty, but which I will not trouble you with in detail, have hitherto prevented me from thanking you for the Biography and all the well-intended flatteries which it contains. But, upon the principle of better late than never, let me thank you now, again and again. I sent it to Graham on the day I received it — taking with it only one liberty in the way of modification. This I hope you will pardon. It was merely the substitution of another brief poem for the last you have done me the honor to quote.

I have not seen your marriage announced, but I presume from what you said in your penultimate letter, that I may congratulate you now. Is it so? At all events I can wish you no better wish than that you may derive from your marriage as substantial happiness as I have derived from mine.

A long time ago I wrote you a long letter to which you have never replied. It concerned a scheme for protecting ourselves from the imposition of publishers by a coalition. I will state it again in brief. Suppose a dozen of the most active or influential men of letters in this country, should unite for the purpose of publishing a Magazine of high character. Their names to be kept secret, that their mutual support might be the more effectual. Each member to take a share of the stock at $100 a share. [*page 2*] Each, if required, to furnish one article each month — the work to be sustained altogether by the contributions of the members, or by unpaid contributions from others. As many of the members as possible to be taken from those connected otherwise with the press: — a black-ball to exclude any one suggested as a member by those already conjoined — this to secure unanimity — These, of course, are mere hints in the rough. But suppose that (the scheme originating with yourself & me) we write to any others or, seeing them personally, engage them in the enterprize. The desired number being made up, a meeting might be held, and a constitution framed. A point in this latter might be that an editor should be elected periodically from among the stockholders.

The advantages of such a coalition seem to me very great. The Magazine could be started with a positive certainty of success. There would be no expense for contributions, while we would have the best. Plates, of course, would be disdained. The aim would be to elevate without stupifying our literature — to further justice — to resist foreign dictation — and to afford (in the circulation & profit of the journal) a remuneration to ourselves for whatever we should write.

The work should be printed in the very best manner, and should address the aristocracy of talent. We might safely give, for $5, a pamphlet of 128 pp. and, with the support of the variety of our personal influence, we might easily extend the circulation to 20,000 — giving $100,000. The expenses would not exceed $40,000 — if indeed they reached 20,000 when the work should be fairly established. Thus there would be $60,000 to be divided among 12 — $5000 per an: apiece.

I have thought of this matter long and cautiously, and am persuaded that there would be little difficulty in doing even far *more* than I have ventured to suggest.

Do you hear anything more about the Lectures?

Truly Yours.

E A Poe

Concerning the biography, see Lowell to Poe, September 27, 1844; it appeared in *Graham's*, February 1845. In his letter of June 27, Lowell apparently spoke of his forthcoming marriage to the poetess Maria White (the MS. letter is unlocated; but W, II, 89, shows an omitted passage which may have been Poe's source of information); the marriage took place in December 1844. In Letter 173 Poe had spoken of the proposed coalition. In connection with the present discussion, see also Letter 186. Lowell succeeded in getting Poe an appointment to lecture before the Boston Lyceum, October 16, 1845 (see Quinn, *Poe*, p. 485). [CL 504]

186 ➤ TO CHARLES ANTHON

[New York, ante November 2, 1844,
probably late October]

†My Dear Sir,

Upon glancing your at this letter you will no doubt be surprised at its length, and

Many years have elapsed since I last wrote you, [*Interlineated;* and had the honor of re] and you will <no doubt> perhaps be surprized — <if not exactly> both at receiving <this> a letter <at   at least and> from me now & receiving one so long. of so great a length. But may I beg your <to> attention for a few moments while I ask of you a favor upon <the> your granting or

refusing which I feel that much of my future prosperity will
depend.† [1]

[*Interlineated*:   who   whose   whose]

Many years have elapsed since my last communication with you,
and perhaps you will be surprised at receiving a letter from me
now — if not positively <discouraged> vexed at receiving one of
so great a length and of such a character. But I trust to your goodness of heart for a patient hearing, at the least.

You will have already seen that, as usual, I have a favor to solicit
<at your hands>. You have, indeed, been to me in many respects
a good genius & a friend — but the request I have to make now is
one of vital interest to myself — so much so that upon your granting it or refusing it, depends, I feel, [*Interlineated*: much if not all
of] the <whole> prosperity and even comfort of my future life.

[*Interlineated*: I have had few friends,]

I cannot flatter myself, that you have felt sufficient interest in
<my humble self> me to have followed <my> in any respect my
literary career, since the period at which you first did me the honor
to <write me a letter communicate with> address me a note me
while Editor of the Southern Messenger. A few words of explanation on this point will therefore be necessary here. [*Interlineated*:
It   It]

[*page 2*] [*Interlineated*: The] As I am well aware that your course
of reading lies ent[i]rely out of the track of our lighter literature,
and as I take it for granted therefore that <yone> none of <my>
the papers in question have met your eye — I have thought it advisable to send you with this letter — a single tale as a specimen.
<You> wil<l think no doubt> This will no doubt put you in
mind of the brick of the sholastikos — but I could not thi[n]k of
troubli[n]g you with more than one. I do not thi[n]k it my best
tale — but it is perhaps the best in <that> its particular vein. Variety has been one of my chief aims.

In lieu of the rest I venture to place in your hands the published
opinions of many of my contemporaries. I will not deny that I have
been careful to collect & to preserve them. They include, as you
will see, the warm commendations yreat number of very eminent
men, and of these commendations, I <am> should be at a loss to
understand why I have not a right to be proud.

---

[1] Matter between daggers was first drafted, and then completely cancelled by Poe.

[*At the bottom of this page occur some scribblings by Poe which we have attempted to reproduce:*]

My D

My Dear   The

Alice My Dear

σκολαστικος

Should you b   upon

I will

[*page 3*] †After a long & desperate struggle with the ills attendant upon orphanage, the total want of relatives, &† <Since quitting the Magazine> <Not long> before quitting the <Mag just mentioned> Mess:, I saw, or fancied that I saw, through a long & dim vista, the <wide and> brilliant field for <a true> ambition which a Magazine of <proper noble & high &> bold & noble aims presented to <any> him who should successfully <accomplish> establish it in America. I perceived that the country from its very constitution, could not fail of affording in a few years, a larger proportionate amount of readers than any <country> upon the Earth. <I perceiv I knew that even then> I perceived that the whole <tendency of the age> [*Interlineated:* energetic, busy spirit of the age tended wholly] was to the Magazine literature — to the curt, the terse, the well-timed, and the readily diffused, in preference to the old forms of the verbose and ponderous & the inaccessible. I knew from personal experience that lying *perdus* among the innumerable plantations in our vast Southern & Western Countries were a host of well-educated <& but little prejudiced> men si[n]gularly devoid of prejudice who would gladly le[n]d their influence to a really vigorous journal provided the right means were taken of bri[n]gi[n]g it fairly within the very limited scope of their observation — per <A> Now, <one of a Magazine Grahams a very true insignifi a journal Full of I> I knew, it is true, that some <dosens> scores of journals had failed (for indeed I looked upon the best success of the best of them as failure) but then I easily traced the causes of this failure in the impotency of their conductors, who made no scruple of basing their rules of action altogether upon what had been customarily done in stead of what was now before them to do, in the

[*Interlineated:*. bu[t]]

[*page 4*] greatly <altered> changed & constantly <alering> changing condition of things.

†But not to trust too implicitly to *à priori* reasonings, I entered a few steps into the field of experiment. I joined the "Messenger" as you know. It had then about 700 subscribers. In short I could see no real reason why a Magazine, if worthy the name, could not be made to <reach a circulation of 50.02.000>. circulate among 20,000 subscribers, embracing the best intellect & education of the land. This was a thought which stimulated my fancy & my ambition. The influence of such a journal would be vast indeed, and I dreamed of honestly employing that influence in the sacred cause of the beautiful, the just, & the true. Even in a pecuniary view, the object was a <great> magnificent one.

The journal I proposed would be a large octavo of 128 pp. <on the finest> printed with <clear> bold type, in single column, on the finest paper, and disdaining everything of what is termed "embellishn"ent with the exception of an occassional portrait of a literary man, or some well-engraved wood design in obvious illustration of the text. Of such a journal I had cautiously estimated the expenses. Could I circulate 20 000 cop. at 5$ the cost wd be about $30.000, estimating all contingencies at the highest rate. There would be a balance of $70.000 per annum. <I thought of these things & reflected that>† ex

But not to trust too implicitly to *à priori* reasonings, and at the same time to make myself thoroughly master of all details <which> which might avail me concerni[n]g the mere business of publication, I entered a few steps into the field of experiment. I joined the "Messenger" as you know which was then in its 2ᵈ year with <It had then> 700 subscribers & the general outcry was that because a Magazine had never succeeded South of the Potomac therefore a Magazine ne[ver] cd succeed. Yet in despite of this & in despite of the wretched taste [*page 5*] of its proprietor which hampered & controlled me at all points I <obtained> in 15 months increased the circulation in 15 months to 5,500. subscribers. <This number the journal had when I left it> paying an annual profit of 10,000 when I left it. This number was never <sur> exceeded by the journal which rapidly went down & <is> may now be said to be extinct. Of "Graham's Magazine" you have no doubt heard. It had been in existence under the name of the "Casket" for 8 years, when I became its editor with a subscribption list of about 5000. In about 18 months afterward its circulation amounted to no less than 50.000 — astonishi[n]g as this may appear. <In> At this period I left it. <an> It is now 2

years since, and the number of subscribers is now *not more* than
25.000. — but possibly very much less. In 3 years it will be extinct.
The nature of this journal, however, was such, that even its 50.000
subscribers could not make it <a> very profitable to its proprietor[s].
Its price was $3 — but not only were its expenses immense owing to
the employment of absurd <plat> steel plates [*Interlineated:* &
other extravagances which tell not at all] but recourse was had to
innumerable agents who recd it at a discount of no less th[a]n 50
per cent & whose [f]reque[n]t dishonesty occasional <great>
enormous loss. But, if 50000 *can* be obtained for a 3$ Maga- among
a class of readers who really read little, why may not 50,000. be
procured for a $5 journal among the true and permanent readers
of the land? [*Interlineated:* Astor House]

Holding steadily in view my ultimate purpose — to <establish>
fou[n]d a Magazine of my own, or in which at least I might have a
proprietary right, — it has been my constant endeavour in the meantime not so much to establish a reputation great in itself as <ef th>
one of that particular character which should best further my special
object[s], and draw attention to my exertions as Editor of a Magazine Thus I have <thus> written no books and [*at this point,
running upside down and between and among the words, occur two
sums:* 20,000

$$\frac{12}{240000} \quad and \quad 8\overline{\left|\begin{array}{c}20,000 \\ 2,500\end{array}\right.}$$
$$60000$$

have been so far essentially a Magazinist — That That [*page 6*]
<putting up not> bearing not only willi[n]gly but cheerfully
<with the thousand> sad poverty & the thousand consequent <ill>s
& contumelies [*Interlineated:* & other ills] which the <the> condition of the mere Magazinist entails upon him in America. — where
more than in any other region upon the face of the globe to be
poor is to be despised.

The one great difficulty resulting from this course, is that <I am
judged by individual papers> unless the journalist collects his various
articles he is <very> liable to <gross misjudgement from on the
part> be grossly misconceived & misjudged by men of whose good
opinion he would be proud — <and> <of> but who <have seen>
see, perhaps, only a paper here & there, by accident, — often only
one of his mere extravaganzas, written <for variety's sake, or> to

supply a particular demand. He loses, too, <the> whatever merit may be his due on the score of *versatility* — a point which can only be estimated by <comparison> collection of his various articles in volume form and altogether. This is indeed a serious difficulty — to seek a remedy for which is my object in my own case in writi[n]g you this letter. [*Here follow some scribblings:*] wh whic extinction b by

<It is very true that I h>

Setting aside, for the present, my criticisms poems & miscellanies (sufficiently numerous) my tales a great number of which might be termed Phantasy Pieces, <and> are in number sixty-six. They would make, perhaps, 5 of the ordinary novel volumes. I have them prepared in every respect for the press; but, alas, I have no money, nor that influence which would enable me to get a publisher — although I seek *no* pecuniary remuneration. My sole im[m]ediate object is the furtherance of my ultimate one. I believe that if I could get my Tales fairly before the public, and thus have <the> an opportun[i]ty of eliciti[n]g foreign as well as native opinion respecting them — I should <by> by their means [*Here occur more scribblings:*] [a]ct volume volu be [*page 7*] be in a far more advantageous position than at present in regard to the establishment of a Magazine. In a word, I believe that the publication of the work would lead forthwith <to an arrangement which I have long held in view with> either directly through my own exertion or indirectly with the aid of a publisher to the establishment of the journal I hold in view.

It is very true that <you> I have no claims upon your attention — not even that of personal acquaintance. But I have <a> reached a crisis of my life, in which I sadly stand in need of <a friend> aid, and without being able to say why, — <I have been always filled> u[n]less it is that I so <much wish> earnestly desire your friendship — I have always felt a half-hope that <I> if I appealled to you you would prove my friend. I know that you have unbounde[d] influence with the Harpers — & I know that if you would exert <that> it in my behalf you could procure me the publication I desire.

[*Here occur more scribblings:*] I [Jou] scarcely but not onl I b but not

[*Unsigned*]

Anthon's reply of November 2, having no apology for delay, implies an October dating for Poe's corrected letter; moreover, Poe to Lowell, March 30, 1844, speaks of a magazine of 120 pp., and to Lowell, October 28, and to Anthon, *supra*, of 128 pp. Poe wrote Lowell, May 28, 1844, that he had written "about 60" tales; he tells Anthon "66." To the 55 titles known to have been written by May 28, 1844 (see Poe's letter to Lowell), we may add the "Literary Life of Thingum Bob" and "The Angel of the Odd" (see Wyllie, *Poe's Tales*, pp. 329, 322), published by the end of 1844. Thus, 57 tales, not "66," are all that we may be certain of, though the four published by July 1845, may have been written by October 1844; also, Poe may have had in mind various articles (he called "Mesmeric Revelation" both tale and essay). [CL 505]

187 ⊁ TO GEORGE R. GRAHAM

[New York, "Early 1845"]

We were square when I sold you the "Versification" article; for which you gave me first 25, and afterward 7 — in all $32 00

Then you bought "The Gold Bug" for 52 00

I got both these back, so that I owed $84 00

You lent Mrs. Clemm 12 50

Making in all $96 50

The review of "Flaccus" was 3¾ pp, which at $4, is 15 00

Lowell's poem is 10 00

The review of Channing, 4 pp is 16, of which I got 6, leaving 10 00

The review of Halleck, 4 pp. is 16, of which I got 10, leaving 6 00

The review of Reynolds, 2 pp. 8 00

The review of Longfellow, 5 pp. is 20, of which I got 10, leaving 10 00

So that I have paid in all 59 00

Which leaves still due by me $37 50

[*Signature missing*]

The "Versification" article was printed as "Notes Upon English Verse" in Lowell's *Pioneer*, March 1843, and later as "The Rationale of Verse" in the SLM, October and November 1848. The review of Thomas Ward's poems, published under the pen name of Flaccus, appeared in *Graham's* for March 1843. The review of William Ellery Channing's poems appeared in *Graham's,* August 1843. The review of Fitz-Greene Halleck's poems was printed in *Graham's,* September 1843 — these three articles forming part of the series of papers entitled "Our Contributors" (reprinted in H, xi). "Lowell's poem" may refer to Poe's review of *Poems* (1844) in *Graham's,* March 1844, though the review was less than two pages in length and Poe's charge implies two and one-half pages; it is possible Poe refers to an article planned at the time of his departure from Philadelphia (see Letter 174), but if completed it was never printed in *Graham's.* The reviews of Reynolds and Longfellow were never printed in *Graham's.* In connection with Longfellow's *Spanish Student,* which seems to be meant by the "review," it is interesting to note that Poe, writing to Lowell, July 2, 1844, said, "Graham has had, for 9 months, a review of mine on Longfellow's 'Spanish Student', which I have 'used up' . . ."; Graham never printed the review, and Poe, therefore, owed Graham $20 more than the amount cited in the letter as "still due by me." [CL 512]

188 ⇥ TO GEORGE BUSH

New York Jan. 4, 45.

Dear Sir;

With this note I take the liberty of sending you a newspaper — "The Dollar Weekly" — in which there is an article, by myself, entitled "Mesmeric Revelation." It has been copied into the paper from a Monthly Magazine — "The Columbian" — in which it originally appeared in July last.

I have ventured to send you the article because there are many points in it which bear upon the subject-matter of your last admirable work on the Future Condition of Man and therefore I am induced to hope that you will do me the honor to look over what I have said.

You will, of course, understand that the article is purely a fiction; — but I have embodied in it some thoughts which are original with myself & I am exceedingly anxious to learn if they have claim to absolute originality, and also how far they will strike you as well based. If you would be so kind as to look over the paper and give me, in brief, your opinion, I will consider it a high favor.

Very Respy. Yr. Ob. St.

Edgar A. Poe.

Please reply thro' the P. Office.

For George Bush, Professor of Hebrew at New York University, see
"Literati" in *Godey's*, May 1846 (reprinted in H, xv, 6–7). "Mesmeric
Revelation" was first published in the *Columbian*, ii (August 1844),
67–70; thus Poe's "July last" probably refers to the appearance of the
magazine. Bush's *Anastasis, or The Doctrine of the Resurrection* is
mentioned by Poe in "Marginalia," April 1846 (see H, xvi, 97–98).
[CL 513]

189 ⊁ TO FREDERICK W. THOMAS

New-York Jan. 4. 45.

Dear Thomas,

I duly received your two letters and "The Beechen Tree", for
which let me thank you. My reason for not replying instanter was
that I was just then making arrangements which, if fully carried
out, would have enabled me to do you justice in a manner satisfactory
to both of us — but these arrangements finally fell through, after
my being kept in suspense for months — and I could find no good
opportunity of putting in a word anywhere that would have done
you service. You know I do not live in town — very seldom visit
it — and, of course, am not in the way of matters and things as I
used to be. As for Benjamin's criticism — although I made all kinds
of inquiry about it, I could meet no one who had ever heard of it.
At the "New-World" Office no paper containing it was even on file.
I am disposed to think you were misinformed, and that no such
critique appeared, in that paper at least. At all events, if there did,
Benjamin, I am assured, did not write it. At the epoch you speak of,
he was unconnected with the "New-World".

In about three weeks, I shall [*page 2*] move into the City, and re-
commence a life of activity under better auspices, I hope, than ever
before. *Then* I may be able to do something.

Virginia & Mrs Clemm are about as usual and beg to be remembered.

I am truly glad to hear of Dow's well-doing. If ever man deserved
prosperity, he does. Give him my respects — in which one word I
mean to include all descriptions of kind feeling.

I remain, Thomas, truly
Your friend,

Poe

In his letter of October 10, Thomas wrote that he was sending Poe a copy of his book, *The Beechen Tree,* which had been reviewed favorably, except by Dunn English and Park Benjamin. Again, on December 10, he asked why Poe had not acknowledged receipt of the poem. Poe had been attempting to get Chivers to join him in publishing the *Stylus* (see Letter 180 and note). A review of *The Beechen Tree* appeared in the New York *Evening Mirror,* November 19, 1844 (Thomas O. Mabbott thinks "the very brief notice may be Poe's — it is complimentary, Poe certainly could have inserted it, and if it is his, it suggests that he found rather more faults than he wished, and perhaps had other reasons than those he told Thomas for failing to write the long review. But it is also possible that Willis anticipated him even in the brief notice, which is not stylistically definitive." Quinn (*Poe,* pp. 435, 414) cites this letter as evidence that Poe was still living on the farm of Patrick Brennan, near what is now the neighborhood of 84th Street, between Amsterdam Avenue and Broadway. Benjamin left the editorship of the *New World* in March 1844 (see Mott, *History of American Magazines,* I, 361), several months prior to the publication of Thomas' poem. Just when Poe moved into New York is uncertain, but he probably went to 195 East Broadway sometime in the spring of 1845. Poe soon became an editor of the new *Broadway Journal* (see Letter 197 and note). Thomas' letter of October 10 spoke of Dow's having become doorkeeper at the House of Representatives in Washington. [CL 514]

190 ✦ TO RUFUS W. GRISWOLD

New-York : Jan. 16. 45.

{Confidential}

Dear Griswold — if you will permit me to call you so — Your letter occasioned me first pain and then pleasure: — pain because it gave me to see that I had lost, through my own folly, an honorable friend: — pleasure, because I saw in it a hope of reconciliation.

I have been aware, for several weeks, that my reasons for speaking of your book as I did (of *yourself* I have always spoken kindly) were based in the malignant slanders of a mischief-maker by profession. Still, as I supposed you irreparably offended, I could make no advances when we met at the Tribune Office, although I longed to do so. I know of nothing which would give me more sincere pleasure than your accepting these apologies, and meeting me as a friend.

If you *can* do this and forget the past, let me know where I shall call on you — or come and see me at the Mirror Office, any morning about 10. We can then talk over the other matters, which, to me at least, are far less important than your good will.

Very truly yours

R. W. Griswold.   Edgar A Poe.

> When Griswold edited the *Works of Edgar Allan Poe* (see Note 111) he failed to print his letter to Poe of January 14, 1845, to which the present letter is Poe's reply. By suppressing his own letter requesting that Poe submit titles of his work and a biographical sketch for inclusion in Griswold's forthcoming *Prose Writers of America* (H, xvii, 197–198), Griswold made it appear that Poe was humbly soliciting favors of him, whereas the situation was actually the reverse. [CL 517]

191 ⯈ TO WILLIAM DUANE

New-York Jan. 28. 45.

Sir,

Richmond is the last place in which I should have hoped to find a copy of either the 1ʳˢᵗ 2d or 3d volumes of the Messenger. For this reason I did not apply there. I have been putting myself, however, to some trouble in endeavouring to collect among my friends here the separate numbers of the missing volume. I am glad that your last letter relieves me from all such trouble in future. I do not choose to recognize you in this matter at all. To the person of whom I borrowed the book, or rather who insisted upon forcing it on me, I have sufficient reason to believe that it was returned. Settle your difficulties with him, and insult me with no more of your communications.

Mr Duane.   Edgar A Poe

> In connection with this letter, see Letter 184 and note. Duane endorsed the present letter: "Bombastes Furioso Poe. Dated January 28, 1845. Received January 31, 1845. Not to be answered." He then restated his note on the earlier letter (Letter 184), and added that Leary sold the volume to "a bookseller in Richmond, Va., who sold it to the publishers of the 'Messenger,' who sold it to a friend of mine . . . whom I had commissioned to purchase me a copy. My name was on the title-page during all these sales" (for the full note, see W, ii, 367–368). Duane's endorsement also includes the statement, "I sent him word that . . ." which may have been transmitted by letter (unlocated), but which was probably sent orally. [CL 520]

VII

NEW YORK

ERA OF THE BROADWAY JOURNAL

February 1845–December 1845

[New York, February 3, 1845]

Dear Shea,

Lest I should have made some mistake in the hurry I transcribe the whole alteration.

Instead of the whole stanza commencing "Wondering at the stillness broken &c — substitute this

Startled at the stillness broken by reply so aptly spoken,
"Doubtless", said I, "what it utters is its only stock and store
Caught from some unhappy master whom unmerciful Disaster
Followed fast and followed faster till his songs one burden bore —
Till the dirges of his Hope the melancholy burden bore,
        'Nevermore — ah, nevermore!' "

At the close of the stanza *preceding* this, instead of "Quoth the raven Nevermore", substitute *"Then the bird said "Nevermore"*.

Truly yours

Poe

Shea was connected with the *Tribune* (see Campbell, *Poems*, p. 248). [CL 521]

New-York, Feb. 24, 1845.

My Dear Griswold,

Soon after seeing you I sent you, through Zeiber, all my poems worth re-publishing, & I presume they reached you. With this I send you another package, also through Zeiber, by Burgess & Stringer. It contains in the way of Essay "Mesmeric Revelation" which I would like to go in, even if something else is omitted. I send also a portion of the "Marginalia", in which I have marked some of the most pointed passages. In the matter of criticism I cannot put my hand upon anything that suits me — but I believe that in "funny" criticism (if you wish any such) Flaccus will convey a tolerable idea of my style, and of my serious manner Barnaby Rudge is a good specimen. In "Graham" you will find these. In the tale line I send you "The Murders in the Rue Morgue" and "The Man that was used up" — far more than enough, you will say — but you can select to suit yourself. I would prefer having in the "Gold Bug" to the "Murders in the R.M", but have not a copy just now. If there is no immediate hurry for it, however, I will get one & send it you corrected. Please write & let me know if you get this. — I have taken a 3d interest in the "Broadway Journal" & will be glad if you could send me anything, at any time, in the way of "Literary Intelligence".

Truly yours,

Poe.

Early in 1845 Griswold was preparing the sixth edition of his *Poets and Poetry of America,* published later in the year (see Jacob L. Neu, "Rufus Wilmot Griswold," p. 133) and Poe had probably been asked at a meeting with Griswold prior to this letter to contribute not only to the *Poets and Poetry of America,* but also to the *Prose Writers of America* (Philadelphia: Carey and Hart, March 3, 1847). The meeting undoubtedly followed Griswold's letter of January 14, in which he requested Poe to submit certain data, and Poe's reply of January 16, in which Poe suggested a meeting. "Zeiber" was George B. Zieber and Co., booksellers, according to P, II, 1685. Burgess and Stringer were carriers in competition with the United States mails. Poe found such carriers more economical than the government mails; for example, he sent packages to Lowell by Harnden's Express. Despite Poe's suggested inclusions, Griswold published only "The Fall of the House of Usher," which first appeared in *Burton's,* v (September 1839), 145–152, and which Poe did not mention in his letter, though Griswold's version of the letter (see Note 193) did; furthermore, Griswold's version omitted any reference to "Marginalia." Poe's "3d interest in the 'Broadway Journal' " dated from February 21, 1845, when the contract with Bisco, the publisher, was signed (see Quinn, *Poe,* p. 751). Griswold's reply to this letter, if made, as Poe requested, is not known. [CL 524]

194 ⋟ TO EDITOR OF THE BROADWAY JOURNAL

[New York] March 8, 1845

In a late lecture on the "Poets and Poetry of America," delivered before an audience made up chiefly of editors and their connexions, I took occasion to speak what I know to be the truth, and I endeavoured so to speak it that there should be no chance of misunderstanding what it was I intended to say. I told these gentlemen to their teeth that, with a *very* few noble exceptions, they had been engaged for many years in a system of indiscriminate laudation of American books — a system which, more than any other one thing in the world, had tended to the depression of that "American Literature" whose elevation it was designed to effect. I said this, and very much more of a similar tendency, with as thorough a directness as I could command. Could I, at the moment, have invented any terms *more* explicit, wherewith to express my contempt of our general editorial course of corruption and puffery, I should have employed them beyond the shadow of a doubt; — and should I think of anything more expressive *hereafter,* I will endeavour either to find or to make an opportunity for its introduction to the public.

And what, for all this, had I to anticipate? In a very few cases, the open, and, in several, the silent approval of the more chivalrous portion of the press; — but in a majority of instances, I should have been weak indeed to look for anything but abuse. To the Willises — the O'Sullivans — the Duyckincks — to the choice and magnanimous few who spoke promptly in my praise, and who have since taken my hand with a more cordial and more impressive grasp than ever — to these I return, of course, my acknowledgements, for that they have rendered me my due. To my villifiers I return also such thanks as they deserve, inasmuch as without what they have done me the honor to say, there would have been much of point wanting in the compliments of my friends. Had I, indeed, from the former, received any less equivocal tokens of disapprobation, I should at this moment have been looking about me to discover what sad blunder I had committed.

I am most sincere in what I say. I thank these, my opponents, for their good will, — manifested, of course, after their own fashion. No doubt they mean me well — if they could only be brought to believe it; and I shall expect more reasonable things from them hereafter. In the mean time, I await patiently the period when they shall have fairly made an end of what they have to say — when they shall have sufficiently exalted themselves in their own opinion — and when, especially, they shall have brought *me* over to that precise view of the question which it is their endeavor to have me adopt.

E. A. P.

Concerning the lecture, see Letter 195, especially the postscript and note. N. P. Willis reviewed the lecture favorably in the *Weekly Mirror,* I (March 8, 1845), 347 (see Quinn, *Poe,* pp. 457–458). John L. O'Sullivan was editor of the *Democratic Review* (see Mott, *History of American Magazines,* I, 677 ff.). For Evert A. Duyckinck, see the note to Letter 201. At the time of the present letter Poe was an editor of the *Broadway Journal,* though his name did not appear on the title page until the following week, March 15, when for the first time the names of the editors were given. [CL 527]

195 ➤ TO J. HUNT, JR.

New-York March 17. 45

Dear Sir,

There is something in the tone of your article on "The Broadway Journal" (contained in the "Archives" of the 13 th.) which induces me to trouble you with this letter.

I recognize in you an educated, an honest, a chivalrous, but, I fear, a somewhat over-hasty man. I feel that you can appreciate what I do — and that you will not fail to give me credit for what I do well: — at the same time I am not quite sure that, through sheer hurry, you might not do me an injustice which you yourself would regret even more sincerely than I. I am anxious to secure you as a friend if you can be so with a clear conscience — and it is to enable you to be so with a clear conscience that I write what I am now writing.

Let me put it to you as to a frank man of honor — Can you suppose it possible that any human being could pursue a strictly impartial course of criticism for 10 years (as I have done in the S. L. Messenger and in Graham's Magazine) without offending irreparably a host of authors and their connexions? — but because these *were* offended, and gave vent at every opportunity to their spleen, would you consider my course an iota the less honorable on that account? Would you consider it just to measure my deserts by the yelpings of my foes, indepently of your own judgment in the premises, based upon an actual knowledge of what I have done?

You reply — "Certainly not," and, because I feel that this *must* be your reply, I acknowledge that I am grieved to see any thing (however slight) in your paper [*page 2*] that has the appearance of joi[n]-ing in with the outcry so very sure to be made by the 'less['] honorable portion of the press under circumstances such as are my own.

I thank you sincerely for your expressions of good will — and I thank you for the reason that I value your opinion — when that opinion is fairly attained. But there are points at which you do me injustice.

For example, you say that I am sensitive (peculiarly so) to the strictures of others. There is no instance on record in which I have *ever* replied, directly or indirectly, to any strictures, personal or literary, with the single exception of my answer to Outis. You say, too, that I use a quarter of the paper in smoothing over his charges — but four-fifths of the whole space occupied is by the letter of Outis itself, to which I wish to give all the publicity in my power, with a view of giving it the more thorough refutation. The charges of which you speak — the charge of plagiarism &c — are *not made at all*. These are mistakes into which you have fallen, through want of time to peruse *the whole* of what I said, and by happening upon unlucky passages. It is, of course, improper to decide upon my reply until you have heard it, and as yet I have only commenced it by giving Outis' letter with a few comments at random. There will be *four* chapters in all. My excuse for treating it at length is that it demanded an answer & no proper answer could be given in less compass — that the subject of imitation, plagiarism, &c is one in which the <subject> public has lately taken much interest & is admirably adapted to the character of a literary journal — and that I have some important developments to make, which the commonest princi- [*page 3*] ples of self-defence demand imperatively at my hands.

I know that you will now do me justice — that you will read what I have said & may say — and that you will absolve me, at once, of the charge of squirmishness or ill nature. If ever man had cause to be in good humor with Outis and all the world, it is precisely myself, at this moment — as hereafter you shall see.

At some future day we shall be friends, *or* I am much mistaken, and I will then put into your hands ample means of judging me upon my own merits.

In the meantime I ask of you, justice.

Very truly yours

To J. Hunt Jr.   Edgar A Poe.

P.S. I perceive that you have permitted some of our papers an[d t]he Boston journals to give you a wrong impression of my Lecture & its reception. It was better attended than any Lecture of Mr Hudson's —

by the most intellectual & refined portion of the city — and was com-
plimented in terms which I should be ashamed to repeat, by the leading
journalists of the City. See Mirror, Morning News, Inquirer New
World &c. The only respectable N. Y. papers which did *not* praise it
<w> throughout, was the Tribune whose transcendental editors or
their doctrines, I attacked. My objection to the burlesque philosophy,
which the Bostonians have adopted, supposing it to be Transcendental-
ism, is the key to the abuse of the Atlas & Transcript. So well was the
Lecture received that I am about to repeat it.

> Poe is replying to a criticism of his Outis paper, "Imitation," in the
> *Broadway Journal,* March 8, 1845, pp. 147–150, by J. Hunt, Jr., in his
> *National Archives* (Ithaca, New York), March 13, 1845. (Hunt's
> *Archives* ran from February 6 to March 13, 1845, and was dead when
> Poe wrote his letter, according to Quinn, *Poe,* p. 456.) Poe's "four
> chapters" in the *Broadway Journal* series were: (in addition to the first,
> already cited) "Plagiarism" (March 15, pp. 161–163); "Mr. Poe's Reply
> to the Letter of Outis" (March 22, pp. 178–182); "A Large Account
> of a Small Matter" (March 29, pp. 194–198); and "A Voluminous
> History of the Little Longfellow War" (April 5, pp. 211–212; Quinn,
> *Poe,* p. 454). There is no evidence of a letter from Hunt in reply to
> Poe's. Poe lectured on "Poets and Poetry of America," announced in
> the *Evening Mirror* (February 27, 1845) for the evening of February
> 28 (Quinn, *Poe,* p. 457); it was delivered in the library of the New
> York Historical Society (see Alexander Crane in the Omaha *Sunday
> World Herald,* July 13, 1902, p. 24, reprinted in part by Quinn, *Poe,*
> p. 458; also Allen, *Israfel,* p. 508. Also, an unpublished letter from
> W. M. Gillespie to Poe, Saturday morning [March 1, 1845] in the
> Boston Public Library, asks permission to copy the characterization of
> Mrs. Osgood, given by Poe in his lecture "last night." Crane also states,
> in the *Sunday World Herald,* that the lecture was repeated, but does not
> give the date. [CL 529]

196 ⊁ TO RUFUS W. GRISWOLD

[New York] Apr. 19 [1845]

Dear Griswold,

I return the proof, with many thanks for your attentions. The
poems look quite as well in the short metre as in the long, and I am
quite content as it is. You will perceive, however, that some of the
lines have been divided at the wrong place. I have marked them right

in the proof; but lest there should be any misapprehension, I copy them as they should be:

Stanza 11.

Till the dirges of his Hope the
Melancholy burden bore

Stanza 12.

Straight I wheel'd a cushion'd seat in
Front of bird and bust and door;

Stanza 12 — again

What this grim, ungainly, ghastly
Gaunt and ominous bird of yore

Stanza 13.

To the fowl whose fiery eyes now
Burn'd into my bosom's core;

Near the beginning of the poem you have *"nodded"* spelt *"nooded"*. In the "Sleeper" the line

Forever with uncloséd eye

should read

Forever with unopen'd eye

Is it possible to make the alteration?

Very sincerely yours

Poe.

PS) I presume you understand that in the repetition of my Lecture on the Poets (in N. Y.) I left out *all* that was offensive to yourself?

This is the only letter Poe is known to have written between March 21 and May 4. He was in New York, as the postal cancellation indicates; and Griswold was in Philadelphia, as the address shows. In its first published form (New York *Evening Mirror*, January 29, 1845), "The

Raven" was printed in long lines, as it was in *The Raven and Other Poems* (New York: Wiley and Putnam, November 19, 1845 — see T. O. Mabbott, "Introduction" to his edition of *The Raven and Other Poems*). [CL 534]

197 ⤗ TO FREDERICK W. THOMAS

[New York, May 4, 1845]

My Dear Thomas,

In the hope that you have not yet *quite* given me up, as gone to Texas, or elsewhere, I sit down to write you a few words. I have been intending to do the same thing ever since I received your letter before the last — but for my life and soul I could not find, or make, an opportunity. The fact is, that being seized, of late, with a fit of industry, I put so many irons in the fire all at once, that I have been quite unable to get them out. For the last three or four months I have been working 14 or 15 hours a day — hard at it all the time — and so, whenever I took pen in hand to write, I found that I was neglecting something that *would be* attended to. I never knew what it was to be a slave before.

And yet, Thomas, I have made no money. I am as poor now as ever I was in my life — except in hope, which is by no means bankable. I have taken a 3d pecuniary interest in the "Broadway Journal", and for every thing I have written for it have been, of course, so much out of pocket. In the end, however, it will pay me well — at least the prospects are good. Say to Dow for me that there never has been a chance for my repaying him, without putting myself to greater inconvenience than he himself would have wished [*page 2*] to subject me to, had he known the state of the case. Nor am I able to pay him now. The Devil himself was never so poor. Say to Dow, also, that I am sorry he has taken to dunning in his old age — it is a diabolical practice, altogether unworthy "a gentleman & a scholar" — to say nothing of the Editor of the "Madisonian." I wonder how he would like me to write him a series of letters — say one a week — giving him the literary gossip of New-York — or something of more general character. I would furnish him such a series for whatever he could afford to give me. If he agrees to this arrangement, ask him to state the length & character of the letters — how often — and how much he can give me. Remember me kindly to him & tell him I believe that dunning is his one sin — although at the same time, I do think it is the unpardonable sin against the Holy Ghost spoken of in the Scriptures. I am going to mail him the "Broadway Journal" regularly, & hope he will honor me with an exchange.

My dear Thomas, I hope you will never imagine from any seeming neglect of mine, that I have forgotten our old friendship. There is no one in the world I would rather see at this moment than yourself; and many are the long talks we have about you and yours. Virginia & Mrs Clemm beg to be remembered to you in the kindest [*page 3*] terms. Do write me fully when you get this, and let me know particularly what you are about.

I send you an early number of the "B. Journal" containing my "Raven". It was copied by Briggs, my associate, before I joined the paper. "The Raven" has had a great "run", Thomas — but I wrote it for the express purpose of running — just as I did the "Gold-Bug", you know. The bird beat the bug, though, all hollow.

Do not forget to write immediately, & believe me

Most sincerely your friend,

Poe

On February 21, 1845, Poe entered into a contract with John Bisco, publisher of the *Broadway Journal,* in which Poe agreed to assist Charles F. Briggs in editing the magazine, to lend his name as one of the editors, to furnish at least one page of original matter each week, and to "give his faithful superintendence to the general conduct" of the *Journal,* for which Bisco agreed to give Poe one third of the profit and to settle with him "as often as every four weeks." The agreement was to last for one year (see a printing of the contract in Quinn, *Poe,* p. 751). Nothing came of Poe's suggested contributions to the *Madisonian.* "The Raven" was reprinted in the *Broadway Journal,* February 8, 1845, the sixth number of the magazine. "The Gold Bug" had appeared in the *Dollar Newspaper,* June 21 and 28, 1843.

On page 3 Thomas wrote concerning Jesse E. Dow, author of "many beautiful fugitive poems." He explained Poe's reference to "dunning" as due to Dow's "pressing need of the money which he had lent to Poe." He then added, as if the note had been made at a date later than that of the letter, "Dow is now dead . . . It was delightful to hear the two talk togeather, and to see how Poe would start at some of Dow's STRANGE notions as Poe called them." (The full note is given in H, XVII, 205, with some inaccuracies.) [CL 535]

198 ⋟ TO FREDERICK W. THOMAS

New-York — May. 14. 45.

My Dear Thomas,

Yours of the 12 th has just reached me & I hasten to send you a translation of the cipher as desired — although I fancy it will turn out to be of no particular importance. It runs thus:

"In September 1843, our respected friend Colonel T. C. Gardner, auditor of the Post Office Department, applied at the Land Office with his warrant. His patent did not render it necessary to reside at the place.

Richard Douglas.

Lieutenant Brewster (or Shrewstead)

Brooklyn Long Island

25 September 1843."

This cryptograph has been written by some barbarously ignorant person who spells "necessary" <for> ["]neseserri" "post office" "puwst ofis" "to" "tuw" [*Marginal addition:* "Brooklyn" "Bruklin"] etc. His name is signed "Rithard Duglas." You will perceive, therefore, that absolute accuracy, in decyphering the cryptograph, is impossible — but I have made it as clear as such a letter would have been *out* of cypher. The words which follow "Lieutenant Brewster" I have not made out & although they *may be* "United States Marine". If more accuracy is required, please forward *the original*. In copying, abundant errors seem to have been made.

I was delighted to hear from you. Do write soon again. (I have not seen Dow yet. Willis is well & going to England next month.) I will write you more fully in a day or two. Yours truly but in haste.

Poe.

On the verso of this letter Thomas wrote: "A gentleman in the land office in Washington inspecting a [*illegible*] in some papers in which he found a letter in cipher, and having heard me speak of my knowledge of Poe's skill in cryptography, asked me to get him to decipher it which I did. T."

Thomas' letter of May 12, 1845 (see Note 198) said that Dow had gone to New York for a visit, and asked if Poe ever saw Willis. Though Poe promises to write in a "day or two," no letter is known until his last to Thomas, February 14, 1849. In connection with Poe's cryptanalysis of "Brewster's" item, see W. K. Wimsatt, Jr., *Publications of* the *Modern Language Association*, LVIII (September 1943), 765–766, in which he says Poe was hasty in his solution and made errors, the original cypher not being done by an ignorant person. [CL 537]

199 ✝ TO JOHN KEESE

[New York]

Mr John Keese,

Dr Sir,

Permit me to thank you for the many expressions of good will in your letter of the 24th — also for the books you were so kind as to send me a few days before — very especially for Mrs Smith's beautiful Poems.

It will give me great pleasure to hand you, in the course of this week, a brief article for "The Opal".

With respect & esteem,
Yr Ob. St.

May 26.th. [1845]　　　　　　　　Edgar A Poe

> The 1846 *Opal: a pure gift for the holy days*, was edited by John Keese, who also edited the one for 1847; neither one, however, has any contribution by Poe (in this connection, see Letter 200). The 1846 *Opal* was reviewed in the *Broadway Journal*, December 27, 1845, p. 386. For Poe's review of the poetry of Elizabeth Oakes Smith, see the *Broadway Journal*, August 23, 1845 (reprinted in H, XII, 228–233); Keese was her editor. [CL 540]

200 ✝ TO JOHN KEESE

[New York]

My Dear Sir,

With this note I have the honor to send you a brief sketch for "The Opal" — and hope that I am not too late.

Whatever you yourself think the value of the article, please remit to the Office of the "Broadway Journal".

With sincere esteem
Yr Ob. S^t

Mr John Keese.　　　　　　　　Edgar A Poe
June 9.th [1845]

> Apparently, Poe's article was too late; at least it was not published in the 1846 *Opal*, edited by Keese, either in the New York printing or

in the Greenfield [Massachusetts] printing (copy in the Newberry Library, Chicago). [CL 544]

201 ➤ TO EVERT A. DUYCKINCK

[New York, June 26, 1845]
Thursday Morning.

My Dear Mr Duyckinck,

I am still dreadfully unwell, and fear that I shall be very seriously ill. Some matters of domestic affliction have also happened which deprive me of what little energy I have left — and I have resolved to give up the B. Journal and retire to the country for six months, or perhaps a year, as the sole means of recruiting my health and spirits. Is it not possible that yourself or Mr Matthews might give me a trifle for my interest in the paper? Or, if this cannot be effected, might I venture to ask you for an advance of $50 on the faith of the "American Parnassus"? — which I will finish as soon as possible. If you could oblige me in this manner I would feel myself under the deepest obligation. Will you be so kind as to reply by the bearer?

Most sincerely yours

E. A. Dyckinck Esqʳ   Edgar A Poe

Evert A. Duyckinck and Cornelius Mathews had edited *Arcturus*, December 1840–May 1842, in New York (see Mott, *History of American Magazines*, I, 711); later, Duyckinck became the editor of the *Literary World*, February–April 1847, which he and his brother George edited and published from October 1848, until December 1853 (see Mott, *History of American Magazines*, I, p. 766). Duyckinck, a frequent contributor to various periodicals of the day, also selected and edited Poe's *Tales*, which Wiley and Putnam had just published (see the note to Letter 237). The advance of $50 on the "American Parnassus" (*Literary America*, see the note to Letter 240) was apparently made (see Letter 215). The bearer was probably Mrs. Clemm, but no written reply is known. [CL 545]

202 ➤ TO EDWARD J. THOMAS

Office of the Broadway Journal
[New York *ante* July 5, 1845]

Edward J. Thomas, Esq.

Sir, —

As I have not had the pleasure of hearing from you since our interview at your office, may I ask of you to state to me distinctly, whether

I am to consider the charge of *forgery* urged by you against myself, in the presence of a common friend, as originating with yourself or Mr. Benjamin ?

Your ob. Serv't.,

Edgar A. Poe

> In *Godey's* for July 1846, Poe belittled the abilities of Thomas Dunn English, poet and editor of the *Aristidean* (1845). In his reply in the New York *Evening Mirror*, June 23, English attacked Poe's character, stating that "a merchant of this city had accused him [Poe] of committing forgery." Poe's rejoinder identified the "merchant" as "a gentleman of high respectability — Mr. *Edward J. Thomas*, of Broad Street." But Thomas' letter (cited in Note 202) makes clear that Thomas merely repeated the rumor of forgery, that he traced it to the originator, who is unidentified, and found it without basis. Apparently, Park Benjamin was in no way responsible for making the charge, and the "common friend" is identified as Mrs. Frances S. Osgood (see Thomas' letter to her, in Quinn, *Poe*, p. 505; see also, Ingram, II, 85, n.). [CL 548]

203 ➤ TO NEILSON POE

New-York: August 8/ 45.

My Dear Sir,

It gave me sincere pleasure to receive a letter from you — but I fear you will think me very discourteous in not sooner replying. I have deferred my answer, however, from day to day, in hope of procuring some papers relating to my grandfather. In this I have failed. Mrs C. has no memoranda of the kind you mention, and all of which I have any knowledge are on file at Annapolis.

I thank you for the kind interest you take in my welfare. We all speak very frequently of yourself and family, and regret that, hitherto, we have seen and known so little of each other. Virginia, in especial, is much pained at the total separation from her sisters. She has been, and is still, in precarious health. About four years ago she ruptured a blood-vessel, in singing, and has never recovered from the accident. I fear that she never will. Mrs Clemm is quite well: — both beg to be kindly remembered.

I regret that I had no opportunity of seeing you during my last visit to Baltimore. Virginia and myself, however, will very probably spend a few weeks in your city during the fall, when we hope to be with you frequently. When you see any of Mr Herring's family, will you say that we are anxious to hear from them?

I rejoice to learn that you prosper at all points. I hear *of* you often. "The B. Journal" flourishes — but in January I shall establish a Magazine.

> Very cordially Yours,
>
> Edgar A Poe

Neilson Poe, son of Jacob Poe, was Maria Clemm's cousin, and Poe's second cousin. Virginia's "sisters" would be her half-sisters, daughters of her father by a former marriage; Josephine Poe, Neilson's wife, was one of them (see Quinn, *Poe*, p. 726). Mrs. Clemm's sister, Elisabeth, had married Henry Herring (see Quinn, *Poe*, p. 17). [CL 553]

---

204 ⊁ TO THOMAS W. FIELD

> New-York: Aug. 9. 45

Dear Sir,

It is nearly a month since I received a note from you, requesting an interview — but, by some inadvertence, I placed it (your note) among my pile of "answered letters". This will account to you for my seeming discourtesy in not sooner giving you an answer.

I have now to say that I shall be happy to see you at any time, at my residence 195 East Broadway. You will generally find me at home in the morning before 10.

> Very Resp^y
> Yr. Ob. S^t

Mr Thomas W. Field.   Edgar A Poe

Thomas W. Field was probably the florist, schoolteacher, and poet who lived in Brooklyn and who is mentioned in the *Dictionary of American Biography* (VI, 376). The present letter shows Poe's address on August 9, 1845; he moved to 85 Amity Street before October 1 (see the note to Letter 215). [CL 554]

---

205 ⊁ TO DR. THOMAS H. CHIVERS

> New-York: Aug. 11th / 45.

My Dear Friend,

Mr Bisco says to me that, with the loan of $50, for a couple of months, he would be put out of all difficulty in respect to the publication of the "Broadway Journal". Its success is decided, and will eventually make us a fortune. It would be, therefore, a great pity that anything of a trifling nature (such as a want of $50) should interfere with our prospects. You know that I have no money at command myself, and therefore I venture to ask <for> you for the loan required. If you *can* aid us, I know you [will]. In 2 months certainly the money will be repaid.

My prospects about "Maga" are glorious. I will be with you in <ten weeks> 6 weeks from [this] date.

Cordially your friend

Edgar A Poe

Please reply as soon as possible. [There is] a [long review] of your Poems in the Southern Patriot. [I presume] you have seen [it]!

> In connection with the plea for $50, see the note to Letter 211. Poe's proposed visit with Chivers in Georgia apparently was not made. For the review of Chivers' *The Lost Pleiad,* see the note to Letter 140. [CL 558]

206 ≻ TO LAUGHTON OSBORN

New York August 15, '45

My Dear Mr. Osborn:

I am neither disposed, nor can I afford, to give up your friendship so easily; and, to preserve it, have no hesitation in overstepping the boundary-line of what is usually called editorial decorum.

In view of the public I am responsible for all that has appeared in "The Broadway Journal," since the period when my name, as one of its editors, was placed upon its title-page. But, in fact, my connexion with the paper during the first six months of its existence, was simply that of contributor. With the making up of the journal — with the reception or rejection of communications — I had no more to do than yourself. The article to which you refer had never been seen by me until you pointed it out. It has the air of having been written by Mr. Benjamin himself.

I am happy in being able to re-assure you that whenever I have had occasion to speak of "The Vision of Rubeta," I have borne testimony

to its high merits. Your "Confessions of a Poet" I read many years
ago, with a very profound sentiment of admiration for its author, and
sympathy with what I supposed his real rather than his fictitious ex-
periences — although until the receipt of your letter, I had been at-
tributing the work to John Neal. In one or two instances I have
written warmly in its defence — . I cannot understand how you can
fail to perceive, intuitively, that I should appreciate your works. I did
not doubt, for an instant, that you would place a proper estimate upon
mine. You will at least see that I am frank.

It is quite a coincidence that, although Halleck is the only poet of
whom we both spoke cordially in approbation, on the night when I
saw you, I should in his case also have been subjected to just such
misconception as arose in your own. Some months ago there appeared
in the "Broadway Journal" a very malevolent and flippant attack on
"Alnwick Castle," and this attack (since I had been known to write
previous criticisms on poetical works, for the Journal) was universally
attributed to me — and even Halleck himself was misled — although
in two biographies, and at least half a dozen long critiques — to say
nothing of a public lecture — I had uniformly treated him with respect. Never[the]less — for the sake of that "editorial courtesy"
which I now violate, and by which I shall never consent to be bound
again, I endured the loss of Mr. Halleck's good will, until by mere
accident, he discovered *that the offensive article had been written by a
brother poet, Lowell,* at the malicious instigation of my former associate, Mr. Briggs — Mr. Lowell especially requesting of Mr. B. that
the critique should not have the name of its author appended (as was
usual with us in all cases of communication) but appear editorially —
although he well knew that the odium would inevitably fall upon
myself. — I hope you will see that you have been hasty. I hope this,
because I am sincerely anxious that we shall continue friends.

With high respect and esteem,

Edgar A. Poe.

The *Broadway Journal* for March 8, 1845 (vol. 1, no. 10) carried for
the first time the names of its editors: C. F. Briggs, Edgar A. Poe,
and H. C. Watson. Poe certainly was the author of the article that
Osborn refers to and that Poe disclaims having seen. Osborn's letter
reads in part: "With the copy of 'Arthur C[arryl]' (1841) which
you had permitted me to present you, I took the liberty of enclosing,

otherwise, 'The Confessions of a Poet' . . . I was under the delusion that Mrs. Poe would take an interest in them . . . You may judge my surprise when the first thing that struck my eyes on opening the nos. of the Journal was that delightable and very dainty passage 'What is the Vision of [Rubeta] . . . gilded swill trough overflowing with Dunciad and water,' above which stands with its associates' names, the name of 'Edgar A. Poe' as editor. Who was the writer of this squill . . ." Osborn's *The Confessions of a Poet* (1835) was noticed by Poe in the SLM, April 1835 (reprinted in H, VIII, 2–3; see also "The Literati," *Godey's Lady's Book*, June 1846, which is reprinted in H, XV, 44–49); for Poe's reference to *Arthur Carryl*, see H, XV, 48. The "Vision of Rubeta" was first published in 1838. Though Poe disclaimed authorship of the "squill" against "The Vision of Rubeta," evidence points to a contrary conclusion. A comparison of the opening paragraph of Poe's review of Wilmer's *The Quacks of Helicon* (*Graham's*, August 1841; reprinted in H, X, 182), of the first paragraph of the anonymous review of Park Benjamin's "Infatuation" under the title of "Satirical Poems" in the *Broadway Journal*, March 15, 1845 (reprinted in H, XII, 107), of the fifth paragraph in "The Literati," *Godey's Lady's Book*, June 1846 (H, XV, 47), where Poe is treating Laughton Osborn, and of the first paragraph of Poe's review of Lowell's *A Fable for Critics*, in the SLM, March 1849, will point to the same author for all the articles. The general tone, point of view, and phraseology are all Poe's. Thus the "anonymous" author of the *Broadway Journal* article, which contains the "squill," is Poe. The squill in the *Broadway Journal* reads: " — and what is the 'Vision of Rubeta' but an illimitable gilded swill-trough overflowing with Dunciad and water?" and in the SLM: " — and what is 'The Vision of Rubeta' more than a vast gilded swill-trough overflowing with Dunciad and water?" The "attack on 'Alnwick Castle' " appeared in the *Broadway Journal*, May 3, 1845. [CL 560]

207 ➤ TO DR. THOMAS H. CHIVERS

New-York: Aug. 29. [1845]

My Dear Friend,

I sit down, in the midst of all the hurry of getting out the paper, to reply to your letter, dated 25th. What can you be thinking about? You complain of me for not doing things which I had no idea that you wanted done. Do you not see that my short letter to you was written on the very day in which yours was addressed to me? How, then, could you expect mine to be a reply to yours? You must have been making a voyage to "Dreamland".

What you say about the $50, too, puzzles me. You write — "Well I suppose you must have it" — but it does not come. Is it possible that you mailed it in the letter? I presume not; but that you merely refer to your intention of sending it. For Heaven's sake do — as soon as you get this — for almost everything (as concerns the paper) depends upon it. It would be a thousand pities to give up just as every thing flourishes. As soon as, by hook or by crook, I can get Wiley & Putnam's book done, I shall have plenty of money — $500 at least — & will punctually repay you.

I have been making all kinds of inquiries about the "broken" money — but as yet have not found it. To day I am on a new scent & may possibly succeed. The "Southern Patriot" *is* published in Charleston. I have no copy — but you can see it anywhere on file [*page 2*] I presume, at Washington. The "Morning News" of this city had, also, a handsome notice, digested from mine in the B. J. Colton's Magazine will also have a favorable one. You may depend upon it that I will take good care of you interest & fame, but let me do it in my own way.

Thank you for the play — poems — and Luciferian Revelation — as soon as I get a chance I will use them. The L. R. is *great* — & your last poem is a noble one. I send on to day, the books you mention.

Virginia and Mrs Clemm send their warmest love to you & your wife & children. We all feel as if we knew your family.

God bless you, my friend.
Truly yours,

Poe

I have not touched a drop of the "ashes" since you left N. Y. — & I am resolved not to touch a drop as long as I live. I will be with you as soon as it is in any manner possible. I *depend on* you for the $50.

At this time Poe was preparing his *The Raven and Other Poems*, which was published by Wiley and Putnam, November 19, 1845 (see Mabbott, *The Raven and Other Poems*, p. xi). Concerning Poe's expectation of $500, see Letter 215. The reference to "broken" money concerns Chivers' request that Poe find the Commercial Bank of Florida, in Wall Street, and obtain certain securities so that Chivers will not lose $210 on October 1 (see Chivers to Poe, September 9, 1845, in H, XVII, 210–215). The *Southern Patriot* reviewed Chivers' *The Lost Pleiad* (see Letter 140). Washington, Georgia, was near Oaky Grove, Chivers' home. Chivers placed a cross after the "L. R." on page 2, and noted at the end of the letter: "Alluding to a M.S. on Poetry, entitled *Lyes Regalio*, then in his possession"; he also placed a cross after "ashes" in the postscript, and noted at the end of the letter: "This was written in allusion to my having asked him in one of my letters touching his intemperance — '*What would God think of that Angel who should condescend to dust his feet in the ashes of Hell?*'" [CL 563]

208 ⊁ TO EVERT A. DUYCKINCK

My Dear Duyckinck,

I leave for you what I think the best of my Poems. They are *very* few — including those only which have not been published in volume form. If they can be made to fill a book, it will be better to publish them alone — but if not, I can hand you some "Dramatic Scenes" from the S. L. Messenger (2d Vol) and "Al Aaraaf" and "Tamerlane," two juvenile poems of some length.

                                        Truly yours
Wednesday 10 th [September, 1845]   Poe.
[New York]

> The moderate success of Poe's *Tales* (New York: Wiley and Putnam, June 1845; see also Letter 237) encouraged the same publishers to bring out Poe's poems as No. VIII in their series, *Library of American Books* (see *The Raven and Other Poems*, ed. Mabbott, opposite p. xiv). "Dramatic Scenes" were five scenes from "Politian," SLM, December 1835– January 1836. [CL 565]

209 ⊁ TO EVERT A. DUYCKINCK

                          [New York, September 11, 1845]
                          Thursday morning
My dear Sir

Your note of yesterday was not received until this morning.

I will call at your home to-night, about 8, in the hope of finding you disengaged.

                                        Very truly yours,
E. A. Duyckinck Esq.   Edgar A. Poe.

> Poe is replying to Duyckinck's note of [September 10, 1845] (un-located), which is the only letter Duyckinck is known to have written to Poe, though other notes or letters were certainly sent. [CL 567]

210 ⤜ TO RUFUS W. GRISWOLD

New-York: Sep. 28. [1845]

My Dear Griswold,

Please do not forget to send the S. L. Messenger — Vol 2. I will take especial care of it.

Truly yours

Poe.

> Since the dramatic scenes from "Politian" were included in *The Raven* volume (pp. 31–51), Griswold must have sent the volume of the SLM as Poe requested; if there was any correspondence in consequence, it is unknown. [CL 568]

211 ⤜ TO RUFUS W. GRISWOLD

New-York : Oct. 26. 45.

My Dear Griswold,

Will you aid me at a pinch — at one of the greatest pinches conceivable? If you will, I will be indebted to you, for life. After a prodigious deal of manoeuvring, I have succeeded in getting the "Broadway Journal" entirely within my own control. It will be a fortune to me if I can hold it — and I can do it easily with a very trifling aid from my friends. May I count you as one? Lend me $50 and you shall never have cause to regret it.

Truly yours,

Edgar A Poe

Reply by return of mail, if possible.

> This is but one of the letters to various correspondents (Chivers, Kennedy, Duyckinck, George Poe, Halleck) in which Poe sought to borrow money with which to keep alive the *Broadway Journal*, into full possession of which he came on October 24, 1845 (see Quinn, *Poe*, pp. 752–753). Only Greeley, Halleck, and perhaps Chivers are known to have loaned him money. [CL 574]

212 ⤜ TO SARAH J. HALE

My Dear Madam,

I have been a week absent from the city, and have been overwhelmed with business since my return — may I beg you, therefore, to pardon my seeming discourtesy in not sooner thanking you for your sweet poem, and for the high honor you confer on me in the matter of your proposed volume? Undoubtedly, it would give me great pleasure to hear from you farther on the subject, or to be of any service to you in any manner that you may suggest. — I *have* some acquaintance with Mess. Clark and Austin, and believe that you will find them, as publishers, every thing that you could wish.

Command me, my Dear Madam, in all things, and believe me

Very Respectfully & Truly Yours

Mrs S. J. Hale.   Edgar A Poe.
New-York : Octo. 26 — 45.

> Poe lectured before the Boston Lyceum, October 16. His "business" was raising money to buy the *Broadway Journal*. Mrs. Hale's "sweet poem" may have been her *Alice Ray*, which he reviewed in the *Broadway Journal*, November 1, 1845, pp. 256–257, praising it generously for "delicacy and fancy," "truthful simplicity and grace of manner," and "point and force of expression." Regarding the "proposed volume," see Letter 225. [CL 575]

213 ⇥ TO JOHN P. KENNEDY

New-York: Octo. 26. 45.

My Dear Mr Kennedy,

When you were in New-York I made frequent endeavours to meet you — but in vain — as I was forced to go to Boston.

I stand much in need of your aid, and beg you to afford it me, if possible — for the sake of the position which you already have enabled me to obtain. By a series of manoeuvres almost incomprehensible to myself, I have succeeded in getting rid, one by one, of all my associates in "The Broadway Journal", and (as you will see by last week's paper) have now become sole editor and owner. It will be a fortune to me if I can hold it — and if I can hold it for one month I am quite safe — as you shall see. I have exhausted all my immediate resources in the purchase — and I now write to ask you for a small loan — say $50. I will punctually return it in 3 months.

Most truly yours,

Hon. J. P. Kennedy.   Edgar A. Poe

At the time of Kennedy's October visit to New York, Poe made at least one attempt to see his old friend, but finding him absent, left a card (see Kennedy's letter cited in Note 213). For Poe's lecture in Boston, see the note to Letter 185. Poe asked loans of various friends at this time, with only partial success. For the failure of the *Broadway Journal*, see Letter 225, and note. Kennedy did not send the money, saying, "Good wishes are pretty nearly all the capital I have for such speculations" (Kennedy's letter, cited in Note 213). However, he closed his letter with a warm invitation to Poe to visit him at any time he came to Baltimore. [CL 576]

214 ⇥ TO [FRANCES SARGENT OSGOOD]

[New York, late October, 1845]

My Dear Madam,

Through some inadvertence at the Office of the B. Journal, I failed to receive your kind and altogether delightful note until this morning.

Thank you a thousand times for your sweet poem, and for the valued words of flattery which accompanied it.

Business, of late, has made of me so great a slave that I shall not be able to spend an evening with you until Thursday next.

[Signature missing]

A floral design appears just above the salutation. Someone, perhaps Griswold, has written at the head of page 1, "Poe to Mrs Osgood," an identification that is not denied by the content of the letter. Mrs. Osgood's (?) note, cited by Poe, is otherwise unknown, its date being merely *ante* late October, 1845. [CL 580]

215 ⇥ TO EVERT A. DUYCKINCK

Thursday Morning — 13th. [November, 1845]
85 Amity St. [New York]

My Dear Mr Duyckinck,

For the first time during two months I find myself entirely myself — dreadfully sick and depressed, but still myself. I seem to have just awakened from some horrible dream, in which all was confusion, and suffering — relieved only by the constant sense of your kindness, and that of one or two other considerate friends. I really believe that I have been mad — but indeed I have had abundant reason to be so.

I have made up my mind to a step which will preserve me, for the future, from at least the greater portion of the troubles which have beset me. In the meantime, I have need of the most active exertion to extricate myself from the embarrassments into which I have already fallen — and my object in writing you this note is, (once again) to beg your aid. Of course I need not say to you that my most urgent trouble is the want of ready money. I find that what I said to you about the prospects of the B. J. is strictly correct. The most trifling immediate relief would put it on an excellent footing. All that I want is time in which to look about me; and I think that it is your power to afford me this.

I have already drawn from Mr Wiley, first $30 — then 10 (from yourself) — then 50 (on account of the "Parnassus") — then 20 (when I went to Boston) — and finally 25 — in all 135. Mr Wiley owes me, for the Poems, 75, and admitting that 1500 of the Tales have been sold, and that I am to receive 8 cts a copy — the amount which you named, if I remember — [*page 2*] admitting this, he will owe me $120 on them: — in all 195. Deducting what I have received there is a balance of 60 in my favor. If I understood you, a few days ago, Mr W. was to settle with me in February. Now, you will already have anticipated my request. It is that you would ask Mr W. to give me, to-day, in lieu of all farther claim, a certain sum whatever he may think advisable. So dreadfully am I pressed, that I would willingly take even the $60 actually due, (in lieu of all farther demand) than wait until February: — but I am sure that you will do the best for me that you can.

Please send your answer to 85 Amity St. and believe me — with the most sincere friendship and ardent gratitude

Yours

Edgar A Poe.

Poe's "embarrassments" probably had to do, in part at least, with his securing loans for the purchase of the *Broadway Journal* (see the note to Letter 211 and Letter 216). Poe lectured in Boston, October 16, 1845 (see the note to Letter 185). Concerning the "Parnassus" (Poe's projected *Literary America*), see Letter 201; also Letter 240 and note). For the publication of the "Poems," see the note to Letter 208. This is Poe's first reference to his Amity Street address (see the note to Letter 239), but in a letter from Laughton Osborn to Poe, October 1, 1845, Osborn speaks of Poe as living at 85 Amity Street. [CL 583]

216 ⊁ TO DR. THOMAS H. CHIVERS

New-York: Nov. 15. 45

My Dear Friend —

Beyond doubt you must think that I treat you ill in not answering your letters — but it is utterly impossible to conceive how busy I have been. The Broadway Journals I now send, will give you some idea of the reason. I have been buying out the paper, and of course you must be aware that I have had a tough time of it — making all kind of maneuvres — and editing the paper, without aid from any one, all the time. I have succeeded, however, as you see — bought it out entirely, and *paid for it all,* with the exception of 140 $ which will fall due on the 1rst of January next. I will make a fortune of it yet. You see yourself what a host of advertising I have. For Heaven's sake, my dear friend, help me now if you can — *at once* — for now is my time of peril. If I live until next month I shall be beyond the need of aid. If you *can* send me the $45, for Heaven's sake do it, *by return of mail* — or if not all, a part. Time with me now, is money & money more than time. I wish you were here that I might explain to you my hopes & prospects — but in a letter it is impossible — for remember that I have to do *everything* myself edit the paper — get it to press — and attend to [*page 2*] the multitudinous *business* besides.

Believe me — will you not? — my dear friend — that it is through no want of disposition to write you that I have failed to do so: — the moments I now spend in penning these words are gold themselves — & more. By & bye I shall have time to breathe — and then I will write you fully.

You are wrong (as usual) about Archȳtas & Orīon — both are as I accent them. Look in any phonographic Dictionary — say Bolles. Besides, wherever the words occur in <poe> ancient poetry, they are as I give them. What is the use of disputing an obvious point? You are wrong too, throughout, in what you say about the poem "Orion" — there is not the shadow of an error, in its rhythm, from α to ω.

Never dreamed that you did not get the paper regularly until Bisco told me it was not sent. You must have thought it very strange.

So help me Heaven, I have sent and gone personally in all the nooks & corners of Broker-Land & such a thing as the money you speak of — is *not to be obtained.*

[*page 3*] Write soon — soon — & help me if you can. I send you my Poems.

God bless you —

E. A. P.

We *all* send our warmest love to yourself, your wife & family.

> For Poe's purchase of the *Broadway Journal,* see the note to Letter 211; for his loss of it, see Quinn, *Poe,* p. 494. In the postscript to Chivers' letter of October 30 is a promise of $45, to be sent "soon"; whether it ever came is unknown. "Orion" was a poem by the Englishman R. H. Horne, and was lengthily reviewed by Poe in *Graham's,* March 1844 (see H, XI, 249–275). Poe's "Poems" refers to *The Raven and Other Poems* (see the note to Letter 207); what he sent Chivers was apparently an advance copy. [CL 585]

217 ⊁ TO GEORGE POE

New-York : Nov. 30. 45.

Dear Sir,

Since the period when (no doubt for good reasons) you declined aiding me with the loan of $50, I have perseveringly struggled, against a thousand difficulties, and have succeeded, although not in making money, still in attaining a position in the world of Letters, of which, under the circumstances, I have no reason to be ashamed.

For these reasons — because I feel that I have exerted myself to the utmost — and because I believe that you will appreciate my efforts to elevate the family name — I now appeal to you once more for aid.

With this letter I send you a number of "The Broadway Journal" of which, hitherto, I have been merely editor and one third proprietor. I have lately purchased the whole paper — and, if I can retain it, it will be a fortune to me in a short time: — but I have exhausted all my resources in the purchase. In this emergency I have thought that you might not be indisposed to assist me. The loan of $200 would put me above all difficulty.

I refrain from saying any more — for I feel that if your heart is kindly disposed towards me, I have already[. . .]

[MS. *cut off*]

No letter is known from Poe to George Poe requesting a loan of $50; however, the request may have been in the letter of July 14, 1839, cited in Sir Edmund T. Bewley's article, "The True Ancestry of Edgar Allan Poe" (*New York Genealogical and Biographical Record*, xxxviii (1907), pp. 55–69); two short passages of genealogy are quoted from the letter, which has never been published in full, and is unlocated. If the July 14 letter contained the request, George Poe's reply is unlocated. Concerning Poe's purchase of the *Broadway Journal*, see Letter 211. For more about George Poe and his previous financial assistance to Mrs. Clemm, see Letter 53. [CL 586]

218 ⊁ TO GEORGE WATTERSTON

Dr Sir,

If I am not mistaken, you were one of the earliest subscribers to "The Southern Literary Messenger", and aided me very materially while it remained under my control. For this reason, and because I am naturally anxious for the support of those whose good opinion I value — because, too, I believe that my objects, as regards our National Literature, are such as your judgment approves — I venture now frankly to solicit your subscription and influence for "The Broadway Journal", of which I send you a specimen number.

With high respect
Yr. Mo. Ob. St.

New-York. Nov. 1845.   Edgar A: Poe.

George Watterston, novelist and critic, contributed to the *Southern Literary Messenger* (see David K. Jackson, *Poe and the Southern Literary Messenger*, pp. 52–54), and was the first librarian of Congress (see Jackson, p. 97). [CL 587]

219 ⊁ TO FITZ-GREENE HALLECK

New York, Dec. 1, 1845.

My Dear Mr. Halleck:

On the part of one or two persons who are much imbittered against me, there is a deliberate attempt now being made to involve me in ruin, by destroying *The Broadway Journal*. I could easily frustrate them, but for my total want of money, and of the necessary time in which to procure it: the knowledge of this has given my enemies the opportunities desired.

In this emergency — without leisure to think whether I am acting improperly — I venture to appeal to you. The sum I need is $100. If you could loan me for three months any portion of it, I will not be ungrateful.

Truly yours,

Edgar A. Poe.

According to James Grant Wilson (*Life and Letters of Fitz-Greene Hal-leck,* pp. 430–431), Halleck sent the money, but it was never repaid. No letter enclosing the loan is known. For Poe's various attempts to borrow money to save the *Broadway Journal,* see his letters for the closing months of 1845. However, the magazine died in January 1846 (see Letter 225, and note). [CL 592]

220 ⤙ TO EVERT A. DUYCKINCK

[New York] Dec. 10 [1845]

[. . . . .]

If you could get the enclosed article (by Mrs. Ellett) in the Morning News, editorially, I would take it as a great favor. . . .

Poe

Though the present item is but a fragment, it seems genuine. The request is similar to others made of Duyckinck; also there seems to be some connection between the present letter and the letters from Mrs. Ellett to Poe of the same period (see the note to Letter 290). [CL 594]

220a ⤙ TO [EVERT A. DUYCKINCK?]

[New York   1845]

Do you know anything of a work on Oil Painting lately published and sent (if I am not mistaken) by Mess. W & P. to the office of the B. J. ?

Yours &c

Saturday Morning.   Edgar A. Poe

The 1rst vol of "The Wandering Jew" you can get from Mr English.

This note seems to refer to a recent publication by Wiley and Putnam, sent for review by Poe in the *Broadway Journal.* Though the correspondent is not identified, he may well have been Evert A. Duyckinck, friend of Poe and reader for the Wiley and Putnam firm. "Mr English" refers to Thomas Dunn English, who at this time was on friendly terms with Poe. [CL 602a]

220b ⇥ TO WILLIAM M. GILLESPIE

[New York]

[1845]

My Dear Gillespie,

An unlucky *contretemps*, connected with the getting out of the "Journal" will, I fear, detain me until after 10 to night — too late for the appointment.

If you can (this evening) see Mrs O. & make any decent apology for me, I will be greatly obliged. Any evening (except to-morrow) I shall be disengaged, and will be happy to accompany you.

In haste Yours truly

Thursday Evening   Poe.
    8. O'clock.

William M. Gillespie, according to Poe in *Literati* (*Godey's*, May 1846; reprinted in H, xv, 19–20), apparently aided Park Benjamin in editing the *New World*. In 1845 Gillespie became Professor of Civil Engineering at Union College, Schenectady, New York (see *Dictionary of American Biography*, vii, 288–289). Gillespie seems to have given the present letter to "Mrs O" (Mrs. Frances Sargent Osgood), who in turn gave it to her grand niece, Miss Helen Tetlow. [CL 602b]

221 ⇥ TO ————

[1845–1846]

[. . . . .]

I am exceedingly anxious. If you would be so kind as to look me up, I will consider it a great favor. You understand the whole story is purely fiction. —

Your opinion is of great consideration. —

Y^r Ob. S^t

Edgar A. Poe

Poe may be referring to "Facts in the Case of M. Valdemar," published in December 1845; or to "Mesmeric Revelation," published in August 1844. [CL 603]